Clothing through American History

Clothing through American History

The Federal Era through Antebellum, 1786–1860

Ann Buermann Wass
and Michelle Webb Fandrich

AN IMPRINT OF ABC-CLIO, LLC
Santa Barbara, California • Denver, Colorado • Oxford, England

Library of Congress Cataloging-in-Publication Data

Wass, Ann Buermann.

Clothing through American history : the federal era through Antebellum, 1786–1860 / Ann Buermann Wass and Michelle Webb Fandrich.

p. cm.

Includes bibliographical references and index.

ISBN 978-0-313-33533-4 (hard copy : alk. paper) —

ISBN 978-0-313-08459-1 (ebook)

1. Clothing and dress—United States—History—18th century. 2. Clothing and dress—United States—History—19th century. 3. Fashion—United States—History—18th century. 4. Fashion—United States—History—19th century. I. Fandrich, Michelle Webb. II. Title.

GT607.W37 2009

391.009'033—dc22 2009029451

ISBN: 978-0-313-33533-4

EISBN: 978-0-313-08459-1

14 13 12 11 10 1 2 3 4 5

This book is also available on the World Wide Web as an eBook.
Visit www.abc-clio.com for details.

Greenwood
An Imprint of ABC-CLIO, LLC

ABC-CLIO, LLC
130 Cremona Drive, P.O. Box 1911
Santa Barbara, California 93116-1911

This book is printed on acid-free paper ♾
Manufactured in the United States of America

Contents

PART TWO: THE ANTEBELLUM ERA, 1821–1860

PART ONE

The Federal Period, 1786–1820

Ann Buermann Wass

Introduction

Part one of this book describes clothing in America during the Federal period, the early years of the independent United States of America from 1786 to 1820. In 1786, The 13 American colonies had just won their independence from Great Britain. These at first formed a loose confederation of states, but the founding fathers went on to develop a new system with a strong central government while allowing the individual states to retain some residual powers. This type of government is a *federal* system, and this is now the name by which we call this era in the United States.

This was a period of great changes in both women's and men's clothing. The changes may appear revolutionary, as if following the political revolutions of the era. However, the transition from the elaborate rococo fashions of 18th-century Europe and colonial America (often manifested in full-skirted, heavily embellished dresses made of silks with intricate woven designs) to the more simple classically inspired styles of the early 19th century was actually more gradual. For the most part American fashions followed the lead of France or England, where a renewed interest in the classical world of Greece and Rome influenced fashions in clothing. By the end of the period, during the first decades of the 1800s, the Romantic movement was under way. The emphasis was now on emotions rather than reason, and on Medieval European culture rather than the ancient world. Elements of Gothic style appeared in dress. More elaborate embellishment, more fullness in the skirt, a return of the waistline to the natural position, and larger sleeves were trends that would continue after 1820.

It did not take long for new styles to make their way across the Atlantic. Nor was there a great time lag in the westward movement of fashions in this country—most Americans seem to have tried their best to keep up with fashion trends. The interpretation of these late-18th and early-19th century styles in the United States is the Federal style. While most costume historians have emphasized the fashions of Europe, the intent of this volume is to describe, for a general audience, how these styles were translated and adapted in the United States.

During this period, the French monarchy ended with a revolution, wherein the trappings of the aristocracy, including elaborate clothing, were overthrown along with the king. Then Napoleon Bonaparte established the French empire, and the fashions of the French Revolution continued to evolve. In Great Britain, the mental instability of King George III necessitated that Parliament establish a regency, naming someone to act in his stead. The king's oldest son, George, Prince of Wales, was named Prince Regent, and he also established himself as a fashion leader. Thus both the French Empire (1804–1815) and the English Regency (1811–1820) have leant their names to styles. While the periods are not exactly contemporaneous, the terms *Empire, Regency,* and *Federal* are roughly interchangeable for clothing fashions of the first two decades of the 19th century.

Sources for the study of clothing of the era include extant garments preserved in museums or private collections. Those more likely to survive are formal clothing, clothing with a special meaning (such as wedding or christening attire), or garments belonging to the wealthy, as working garments wore out and were discarded. One challenge of studying actual garments is that the precise date is not always known but must be determined by studying characteristics of the garments themselves. Another is that, because fabric was expensive, garments were often remade as styles changed. This could be as simple as minor alterations or as extensive as taking a garment entirely apart and cutting a new garment from the pieces. Clothing historians look for clues such as stitching marks, fold lines, or piecing (sewing small segments together into a larger fabric) for evidence of such re-working.

Paintings, drawings, and prints also supply information. Subjects of formal portraits tended to be wealthy, although by the early 19th century, members of the growing middle class began to commission portraits. One advantage of studying formal portraits is that the date is usually (although not always) known. Portraits must be used with caution, as sometimes painters had sitters wear studio props or some form of costume or fantasy dress; however, the majority of portraits provide a view of what was actually in the subject's wardrobe. Genre paintings, or scenes of everyday life, more often show middle- or working-class individuals depicted in a variety of settings, both indoors and out. Unfortunately, although genre painting was well established in Europe, there were only a few genre painters in the United States during the Federal period. Satirical prints, though exaggerated, also provide clues. As photography was still in the future, this valuable documentation source is not available for this period.

Another rich source of information are magazines with engraved illustrations and fashion commentary. Such features in American publications were generally short-lived during the Federal era. However, Americans had access to a number of British and French publications. As these depicted high-style, sometimes imaginary garments, caution must be used in accepting the illustrations at face value, but they certainly provided American women with ideas for making their clothing.

Advertisements in newspapers list what was available for sale in American shops. Masters also placed advertisements in newspapers seeking the return of slaves who ran away to seek freedom, and these sometimes include descriptions of the clothing the person was wearing as well as extra clothing taken—common language was "had on and took with her/him."

Other written sources include letters, diaries, and travelers' accounts. (When such materials are quoted in this book, the original spelling and syntax are preserved.) Some legal documents also provide information. Probate inventories, for example, were lists made of a deceased person's goods as part of the process of settling an estate. The people assigned to do the inventory sometimes made detailed lists of clothing items; unfortunately, though, the clothing is often lumped together as "wearing apparel of the deceased." As clothing was valuable, sometimes it was specifically mentioned as a bequest in a will.

Some instruction manuals or guidebooks were published during this period. Tailors' manuals provide insight into the cut and construction of men's clothing. Guidebooks for charity sewing provide valuable details about children's and women's clothing.

As clothing must be understood in context, the timeline highlights important dates and chapter 1 of this book provides a brief overview of the political and economic history of the country during the Federal period. Chapter 2 addresses social and cultural events that influenced how Americans dressed. Chapters 3 and 4 survey women's and men's fashions, respectively, with consideration of all social classes, urban and rural inhabitants, enslaved African Americans, and American Indians. Chapter 5 surveys children's fashions. Illustrations have been carefully chosen to extend the descriptions in the text. The glossary defines words that may be unfamiliar to the general reader. The resource list includes not only books, but also museum collections and Web sites where the reader can look for further information, and a list of motion pictures featuring authentic clothing of the period.

Acknowledgments

I thank my husband, Jim, my boss, Edward Day, my friends Martha Kelly and Lucy Younes, who provided encouragement, and Alden O'Brien, who both cheered me on and shared her considerable knowledge with me. I also thank Lynne Bassett for drawing me in to this project. Others who have provided invaluable assistance include Sally Bennett, Anne Bissonnette, Karin Bohleke, Elizabeth Bowling, William L. Brown III, Ellen Donald, Mary Doering, Susan and Bruce Greene of American Costume Studies, Karen Harris, Mela Hoyt-Heydon, Carol Kregloh, Joyce McDonald, Marla Miller, Robert J. Moore Jr., Jane Nylander, Louisa Pineault, Myron Peterson, Nancy Saputo, Joyce White, and Kevin Windsor. I also thank members of four Yahoo! Groups electronic lists, 18cWoman, 1812Civilian, H-COST, and NativeList, who were always willing to answer my questions. Collections that generously opened their doors to me include the Daughters of the American Revolution Museum, the Mashantucket Pequot Museum and Research Center, the Missouri Historical Society, and the Western Reserve Historical Society.

Timeline

THE FEDERAL PERIOD, 1786–1820

1787 Shays's Rebellion highlights the weaknesses of the Articles of Confederation. States send delegates to Philadelphia to discuss modifications to the Articles and instead decide to write a new constitution.

1788 The new constitution goes into effect with the ratification by the ninth state, Virginia. Grand Federal Procession in Philadelphia features calico printer John Hewson on a float.

1789 George Washington is elected the first president. At his inauguration, he wears a suit of American-made wool. The storming of the Bastille in Paris begins the French Revolution.

1790 Rhode Island is the last state to ratify the Constitution.

1791 English immigrant Samuel Slater builds the first water-powered cotton-spinning mill in the United States at Pawtucket, Rhode Island. Secretary of the Treasury Alexander Hamilton compiles a report on manufactures, as he advocates that the United States should no longer depend on foreign manufactured goods.

1793 The invention of the cotton gin makes the processing of cotton fibers easier and will lead to an expansion in growing cotton (and enslaved labor) in the southern United States.

1794 The Whiskey Rebellion tests the new federal government. Nicholas Heideloff begins publication of *The Gallery of Fashion,* with some Americans among the subscribers.

1796 John Adams is elected president.

1797 The French *Journal des Dames et des Modes* begins publication. Four engraved fashion plates are published every two weeks. American women obtain copies from friends and family abroad.

1798 Congress passes the Alien and Sedition Acts. These are unpopular and virtually ensure that Adams will not be reelected.

1799 George Washington dies in December, and people all over the country wear mourning clothes.

1800 Thomas Jefferson is elected president.

1803 The United States purchases the Louisiana Territory from France. Anthony Merry arrives in the United States as minister from Great Britain and encounters Thomas Jefferson's Republican style of etiquette. Elizabeth "Betsy" Patterson of Baltimore marries Jerome Bonaparte, Napoleon's younger brother. Her gowns in the latest French fashion attract attention, much of it negative, in Baltimore and Washington, D.C. society.

1804–1806 Meriwether Lewis and William Clark lead an expedition through the northwest Louisiana Territory and on to the Pacific Ocean. They record their observations of the dress of various tribes of Plains Indians and those of the Pacific Northwest.

1804 Napoleon Bonaparte crowns himself emperor of France. He attempts to stimulate native industries by requiring women to wear gowns of French-made silks, rather than fashionable English and Indian cottons, at court.

1807 In response to European restrictions on trade, Jefferson declares an embargo on trade to and from all U.S. ports. This results in a shortage of imported fabrics and stimulation of American textile manufacturing.

1809 James Madison is inaugurated as the fourth president, and he, like George Washington, wears a suit of American-made wool fabric. President Madison's wife, Dolley, enthusiastically wears French fashions and is much admired.

The trade embargo is lifted and is replaced by a non-intercourse act prohibiting trade with England and France and their colonies but permitting it with the rest of the world.

1810 Secretary of State Albert Gallatin reports on the state of American manufacturing. He finds that, while textile manufacturing is growing, production is not enough to meet the needs of the country.

1811 George, Prince of Wales, is named Prince Regent by the British Parliament as, due to mental illness, King George III is unable to fulfill his duties.

1812 The United States declares war on Great Britain, beginning the War of 1812. This shuts down legal trade with the British Empire. At the same time, there is increased demand for fine-quality wool fabrics to clothe American soldiers and sailors.

1814 The British burn many of the public buildings in Washington, including the President's House and the Capitol. The American commissioners negotiating for an end to the War of 1812 in Ghent are directed to wear diplomatic dress. The Treaty of Ghent, which ends the war, is signed on December 24.

1815 The Treaty of Ghent is ratified, and formal relations with Great Britain are resumed. British manufactured goods begin to flood the American market. Napoleon I is defeated at the Battle of Waterloo, leading to peace in Europe. The first American mill with power looms begins operation in Waltham, Massachusetts.

1816 With the Federalist Party virtually gone, Republican James Monroe has no real opposition and his election as president ushers in the "Era of Good Feeling."

1818 James and Elizabeth Monroe re-open the newly refurbished President's House to the public on New Year's Day.

1819 The country faces the Panic of 1819, the first widespread economic crisis.

1820 Congress passes the Missouri Compromise, with the admission of Missouri as a slave state and Maine as a free state, and the thorny issue of the expansion slavery into new U.S. territories is temporarily laid to rest.

CHAPTER 1

The United States in the Federal Period

CREATING A NEW GOVERNMENT

From 1786 to 1820, the United States faced the tasks of establishing a sound system of government and a robust economy. After a false start under the Articles of Confederation, the United States laid the foundations for a strong federal government with a new constitution. During this Federal period, the country's geographic area expanded across the North American continent to the Pacific Ocean. Settlers followed explorers into the new territories, with the inevitable displacement of many of the native peoples. In 1790, the first census numbered the population at nearly four million and this more than doubled by 1820, while the number of states increased from 13 to 23.

The United States struggled to hold its own on the world stage as almost constant warfare between France and Great Britain and their respective allies raged over much of Europe and around the world. The United States came close to war with France and then, in 1812, did go to war with Great Britain.

Meanwhile, Americans disagreed on the direction the economy should take. Thomas Jefferson, the first secretary of state, second vice president, and third president, believed that the basis of the economy should be yeoman farmers tilling the soil on their own small farms. (He and many others in the largely agrarian Southern states, however, were coming to rely on an enslaved African-American labor force.) Alexander Hamilton,

Liberty. In the form of the goddess of youth, giving support to the bald eagle, **painted and engraved by E. Savage. 1796. The United States was often personified as a woman called Liberty, Freedom, or Columbia. Liberty's dress, while reminiscent of the styles of ancient Greece and Rome, is up-to-the-minute 1790s fashion.** Courtesy of Library of Congress.

the first secretary of the treasury, on the other hand, promoted manufacturing to free the United States from dependence on foreign-made goods. This and other fundamental differences in the philosophy of the role of government led to the formation of political parties. As a result, after the unanimous election of George Washington as the first president, future presidential elections were usually contentious.

The Articles of Confederation

After independence, the 13 states continued to operate much as they had during the Revolutionary War. Under the Articles of Confederation, there was a legislative body, Congress, and each state had one vote. Congress did not have the power to levy taxes but could only requisition individual states for funds. Positive votes from 9 of the 13 states were required to make certain decisions, such as those dealing with treaties, coinage, or war. Furthermore, any amendments to the articles required unanimous consent. The government had no executive branch and no courts. The presiding officer of Congress was elected yearly, and most of the administrative work was done by Congressional committees. Much of the business of government was conducted at the state, rather than the national, level.

Since Congress could not levy taxes, it had no sure source of income to pay the debt incurred during the war. Adding to economic instability, the individual states created their own economic policies, such as levying tariffs on imported goods, and this meant higher prices. Some states printed large amounts of paper money, leading to inflation. Others enacted legislation postponing the payment of debts and foreclosure of mortgages to offer some relief to their citizens. Not all did so, however. In Massachusetts in 1786, farmer Daniel Shays, a debt-ridden Revolutionary War veteran, led a mob that broke up the Massachusetts state Supreme Court, while others closed lower courts to prevent foreclosure proceedings. In January 1787, Shays and his followers attempted to seize the Springfield Arsenal but were repulsed by the state militia.

The Constitution

Shays's rebellion served to highlight weaknesses of the Articles of Confederation. Political leaders called for revisions to the Articles, and 12 of the 13 states sent representatives to Philadelphia to discuss revisions in 1787. (Rhode Island did not send delegates.) The delegates decided not to amend the Articles, but rather to start over again and draft a new constitution. George Washington was the presiding officer. The delegates included such prominent citizens as James Madison and George Mason of Virginia, James Wilson of Pennsylvania, Elbridge Gerry of Massachusetts, Gouverneur Morris of New York, Luther Martin of Maryland, and Roger Sherman of Connecticut. Benjamin Franklin literally served as elder statesman. Thomas Jefferson and John Adams, two of the great thinkers of the Revolutionary War, were abroad as diplomats and could not attend. Alexander Hamilton of New York, who would later be a major force in shaping the constitutional republic, was forced to leave when his fellow delegates withdrew over the issue of states' rights.

How to balance a strong federal government with the rights of the states was a thorny issue and the delegates made a series of compromises. The resulting document gave the federal government the power to levy taxes, regulate commerce, and raise an army and navy. This new government was to have three branches: legislative, executive, and judicial. One of the compromises was the formation of a bicameral legislature, consisting of the senior Senate, with equal representation for each state, while members of the junior House of Representatives were apportioned according to state populations. This appeased both the large states, who wanted representation by population, and the smaller states, who wanted equal representation for all. There was a chief executive, the president. Federal courts were also provided for in the third, judiciary, branch of government. A series of checks and balances were designed to insure that the power of each of the three branches was kept within bounds.

The issue of slavery caused much contention between northern and southern states, and again, the delegates compromised. It was agreed in Article I, section 2, that, for apportionment of both members of the House of Representatives and direct taxes, three-fifths of the number of "all other persons" (that is, enslaved people), would be added to the whole number of "free persons." Further, Article I, section 9, stated that the importation of slaves would not be outlawed before 1808, but a tariff could be levied on those imported.

The new document required ratification by nine states. Spirited debate for and against ratification appeared in the public press. The Federalists, who supported it, included Alexander Hamilton, James Madison, and John Jay. Their anti-Federalist opponents, including Patrick Henry, Richard Henry Lee, and Samuel Adams, expressed concerns, including the lack of protection for individual liberties and states' rights. However, the ninth state, Virginia, ratified the new constitution on June 25, 1788, allowing it to officially take effect. Powerful New York finally approved it in July of that year. North Carolina, however, did not vote for ratification until 1789, and Rhode Island was the last to ratify in 1790.

In the first session of the new Congress, James Madison addressed the concern that individual liberties were not sufficiently protected in the new document by drafting the first 10 amendments to the Constitution. These became known as the Bill of Rights, and spell out those freedoms Americans consider fundamental to their way of life, such as the First Amendment's freedom of speech, the press, and religion, and the Sixth Amendment's right to a jury trial. Further, the Tenth Amendment specified that powers not given to the U.S. government were "reserved to the individual states, or to the people."

George Washington's Administration

The Constitution provided for the president to be chosen by electors from each state, rather than by popular vote. The electors unanimously

The Washington family—George Washington, his lady, and her two grandchildren by the name of Custis, **painted and engraved by E. Savage. 1798. Martha Washington's grandchildren are George Washington Parke and Elinor. The man at right may be Edward Lee, an enslaved servant.** Courtesy of Library of Congress.

chose George Washington, the hero of the Revolutionary War, as the first president, and he took the oath of office on April 30, 1789. The vice president was John Adams. Washington appointed the heads of the four departments, or cabinet officers: Thomas Jefferson, secretary of state; Alexander Hamilton, secretary of the treasury; Henry Knox, secretary of war; and Edmund Randolph, attorney-general. The new government convened briefly in New York but then moved to Philadelphia for the next 10 years.

The location of the permanent capital, Washington, D.C., was the result of another compromise. In order to put the new government on a sound financial footing, Alexander Hamilton considered it of primary importance to fund the nation's Revolutionary War debt—that is, to pay off government bonds at face value, plus interest. This plan aroused some opposition because many people, fearing that their bonds would never be redeemed at full value, had sold them to speculators for a fraction of their worth. Therefore, speculators, primarily in the north, would benefit the most. Hamilton also advocated assumption of the individual states' debts, a measure that caused controversy among the states. Virginia, for example, had been prudent in managing its own debt, while Massachusetts had not. Ultimately, Virginians Jefferson and Madison agreed to support all of Hamilton's measures in exchange for locating the permanent national capital in the South, on the banks of the Potomac River, the border between Maryland and Virginia.

Portrait of Alexander Hamilton, first Secretary of the Treasury. From a painting by John Trumbull. Hamilton was the first Secretary of the Treasury and one of the leaders of the new Federalist Party. Courtesy of Library of Congress.

Hamilton needed funds to pay the debt, and one source of revenue was an excise tax on domestically produced whiskey. Back-country farmers, who found it more profitable to distill their bulky grains into liquor than to ship them to market, were hit hard by this tax. In 1794, farmers in four Pennsylvania counties fought back, terrorizing Federal revenue collectors. Washington saw this as a threat to federal authority, mustered the militia from surrounding states, and personally led the troops to put down the insurrection. This Whiskey Rebellion quickly collapsed, and federal authority was validated.

The other major source of revenue was a tariff on imported goods. This

Factions Become Parties

The founders of the Republic, students of the Enlightenment, distrusted the English political party system. They believed that reason should provide a single solution to any problem and those in opposition must be motivated by self-interest. But it did not take long for factional disagreements to arise.

The first was over Alexander Hamilton's proposal for a national bank. Washington, uncertain about its propriety, solicited opinions from his cabinet. Jefferson argued that the Constitution did not give the United States the power to charter a bank and, further, that the Tenth Amendment prohibited it. His reading of the Constitution has come to be called strict construction. Hamilton, on the other hand, said that the power of the federal government to charter a bank could be inferred. This loose construction view won out.

Differences in foreign policy cemented the factions into parties. Jefferson, a southerner and former minister to France, supported the philosophical ideals of the French revolutionary government. Meanwhile, northern sentiments were more closely aligned with Great Britain, France's enemy.

By the end of Washington's administration, party lines were drawn. Hamilton, John Adams, and Washington were styled Federalists. Primarily from the Northeast, they wanted policies that favored commerce and manufacturing. Jefferson and James Madison led the Republicans (sometimes called the Democratic-Republicans, to distinguish them from the modern Republican Party). Primarily from the South, they upheld the agrarian way of life. Unabashedly partisan newspaper editors fueled the debate with personal attacks. Although the names and platforms of the parties would change through America's history, and third parties would emerge occasionally, the two-party system remains firmly in place.

had the benefit of stimulating domestic manufacturing, as, without the added cost of a tariff, domestically produced goods could be purchased more cheaply than imported ones. Congress enacted the tariff laws, and, with increased revenue, the government did begin to pay off the war debt, and the country was on its way to economic prosperity.

JOHN ADAMS, THE SECOND PRESIDENT

In 1796, Washington chose to retire rather than run for a third term, thus setting a two-term precedent that would last nearly 150 years. The Federalists chose Vice President John Adams as their presidential candidate, while the Republicans chose Thomas Jefferson. The drafters of the Constitution had not foreseen selection of candidates by party; rather, the president was the person who received the most electoral votes, with the runner-up being vice president. This put Adams, who received the most votes, in the uncomfortable position of having his opponent, Jefferson, who came in second, as his vice president.

Adams had to deal with an increasingly volatile situation with France. During his presidency, the French broke off diplomatic relations with the United States and preyed on American shipping. This undeclared war is now often known as the quasi-war with France, and Adams built up American defenses in response. He authorized the building of six large Navy ships as well as a 10,000-man army.

Anti-foreign feeling ran so high that the Federalist Congress passed a series of laws in 1798, the Alien and Sedition Acts, aimed at both foreign and domestic enemies. Members of the Republican party were especially outraged by the Sedition Act because it made it a crime to publish "any false, scandalous, and malicious writing or writings" against the government, Congress, or the president. They viewed the Act as an infringement on the freedom of the press granted in the First Amendment to the Constitution.

Portrait of John Adams, second president of the United States, published in *Pendleton's Lithography,* circa 1828, from a painting by Gilbert Stuart. Adams's shirt with lace ruffles is old-fashioned for the 1790s. Courtesy of Library of Congress.

THE ELECTION OF 1800

President Adams was not personally popular, and the Alien and Sedition Acts assured that he would not win re-election. Thomas Jefferson and Aaron Burr formed the Republican ticket. However, once again, a flaw within the electoral system was revealed when Jefferson and Burr received the same number of electoral votes. The election had to be decided in the House of Representatives, where the Federalists had a small majority. Alexander Hamilton threw his support to Jefferson, who emerged as president, with Burr as vice president. After this election, the Twelfth Amendment, requiring that electors cast separate votes for president and vice president, was added to the Constitution. (Aaron Burr was thoroughly discredited by the time of the 1808 presidential election. He killed Alexander Hamilton in a duel in 1804 and then was involved in a plot to establish an empire in the Louisiana territory. While he was acquitted of both murder and treason, his political career was over.)

The Louisiana Purchase and Westward Expansion

Probably the greatest accomplishment of Jefferson's administration was the purchase of the Louisiana territory. Settlers were already flooding to the U.S. territory west of the Appalachian mountains. Farmers in what would become the states of Kentucky, Tennessee, and Mississippi found that the best way to get their produce to market was to send it down the Mississippi River to New Orleans. From there, it could be loaded onto ocean-going vessels and shipped anywhere in the

> ***"A Foolish Circumstance of Etiquette"***
>
> Thomas Jefferson was no stranger to the niceties of etiquette, as he had been minister to France in the last years of the monarchy as well as Washington's secretary of state. But as president, he determined to establish less formal "republican" manners.
>
> His treatment of Anthony Merry, the British minister to the United States, almost led to an international crisis. When Merry, in formal diplomatic dress, presented his credentials, he was shocked to find Jefferson "not merely in undress, but *actually standing in slippers down at the heels,* and both pantaloons, coat, and under-clothes indicative of utter slovenliness and indifference to appearances and in a state of negligence actually studied" (Allgor 2000, 36).
>
> More upsets awaited. When Merry and his wife went to dine with Jefferson, they learned that he was eliminating the etiquette of precedence. Mrs. Merry, as the female guest of honor, should have been escorted to dinner by the president. Instead, he took the woman closest to him, Dolley Madison, wife of Secretary of State James Madison; nor was Mr. Merry accorded an honored position at the table. Jefferson also invited the French chargé d'affaires, another insult, as Great Britain was at war with France.
>
> Merry, interpreting this new etiquette as an affront to his country, announced that he and his wife would not attend any further social functions. Jefferson and Madison realized they would have to relent if diplomacy was to continue and so the Merrys re-entered the social scene. However, Merry's views of the United States were colored by what Madison called a "foolish circumstance of etiquette" (Lester 1978, 36–39).

world. Spain controlled the river and New Orleans, but Thomas Pinckney had negotiated a treaty in 1795 that gave Americans the right to navigate the river and the right of deposit in New Orleans, that is, use of the port without paying duty on the goods. However, Spain ceded the Louisiana territory to France by the Treaty of San Idlefonso in 1801.

The treaty was secret, but there were rumors that Napoleon Bonaparte, the virtual dictator of France, had his eye on this North American territory. (At this time, Napoleon's title was First Consul for Life; he would declare himself emperor in 1804.) He sent troops to establish a base of operations on the French Caribbean island of Saint Domingue (present-day Haiti). This was an ill-fated action. The former slave Toussaint L'Ouverture was fomenting rebellion among the black population there. While he claimed to be a loyal subject of France, his followers fought Napoleon's army. What the rebels did not accomplish, yellow fever did, with many of the French soldiers succumbing to the disease. Napoleon decided that North America was not worth the price and turned his efforts back to the domination of Europe.

In France, American minister Robert Livingston had begun negotiations about the future of New Orleans. Jefferson sent James Monroe to join him, with instructions to buy New Orleans and Florida (it was not yet known that Spain had not ceded Florida), or at least to guarantee the right of deposit. The Americans were stunned when Napoleon offered to sell the entire Louisiana territory. Even though it exceeded their instructions, they decided they should go ahead with the purchase.

When Jefferson heard the news, he faced a dilemma. He wanted to see the territory of the United States peacefully expanded to the Pacific Ocean. But, as a strict constructionist of the Constitution, he felt he did not have the authority to purchase the territory and guarantee that its inhabitants would become American citizens. Passage of a constitutional amendment allowing this would be a lengthy process, and prompt action was needed as Napoleon was already expressing misgivings about the transaction. So Jefferson presented the agreement with France to the Senate in the form of a treaty, where it was ratified on October 20, 1803. The territory was transferred to the United States on December 20.

***Meriwether Lewis* engraved by Stuckland for the *Analectic Magazine,* 1815, from an 1807 watercolor by Charles B.J.F de Saint-Mémin. Lewis wears a fur tippet that may have been given to him by Shosone Indians.** Collection of the author.

Jefferson had already been planning an army expedition under the command of his secretary, Meriwether Lewis, to explore the Northwest. Starting in St. Louis, where the Missouri River flowed into the Mississippi, the explorers were to go up the Missouri and search for a water passage to the Pacific Ocean. Finding a northwest passage, or water route across the continent, had been a quest from the earliest days of the exploration of North America. This was not actually American territory when Jefferson asked Congress to appropriate money for the expedition, but that changed with the acquisition of the Louisiana territory. Lewis and his co-captain, William Clark, and their corps set out in 1804. They were gone over two years. They did not find a northwest passage, although they did reach the Pacific Ocean by way of the Columbia River. They also observed and recorded many new species of plants and animals that greatly excited Jefferson, who was an avid naturalist. They also established relations with many Indian tribes along the way. Even before the expedition, settlers had begun moving into the new territory. In what Americans would come to see as their destiny, more settlers soon began working their way west.

Foreign Affairs

Jefferson also had some difficult foreign issues to deal with. On the northern, or Barbary, coast of Africa, the rulers of Morocco, Algiers, Tunis, and Tripoli, parts of the Islamic Ottoman Empire, controlled access to the Mediterranean through the narrow Straits of Gibraltar. They demanded payment, or tribute, on behalf of the Ottoman sultan, to allow ships to pass. Although the newly independent United States, no longer protected by British payments, had agreed to pay tribute rather than have their ships captured, the bashaw of Tripoli (part of modern-day Libya), unhappy with the amount of tribute he was receiving, declared war on the United States in 1801. Jefferson sent a squadron of warships to blockade the coast. One of these, the frigate *Philadelphia,* ran aground, and her crew was captured and held for ransom.

Meanwhile, William Eaton, the American consul to Tunis, put together a force to attack from neighboring Egypt. This motley crew of Greek, Turkish, and Arab mercenaries included a handful of U.S. Marines. The capture of the harbor fortress of Derna was immortalized in the words of the Marine Hymn, "to the shores of Tripoli." Unknown to Eaton, however, a diplomatic solution was being worked out with the bashaw. The United States agreed to pay $60,000 ransom for the crew of the *Philadelphia,* but no additional sum as either a treaty payment or tribute.

Jefferson also had to deal with the major European powers. By this time, Napoleon had declared himself emperor of France and was trying to conquer Europe and Great Britain and her allies, including Austria and Russia, were trying to stop him. The United States was caught in the middle. The British Orders in Council called for the seizure of any

***The happy effects of that grand systom of shutting ports against the English!!* Caricature by one of the English satirists of the Cruikshank family, 1808. Thomas Jefferson defends the trade embargo to a group of irate citizens. Napoleon encourages Jefferson, whose pro-French sentiments were not universally popular.** Courtesy of Library of Congress.

vessel bound for Europe that did not first call at a British port. The French countered with the Berlin and Milan decrees ordering the capture of any ship stopping in Britain on the way to the Continent. Thus, American shipping was subject to attack by either belligerent. In 1807, Jefferson's response was an embargo on all trade from American ports. His aim was to make the European powers feel the lack of American food and raw materials, but resourceful smugglers continued to provide goods and the main sufferers were law-abiding Americans who obeyed the embargo. Jefferson repealed it shortly before he left office in 1809.

Another cause of trouble was the British policy of impressment. The British often stopped American ships, removed sailors, and put them onto their warships. Life on Royal Navy ships was brutal, and men did sometimes desert for the relatively better service on American merchant vessels. Even if the deserters claimed to be naturalized American citizens, the British did not recognize them as such, maintaining that they were still British subjects. Together, these issues of trade and impressment were to drive the next administration with the rallying cry of "Free Trade and Sailors' Rights."

JAMES MADISON'S ADMINISTRATION AND THE WAR OF 1812

Jefferson's secretary of state, James Madison, won the 1808 election. As the conflict in Europe continued, he tried a different solution to the problem of free trade. The Nonintercourse Act reopened trade with all countries except France and Great Britain, but this was as ineffective as Jefferson's embargo had been.

While the United States had almost gone to war with France in the late 1790s, now Great Britain was seen as a bigger enemy. In addition to their violation of neutral shipping rights, the British were inciting American Indians to warfare on the western frontier. A group of militant young congressmen, led by Henry Clay of Kentucky, agitated for war. Not only were these War Hawks looking to avenge wrongs done by the British, they also coveted the territories of Canada and Spanish Florida. In 1812, Madison agreed to send Congress a war message if the War Hawks supported him for reelection that year. He sent the message on June 1, Congress declared war on June 18, and Madison was re-elected.

The United States was not well prepared for war against one of the greatest powers on Earth and the war started badly. The U.S. Army and Navy were small, and the Federalists in the northeast did not support the war effort. The Americans tried to attack Canada before British reinforcements could arrive, but instead the British captured American garrisons at Detroit and Fort Mackinac and Indians, with British support, slaughtered the defenders of Fort Dearborn (the site of present-day Chicago).

Portrait of James Madison, engraving by David Edwin from a painting by Thomas Sully, 1809–1817. Madison wears his characteristic old-fashioned knee breeches and powdered hair. Courtesy of Library of Congress.

Surprisingly, though, the U.S. Navy won some successes against the British Navy, then regarded as the mistress of the seas. On August 19, 1812, USS *Constitution* defeated HMS *Guerrière,* thus earning her nickname, "Old Ironsides." In September 1813, Oliver Hazard Perry won another victory, reporting, "We have met the enemy and he is ours" at the Battle of Lake Erie. Perry's ships then ferried 5,500 troops under the command of William Henry Harrison across the lake, where they defeated combined British and Indian forces.

In Europe, however, Napoleon surrendered to the British and their allies in April 1814. This freed more British forces to be sent to the United States. A British fleet sailed into the Chesapeake Bay and raided up and down the coast throughout the summer. In late August, they landed a force in southern Maryland that marched on Washington, meeting the American army en route at Bladensburg on August 23. The Americans were poorly trained, poorly equipped, and poorly led, and could not stand up to the British, who then went on to enter the capital. There, they burned the Capitol, the President's House, and other public buildings.

The British then sailed to Baltimore, and in September they bombarded Fort McHenry. They were not successful there, however; they gave up after a day and a half and sailed away, leading Francis Scott Key to immortalize the event in a poem that was set to music and is now known as "The Star-Spangled Banner," the national anthem of the United States. On the northern front, the Americans also won an important victory on Lake Champlain.

At this time the British began to think of peace. Emissaries from both countries met in Ghent (a city in modern-day Belgium) and signed a treaty on December 24, 1814. Because neither side had decisively won, the representatives agreed to the restoration of conditions as they had been before the war. Before word of the treaty could reach the United States, one last battle was fought in New Orleans, where Andrew Jackson's troops soundly defeated the British. (One of the provisions of the treaty was that it would not go into effect until it had been ratified by both sides; therefore, technically, the two nations were still at war when this battle was fought.)

Peace came just in time. Napoleon escaped from exile on Elba and returned to the European continent, where the British and their allies had to face him once last time—at Waterloo, where he was soundly defeated. The Treaty of Ghent did not secure American maritime rights, but with the end of the conflict in Europe the British no longer had any need to harass American shipping. The United States did not win any new territory, and the attempted invasion of Canada merely stimulated Canadian nationalism. However, Florida was acquired peacefully in 1819, when Spain sold it to the United States. Additionally, the War of 1812 proved that the upstart United States could hold its own on the world stage.

JAMES MONROE AND THE ERA OF GOOD FEELINGS

James Monroe, Madison's secretary of state, was the logical presidential candidate in 1816. He was opposed by Federalist Rufus King but won an overwhelming victory. By this time, the Federalist party was very weak and would soon dissolve altogether, leaving Monroe's term virtually free of partisan politics. In fact, a Boston Federalist newspaper, the *Columbian Sentinel,* declared an "Era of Good Feelings" at the beginning of his term.

But despite the lack of partisan opposition, Monroe faced several challenges during his administration. First, there was a problem in the Southeast. As Spain's Latin American colonies began to fight for their independence, Spain was forced to withdraw troops from its Florida territory. This resulted in general lawlessness along the border with the United States, and the Seminole Indians in particular began raiding into Georgia. Monroe sent General Andrew Jackson, the hero of the Battle of New Orleans, to deal with the Indians. Jackson did so, but also exceeded his orders, executing two Indians without trial and attacking Spanish posts. Monroe's administration debated what to do, finally deciding not to reprimand the popular general. Meanwhile, Spain, fearing that the United States would take Florida by force, agreed to sell it to them instead.

A second challenge for the Monroe administration was the Panic of 1819, the country's first great economic crisis. As economic historian Murray Rothbard explained it, "the War of 1812 and its aftermath brought many rapid dislocations to the young American economy" (1962/2002, 1). The government had borrowed heavily from banks throughout the country to finance the war. It had been assumed that the banks would retain adequate reserves of specie, or hard currency in gold or silver, so that at any time bank notes could be redeemed for hard currency. The banks, however, issued more and more paper money without adequate reserves, leading to inflation, as paper notes without backing were discounted—that is, they were traded at less than their face value. The revival of foreign trade after the war also brought floods of goods into the United States, leading to lower prices on domestic commodities.

An expansion of credit allowed speculators in western lands to buy on liberal terms, and there was heavy borrowing to pay for internal improvements. The government also effectively extended credit by allowing a time lag in the payment of duties on imported goods. Concern over mounting problems prompted Congress to charter a second Bank of the United States, and this began operation in 1817. But it at first added to the problems with expansionary policies, accepting paper notes from various state banks, rather than specie, as payment. Another factor was the scheduled repayment of the Louisiana debt—the United States had borrowed money from Great Britain to buy the Louisiana territory, and payments of $4 million, in specie, were due in 1818 and 1819.

The Bank of the United States was forced to initiate a series of deflationary moves. The bank's branches were ordered to redeem notes from state banks. State banks, in turn, had to call in loans, leading to a wave of bankruptcies. Prices fell, including the prices of important export staples such as cotton, wheat, and tobacco. Merchants were left with heavy stocks of goods that no one could afford to buy, even at bargain prices. Even though most Americans still lived in rural areas, those in the cities faced widespread unemployment and accompanying distress. While farmers could revert to making do with what they could produce themselves or obtain by barter, urban workers did not have this flexibility. Ultimately, however, the deflationary moves were successful, and the depression began to abate in 1821.

One more challenge, the expansion of slavery, faced the Monroe administration. In 1819, Missouri applied for statehood. Missouri was the second state to be formed from the Louisiana territory, and, as many of the settlers owned slaves, the proposed state constitution allowed slavery. Even though political factions had temporarily been laid aside, this issue awakened regional differences between northern and southern states. The population of the northern free states was growing more rapidly than the southern slave states, and, therefore, the North controlled the House of Representatives, where representation was based on population. However, the admission of Missouri would give the South a majority in the Senate. James Tallmadge, representative of New York, proposed that the introduction of more slaves into Missouri be prohibited and that the children of those already in Missouri be freed at age 25. This restriction passed the House but not the Senate. Senator Jesse Thomas of Illinois proposed a compromise. Missouri could allow slavery, but Maine, which had also applied for statehood, would be admitted as a free state, keeping the balance of northern and southern states even in the Senate. Further, slavery would be prohibited in any new states to be formed in the Louisiana territory that were north of the southern boundary of Missouri, the latitude of 36°30′. This came to be known as the Missouri Compromise. (Missouri would not actually be admitted to the union until 1821, after a further compromise, proposed by Kentucky representative Henry Clay, specifying that Missouri must not deprive the citizens of any state of their Constitutional rights.)

The question of the expansion of slavery seemed settled for the moment; however, already there were indications that this issue would one day tear the country apart. Thomas Jefferson wrote to John Holmes on April 22, 1820, "But this momentous question, like a fire bell in the night, awakened and filled me with terror. I considered it at once as the knell of the Union. It is hushed, indeed, for the moment. But this is a reprieve only, not a final sentence." And Secretary of State John Quincy Adams, son of former President John Adams, who would himself be elected the next president, wrote in his diary on March 3, "If the Union must be dissolved, slavery is precisely the question upon which it ought to break. For the present, however, this contest is laid asleep."

References

Allgor, Catherine. 2000. *Parlor Politics: In Which the Ladies of Washington Help Build a City and a Government.* Charlottesville: University Press of Virginia.

Lester, Malcolm. 1978. *Anthony Merry* Redivivus*: A Reappraisal of the British Minister to the United States, 1803–6.* Charlottesville: University Press of Virginia.

Rothbard, Murray N. 1962. *The Panic of 1819: Reactions and Policies.* New York: Columbia University Press. Online edition Ludwig von Mises Institute, 2002.

CHAPTER 2

Society, Culture, and Dress

In 1790, the population of the United States was largely rural, with only about 5 percent of Americans living in cities. That number increased to about 7 percent in 1820; the vast majority of Americans still lived in rural areas by the end of the Federal era (U.S. Bureau of the Census 1990).The five largest cities in 1790 were New York, Philadelphia, Boston, Charleston (South Carolina), and Baltimore. In 1820, New York remained the largest city with a population surpassing 100,000. Completing the top five were Philadelphia, Baltimore, Boston, and New Orleans, which had not been part of the United States in 1790 (U.S. Bureau of the Census 1998).

European travelers observed that Americans seemed to be putting their ideal of equality into practice. In 1794, Englishman Henry Wansey observed, "In these States, you behold a certain plainness and simplicity of manners, which bespeak temperance, equality of condition, and a sober use of the faculties of the mind" (Wansey 1796/1969, x). A few years later, Scotsman John Melish wrote, "the inhabitants have a spirit of independence, and will brook no superiority.... As the people will bend to no superiority, they really affect none" (1818/1970, 48–49). This equality extended to dress, so that it was sometimes difficult to determine any class distinctions at all. Rosalie Stier Calvert wrote in 1806, "My chambermaid (a stout, pretty girl) dresses as well as I do," and in 1818, Scotsman James Flint observed in Philadelphia, "On Sundays it

***Tontine Coffee House, Wall & Water Streets, circa 1797,* print from a painting by Francis Guy. The Tontine Coffee House in New York, the largest city in the United States, was the forerunner of the New York Stock Exchange.** Courtesy of Library of Congress.

would be difficult to discriminate betwixt the hired girl and the daughter in a genteel family, were drapery the sole criterion" (Callcott 1991, 151; Flint 1822/1970, 39).

Foreign travelers also noted a lack of poverty in the United States. Wansey wrote, "I never observed a single person in rags, or with any appearance of distress or poverty; yet I looked into all the poor habitations I could find, which were very few indeed" (1796/1969, 61). James Flint wrote in 1818, "Beggars do not abound here as in some countries in Europe" (1822/1970, 6).

However, despite the perceived equality and lack of poverty, society was not altogether unstratified. Englishman John Lambert described "three distinct classes" in New York, and this was probably similar elsewhere. First, he said, were "the constituted authorities and government officers; divines, lawyers, and physicians of eminence; the principal merchants, and people of independent property." The second class was the "small merchants, retail dealers, clerks, subordinate officers of the government, and members of the three professions" [that is, medicine, law, and clergy, but not those "of eminence"]. The third was the "inferior orders of the people," such as laborers, domestic servants, common sailors, and, in rural areas, landless agricultural workers (Lambert 1810, 2:195).

In some areas of the country, the Native Americans were beginning to assimilate. In New England, there were small communities of such Indian tribes as the Abnakis, Pequots, and Wampanoags, who preserved their languages and traditional crafts but lived in modern frame houses and adapted features of European dress to their own wardrobes (Larkin 1988, 4–5). They no longer wore clothing made of skins, as these were valuable trade items, but rather used English-made wool fabrics for their matchcoats or robes, loincloths, and leggings. Both men and women wore variations of the Anglo European man's white linen shirt, but often made of brightly colored fabric instead. Tribes in the Southeast maintained communities at this time, although they would be forcibly removed later in the 19th century. They, too, had adopted many European ways, including the clothing. Major John Norton noted in 1816 that Cherokee women wore "the European dress with that variety which their circumstances in life may admit" (Klinck and Talman, 1970, 134). In the Northern Plains, the Lewis and Clark expedition encountered tribes such as the Sioux, Mandans, Cheyenne, and Shosone. The tribes had contact with European traders, trappers, and hunters, but they retained a great deal of their traditional cultures, including clothing—they, unlike the northeastern Indians, still made most of their garments from animal skins. Lewis and Clark also encountered the Chinook and the Umitilla of the Pacific Northwest. They traded with other Indians up the coast into present-day Canada and Alaska and also had contact with the outside world through visits from Spanish, Russian, and British ships. Some Indian men wore European clothes acquired in trade from the visiting sailors, that "they appear[ed] to prise highly" (Moulton 1983, 6:76).

MARRIAGE AND THE FAMILY

The Family

Almost all adults married and had children in the Federal era. Men and women were beginning to marry for love, rather than merely for economic necessity. Parents recognized the importance of this and generally left the choice of a mate to their children. Susan Kittredge wrote to her daughter in 1792, "she should not wish any friend of hers to give their hand where they could not give their heart" (Rothman 1984, 30). John Lambert wrote in 1810, "parents are not apt to force the inclinations of their children from avaricious motives" (Lambert 1810, 2:207). Courting couples were allowed private time together, as well. For example, in 1807, Mary Guion's suitor, Samuel Brown, came to call. "After tea, Samuel came here we were all reading in the Parlor when he came but they [her family] soon took a walk but him who chose to stay with me, we read, sung, and discoursed...till they returned" (Rothman 1984, 26).

Even though young people made their own decisions, parental approval was still important. Eliza Southgate met her future husband, Walter Bowne, while away from home, and wrote her mother that she "went so far as to tell him I approved him as far as I knew him, but the decision must rest with my Parents, their wishes were my law" (Bowne 1887/1980, 140).

A man generally did not decide to marry until he knew he could support a family, and most men therefore married in their middle to late 20s. Women tended to be slightly younger. Weddings were usually held at the home with family and a few friends in attendance, although related festivities could continue for several days. Debby Cochran described the wedding of her niece in Baltimore in 1817, "on Thursday Evening last about eight o'clock the ceremony was performed by the Bishop in the company of forty odd." She added that they sat down to a superb supper at 9:30 that night, and there were over one hundred people the following day for "Punch drinking" (Cochran 1817).

While a woman often wore a new dress for her wedding, she did not have the luxury of wearing it just once. Her wedding dress likely

***Country Wedding; Bishop White Officiating,* by John Lewis Krimmel, probably 1814. Oil on canvas. The genre painter Krimmel illustrates a typical wedding taking place in the bride's home with a small number of family and friends present. The bride wears a simple white dress and mitts and no head covering.** Courtesy of the Pennsylvania Academy of Fine Arts, Gift of Paul Beck, Jr.

remained the best dress in her wardrobe for a long time afterwards. It was also the custom in some parts of the country for the newly married woman to wear her wedding dress to church the first Sunday after the wedding, as well. Men did buy some new clothes for the wedding, but also continued to wear them for some time after—perhaps forever. George Wingate Chase wrote that a man purchased a new top hat "with his wedding coat, and in most cases he never had occasion to replace it. It was worn only to meeting, and on great and special occasions" (1861, 541).

Enslaved African Americans were not allowed to be legally married. Nonetheless, many did live as husband and wife after first seeking the consent of their master or mistress. Enslaved families faced the possibility of separation by sale—husbands might lose their wives, or mothers their children. Occasionally, one of a couple was able to earn freedom and would then work and save to buy his or her spouse and children.

In general, people married at a younger age than Western Europeans and had more children. Four to five children seems to have been the average family size in New England, while the number was higher in the South. Birth rates began to decline during the Federal period, especially in urban areas. At the same time, parents began to feel a new affection for their children and to adopt a new view of childhood as a distinct stage of life. The idea that children were not just small adults extended to their clothing, as parents no longer dressed their children in miniature versions of adult fashions. Rather, distinctive clothing styles for children allowed them more freedom of movement as they engaged in active play (see chapter 5).

Overall, enslaved African Americans in the United States had a high rate of natural increase. However, cases of unexpected miscarriage suggest that some women knew folk methods for inducing abortion and did so as a means of resistance against their masters.

The Polish traveler Julian Niemcewicz, writing in the last years of the 18th century, observed that American families "perhaps do not enjoy as much pleasure and amusement as Europeans do, but calm and moderate in their emotions, they pass their life in sweet tranquility." He also found that "infidelities on the part of the women are almost unknown and those of the men extremely rare" (1965, 21–22). John Lambert similarly wrote, "I understand that unhappy marriages are by no means frequent" (Lambert 1810, 2:207). Divorces were rare but did occur, perhaps in part because of the new emphasis on happiness in marriage. In 1804, Eliza Law, step-granddaughter of George Washington, and her husband, Thomas, agreed to separate. Mrs. Calvert, who was Mrs. Law's aunt, wrote, "Mrs. Law and her husband separated amicably.... They don't accuse each other of anything except not being able to get along together" (Callcott 1991, 92). As was usual in cases of divorce involving children, the father received custody of their daughter.

The Household

There were likely to be one or more unrelated people living in a household at any one time. Men who ran their own businesses would likely have apprentices who would live with the family. Even families who were not very prosperous might have a young woman helping with domestic chores. This could be considered an informal form of apprenticeship, as a young woman learned housekeeping skills before marriage. More prosperous households might also have hired male servants. However, no doubt because of the American spirit of equality and equal opportunity, servants were notorious for being independent and not staying in any one position for very long. Henry Wansey wrote that a woman in Newark, New Jersey, told him of the "difficulty of getting domestic servants; they will only agree by the month, at very high wages" (1796/1969, 99). William Cobbett in 1818 observed, "Neither men nor women will allow you to call them *servants.*" He added, "Domestics of both sexes are far from good. They are *honest;* but they are not *obedient*" (1818/1964, 187–88). Likewise, James Flint found, "Servants are not here so attentive to their duty as elsewhere.... *Master* is not a word in the vocabulary of hired people. *Bos,* a Dutch one of similar import, is substituted" (1822/1970, 9). In the South, domestic servants were for the most part enslaved and could not, therefore, be so independent.

The majority of the population lived in modest dwellings, from one-room log houses on the frontier, to one to four room frame houses in more settled villages, towns, and cities. One main room generally served for cooking, eating, and sitting. Children, apprentices, and hired help might also sleep there, or in a loft. If a man was engaged in a craft, trade, or profession, another room in the house was likely his place of business. Adults sometimes had the luxury of a separate chamber for sleeping. In the South, a separate kitchen building was fairly common, as the kitchen fireplace would heat up the main house as well as posing a risk of fire to the structure. Most houses were built of wood, with brick or stone fireplaces and chimneys. Only about 10 percent of the population lived in substantially built two-story houses with six or seven rooms, and only an elite 1 percent had elegantly built and furnished town houses or large manors on country estates or plantations (Larkin 1988, 113). These grand houses might be built entirely of brick, usually made on site.

Furnishings, too, varied, with the more well-to-do having stylish furniture, either imported from Europe or, increasingly, made by American craftsmen. They could keep their clothing and household textiles in chests with drawers or in presses—large pieces of furniture with shelves. For example, when Margaret Dickie died in 1799, those who inventoried her estate listed the clothing that was found in the drawers of her large chest (Hersh and Hersh 1995, 154). Most people, though, had few pieces of furniture. They might hang their outerwear on a peg by the door and store their other clothing in a simple box or trunk. Window and floor coverings were also luxuries, with most homes having bare windows and floors.

DAILY LIFE

Religion

Many settlers had come to the American colonies seeking freedom to worship in their own way. The new nation saw a proliferation of religious sects. In the early 1800s, John Melish described Newport, Rhode Island, as having "four baptist churches, two for congregationalists, and one each for episcopalians, quakers, Moravians, and Jews" (1818/1970, 65). A strong spiritual revival, known as the Second Great Awakening, began in the 1790s and continued into the 1840s. This, coupled with westward expansion and the independence of the pioneer spirit, contributed to the diversity of religious thought and the formation of new Protestant denominations. The following are some of the most significant religious entities during the Federal era.

After independence, members of the Church of England, or Anglican Church, reorganized as the Episcopal Church in America. Separation of church and state meant that, rather than being supported by the state, as it had been in England, the new church had to compete with other denominations for adherents.

Catholics were among the first settlers to the American colonies, coming to Maryland in 1634. The number of Catholics in the United States was not large, although it increased as the anti-clerical sentiment of the French Revolution drove priests and other observant Catholics into exile. The addition of New Orleans to the United States in 1803 also increased the number of Catholics within the borders of the country.

Methodism began as a reform movement within the Anglican Church in the early 1700s. English Methodist missionaries came to the American colonies, and one, Francis Asbury, remained after the War for Independence. Asbury and his followers were very successful in gaining converts. By the 1790s, the Methodist Episcopal Church was ordaining ministers, had established a publishing house, and had appointed Asbury as a bishop.

In New England, Congregationalists were the legacy of the early Puritan settlers. The Congregationalists were the first American denomination to send missionaries abroad. Some disaffected Congregationalists were attracted to Presbyterianism, as were many Scots-Irish immigrants. Both Presbyterians and Baptists followed the settlers as they moved west. Baptist preachers were not required to have formal training, which allowed their numbers to proliferate. Further, they supported the separation of church and state and congregational independence, ideas that likely appealed to independent-minded pioneers.

In Philadelphia, Richard Allen, a freed African American, attracted crowds to Saint George's Episcopal Church with his preaching. The white members of Saint George's hastened the departure of their African American members by directing that they sit only in the newly built church gallery. In response, Allen and his followers started the African Methodist Episcopal Church in 1794.

William Penn had founded the colony of Pennsylvania as a refuge for Quakers, or members of the Society of Friends, and their presence was still strong in Philadelphia. Quakers were pacifists and opposed to slavery, and were therefore active in the abolitionist movement.

Moravians came from the German state of Saxony to Pennsylvania in the early 1700s. (This sect, like the Lutherans, had its origins in protests against the Roman Catholic Church in Europe.) The Moravians also settled in North Carolina.

The number of Jews in the United States was very small throughout the Federal era. It would only be later, when there was increased immigration of Jews from Eastern Europe, that their numbers would grow significantly. The first Jewish settlers in the American colonies were Sephardic Jews from Western Europe, although some Ashkenazim from Eastern Europe did immigrate during the colonial period.

Education

The rate of literacy was rising in the early 19th century; even the poor generally learned the rudiments of reading, writing, and arithmetic. (Reading and writing were regarded as separate skills, so at a given time, more people might know how to read than how to write.) About 75 percent of white male Americans were literate (Larkin 1988, 35). In New England, primary schools were often supported by a mix of public and private funds, but elsewhere, parents had to pay for their children's educations. Mothers, if they had the time and inclination, often taught their children the basics themselves. Enslaved African Americans generally had little formal education. However, laws actually forbidding slaves to read and write would not be passed until later in the 19th century, in response to the perceived threat of slave rebellions.

In well-to-do families, boys received a classical education. That is, they learned to read both Greek and Latin literature in the original languages. They might learn from a private tutor at home, from a local teacher (often a clergyman), or at a boarding school. Other subjects in the curriculum of a well-educated young man included English grammar, mathematics (algebra, geometry, and trigonometry), logic, public speaking, science (biology, botany, physics, or geology), and geography.

***The May Queen (The Crowning of Flora),* by Jacob Marling, 1816. Oil on canvas. At these end of the school year ceremonies, students demonstrated the progress they had made and a worthy student was crowned queen. This may depict the Raleigh Academy in North Carolina, where Marling taught art. Most of the girls wear fashionable white dresses.**
Courtesy of the Chrysler Museum of Art.

Girls, too, were sent to school and taught at least basic academic subjects, although the classics, sciences, and higher mathematics were often omitted. (In 1806, a writer in the *Charleston* [SC] *Spectator* echoed the common belief that, "an inquiry into abstract and speculative truths, into the principles and axioms of the sciences...is not the province of women....neither have they sufficient attention and precision to succeed in mathematics.") Modern scholars have coined the term "Republican Motherhood" for the belief that girls should have a good basic education because, as mothers, they would then educate their sons to be good citizens.

It was considered important for a girl to learn elegant handwriting, since letter writing was a primary means of communication. Girls also learned what schoolmistresses advertised as "useful and ornamental" subjects. Basic sewing, for example, was a useful skill, as even well-to-do women sewed much of the basic family clothing and household textiles, or at least supervised the work of others. Girls, therefore, learned basic plain sewing, but they also learned ornamental needlework. A completed needlework picture, framed and proudly hung in the home, was tangible evidence that the family had the means to send their daughter away to school.

Among genteel families, both boys and girls learned dancing—an important social skill. Children learned manners and deportment along with the dance steps. Both sexes also learned drawing and music. French and Italian might be added to the curriculum, especially among those who planned to send their children to Europe.

Young men could continue their education at a college. Harvard and Yale, founded to train ministers in the north, and the College of William and Mary in Virginia were the oldest institutions of higher learning in the nation, and, John Lambert pointed out, in the early 1800s colleges were "multiplying very rapidly" (1810, 2:201).

Young men (and some young women) commonly learned their trade or craft through apprenticeship. Apprenticeship was usually a legal agreement, or indenture, made between the craftsman and the father of the child. The child was to be taught the trade or craft, and perhaps some academic subjects as well, and provided room, board, and clothing. Not only were clothes to be provided during the apprenticeship, but it was customary for an apprentice to be given a new outfit upon completion of the term. Poor orphaned children were often bound out by the local government, thus relieving the state of the burden of support. In some trades, the former apprentice next became a journeyman, one who was paid for his work but was not yet ready to be a self-sufficient businessman. In 1820, Everard Peck had five journeymen and apprentices in his Rochester, New York, bookbinding shop, and they all lived in his household (Larkin 1988, 9).

In the days before the mass production of ready-to-wear garments, people often had professionals make their fitted and formal garments to order. Both boys and girls engaged in apprenticeships in the needle trades. (In fact, this was one of the few areas open to females.) Girls could apprentice as *mantua-makers* (named after the *mantua,* a loose-fitting dress), making women's garments. Later the term became *dressmakers.* Tailors were primarily men, although there were some women in the trade. Tailors made men's coats, overcoats, and leg wear as well as women's masculine-style riding habits. As there were no commercial patterns, apprentices in both trades had to learn to take a client's measurements, cut the garment pieces, sew them together, and fit them to the body.

Young men learned even the professions by studying with an established practitioner, although they might attend a college first. New Hampshire statesman Daniel Webster, for example, learned law by clerking for Christopher Gore, a prominent attorney who later served as governor of Massachusetts. In 1800, Daniel Drake began to study medicine with Dr. William Goforth of Cincinnati, who himself had studied with a Dr. Young in New York (Mansfield 1855/1975, 50).

Health

It is difficult to determine what an American's life expectancy was during the Federal period, as birth and death dates were not consistently recorded. However, in the Northeast, it appears that, if people survived childhood, they could expect to live into their 60s (Larkin 1988, 74). People frequently died from infectious diseases and complications from injuries and accidents, and women often died from complications of childbirth. A yellow fever epidemic hit Philadelphia in 1793, killing about 10 percent of the population, and there were other outbreaks in Philadelphia, New York, Boston, Baltimore, and New Orleans before the end of the Federal period. Tuberculosis, or consumption, was another leading cause of death.

Malaria was endemic in the South. It was seldom fatal, but the recurring chills and fever symptomatic of the disease were debilitating. John Melish stopped at a tavern in South Carolina where first a doctor and then the landlord were seized with ague fits, or shaking and fever, which were most likely caused by malaria (1818/1970, 194). Smallpox was disfiguring, debilitating, and sometimes fatal. A form of inoculation, where people were given a mild form of the disease, had been developed in the middle of the 18th century. When physician Edward Jenner discovered in 1796 that inoculation with the related disease cowpox gave immunity with less risk, this method became widespread.

Poor sanitation doubtless played a role in illness. Running water and indoor toilets were very rare during the Federal period. Not everyone had a privy or outhouse, either. Often, people just let their waste accumulate in the yard or in the streets. Even in cities, livestock roamed the streets and, along with the horses, deposited their waste.

Medical treatment was likely to do more harm than good. Physicians still followed the teachings of the Greek physician Galen. According to his theory, good health was maintained by a balance of the four humors in the body: black bile, yellow bile, phlegm, and blood. Illness was caused by an imbalance of the humors, necessitating bleeding, blistering, or purging (inducing vomiting or diarrhea), to correct the imbalance. When Charles Stier, in Philadelphia, had a fever, he went to one of the most famous physicians in the United States, Benjamin Rush. Stier noted that he was bled repeatedly, purged, and blistered (Callcott 1991, 5). Amputations and other surgery were performed without anesthesia. Also, as germ theory was unknown, there was no attempt at antiseptic or aseptic conditions. Infection was common.

Many of the medicines that physicians used also caused harm. Drugs included calomel, or mercurous chloride, which can cause tooth damage, and laudanum, an opium derivative. People who could not afford a doctor, did not have access to one, or simply mistrusted the treatments of the professional, sometimes sought out natural remedies. Some of these were actually effective. Willow bark, for example, contains a chemical similar to aspirin with pain relieving and anti-inflammatory properties.

Dentistry was also primitive. Tooth decay was common, and having a tooth pulled was an ordeal, as there was no medication for pain and there was high risk of infection. George Washington suffered from life-long dental problems, including infected and abscessed teeth and gums and multiple extractions. He tried several sets of dentures variously made with real human teeth or ivory, but none was really satisfactory. (Contrary to later popular belief, he did not have false teeth made of wood.)

ARTS AND ENTERTAINMENT

Painting

Students of dress find the work of portrait painters a valuable resource for information about clothing and appearance. Traditionally, only the very wealthy could afford to hire an artist to have a portrait painted. However, during the Federal era, a broader spectrum of American citizens were able to do so. A number of portrait painters who had been educated in Europe brought their skills back to the United States.

***The Accident in Lombard Street,* by Charles Willson Peale, 1787. Etching. The patriarch of the artistic Peale family here depicts ragged chimney sweeps laughing at a girl who has dropped a pie she was taking home from a bake-house.** Courtesy of Library of Congress.

Ralph Earl was born in Massachusetts, but went to England during the War for Independence. Earl returned to the United States in 1785, eventually settling in Litchfield, Connecticut. He did not have a studio, but rather painted his subjects in their homes, thereby providing a glimpse of their household goods as well as themselves.

Charles Willson Peale of Maryland also studied in England, returning to the American colonies in 1769. By the beginning of the Federal era, he was well-established as a painter. In 1791, he founded his Philadelphia Museum, the first in the United States, to depict the "world in miniature." On display were a variety of natural specimens, including animals, plants, minerals, Peale's portraits of famous Americans, and the skeleton of a prehistoric mastodon that he exhumed near Newburgh, New York, in 1801 (Miller 1996, 22–27). Peale's brother, James, and Peale's second son, Rembrandt, were also successful portrait painters.

Gilbert Stuart was born in Rhode Island and spent a number of years in Great Britain before returning to the United States in 1793. He was a prolific portraitist, painting a number of wealthy clients in New York, Philadelphia, Washington, D.C., and Boston. He also had a lucrative

***Bank of Pennsylvania, South Second Street, Philadelphia,* from an engraving by William Birch, 1804. Benjamin Henry Latrobe's design for this building, suggesting a Greek temple, is typical of the classical style of architecture that was fashionable in Federal America.** Collection of the author.

Classicism

Much of Western architecture, philosophy and scientific knowledge is derived from the classical world of ancient Greece and Rome. During the 18th and 19th centuries, this knowledge was central to the education of upper class Western Europeans and Americans, who studied Greek and Roman literature in the original languages. In the first half of the 18th century, the excavations of the Roman cities of Herculaneum and Pompeii fueled this interest as they revealed intact paintings and furniture.

The ideals of Greek democracies and the Roman Republic had inspired the American Revolution. To provide a proper setting for the new American Republic, architects such as Benjamin Henry Latrobe and Thomas Jefferson designed buildings using Greek or Roman temples as models. Furniture makers borrowed both the forms and applied ornament of the classical world. (This style is often called neo-classical, but that term was not used at the time.) Symmetry and proportion were of prime importance in classical design.

The French revolutionaries carried their idolization of the ancients a step further. Women began to dress in "Greek" or "antique" style, wearing narrow dresses that clung in folds suggestive of ancient statues. Greek and Roman decorative motifs embellished both men's and women's clothing.

By the end of the Federal era, classicism began to give way to romanticism. The emphasis was on emotion rather than reason and inspiration came from Gothic or Medieval Europe rather than the ancient world.

business painting portraits of George Washington. Other well-known portrait painters included Thomas Sully, who studied in England, and John Vanderlyn, who studied in France and Italy.

Painters who did not have the benefit of a European education included Joseph Eichholtz, John Wesley Jarvis, and Joshua Johnson. Eichholtz was a Pennsylvania German who began his professional life as a coppersmith but later turned to portrait painting, depicting members of the growing middle class in Pennsylvania, Maryland, and Delaware (Ryan 2003, 1, 11). John Wesley Jarvis became the leading portrait painter in New York City, and the city government commissioned him to paint heroes of the War of 1812 for public display (Baigell 1984, 53–54). Joshua Johnson, a free man of color in Baltimore, painted a number of portraits of individuals, families, and children of the rising middle class through the first quarter of the 19th century.

Folk artists, largely self-trained and often anonymous, provide us with a broader range of images. Ammi Phillips, for example, painted portraits of residents along the New York-Massachusetts border, including prosperous farmers and their wives (Chotner 1992, 171).

Genre painters portray scenes of ordinary life and therefore provide information on how people of different walks of life dressed when engaged in a variety of activities. While genre painting was well established in Europe, only a few American painters worked in this style during the Federal period. (Genre painting became much more popular in the second quarter of the 19th century.) The foremost genre painter of the Federal era was John Lewis Krimmel, who came to Philadelphia from Germany in 1809. He painted a number of scenes of both everyday life and special occasions, portraying a cross-section of society.

Entertainment, Amusements, and Pastimes

In 1810, John Lambert wrote, perhaps with tongue in cheek, that while the young women in New York were accomplished in music, drawing, and dancing, "among the young men these accomplishments are but little cultivated. Billiards and smoking seem to be their favourite amusements" (1810, 2:205). However, men as well as women read books, newspapers, and magazines, and attended the theater.

Literature

Lambert did recognize that, "A taste for reading has of late diffused itself throughout the country" (1810, 2:202). People in the United States often read books published in England, but there were some accomplished American writers. Among these, three historians stand out. Mercy Otis Warren was one of the literary greats of the day. She wrote poems and two plays, and her master work, published in 1805, was a three-volume *History of the Rise, Progress, and Termination of the American Revolution.* She wrote from the viewpoint of the Jeffersonian Republicans. Chief Justice John Marshall, on the other hand, wrote his five-volume biography of George Washington from the Federalist point of

***Billiards at a Country Tavern,* by Benjamin Henry Latrobe, circa 1796. A working man has removed his coat and shoes to play billiards with more well-dressed opponents.** In *The Journal of Latrobe,* 1905, New York: D. Appleton and Company.

view. David Ramsay, of South Carolina, wrote histories of that state and the American Revolution and a biography of George Washington.

Charles Brockden Brown was one of the first American writers of fiction. He wrote in the style of the popular English Gothic novels, adapting the form to American themes and settings. For example, he set *Arthur Mervyn* in Philadelphia during the yellow fever epidemic of 1793 (Vickers 2002, 165). Brown also published two literary magazines, the *Monthly Magazine and American Review* and the *Literary Magazine and American Register.* Both of these were short-lived. Often, material in both magazines and newspapers was copied from English publications. Other literary, general interest, and women's magazines also came and went during the period. The women's magazines included information on European fashions so that American women could be in style. The *Boston Magazine/Boston Weekly Magazine,* in print from1802 to 1805, ran articles on the fashions current in both London and Paris. However, the news from London was one to three months old, with fashions for September being reported at the end of October, 1802, and fashions from October being described in the December 4, 1802, issue. In New York, the *Lady's Monitor* appeared briefly in the early years of the 19th century and reported on London fashions. The Philadelphia general-interest magazine, the *Port Folio,* reported on European fashions for a few years early in the century but then dropped this feature.

Newspapers were widespread. Many editors took full advantage of the freedom granted the press in the First Amendment to the Constitution and were unabashedly partisan. Attacks on political opponents could be nasty and have little basis in fact. James Flint wrote, "the style of many communications and advertisements that appear in them, shews that the *public* are not far advanced in taste" (1822/1970, 19). The distribution of newspapers and magazines was expanded when legislation allowed them to be delivered by the postal service at moderate rates.

Theater

Large cities had theaters frequented by a cross-section of society. In New York, the John Street Theatre had been established before the Revolutionary War. In 1787, it was the venue for Royall Tyler's *The Contrast,* generally regarded as the first distinctly American play. Comic actor Thomas Wignell established the Chestnut Street Theatre in Philadelphia in the 1790s. (George Washington was a frequent visitor, and Wignell set aside a presidential box and always greeted Washington personally.) Henry Wansey wrote, "it is an elegant and convenient theatre, as large as that of Covent Garden" (1796/1969, 126). Boston, Charleston, and New Orleans all had theaters. Touring companies visited smaller cities that did not have permanent troupes.

Holidays

In agrarian societies, mid-winter was a time when the workload was lighter and food was plentiful; the crops had been harvested and livestock butchered. It was, therefore, natural for the winter holidays of Christmas and New Year's Day to be a time of celebration. John Lambert found that Christmas was celebrated in New York much as it was in England, except that people did not necessarily attend church. In 1807, a group of clergymen of several denominations recommended that the day be "a day of solemn *thanksgiving and prayer,*" and as a result, people did indeed attend church and the day "was religiously and strictly observed" (1810, 2:216).

In contrast, "all the complimentary visits, fun, and merriment of the season" were reserved for New Year's Day. The mayor of the city held an open house where cakes, wine, and punch were served (Lambert 1810, 2:217). In Washington, D.C., people called at the President's House. Rosalie Stier Calvert wrote of her visit in 1818, "Everyone goes there on that day. There was such a crowd in the room where Mrs. Monroe was that we could hardly move, either forward or backward" (Callcott 1991, 331; Mrs. Calvert added, "Because it was morning, people were not very dressed up." These "morning calls" were actually made in the early afternoon, and people would not wear their most formal clothes for such visits). Even in less exalted circles, people exchanged visits on New Year's Day.

Christmas was not universally celebrated in New England, as it was generally not recognized in the Puritan/Calvinist religious tradition. In 1816, Sylvia Lewis Tyler of New Hartford, Connecticut, recorded in her diary, "Christmas some kept the day." She did, however, visit neighbors, where they had "an Oyster supper & walnuts & Apples in the Evening." In 1812, although she "did house work," she added, "it being Christmas I dressed a Turkey and we ate it for supper."

Celebrating the holidays with the noise of gunfire was a practice in the South and on the frontier. Mary Boardman Crowninshield of Salem, Massachusetts, was in Washington, D.C., on Christmas Day in 1815. She wrote, "Christmas morn. It seems more like our Independence—guns firing all night" (Crowninshield 1935, 30). James Flint was in Washington, Ohio, on Christmas day in 1818. He wrote, "About five o'clock I was awakened by the firing of guns and pistols." He was in another town on January 1, 1819, where, once again, "the boys of the town made a great noise by firing guns and pistols.... During the night I heard much noise of fighting and swearing amongst adult persons" (1822/1970, 122, 126; the latter was no doubt related to the consumption of alcohol).

Traditionally, slaves on plantations were given a holiday for the week between Christmas and New Year's Day. However, former slave Charles Ball found that, as cotton was ready to harvest at this time of year, those on cotton plantations did not generally get time off. They did, however, get "a dinner of meat, on Christmas-day," and the winter allowance of clothing was distributed (1837/1969, 268).

Americans celebrated their independence on the fourth of July, and it was evidently quite a celebration by 1819. John Lewis Krimmel's painting depicts a carnival atmosphere in Philadelphia's Centre Square. Tents display scenes from both Revolutionary War battles and the War of 1812. Krimmel noted that vendors sold Seville oranges, lemons, pies and breads, gingerbread, oysters, lobsters, crawfish, pretzels, sausages, lemonade, and beer, and that amusements included dice throwing and an optic show (Harding 1994, 168–70). Speeches and recitations of patriotic poetry might also have marked the day.

Thanksgiving was not a national holiday until later in the 19th century. However, governors of individual New England states did proclaim a Thursday in November as a holiday. Sylvia Lewis Tyler usually mentioned the day in her diary. On November 27, 1812, she wrote, "It being Thanksgiving I Baked" and then she went to her in-laws' house for supper. Thanksgiving was on November 30 in 1814, and she "prepared some victuals Baked an Oven full."

TRANSPORTATION, COMMUNICATION, COMMERCE, AND MANUFACTURING

James Flint wrote in 1818, "America has a full proportion of enterprizing citizens, and such as are essential to the progress of a new country" (170). The Federal era saw improvements in transportation and communication as the new country expanded westward. Enterprising Americans also began to put Alexander Hamilton's theory of self-sufficiency into practice, establishing fledgling industries to replace imported goods with American-made ones.

Transportation

The movement of passengers, agricultural commodities, and finished goods depended on reliable methods of transportation. Improved roads were built by private corporations who sold shares to fund construction and then charged tolls for passage. Pikes, or gates, were placed at intervals where a keeper would collect the toll and open, or turn, the pike to let travelers pass. The first turnpike was constructed from 1793 to 1795 and connected Philadelphia to Lancaster, Pennsylvania. By 1811, work had begun on the National Road to connect Cumberland, in western Maryland, to Wheeling (then in Virginia, but today in West Virginia.) In 1813, the Baltimore-Washington Turnpike was also under construction to connect the new national capital to the third largest city in the United States. (Today, the National Road is remembered as US Route

40 and Interstate Highway 68, while the Baltimore-Washington Turnpike is US Route 1.)

Permanent bridges across bodies of water replaced ferries or floating bridges. In Massachusetts, a bridge over the Charles River connecting Boston with Charlestown was built in 1786. The first suspension bridge (a bridge with the roadway suspended from spans of ropes, chains, or cables attached to supports) was built in Pennsylvania in 1796.

Travel on inland waterways was made easier and faster by the invention of a practical steam-powered boat that could reliably travel upstream against the current. Robert Fulton's *Clermont* made its maiden voyage up the Hudson River in 1807. On the ocean, sailing ships were still the only method of travel. Americans improved the design of their ships to make them both larger, to carry more cargo, and faster.

Communication

The American colonies had established a postal system with Benjamin Franklin as postmaster. The Articles of Confederation gave Congress the power to establish post offices in the new United States, and Postmaster General Ebenezer Howard developed inland service, contracting with stagecoach companies to carry the mail. He also opened a route west to Pittsburgh, then on the frontier, and he reestablished monthly mail service to Europe. The postal service continued under the new Constitution. Mail delivery remained primarily from post office to post office, where individuals would have to pick up their mail. Some cities, though, did provide home delivery for an extra fee.

Commerce

Americans, primarily Yankees from the northeastern states, carried on lively overseas trade with Europe, the East and West Indies, Africa, and China. Goods from the United States that were in demand around the world included grain, lumber, horses, cattle, beef, pork, fish, poultry, butter, and cheese. In addition to manufactured goods that were not produced domestically, the ships brought back produce from the East and West Indies, such as citrus fruit and spices, dyestuffs from Central and South America, such as logwood and Brazilwood, and slaves from Africa. (Jefferson's trade embargo [see chapter 1] was especially damaging to law-abiding Yankee traders. Others engaged in smuggling. In addition, despite the 1808 law prohibiting it, smugglers also continued to import slaves from Africa long after the end of the Federal period.)

Large cities had shops featuring both imported and locally produced goods. Mary Bagot, wife of the British minister to the United States, went shopping in Philadelphia in 1816 and "found every sort & kind of French, Indian & English goods to be had—excellent of their kind & not dear" (Hosford 1984, 43).

Even small settlements had shops or stores, as surrounding farmers needed a place to sell their goods and buy the necessities they could not produce themselves. The storekeeper played another important role, as there was usually a shortage of currency and coin during the Federal era, and most commercial transactions were recorded as credits and debits in the shopkeeper's books. For example, a shopkeeper in a small farming town might also own a gristmill. A farmer would bring his crop of wheat to the mill, where it was ground into flour. The shopkeeper recorded a credit of the value of the wheat to the farmer's account, subtracting the cost of the milling and the cost of shipping the flour to market (either to a larger town to be sold there, or to a port for shipment overseas.) Then the farmer could use the credit for items such as muslin for a gown for his wife, nails, sugar, salt, or whiskey. Further, the shopkeeper might keep private transactions on his books, if, for example, one farmer borrowed money from another. He might also loan small sums of money when hard currency was required, for example, for tax payments (Martin 2008, 72).

Manufacturing

Great Britain had established colonies both as a source of raw materials and as a market for manufactured goods. As such, manufacturing was discouraged in those colonies, and the fledgling United States had no large-scale manufacturing. The fabrication of goods was mostly home-based. By 1810, however, larger-scale industry was developing. That year, Secretary of the Treasury Albert Gallatin presented a report to Congress on American manufactures. Industries that met domestic demand included wood and wood products (such as furniture, coaches and carriages, and ship building); leather and leather goods (especially shoes); refined sugar; coarse earthenware; and snuff, chocolate, and mustard. Soap and tallow candles were also on this list, even though much of this production was still done in the home.

Industries that did not meet domestic needs included iron products, paper making and printing, brewing and distilling, gun powder, and window glass. Cotton, wool, and flax textiles were also on this list. As these are most significant to the subject of this book, the development of this industry will be addressed in detail.

Textile Manufacturing

Much textile production was still done in the home. There were professional weavers, but even they worked on a small scale, primarily working to order with the client providing the materials. They combined weaving with other pursuits, such as farming. Women spun and wove at home in addition to their other domestic tasks, producing utilitarian fabrics such as linens for undergarments and household use. Sometimes they did so to clothe their families, but also exchanged their home-produced utilitarian fabrics for finer, imported fabrics or other goods at the local store. Americans also made some all-wool and all-cotton fabrics, as well as mixtures of linen and cotton or cotton and wool. High quality clothing fabrics, such as wool broadcloth for men's wear and silks and printed linens and cottons for women's wear, were imported.

After the Revolutionary War was over, England eagerly began to send its manufactured goods to the former colonies. Even in rural Virginia, "The staid and sober habits of our ancestors, with their plain home-manufactured clothing, were suddenly laid aside, and European goods of fine quality adopted in their stead" (Tryon 1917/1966, 127). Many people in the United States hoped to see the country no longer dependent on imported fabrics; in 1809, a commentator in the *Raleigh Register* wrote, "We anxiously look forward to the day, when a man may furnish himself with a good Coat, for either winter or summer, without being obliged to send 3000 miles for the Cloth." But self-sufficiency was not possible with small-scale home-based production.

In England, the Industrial Revolution was underway, led by the development of new machinery in the textile industry. John Kay's flying shuttle, in 1733, simplified the weaving of broadloom fabrics. Prior to this, a weaver required an assistant to help pass the shuttle back and forth. In 1767 James Hargreaves invented the spinning jenny, a mechanism that made it possible for a spinner to spin several threads at once, although it was still hand-powered. However, the thread produced by the jenny was not strong enough to be used for warp threads, which still had to be spun individually by hand. Richard Arkwright's 1768 spinning

Ipswich Lace

The production of bobbin lace in Ipswich, Massachusetts was a serious commercial endeavor. (Bobbin lace is produced by intertwining a number of individual threads, wound on bobbins. A paper pattern is placed on a small pillow and the motifs are marked with pins, with the threads being intertwined around them.) This was truly a cottage industry, with women making lace in their homes. Between August 1789 and August 1790, over 600 women produced 41,979 yards of lace, averaging seven inches of lace a day. Given the effort needed to produce it, this was an impressive quantity (Cotterell 1999, 82–85).

Ipswich had been a thriving port, but shifting sands at the mouth of the Ipswich River made it impossible for ocean-going ships to enter. Residents looked for other means to earn their livelihood and, about 1750, women began to make lace. Lace was a good choice because it was small and easily portable but had great value. When the Revolutionary War cut off the supply of English lace, the lacemakers of Ipswich were ready to fill the demand.

Their products included narrow white edgings for garments such as women's caps and baby clothes. These white laces were made of linen threads. By the late 18th century, the women were also making fashionable black lace from silk thread. They also made some blonde lace from natural-colored silk thread.

Surviving garments incorporating Ipswich lace include a shawl belonging to Martha Washington, with two kinds of lace, and a black silk cape with lace trim worn by Abigail Winship Robbins (Raffel 2003, 117–20). The industry died out by the 1840s, as machine-made lace replaced handmade lace in fashion.

frame produced stronger threads that could be used for the warp. This machine was powered by water and so became known as a water frame, and it opened the door to large-scale mechanized factory production. Before fibers could be spun into thread or yarn, they had to be carded. Carding is the preliminary alignment of the short individual fibers. They are made into a thin web and then formed into a roll called a sliver, which is then spun. Carding was done by hand using pairs of wooden cards with wire teeth until Lewis Paul invented a hand-driven carding machine in 1748. Arkwright designed an improved machine in the 1770s.

The English, eager to keep their secrets, refused to sell machines abroad or allow workers to leave the country. However, enterprising Americans made attempts to set up factories and recruited English technicians who emigrated despite the prohibitions. Some Americans also visited England and directly observed the machinery in operation. It was difficult for entrepreneurs in the United States to compete with those in England as domestically made fabrics could not be sold as cheaply as imported ones. Secretary of the Treasury Alexander Hamilton thus proposed increased duties, or taxes on imported goods, which would increase revenue for the government and also add to the cost of imported fabrics, allowing American fabrics to be priced more competitively. Another economic incentive was to pay a bounty on domestic manufactures. Hamilton also recommended payment of a bounty, or subsidy, on some domestically manufactured goods, such as sail cloth, as an incentive to producers.

Domestic manufacturing received another boost with President Thomas Jefferson's embargo on trade with Great Britain and France in 1807 (see chapter 1). With supplies of fabrics from these countries cut off, more Americans entered the business with a ready-made market for their goods. Jefferson's successor, James Madison, put similar legislation in place to restrict trade and finally declared war on Great Britain in 1812. Not only did the war cut off trade, but it also created a demand for wool fabrics, formerly overwhelmingly British-made, for military uniforms. However, both privateers and smugglers continued to bring some imported goods into the country.

With the end of the war in 1815, England again flooded the American market with goods as they had done after the Revolutionary War. Only the most efficiently run American factories could continue to compete. The general economic slow down of the Panic of 1819 further hurt the textile industry in the United States, although it went on to thrive in the next two decades.

Cotton was best suited to early mass production. Production of wool, linen, and silk fabrics lagged behind. The following is a brief overview of how industrialization began for these primary textile fibers in the United States.

Cotton

The new textile machinery had been designed for cotton manufacturing. In 1789, mechanic Samuel Slater, who had worked at an English cotton mill, emigrated to the United States in secret, carrying plans for the machines in his head. He found backing with Moses Brown and his son-in-law, William Almy. Slater built Arkwright-style water-powered spinning frames that produced the stronger threads suitable for warp use. In 1790, these machines were first installed in an existing building in Pawtucket, but later a new building housing additional new equipment was built. Slater insisted on being a partner, rather than a hired mechanic, and the firm became Almy, Brown, and Slater. In this first mill, carding and spinning were both done under one roof. Weaving, though, still accomplished on hand looms, was done in separate weaving sheds where several professional weavers worked together. This arrangement was not successful and the company turned to putting out warps, that is, sending thread out to be woven to individual weavers. This was the common system by 1803. Also, thread was sold to dealers and later to agents who took over the management of putting out warps to weavers.

At first, the Pawtucket mill had to rely on imports of West Indian cotton because cotton grown in the United States was of poor quality. However, in the middle of the 1790s, domestic quality improved with the introduction of sea island cotton in Georgia. The 1793 invention of the cotton gin also made the separation of cotton fibers from seeds more efficient. Soon, cotton cultivation spread throughout the South, resulting not only in enough fiber for domestic use, but also for export to Great Britain.

The next significant development in the American textile industry was the implementation of power looms. Boston merchant Francis Cabot Lowell visited England in 1810 to look at textile machinery. On his return to the United States, he established a vertically integrated factory—that is, where all the processing, spinning, and weaving of the cotton was done under one roof, and all the machinery was powered by water. His Boston Manufacturing Company was in Waltham, Massachusetts, and was to set the pattern for New England textile mills, including those in the town bearing Lowell's name, in the second quarter of the 19th century

The fabrics produced in both Rhode Island and Massachusetts were primarily utilitarian fabrics such as shirting and sheeting. Power looms were not yet advanced enough to make more than simple plain weave fabrics in solid colors or vertical stripes. Hand weavers could produce more complex patterns and weaves such as ticking, check, and plaid, and so continued to find work even as power looms were being widely adopted.

Printed cotton fabrics were first imported from India and then from England. However, by the beginning of the Federal period, John Hewson, an English immigrant, was producing high quality printed cotton fabrics in Philadelphia. He had actually started his business before the American Revolution, but joined the Continental forces during the war and was captured by the British. After the war, he once again set up his printing business. He was featured in action on the manufacturing float in the Grand Federal Procession held in Philadelphia on July 4, 1788. His wife and four daughters, all dressed in Hewson's printed cottons, also rode on the float.

Wool

The demand for good quality wool fabrics, the staple of men's apparel, was very great. Americans therefore tried to manufacture such fabrics domestically, rather than relying on British imports. These fabrics required expert finishing, or dressing, as well as spinning and weaving. Those who performed all the steps of finishing were called clothiers. (The term *cloth* at this time was mainly used to refer to fabrics made from wool, unlike today, when the term can mean any woven textile.) Fulling, the process of washing, shrinking, and felting the fabric, resulted in a dense, tightly woven textile. The fabric was then napped, a process of raising the fibers on the cloth to improve the feel, and then sheared, to insure that the napped surface was even. All of these processes required skill and control to produce a good result. The same craftsmen also often dyed the fabric, a process that required expertise to achieve a uniform color that was fast, or able to withstand exposure to light and cleaning. Fulling mills were established for individual weavers to bring their fabrics to be finished. Fullers also cleaned and re-dyed finished garments.

In 1788, A group of entrepreneurs established the Hartford Woollen Manufactory in Connecticut. George Washington wore a suit of fabric from this firm when he was inaugurated on April 30, 1789, and later that year he visited the factory. Despite reports that the fabric produced by the factory was as good as English imports and was priced competitively, it did not sell well. The factory closed in the middle of the 1790s.

As the Hartford factory was winding down, brothers Arthur and John Scholfield, who were clothiers in England, immigrated to the United States. They established a water-powered mill in Byfield, outside of Newburyport, Massachusetts, that attracted other English immigrants. The factory housed a carding mill and spinning, weaving, and finishing workshops that utilized the most current technology. This factory, though, was not profitable and, in 1798, the Scholfields moved to Montville, Connecticut, and established a new mill there. Later, Arthur set up on his own in Pittsfield, Massachusetts. It was the Pittsfield factory that provided the wool broadcloth that James Madison wore for his 1809 inauguration as president.

One of the problems faced by manufacturers of wool fabric was the availability of good quality raw wool. American sheep did not produce abundant, high-quality fleece. There were attempts to cross different native American breeds to improve the quality and yield of the wool. By the second decade of the 19th century, though, Merino sheep were imported from Spain. The fleece of the Merino was regarded as the best quality for the production of fine wool fabrics and this breed became dominant.

The trade embargos and subsequent war spurred the growth of wool manufacturing. The 1816 report to the congressional committee of Commerce and Manufactures stated that there were 25 wool factories in Connecticut. However, according to the report, there continued to be large amounts of yardage made in private homes.

Flax and Linen

Production of linen fabrics, from processing the fibers of the flax plant through spinning the yarns and weaving the finished yardage, was largely home-based and home production of plain fabrics for utilitarian uses continued to be important through the Federal era. Flax grew very well in the cooler climate of New England and upstate New York, and women often wove their own sheets and towels. The weavers often traded excess linen yardage at the local store for such mass-produced goods as printed cotton dress fabrics.

Flax was important as the raw material for sailcloth that was required in great quantities for ships. In the early 1790s there was a flourishing sail cloth factory in Boston. Sailing ships also required large amounts of cordage, or ropes, for rigging. The plant fibers hemp and sisal were used for this purpose, as well as to make ropes for other uses.

Silk

There would be sporadic efforts to raise silkworms and produce silk fabrics in the United States for the next several decades, but they were never successful on a large scale. Occasionally, an enterprising woman might produce enough silk to knit a pair of stockings, for example.

References

Baigell, Matthew. 1984. *A Concise History of American Painting and Sculpture.* New York: Harper & Row.

Bowne, Eliza Southgate. 1887. *A Girl's Life Eighty Years Ago: Selections from the Letters of Eliza Southgate Bowne.* Repr., Williamstown, MA: Corner House Publishers, 1980.

Callcott, Margaret Law, ed. 1991. *Mistress of Riversdale: the Plantation Letters of Rosalie Stier Calvert 1795–1821*. Baltimore: Johns Hopkins University Press.

Chase, George Wingate. 1861. *The History of Haverhill, Massachusetts.* Haverill, MA: published by author.

Chotner, Deborah. 1992. *American Naive Paintings.* Washington, D.C.: National Gallery of Art.

Cobbett, William. 1818. *A Year's Residence in the United States of America.* Repr., Carbondale: Southern Illinois University Press, 1964.

Cochran, Debby, to Ruth Hollingsworth, March 23, 1817, MS 1849, Lydia E. Hollingsworth Correspondence, Maryland Historical Society.

Cotterell, Marta M. 1999. "The Laces of Ipswich, Massachusetts: An American Industry 1750–1840." In *Textiles in Early New England: Design, Production, and Consumption,* ed. Peter Benes, 82–99. Boston: Boston University.

Crowninshield, Francis Boardman, ed. 1935. *Letters of Mary Boardman Crowninshield 1815–1816.* Cambridge, MA: Riverside Press.

Flint, James. 1822. *Letters from America.* Repr., New York: Johnson Reprint Corporation, 1970.

Gallatin, Albert. 1810. *Report of the Secretary of the Treasury on American Manufactures Prepared in Obedience to a Resolution in the House of Representatives.*

Harding, Annaliese. 1994. *John Lewis Krimmel: Genre Artist of the Early Republic.* Winterthur, DE: Henry Francis du Pont Winterthur Museum.

Hersh, Tandy, and Charles Hersh. 1995. *Cloth and Costume 1750–1800 Cumberland County, Pennsylvania.* Carlisle, PA: Cumberland County Historical Society.

Hosford, David. 1984. Exile in Yankeeland: The Journal of Mary Bagot, 1816–1819. *Records of the Columbia Historical Society* 51: 30–50.

Klinck, Carl F., and Talman, James, J. ed. 1970. *The Journal of Major John Norton.* Toronto: The Champlain Society.

Lambert, John. 1810. *Travels through Lower Canada, and the United States of North America, in the Years 1806, 1807, and 1808.* 3 vols. London: Richard Phillips.

Larkin, Jack. 1988. *The Reshaping of Everyday Life 1790–1840.* New York: HarperPerennial.

Mansfield, Edward D. 1855. *Memoirs of the Life and Services of Daniel Drake, M.D.* Repr., New York: Arno Press, 1975.

Martin, Ann Smart. 2008. *Buying into the World of Goods: Early Consumers in Backcountry Virginia.* Baltimore: Johns Hopkins University Press.

Melish, John. 1818. *Travels Through the United States of America.* Repr., New York: Johnson Reprint Corporation., 1970.

Miller, Lillian B., ed. 1996. *The Peale Family: Creation of a Legacy 1770–1870.* New York: Abbeville Press.

Moulton, Gary E., ed. 1983. *The Journals of the Lewis and Clark Expedition.* Vol. 6. Lincoln: University of Nebraska Press.

Niemcewicz, Julian Ursyn. 1965. *Under Their Vine and Fig Tree,* ed. and trans. Metchie J. E. Budka. Elizabeth, NJ: The Grassmann Publishing Company.

Raffel, Marta Cotterell. 2003. *The Laces of Ipswich.* Hanover, NH: University Press of New England.

Rothman, Ellen K. 1984. *Hands and Hearts: A History of Courtship in America.* New York: Basic Books.

Ryan, Thomas R., ed. 2003. *The Worlds of Jacob Eichholtz, Portrait Painter of the Early Republic.* Lancaster, PA: Lancaster County Historical Society.

Tryon, Rolla M. 1917. *Household Manufactures in the United States, 1640–1860.* Repr., New York: Johnson Reprint Corporation, 1966.

Tyler, Sylvia Lewis. Diaries, 1801–1820, transcribed by Alden O'Brien. Acc. 2889, Americana Collection, National Society of the Daughters of the American Revolution, Washington, D.C.

U.S. Bureau of the Census. 1990. Population: 1790–1990. http://www.census.gov.

U.S. Bureau of the Census. 1998. Population of the 100 Largest Cities and Other Urban Places in the United States: 1790–1990. http://www.census.gov/population/www/documentation/twps0027/twps0027.html.

Vickers, Anita. 2002. *The New Nation.* Westwood, CT: Greenwood Press.

Wansey, Henry. 1796. *The Journal of an Excursion to the United States of North America in the Summer of 1794.* Repr., New York: Johnson Reprint Corporation, 1969.

Weekley, Carolyn J., and Stiles Tuttle Colwill. 1987. *Joshua Johnson: Freeman and Early American Portrait Painter.* Baltimore: Maryland Historical Society.

CHAPTER 3

Women's Fashions

EVERYDAY AND SPECIAL OCCASION CLOTHES

At the beginning of the Federal era the style of women's clothing was similar to that of the late Colonial period. Changes were happening gradually but would become more radical in the next decades. The full-skirted silhouette (or overall shape) would be completely replaced by a slender, tubular silhouette in the early 19th century. With their close ties to England, the former mother country, American women were influenced by English styles, but they also looked to France, the acknowledged leader in fashion. Later, as a violent revolution swept France and Europe was plunged into war, communication would be more difficult but still not impossible for those determined to have the latest styles. In 1799, Margaret Manigault of Charleston, South Carolina, commented on changing fashions in a letter to her friend Josephine du Pont, then living in Paris, "Our modes change almost as rapidly here as they do with you" (Low 1974, 50). Perhaps because he was French, Constantin François Volney observed in the 1790s that American women wore French styles, but with a time lag, "the Parisian dress of 1793 [was] in full vogue at Philadelphia in 1795, and that of 1794 did not reach that city till 1796. Enquiring into their history, for the intermediate years, I discovered that they were obliged to pass over to London, before they could meet with a kind reception in America" (Volney 1804/1968, 224).

Where did this leave American women when France and England went to war for much of the era, causing their styles to diverge? Sometimes they had to choose one or the other. Englishman John Lambert, who toured the United States and Canada from 1806 to 1808, wrote about New York:

> The ladies in general seem more partial to the light, various, and dashing drapery, of the Parisian belles, than to the elegant and becoming attire of our London beauties, who improve upon the French fashions. But there are many who prefer the English costume, or at least a medium between that and the French....
>
> ...methought I could discern a pretty *Democrat* à la mode Françoise, and a sweet little *Federalist* à la mode Angloise. I know not whether my surmises were just; but it is certain that Mrs. Toole and Madame Bouchard, the two rival leaders of fashion in caps, bonnets, feathers, flowers, muslin, and lace, have each their partizans and admirers: one because she is an Englishwoman, and the other because she is French; and if the ladies are not really divided in opinion as to politics, they are most unequivocally at issue with respect to dress. (1810, 2:196–97)

David Ramsay wrote about Charleston, South Carolina, in 1808:

> There is no standard for dress in Carolina. The models of it are not originally american, but are copied from the fashions of London and Paris. Milliners and taylors have more influence in regulating it than the court at Washington. These keep up a regular correspondence with Europe, and import new dresses to Charlestown as soon as they are introduced in the capital of France or England. The ladies of Carolina dress with taste, but approximate nearer to the french than english style. They often improve on imported fashions, but few of them have resolution enough to follow their own correct ideas without any reference to french or english models. (1809, 409)

Englishman John Palmer observed in Philadelphia in 1817, "The dress of both sexes is English, or closely bordering thereon." In New York, though, he found, "many follow French fashions, particularly the ladies in their head-dresses" (1818, 283,329).

While it might be supposed that women in the United States were not able to keep up with foreign modes, this was not the case. In 1803, it was reported that Fanny Erskine's American clothes were "much admired and copied in England." Philadelphian Frances (Fanny) Cadawalader had married Englishman David Erskine in 1799. On their return to England, Mrs. Erskine "saw no fashions...equal to what she took with her" (de Vallinger and Shaw 1948, 222). And even out west in Ohio, Scotsman James Flint found in 1820, "I have seen some elegant ladies by the

***Madame Récamier,* 1800. By Jacquet, after Jacques-Louis David. Juliette Récamier was one of the fashion leaders of post-Revolutionary France.** Courtesy of Biographical Images.

way. Indeed, I have often seen among the inhabitants of the log-houses of America, females with dresses composed of the muslines of Britain, the silks of India, and the crapes of China" (Flint 1822/1970, 286).

Most women's dress fabrics were imported from Europe or Asia, and a wide variety of goods were available in the larger cities. The infant textile industry in the United States was not yet capable of producing the fine quality wool fabrics, elaborately patterned silks, block printed linens and fine cottons that, at various times, would be fashionable for women's apparel. As styles changed, thrifty women altered or even completely remade older garments, using the precious fabric to keep up with the newer styles.

Main Garments

1786–1800

In 1786, the woman's primary garment was called a gown or robe. The style called the open robe had also been the fashion in the colonial period, but the form changed by the 1780s. The bodice center front edges were often joined, either with hooks or pins, instead of being open with a separate piece called a stomacher filling in the gap. The bodice met edge to edge—that is, the two sides did not overlap. The skirt of the open robe revealed a separate petticoat. An alternative style was the closed robe with a falling front panel of the same fabric, also called an apron front or drop front, so no separate petticoat was required. The front panel of this apron front style was open for several inches on both sides, forming a flap opening that allowed the skirt to fit over the hips. The flap was pulled up to the waist position and secured with a drawstring. This style was later called a round gown.

By the 1780s, the back of the gown was most often cut in the style called the *English back (à l'Anglaise)*, or *en fourreau* (that is, tightly fitted). The center back bodice section was cut in one with the skirt, and small pleats were stitched to a lining to fit the bodice to the wearer. (An earlier style, the *sack* or *robe à la Française,* or "in the French style" had larger, unstitched pleats that flowed down the back. This type of gown was largely out of fashion by the late 1780s.) While the sack back was especially suited to show off large-scale elaborately woven patterned silk fabrics, such as brocade, the gown styles of the 1780s were more suited to lighter weight, small scale patterned or solid silks, fine quality wool, or printed cotton or linen fabrics. Formal gowns often had rows of self-fabric ruffles or ruching, perhaps with additional embellishment, such as lace, around the neck and sleeve edges. If the gown had an open bodice, the trimming might also be applied all the way down the front edges.

The skirt of the 1780s was full all around, but many styles showed more concentrated fullness in the back. This was often achieved by arranging the back skirt of the gown in looped up puffs, called by the French name *à la Polonaise.* Sometimes a pad called a bum roll was tied around the waist under the skirt to emphasize the back fullness (*bum* is a rather vulgar word for the buttocks). The sleeves of the gown were usually closely fitted to the arm. They were elbow length at the beginning of the period but long and tightly fitted by the late 1780s. A gown in the collection of the Wadsworth Antheneum, dated circa 1785, is characteristic of the style at the beginning of the Federal era. It is made of a brown block-printed, painted, and glazed cotton with a front opening bodice, a one piece center back panel, a drop front skirt, and below-elbow-length sleeves (McMurry 2001, 28).

The open robe required a separate petticoat, sometimes called a coat, underneath. In very formal ensembles the gown and petticoat were made of the same expensive fabric, with elaborate ruched or ruffled trimming similar to that of the gown also applied to the petticoat. Most women were more likely to own a few solid color petticoats and wear them with various gowns. Sarah Allen of Pennsylvania, for example, in 1794 had six gowns and at least nine petticoats, but only one gown and petticoat were of the same fabric (Hersh and Hersh 1995, 138). Women wore quilted petticoats into the 1790s, but they went out of style as lighter fabrics and a slimmer silhouette became fashionable. As became very popular with bed quilts, women often worked together to quilt a petticoat; groups of women came to quilt with Ruth Henshaw Bascom in 1789, for example (M. Miller 2006, 106). However, women could also buy petticoats that had been quilted in England. The stitched design could be very elaborate, with flowers, birds, or fantastic animals, or just a simple diamond pattern. The fabrics were usually either silk or glazed wool, which had a shiny surface. The batting was most often wool, and the lining linen or wool. Petticoats with wool batting were very warm in the winter and hence were common in the Northeast.

A variation of the gown that appeared in the late 1780s was influenced by the man's overcoat called a greatcoat. This women's garment was also called a greatcoat or by the French name *redingote.* This garment had a large turned-back collar and long sleeves. Lucinda Lee, writing from Virginia in 1787, said, "my Great-Coat shall be my dress today," and later, her cousin wore a pink "Great-Coat" (Mason 1871/1976, 14,

***The Artist and His Family,* by James Peale, 1795. Oil on canvas. The artist's wife, Mary Claypoole, wears an open robe and petticoat. Seven-year-old Maria wears a white dress with a blue underdress and sash, while four-year-old Anna Claypoole's underdress is bright pink.** Courtesy the Pennsylvania Academy of the Fine Arts.

36). In 1790, Ralph Earl painted Abigail Taylor in a light gray greatcoat-style dress (Kornhauser 1991, 165).

While elaborate styles continued to prevail through the 1780s and into the 1790s, women's fashions became less formal. One new style that appeared in the 1780s was the chemise gown. This was a precursor of the light, filmy styles popular at the turn of the 19th century and was so named because it was reminiscent of the woman's basic undergarment, the shift, called *chemise* in French. Queen Marie Antoinette is credited with introducing this style in France, where she wore it at her rural retreat, the Petit Trianon, although she probably borrowed the idea from the Creoles—women of French heritage who lived in the hot and humid colonies of Martinique, Guadeloupe, and Saint Domingue (Haiti) in the Caribbean. The queen created a stir when she wore a chemise to have her portrait painted, circa 1783, because it was regarded as a very informal garment. In 1784, she sent a chemise to her good friend, Georgiana, the Duchess of Devonshire, another leader in fashion, and the style caught on in England. So rapid was the spread that, later that same year, a London merchant's wife appeared in one (Arnold 1989, 133). The date the style came to the United States cannot be precisely pinpointed; however, Catherine Yates Pollock sat for her portrait by Gilbert Stuart in 1793/94 wearing a variation of the chemise. As the chemise continued to be regarded as rather informal, most women would not have chosen to wear one when having a portrait painted, a fact that adds to the difficulty of determining their popularity. The chemise gown was made from full widths of fabric, with minimal cutting and sewing; therefore, it would have been easy for a woman to take one apart and use the yardage for something else. This is probably why so few chemise gowns exist today, another fact that makes it difficult to determine just how widespread the style really was. However, these relatively unstructured dresses, made of filmy cotton fabrics, certainly influenced later neoclassical styles.

Another less formal ensemble was the separate short bodice or jacket, worn with a matching or contrasting petticoat that had been popular for working and informal wear since the 1770s. The front of the bodice was cut along the same lines as the dress bodice, opening in the front with the waist ending in a **V.** Earlier in the period, the jacket, like the long gown, was worn with a stomacher filling in the front. The back was shaped with separately cut curved pieces, unlike the style of gown that had a one-piece back shaped with pleats. A short skirt, or peplum, was either cut as part of the bodice or sewn on separately at the side front waistline and continuing around the back, emphasizing the fashionable silhouette of back fullness. By about 1790, jackets were most often made with the long tight sleeves that were becoming fashionable. An elegant two-piece ensemble made of a brightly printed Indian cotton was worn in Albany, New York, around 1790 (Baumgarten 2002,

80), and Sarah Allen, in Pennsylvania in 1794, had a jacket and petticoat ensemble (Hersh and Hersh 1995, 138).

Women also adopted more simply constructed dresses or gowns similar to those worn by children. These were less rigidly constructed than formal silk gowns and were often of the apron front, or closed robe style. Like chemise gowns, they were often made of the very fine, lightweight, almost sheer cotton fabric called muslin. And, like her children, a woman often tied a wide colored silk sash around her waist when she wore one of these dresses. The child-like appearance of this style was emphasized in a 1789 *Lady's Magazine,* "All the sex now—from fifteen to fifty upwards (I should rather say downwards) appear in their white muslin frocks with broad sashes" (Arnold 1970, 19). Through the 1790s, as the sash became wider, the waistline of the dress at first appeared to be at the higher position of the top edge of the sash and gradually was actually constructed with the waist seam at a raised position. The back pleated shaping was disappearing and the new gowns opened in the back, again resembling children's clothes (although they were not open completely down the back, as children's dresses usually were). Another change was that the bodice was cut separately from the skirt instead of having a continuous center back panel from neck to hem.

The fabric called muslin is not the same as the rather coarse, often unbleached, fabric we call muslin today. Muslin at the time referred to fine, lightweight woven cotton fabrics, and, at the beginning of the era, the best came from India. The British also began to produce good quality cotton fabrics during this period. The quality of muslin did vary, though. The English author Jane Austen wrote in 1799, "had no difficulty in getting a muslin veil for half a guinea, & not much more in discovering afterwards that the Muslin was thick, dirty & ragged" (Byrde 1999, 65).

The decade of the 1790s was a period of transition, and portraits and extant garments suggest that women wore a variety of styles, sometimes re-making older garments to be more up-to-date (for more on this, see "Making and Acquiring Clothes," below.) For example, in her 1790 portrait, Mary Floyd Talmadge wears a very elaborate blue satin open robe and petticoat with a very full skirt. The open robe and petticoat are typical of the 1780s, but the waist sash, tight sleeves and low round neck suggest the styles to come. William Jennys painted Hannah Plant Benjamin in 1795. She wears a pink silk gown with tight sleeves and the neckline is so fashionably low that her handkerchief ends below her bosom (National Gallery of Art, http://www.nga.gov).

As the decade progressed, the French Revolution influenced fashion, with French women borrowing from ancient Greek statues, wearing dresses *á l'antique.* These had high waists, long narrow skirts, and short sleeves, and left the arms bare. Lightweight muslin that clung to the figure in sculptural folds continued to be a popular choice of fabric. As the

Les Merveilleuses

The French Revolution is generally credited for the apparent revolution in women's fashions. However, the change in styles was actually more gradual, beginning in the middle of the 1780s when Queen Marie Antoinette began to wear simple muslin gowns. During the Revolution, it became dangerous for anyone to wear the elaborate clothes of the old aristocracy, and even the wealthy adopted more simple fashions in the early 1790s. The *Journal de la Mode et du Goût* advocated the jacket and skirt ensemble, with its resemblance to working women's attire; however, this outfit was already fashionable (Ribeiro 1988, 58). As the revolution progressed, elaborate public pageants called for Greco-Roman-style costumes. Some young women wore extreme versions of these styles, appearing in sheer white high-waisted dresses that trailed the ground, minimal undergarments, and sandals on their otherwise bare feet. These women were called *merveilleuses* (those exciting wonder or astonishment). New fashion leaders emerged after the Revolution, including the Creole widow Josephine Beauharnais, who would later marry the rising star Napoleon Bonaparte; Thérèse Tallien, mistress of Paul François de Barras, an ex-aristocrat who was a powerful government figure in the late 1790s; and Juliette Récamier, wife of an influential banker. Portraits of these women in their sheer white high-waisted dresses have come to epitomize what is now called the Empire style.

remains of ancient statues that came to light were white marble, white remained the most dress popular color. (However, recent discoveries suggest that this was a misinterpretation, as Greek statues were actually brightly painted, although most of the color has disappeared over the centuries [Gurewitsch 2008, 66]).

These new fashions made their way across the Atlantic to the United States. In 1797, Elizabeth Drinker, a Philadelphia Quaker, wrote, "a Woman was here yesterday dress'd very fine in but a middleing way, gold ear-bobs, white french dress and a vail on" (1994, 179). That her dress was "middling" suggests that she was not on the cutting edge of fashion, so the "French style" must have appeared sometime before; however, as Mrs. Drinker commented on it, it must not yet have been the norm. Mrs. Cadwalader wrote from Philadelphia, "Nothing is seen here on genteel People but white and certainly nothing is so pretty" (de Vallinger and Shaw 1948, 166). In Maryland, Rembrandt Peale painted Ann Ogle Brewer in a very high-waisted, low-necked gown, although she fills in the neckline with a modest frill of lace (Weekley and Colwill 1987, 169). A white embroidered muslin dress probably made in the very late 1790s is in the collection of the Richmond (Virginia) History Center. It has a center front closure that fastens with drawstrings at the neck and high waist, a slit opening continuing into the skirt, and short sleeves. In 1800, Josephine du Pont described an acquaintance in New York as, "an Irish lady who spent 3 years in France, loves everything French, even the Greek style which incidentally made her seem somewhat ridiculous on her return because her appearance did not lend itself naturally to it" (Low 1974, 59).

The short sleeves favored by Frenchwomen of this period also appeared in the United States. In 1797, John Marshall visited the home of William and Anne Bingham outside Philadelphia, and wrote, "Mrs. Bingham is a very elegant woman who dresses at the height of fashion. I do not however like that fashion. The sleeve [does] not reach the elbow or the glove come quite to it. There is a vacancy of three or four inches & just [above] the naked elbow is a gold clasp." Anne Bingham wears a dress with similar sleeves in her portrait by Gilbert Stuart (Barratt and Miles 2004, 196–97).

While white dresses continued to be common, they could be embellished with bright colors. In 1799, Margaret Manigault wrote, "I have worked several gowns au tambour–that is, a border in color'd worsteds" (Low 1974, 50; tambour work is a type of embroidery where the stitcher uses a small hook to make rows of chain stitches, in this case with worsted wool yarns, on the surface of the fabric.) In 1800, Mrs. Manigault asked her friend, recently returned from France, "Were embroidered borders to gowns much the fashion when you left France? We are mighty fond of them here, and I am quite expert in finding out grecian patterns" (Low 1974, 55).

Abigail Adams lamented the popularity of white muslin gowns, "I wish anything would persuade the Ladies that muslin is not a proper winter dress. So far as example goes, I shall bring in the use of silks" (Mitchell 1947, 218). Women did wear fabrics other than muslin, though. In 1799, Ann Ridgely wrote her mother from Philadelphia that she had a pink and white chintz as well as "a handsome white japan'd muslin" waiting to be made into gowns; both of these were cotton fabrics. Her mother later suggested that she buy "a plain thick (Cambrick) muslin...or a handsome fine Chintz," with a white figure on a blue ground (de Vallinger and Shaw 1948, 191,198). Women in New England adapted to their cold climate by wearing wool gowns. They used *camlet* or *camblet,* a wool or wool and mohair blend glazed fabric—that is, the fabric has a shiny surface and often also has a *watered* finish, with an embossed wavy design giving the impression that the fabric is wet. *Russel* was another fabric used for gowns. Russel is a wool damask, a fabric with an elaborate pattern woven in, but usually all in one color.

Napoleon Bonaparte's Egyptian campaign of 1798–1799, while not a military success, inspired other new styles. In 1799, Margaret Manigault wrote from Charleston to her friend in New York, "Do they wear Mamelouc cloacks, & Egyptian head dresses with you? Our fashions make momies [mummies] of us" (Low 1974, 51; the Mamelukes were a class of fierce warriors in Egypt, then under the control of the Ottoman Empire. Napoleon formed his own detachment of Mamelukes in France, and their uniforms, with Egyptian, Turkish, and Middle Eastern elements, influenced both military and civilian fashion).

1800–1820

By 1800, the slender, high-waisted silhouette was widespread in the United States. In June of that year, Margaret Manigault wrote from

Charleston, "We have Chemises à l'antique" (Low 1974, 65). In 1803, Eliza Bowne wrote from New York, "I see nothing new or pretty....very short waists" (Bowne 1887/1980, 151).

By this time, too, the term *dress* was becoming more common than *gown* to describe a woman's main garment. While the skirt of the dress was cut as a tube, the front was applied more or less flat, with the bulk of the fullness gathered or pleated in the back. Dresses were often constructed with what we now call a bib front. The bodice side front pieces, made of the outer fabric, were attached to flaps of lining fabric that were pinned in place across the bosom. A rectangular bodice piece of the outer fabric (the bib) was attached to the center front skirt panel, while the skirt seams were open about nine inches down each side. The bib was pulled up over the flaps and pinned or buttoned in place. There were other variations—instead of a bodice bib, the dress bodice pieces might cross over each other, or the bodice pieces might meet at center front and tie or pin shut, and the skirt was then tied in place at the waist. Another style had the bodice and skirt attached all the way around, with the center front bodice opening continuing into a slit in the center front of the skirt. A drawstring at the waist was then drawn up to fit and tied in place. A gown in the collection of the Wayne County Historical Museum in Richmond, Indiana, is made this way. The fabric is white cotton and linen with red, dark blue, and light blue woven stripes (Altman 1997).

Some dresses had a back closure, a style that became more common over the rest of the Federal period. A white cotton, long-sleeved dress in the Costume Institute of the Metropolitan Museum of Art (hereafter referred to as the Costume Institute), dated 1804 to 1810, has a back opening (McMurry 2001, 121–23).

Walking or daytime dresses often had trains in the first few years of the 19th century. While a train may look elegant on a formal dress, it is rather impractical for daywear and the styled was short-lived. As early as June 26, 1802, the *New-York Herald* reported:

> There has been a sudden and general revolution in the female dress. The ladies have all abandoned the long *queues* or trains to their gowns, of which they were lately so fond. They now all wear short round gowns, very richly trimmed with lace; a *mode* which is found to be more convenient, as well as more becoming than the former.

In 1805, Ann Ridgely wrote that she was glad to hear no "trails" were being worn in Philadelphia as she disliked the "long clothes" (de Vallinger and Shaw 1948, 267).

Trains did remain in style for formal occasions for some time. Margaret Bayard Smith reported that on March 9, 1809, when James Madison

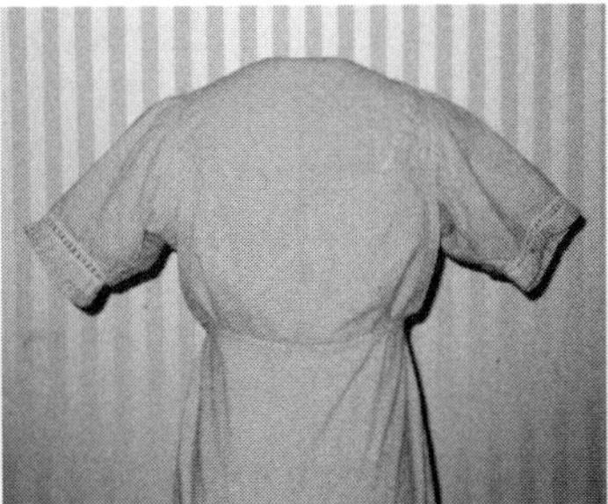
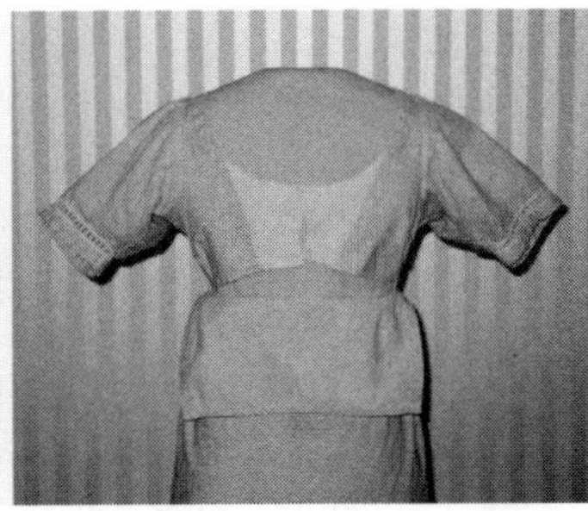

White cotton bib front dress printed with purple, 1800–1805. Left to right: full length view of dress from the back–short trains were fashionable for day wear early in the century; bodice with bib pinned in place; bib of bodice folded down, showing lining flaps of bodice. Courtesy of Nancy Saputo.

was inaugurated as president, Mrs. Madison wore "a plain cambrick dress with a very long train" during the day, and "a pale buff colored velvet, made plain, with a very long train" in the evening (Smith 1906/1965, 58, 62). Dolley Madison's white silk dress that is preserved in the National Museum of American History's First Ladies Collection has a train. However, by the end of the second decade of the century, trains were evidently no longer worn at all, even for formal occasions. Rosalie Stier Calvert wrote about the dress her sister sent from Europe in 1817, "I will say that I regret that my full-dress gown is trailing. I don't think anyone is wearing them like that here, so I will shorten it all around" (Callcott 1991, 326–27).

Short sleeves continued to be fashionable in the early years of the new century. In 1803, Mrs. Calvert wrote to her sister in Europe, "According to your description, our fashions are about the same. I wear my sleeves half-way up the arm; those who follow the exaggerated fashion wear them even shorter and very transparent" (Callcott 1991, 72). However, in 1803, Eliza Bowne described the fashion in New York, "Long sleeves are very much worn, made like mitts; crosswise, only one seam and that in the back of the arm, and a half drawn sleeve over and a close, very short one up high, drawn up with a cord" (Bowne 1887/1980, 167; "crosswise" probably meant cut on the bias—that is, with the pieces cut at a forty-five degree angle to the lengthwise and crosswise threads, allowing a close yet comfortable fit, as the fabric would have more give). Long sleeves generally reached almost to the knuckles. The long straight sleeve under a short, often decorated, oversleeve such as Mrs. Bowne described continued to be fashionable through the rest of the period. Mary Ridgely reported that long sleeves were fashionable in Philadelphia in 1805 "cut cattercorner ways of the muslin and fit the arm nicely" (de Vallinger and Shaw 1948, 264; "cut cattercorner ways" also means the sleeves were cut on the bias).

White continued to be a fashionable color for dresses through the first two decades of the 19th century. The fashion commentary in the November 1801 Philadelphia *Port Folio* stated, "White dresses are the most prevalent." Lightweight muslin remained a popular choice, but percale, a heavier cotton fabric, was also fashionable. In 1800, Margaret Manigault wrote, "Dimity, Percale, Cotton batiste—do you know that merchandise? We wear only that. It is extremely handsome, fine light, white" (Low 1974, 68). More utilitarian dresses were made of cotton or linen in darker solid colors or had printed designs on white or colored backgrounds. A front-opening long-sleeved dress in the Costume Institute, dated 1800 to 1804, is white cotton printed with a wavy black or dark brown stripe (McMurry 2001, 96–98). However, Fanny Erskine, the American just returned from England, could not "bring herself to wear calico in the morning as even fashionable people do in England," suggesting that wearing these more utilitarian fabrics was not fashionable in Philadelphia (de Vallinger and Shaw 1948, 226). *Calico* referred to a variety of cotton fabrics, sometimes in solid colors and sometimes printed, checked, or striped. In general, these were a heavier weight and a lesser quality than muslin.

Sheer white fabrics might have included woven patterns of heavier white threads in checks or stripes. Sprigged muslin had small printed, woven, or embroidered flowers or other small designs, and spotted muslin had printed, woven, or embroidered dots. Eliza Southgate wrote her mother in 1800:

> I must again trouble my Dear Mother by requesting her to send on my spotted muslin. A week from next Saturday I set out for Wiscassett....so long a visit in Wiscassett will oblige me to muster all my muslins, for I am informed they are so monstrous smart as to take no notice of any lady that can condescend to wear a calico gown, therefore, dear mother, ensure me a favorable reception, pray send my spotted muslin in the next mail. (Bowne 1887/1980, 28–29)

(Wiscassett was a thriving port in the part of Massachusetts that later became the state of Maine. According to John Hannibal Sheppard, "It was a very gay and extravagant place," so Eliza had cause to be concerned about her appearance [Banks 1998, 811].) After her marriage and move to New York in 1803, Eliza bought her sister a "pretty India spotted muslin" (Bowne 1887/1980, 157).

Embroidery continued to be a popular embellishment on plain white dresses. This was often done in white thread, and sometimes the embroidery was done with heavier white cotton or colored wool or silk threads. In 1800, Margaret Manigault wrote that her children's nurse "embroidered a charming dress for me while I was away. It is a lovely Etruscan design worked in lilac silk on an India muslin" (Low 1974,

70; the "Etruscan" design, inspired by the ancient pre-Roman culture, was another reflection of the classical influence). One could acquire flat fabric with embroidery already done and make it up into a dress. Some dresses seem to combine both pre-embroidered portions and embroidery added later, after the dress was constructed. Strips of trimming could also be purchased—Rosalie Calvert wrote that her daughter had a muslin gown "with one of the embroidered muslin trimmings" that her sister sent from Europe (Callcott 1991, 331). Magazines also published patterns so women could do this kind of needlework themselves (Shep 1998, 151–56, 200–204). In 1816, Mary Bagot occupied herself doing fancy embroidery like this, recording in her diary, "Began the third breadth of a gown I had begun working for dearest Moma" (Hosford 1984, 36; a breadth was a panel cut the full width of the fabric). Margaret Manigault also described percale dresses "with very pretty little painted borders" rather than embroidered ones (Low 1974, 70). By the second decade of the 19th century, color could be added with a colored lining or underdress worn under the sheer muslin. In 1815, Elizabeth Monroe was "dressed in a very fine muslin worked in front and lined with pink."

While cotton was fashionable for even formal occasions, silk had not gone completely out of style. From portraits, it is apparent that women had dresses made of lustrous silk fabrics. Older married women seem to have favored darker colors: Jacob Eichholtz painted Susannah Burkhart Mayer in 1814 in a brown dress, Catherine Eichholtz Lemon in 1813 and Catherine Breissler Frey in 1815 in gray, and Ann Mary Boyer Hoff in 1816 in dark green. Eliza Schaum, engaged to be married in 1816, on the other hand, wore light blue (Ryan 2003, 49, 110, 113, 115, 116). In 1818, Charles Willson Peale painted Angelica Peale Robinson in mustard yellow (L. Miller 1996, 49).

Silk crêpe, which is lightweight and fluid, was evidently another popular choice, as several crêpe gowns from this period still exist. (The fabric was usually called *crape* during the period. The fabric is made with tightly twisted yarns, giving it a crinkled surface. It was made with silk that did not have the natural gum washed out, giving it a different texture from other silks.) In 1805, Baltimore milliner Miss Hunter advertised in the *American and Commercial Daily Advertiser* that she had "Black, white and colored Sufflee Crapes" for sale. ("Sufflee" is probably a form of *souflée,* meaning that the fabric had a puffy appearance. In the 18th and early 19th centuries, milliners sold a wide range of merchandise, including fabrics and all kinds of trimmings, as well as hats. Later, the term would come to be applied to one who sold only hats.) Sarah Bryant made herself a "crape" dress in 1817 (Nylander, n.d.).

A more tailored style of dress, opening up the front and resembling the outer garment called the French *redingote* or English *pelisse,* continued to be an alternative style throughout this period. Josephine du Pont in 1800 had "a gray taffeta redingote" style dress, edged with white fur (Low 1974, 73). In 1815, Mrs. Crowninshield had a pelisse gown made by a Washington mantua-maker. "I was disappointed in my pelisse. First it was made too short—it was then pieced down and the border quilted; it really looked handsomer, but she charged me ten dollars more than she engaged to make it for, so I sent it back" (Crowninshield 1935, 36).

The silhouette of the dress began to change in the middle of the second decade of the 19th century. Fullness was added to the hem of the skirt in the form of gores, triangular shaped pieces of fabric that added fullness at the hem but not at the waist. The gores, inserted between the center front and center back panels, were usually more angled in the back than the front, thus maintaining the flat front of the skirt and throwing the fullness to the back. Rather than giving the appearance of a straight tube, the skirt assumed a cone shape. A white muslin long-sleeved dress in the Costume Institute has two gores on each side and one in the Richmond History Center has one gore on each side (McMurry 2001, 131–35).

Fashion plate, *Ackermann's Repository,* April 1817. The lilac spencer is trimmed à la Hussar. The elaborate flounces on the skirt and the large bonnet typify the style changes at the end of the Federal era. Collection of the author.

Later in the decade padded cording (or a *rouleau*) was sometimes added around the hem to make it stand out. A dress in the Costume Institute, made in England around 1820, has silk padded cording around the hem and also sewn in a scalloped design on the skirt, giving body to the yellow silk gauze fabric (Wallace et al. 1986, 86). Rows of trim around the skirt emphasized the new shape. Fashionable women chose rows of self-fabric or embroidered ruffles or flounces, flowers, or lace for trim. Jane Austen wrote to her sister in 1813, "Miss Chapman had a double flounce to her gown.—You really must get some flounces. Are not some of your large stock of white morn'g gowns just in a happy state for a flounce, too short?" (Byrde 1999, 58). Mrs. Crowninshield wrote in 1815 that she "got in Philadelphia a beautiful gold trimming" for her gold muslin gown (Crowninshield 1935, 25). Very elaborate trimmings with a three-dimensional effect were made of the same or contrasting fabric padded, shaped, and corded in a variety of ways. These new fashions were influenced by the Romantic movement in the arts that looked back to the Gothic or Medieval period for inspiration. Two examples with known American history suggest some of the many ways dresses were trimmed during the period 1815 to 1820. An aqua silk dress in the collection of American Costume Studies has a zigzag self fabric edging (often called Vandyke edging, as it suggested the pointed lace collars and cuffs worn by sitters in paintings by 17th century Flemish painter Anthony Van Dyke or Van Dyck). The caps of the sleeves are trimmed with triangular self-fabric tabs tied with ivory silk ribbon bows, and the lower edge of the sleeves and skirt are trimmed with a series of horizontal tucks (folds of fabric). A gold, long-sleeved, silk dress, made and worn in upstate New York around 1820, has strips of plush as cuffs, short oversleeves, and a trim around the hem. (Plush is a silk pile fabric that resembles fur, and this plush incorporates gold, pink, and white yarns.) Three shirred self-fabric strips on the bodice add further three-dimensional trim to the dress (McMurry 2001, 161–62, 174–75).

It can be difficult to differentiate between less formal and more formal women's attire from the Federal period. There were no doubt some very expensive, highly decorated ensembles that were reserved for formal occasions. (Not all such occasions happened in the evening—Americans often ate dinner in the early afternoon.) There were also very plain utilitarian garments that women most likely wore to work in the house or garden. But other garments could be, in the words of Rosalie Stier Calvert, "more or less dressed up" (Callcott 1991, 327). She was referring to a dress that had short sleeves with detachable long undersleeves. The long sleeves would be "less dressed up," for daytime wear. Women also got double duty from dresses with low necklines, suitable for evening wear, by filling in the neckline with a matching or contrasting handkerchief, chemisette, or tucker (see Neckwear and Sleeves section). An orange, white, and black printed, short-sleeved, bib front dress in the collection of Old Sturbridge Village has a matching neck piece and long sleeves (Old Sturbridge Village, http://www.osv.org).

Undergarments

The Shift or Chemise

The shift was the undergarment that a woman wore next to the skin. (The French word, *chemise,* also means shirt, and the garment was analogous to the man's shirt. The word *smock* is also occasionally used to refer to this garment but seems to have been more common in rural England.) The shift was initially made of linen, with the quality depending on the means of the wearer. (Because linen was an almost universal fiber for underwear until the 19th century, the terms *linen* or *body linen* often refer to undergarments, and this gives rise to the phrase, "airing one's dirty linen in public.") The shift was cut as a single long rectangle, with a rounded cut opening for the neck and smaller rectangles for sleeves. To add room for movement, square pieces called *gussets* were inserted under the arms. To add width at the lower edge, long triangular gores were sewn into the side seams. (If the fabric was particularly wide, the sides were sometimes cut in the triangular shape; however, most linen was 36 inches, or a yard, wide; 31-1/2 inches, or 7/8, of a yard wide; or 27 inches, or 3/4 of a yard wide. These widths required separately cut gores.) At the beginning of the Federal period, the neckline included a drawstring to gather in the fullness, and there was often a self-fabric ruffle or lace around the neck edge that showed above the neck of the dress. Similarly, a sleeve ruffle might show under the dress sleeve.

Many existing shifts are marked with the wearer's initials and a number stitched or written or stamped in ink. (Household linens, such as sheets, were also marked this way.) In a household with several women, this marking helped the individuals keep track of their similar undergarments. The marks also identified a person's garments if she had to send her laundry outside the home, as was often the case in urban areas. The number might also serve to keep track of inventory or, perhaps, to insure that linens were rotated.

As the dress shape changed in the late 18th century, so did the shift. The neck was cut wider to accommodate the more bare neckline of the dress. It often did not have a drawstring but simply rested on the shoulders. The sleeves were shorter and more narrow, to fit under the tighter, shorter sleeves of the dress. A shift in the collection of the Chester County Historical Society has short tight sleeves, indicating that it was made to fit the sleeve shape of dresses after 1790 (Burnston 1998, 44). Both contemporary written reports and existing portraits suggest that some very daring women did not wear shifts with the new classical style of garments, but this was probably not a common practice in the United States.

"An Almost Naked Woman"

Women's fashions at the turn of the 19th century elicited comment because they were so revealing. A dress with a slim silhouette, made of a fabric that clung to the body, looked very different from the fashions of 15 years earlier. In 1800, Abigail Adams described a dress "made so strait before as perfectly shows the whole form" (Mitchell 1947, 241), and Margaret Bayard Smith described a woman she called "Madame Eve, and called her dress the *fig leaf*" (1906/1965, 19). In 1801, the *Port Folio* quoted the English writer Hannah Moore on women's dress, that with "its seemingly wet and adhesive drapery, so defines the form." It has since been said that women actually dampened their dresses, but it is doubtful this happened, as the lightweight fabrics needed no assistance to "define the form." Rosalie Stier Calvert wrote to her European brother in 1802,

> I am surprised that an art-lover like yourself should not approve of the clinging dress which gives the painter and sculptor opportunity to contemplate and study beauties formerly left to their imagination. In this more virtuous land only the contours are perceived through filmy batiste—a subtler fashion. (Callcott 1991, 34)

In 1803, Elizabeth (Betsy) Patterson of Baltimore married Jerome Bonaparte, Napoleon's younger brother, and people talked about her appearance in her French-made gowns. Mrs. Calvert said she wore "no chemise at all," and Mrs. Smith wrote, "mobs of boys have crowded round her splendid equipage to see what I hope will not often be seen in this country, an almost naked woman" (Callcott 1991,77; Smith 1906/1965, 46–47).

Stays and Corsets

The fashions of the late 18th century were shaped by the foundation called stays. Stays were designed to give a woman's body the proper conical shape for the bodice of the dress as well as to promote the fashionable posture and carriage, or way of holding and moving the body, keeping the torso straight and forcing the shoulders backwards, creating the appearance of a very narrow back. Both boys and girls wore modified versions of stays when young to encourage the correct posture. Grown men generally did not wear them (although some very heavy men may have), but the man's coat was cut so that he had to maintain this stance. The stays certainly did constrict the waist somewhat, but the goal was not an extreme reduction of the waistline. (One extant set of stays in the collection of Colonial Williamsburg have a waist measure of 34-1/2 inches [Baumgarten 2002, 40].) Stays were constructed of two layers of durable fabric and sometimes were covered with another finer fabric, such as a silk brocade. Channels were stitched through the two layers for what were called bones or whalebones. These were actually made from baleen, the horny plates in the mouth of some types of whales that sieves their food, tiny marine animals, out of the water. Baleen was split into slender pieces, softened with steam, and shaped to accommodate the curves of the body. Sometimes the stiffening was provided by strips of wood or reeds instead, but these were less satisfactory materials. What we now call fully boned stays were stitched with boning channels all around the body. Half-boned or partially boned stays did not have channels all the way around. A woman may have worn these more comfortable stays for less formal occasions or perhaps for pregnancy. There is a pair of white cotton partially boned stays in the collection of Colonial Willamsburg (Baumgarten 2002, 211; the bones are wood or cane). The edges of the stays were usually bound with soft leather to prevent the bones from poking through. Stays were fastened with laces threaded through stitched holes, or eyelets, and usually laced up the back, thus requiring a woman to have someone to help her dress. Some styles laced in the front, however, and some, especially earlier 18th-century styles, were made in two sections and joined with laces at the front and the back. Stays of this period generally also had shoulder straps. When the gown worn over the stays had the waist at the natural position, the lower edge of the stays was cut into tabs to allow them to fan out over the hips.

The transitional styles of gowns or dresses of the last decade of the 18th century required changes to the stays. They became shorter as the waistline of the dress rose above the natural position, and eventually the tabs were no longer required. Often these new stays were not completely boned. The Daughters of the American Revolution Museum has a pair from this period, believed to date to the 1792 wedding of Ruth

Stephens to Levi Adams. The stays are made of two layers of yellow linen with wood boning and leather binding and are still fully boned and have waist tabs, but no shoulder straps (O'Brien 1998).

The period of transition continued into the next century, and evidently some women did stop wearing any type of stays or corset altogether. While this was probably more prevalent among the fashion leaders in France, Abigail Adams wrote in 1800 that women in Philadelphia appeared in gowns with "nothing beneath but a chemise.... without stays or Bodice" (Mitchell 1947, 241; "Bodice" is probably a variant of "bodies," an earlier term for stays). The lining flaps of bib front dresses may have provided adequate support for women with smaller busts. It is unlikely that all women immediately discarded the older styles of stays and other women evidently modified the old forms for the new styles. The Daughters of the American Revolution Museum has stays that Quaker Ann Taylor wore at her 1804 wedding. They are boned but are shorter than 18th-century corsets, no doubt to accommodate the new raised waistline, and do not have hip tabs or shoulder straps.

However, the slender gowns of the early 19th century generally required a slender shape underneath, and entirely new support garments, now called by the French name *corsets,* developed. The new silhouette also required the breasts to be lifted up and separated (in fact, one style was called the *divorce* because it aided this separation). The new corset was made of one or two layers of a sturdy fabric, often a twill weave cotton called *jean.* Triangular gussets were inserted to allow shaping for the bust. Some styles have one gusset on each side, and some have two. Rows of closely placed stitching, sometimes with cording inserted, under the bust and in the waist area helped to push the bust up. Some also had

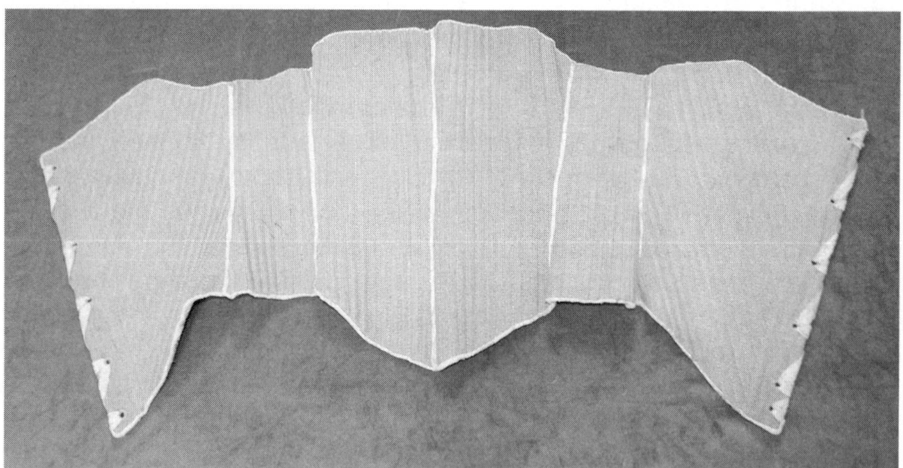

Brown linen stays with white kid leather binding, c. 1790–1800. The short waistline of these stays indicates that they are from the very late 18th century. They are fully boned. Courtesy of American Costume Studies.

gussets at the hip. There were shoulder straps, sometimes stitched onto the body of the corset and sometimes tied on, or stitched on the back and tied in the front. Sometimes bones were added along the seams, especially for women with fuller figures. These new corset styles generally laced up the back through thread eyelets, and there were often bones along the back beside the eyelets. Circular bone inserts for the eyelets were developed towards the end of the Federal period. (Metal eyelets were an invention of the 1820s.) Rosalie Stier Calvert described the fit of a corset that was sent from Europe in 1818, "mine is about three inches too small. When it is laced as tight as I can stand it, it is open four inches," which suggests that it was to be open about an inch up the back (Callcott 1991, 330). There was generally a pocket of fabric up the center front for a *busk,* a piece of wood or metal that ensured an upright posture and a flat stomach. Some busks were straight, while others were curved to fit the contours of the body. (Men sometimes elaborately carved busks as gifts for their sweethearts, but these may have been saved as keepsakes instead of actually being worn.) An alternative style of corset during this period laced up the front and may have been developed to wear with dresses with front openings (Altman 2000).

The Scottish physician, William Buchan, wrote early in the 19th century that the old boned stays were hazardous to women's health, "It is, indeed, impossible to think of the old straight waistcoat of whalebone, and of tight lacing, without astonishment and some degree of horror" (1807, 10). Physicians continued to object to tight lacing throughout the 19th century as different styles of boned corsets came and went. (Dr. Buchan died in 1805, and his *Advice to Mothers* was first published in Great Britain in 1803. However, it was re-published many times, including an edition in Charleston in 1807 and one in Boston in 1811, making his advice available in the United States long after his death.)

Petticoats

At the beginning of the Federal era, women often wore separate skirts, or petticoats, that showed because the front of the gown was open. They did also apparently wear under-petticoats. These seem to have been simple white linen and were made to fall to about mid-calf length. They may have been embellished with ruffles or embroidery. While large boned petticoats, or hoops, had gone out of style by the 1780s, the very full skirts at the beginning of the Federal period probably still featured some support underneath. Under-petticoats made of the fabric called Marseilles, which was loom-woven to resemble hand quilting, are known to have been worn earlier in the century and would have provided shaping for this era's full skirts. Also, as the fullness of skirts shifted to the back, women wore *bum rolls* or *rumps,* pads that tied on around the waist to hold out the back of the skirt, much like the later bustle. The pads were sometimes made of cork.

As the silhouette of the dress became more narrow, so did the under-petticoat. As it is difficult to keep a separate skirt in place at a raised waist position, some under-petticoats were attached to sleeveless bodices. Others had tape straps attached, much like suspenders, to allow the petticoat to hang from the shoulders. Some under-petticoats in the collection of the National Museum of American History have tape straps like these. Under-petticoats were still primarily made of white linen or cotton. However, the "Lady of Distinction" recommended that women should adjust their dress to the cold climate of Great Britain, and women in New England most likely did so as well. "During the chilling airs of spring and autumn, the cotton petticoat should give place to fine flannel" (Lady of Distinction 1811/1997, 79; flannel is a soft, spongy wool fabric, often bleached white).

Some period sources mention a *slip,* but this seems to have been a garment, cut like a dress, that was worn under a sheet outer dress. Early in the 19th century, a slip might be peach or pale pink to suggest a nude look, but later other colors were fashionable. A sheer white dress in the collection of Old Sturbridge Village was preserved with its peach-colored silk slip. A white dress, for example, might be trimmed with pink flowers to match the pink slip underneath.

Other

Women evidently did wear additional warm undergarments called *waists, waistcoats,* or *underwaistcoats.* In 1797, Eliza Southgate wrote her mother asking for a "flannel waist," (Bowne 1887/1980, 11). In July 1805, Mrs. Bryant "finished white flannel underwaistcoat for myself" (Nylander n.d.). Soft wool flannel would have kept Mrs. Bryant warm in the cold Massachusetts winter. The 1808 probate inventory of Abigail Keyes, of Hartford, Connecticut, listed a flannel waistcoat. Women in general did not wear any form of underpants during this period. (Young girls, though, were beginning to wear them. Please see chapter 5 for more information on these garments.)

Nightwear

Women often slept in their shifts. However, more well-to-do women did have distinctive nightgowns. These were generally made of white linen and cut like a man's shirt, with long sleeves and a collar and ruffled or lace trim. In the 18th century, women may have worn loose robes, similar in cut to men's *banyans* (see chapter 4) for informal wear, perhaps after rising in the morning but before getting dressed for the day (or perhaps all day long in the hot and humid South, if they knew they would not have visitors). The fabrics of men's and women's banyans were probably similar—expensive Indian cotton chintz, printed cotton calico, wool damask, or various silks. New styles of informal wear emerged in the early 19th century. These echo the slim silhouette of dresses of the period. There are extant examples of long white garments, some with fold-over collars, that open in the front and are edged with ruffles. They probably functioned as robes or dressing gowns. A similar style, but waist length, may have been designed for a woman to wear after childbirth, when she would be receiving visitors in bed.

Outerwear

At the beginning of the era, women primarily wore some form of cloak or cape as outerwear, as a more fitted outer garment would not have fit over the full skirts of dresses of the period. Many of these cloaks had hoods and were often made of wool broadcloth for warmth. (Wool broadcloth is so-called because it is woven on a wide loom, usually 54 inches wide. It is also heavily fulled, or treated so that the fabric shrinks up slightly and becomes very dense, almost like non-woven felt. This treatment, in addition to the natural oils in wool that make it water repellent, would help to keep out the wind and the rain.) The hoods of these cloaks were probably generally lined and the fronts might have been faced, but the bodies were not fully lined. The raw edge of the broadcloth would not ravel, so the cloak would not need to be hemmed. Red was a favorite color and these cloaks were often called *cardinals.* Cardinals were worn from at least 1750 (well before the Federal period) into the early 19th century. There is an extant red cloak in the collection of Colonial Williamsburg dated 1750 to 1810 (Baumgarten and Watson 1999, 54–56), and another survives in the Ross County Historical Society in Ohio (Bissonnette 2003, 144). An Alexandria, Virginia, merchant advertised in the *Virginia Gazette* in 1787, "Cardinals trimmed with snail and ermine" indicating that these cloaks could be bought ready-made. (*Snail* is chenille, a kind of cord having short threads of silk or wool standing out at right angles from a core of thread. It was stitched onto garments as an embellishment.) Joel Jones recorded the clothing of his deceased wife in 1795, including "One Red Broad Cloth Cloak," and in 1797, Sarah Snell Bryant made a scarlet cloak for herself (Smith 1925, 50; Nylander n.d.). In 1799, Abigail Adams wrote, "I should certainly use Some Red Broad cloth if I could come at it, for red cloth Cloakes are all the mode, trim'd with white furs" (Mitchell 1947, 218). It appears that New England women called a cloak with an attached hood a *riding hood.* As New Englanders also used the term *cloak,* it is not known how they distinguished between these two types of garments.

A lighter weight silk cloak was an option when a heavy wrap was not required. Sarah Allen of Pennsylvania had two black satin cloaks (Hersch and Hersch 1998, 138). There are two cloaks, made of dove gray (tannish-gray) silk, in Pennsylvania collections that might be distinctively Quaker garments. Subdued colors such as dove gray and drab (a dull light yellowish-brown) were common choices for Quaker women (Burnston 1998, 32–34).

As the silhouette of women's dresses changed, so did outerwear. Shawls were one option. Shawls were compatible warm coverings and provided colorful accents to plain white dresses made of soft, flowing fabrics. Cashmere shawls from India first appeared in England in the 18th century. These were woven in the Indian province of Kashmir from the soft fine fleece of the Central Asian mountain goat. The patterned weaving technique was labor-intensive, and these shawls were very expensive. They seem to have become popular in France when soldiers on Napoleon Bonaparte's 1798 Egyptian campaign began sending them back home. An elegant woman was expected to be able to gracefully drape a shawl, and the Empress Josephine bought a great number of them. (She also had them made into dresses, a style that evidently also came to the United States. Mary Boardman Crowninshield reported in 1816 that Lucretia Hart [Mrs. Henry] Clay wore "a white merino dress with a deep border and a shawl to match. Mrs. [Pamela, wife of General Jacob] Brown, an orange dress of the same kind" [Crowninshield 1935, 36]).

These shawls became very popular, but supply could not keep up with demand. French weavers, as well as weavers in Norwich, England, and Paisley, Scotland, began to make less expensive reproductions of the hand-woven shawls. (Thus today we call the distinctive bent-tip swirling cone design that was frequently used as a motif on cashmere shawls a paisley.) Fridge & Morris, Baltimore merchants in 1810 advertised "Imitation Shawls" among their goods. The advertisement mentions that goods had been received from Glasgow, Liverpool, and London, so these could have been either Scottish or English machine-woven shawls.

Women in the United States also reported buying merino wool shawls. Wool from Merino sheep is of high quality, but not as fine and soft as cashmere. Ellen Wayles Randolph wrote her mother about the purchase of a merino shawl as she prepared for a trip to Washington, D.C., in 1811:

> I was tempted in Richmond by some very elegant merino shawls. their price was 35 dollars. they were very large and had the richest borders I ever saw. they were rather more fashionable and I thought cheaper than the pellisse [pelisse—outerwear like a coat] I should get in Baltimore. in short I bought one of them; I had not finished folding & unfolding. gazing & admiring, counting the large roses in the broad border & the little roses in the narrow border, when a letter arrived from Mrs S. saying that handsome pelisses were only 25 dollars in Baltimore.... but the worst was yet to come; when I arrived here I put on the shawl and sallied out, every

> body admired it, Mr P. Todd declared he had seen nothing so elegant in the Parisian shops; the fashionable milliner Mrs Mc. Daniel was in raptures and said she had sold several not as handsome for 60 dollars. this praise was very gratefull to me, but alas it could not keep me warm, neither could the shawl. the spectators admired and I shivered.

In 1816, Mary Boardman Crowninshield received "two young ladies... dressed in white cambric high in the neck, ruffled round, merino shawl, both alike, and very pretty white satin bonnets, "and Mary Bagot, the wife the British minister, paid a call wearing a scarlet shawl over her white dress. (Crowninshield 1935, 48, 62). Caroline Calvert wore "a pretty white shawl of French merino wool with a border of flowers" in 1818. This was not among the items her sister sent from Europe and must, then, have been purchased in the United States.

While cashmere shawls (and their imitations) were very fashionable by the beginning of the 19th century, women also wore other kinds of shawls. Martha Washington had a shawl made of assorted patterns of black lace and in 1800, Margaret Manigault requested some black lace "to trim a shawl" (Raffel 2003, 117–19; Low 1974, 62). Shawls were also made of silk gauze, crêpe, or embroidered muslin. In 1800, Anna Maria Brodeau Thornton made at least two netted shawls; she made one of them from blue cotton (Thornton 1907, 101, 133).

A new form of outerwear, the spencer, developed in the 1790s. This short jacket without tails is named for George Spencer, 2nd Earl Spencer, and there are various stories about its origin, although none can be documented. One is that the Earl got too close to the fire and burned the tails of his coat, and another is that the tails of his coat got caught in brambles while he was riding. In either case, he is supposed to have cut or ripped the tails off his coat and proclaimed a new fashion. After women adopted the style, they seem to have worn it more frequently than men. In 1797, Rosalie Stier, who lived in Annapolis, described the jacket of her riding habit as "a Spencer of nankeen from the Indies" (Callcott 1991, 14). In 1798, Williamina Cadwalader, in Philadelphia, suggested that Ann Ridgely, in Dover, make her own spencer at home (de Vallinger and Shaw 1948, 186). Margaret Manigault in 1800 described an acquaintance in Charleston, "On horse back with a red Spencer" (Low 1974, 51).

The English *Lady's Magazine* for 1803 stated, "Cloaks now wholly disappeared, and given place to Spencers of every description, but the most fashionable is the military Spencer made of velvet" (Pineault 2002, 313). Spencers were certainly one practical solution to staying warm while wearing lightweight muslin dresses. In 1808, Jane Austen wrote, "My kerseymere spencer is quite the comfort of our eveng walks" (Modert 1990, F149, p. 1; *kerseymere* or *cassimere* is a soft twill-weave wool fabric). Even in June, the evening could be chilly in England. Spencers could be decorative as well as functional. In 1815, Mrs. Crowninshield described her first meeting with Dolley Madison (Whose husband was then president):

> She was dressed in a white cambric gown, buttoned all the way up in front, a little strip of work along the button-holes, but ruffled around the bottom. A peach-bloom-colored scarf with a rich border over her shoulders by her sleeves. She had on a spencer of satin of the same color, and likewise a turban of velour gauze, all of peach bloom. She looked very well indeed. (Crowninshield 1935, 16)

The *canezou* was similar to a spencer. While it has not been determined exactly what was called by this name during the period, it seems to have been a short jacket cut like a spencer but made of lightweight muslin fabric. It may have been intended as light outerwear in summer, or as another layer to wear indoors for warmth or for style. In 1817, Rosalie Stier Calvert wrote, "the percale canezou with little pleats....was too small. I opened the bodice under the arm and inserted a small piece there as well as in the sleeve, and now it fits her quite well" (Callcott 1991, 329).

As the silhouette of the dress became more slim, women adopted a form of outer coat often called a *pelisse.* These garments were also sometimes called by the French term *redingote* (which also referred to a coat-style dress) or the English term *greatcoat,* which was also the general name for a man's overcoat. Pelisses had long sleeves and buttoned down the front. They were often of wool, but silk was also fashionable and silk pelisses were often *wadded,* or interlined with wool or cotton batting, for warmth. (Another French term, *douillette,* was also used for this style). There is an elegant wadded lavender silk brocade pelisse in the collection on the New Castle (Delaware) Historical Society that has matching lavender plush trim. In 1807, Eliza Southgate Bowne wrote from New York, "Fashions:—Ladies wear fawn-colored coats and bonnets of the same trimmed with velvet trimming, same color with lappets, cape and inner waistcoat" (Bowne 1887/1980, 220). Mary Boardman Crowninshield was in Washington in the winter of 1815–1816, and observed a variety of outerwear, "beautiful bonnets and pelisses, shawls, etc." such as Susanna Gerardine Crawford's "light green pelisse with bonnet," and others wearing "a light pelisse trimmed round with velvet the same color" and "a brown merino pelisse trimmed with a rich trimming all colors" (Crowninshield 1935, 35, 30, 36). Sylvia Lewis Tyler, in Connecticut, recorded making a number of "great coats" for family members and clients of her sewing business in the early 19th century (Tyler Diaries 1801–1820). Sarah Snell Bryant made herself a great coat in addition to her cloak in 1799. A durable wool great coat could last a long time. Mrs. Bryant next made herself another one in 1808, and altered one (probably the same one) in 1817. She recorded making a silk pelisse, with some assistance, in 1820 (Nylander, n.d).

Accessories

Headwear

In the second half of the 1780s, women's hairstyles were both high and wide, and hats and caps became correspondingly larger than they had been earlier in the century. Women in the United States must have emulated their European counterparts. Straw hats had earlier gone from being strictly country wear to being English high fashion, and illustrations show women wearing large and elaborately decorated ones (Rothstein 1987, 75, 76, 78). (To make a straw hat, straw is braided, or plaited, into long rolls. Beginning at the center of the crown, the plait is coiled into shape and the edges are stitched together to form the hat. *Chip* hats, made of thin strips of wood woven to shape, were a less expensive alternative to straw [Mackenzie 2004, 8].) Englishwomen Elizabeth Stephen Hallett and Sarah Siddons both wear black hats with large brims and low crowns, trimmed with ribbons and feathers, in their portraits by Thomas Gainsborough (National Gallery, http://www.nationalgallery.org.uk); such hats would come to be called *Gainsborough* hats when they were revived in the late 19th century).

Another style of hat had a large, puffy fabric crown, and this was sometimes called a *balloon* hat, commemorating the first ascension of hot air balloons in Paris in 1783 and London in 1784. French fashion plates also depict women in large hats in the late 1780s (Ribeiro 2002, 230). One early American image that depicts a similar large hat, trimmed with feathers, is *Miss Denison of Stonington, Connecticut,* painted circa 1790 (National Gallery of Art, http://www.nga.gov). By the early 1790s, women began wearing bonnets, which differ from hats in that they fasten with ties under the chin.

As this decade progressed, women's hairstyles began to change. Large powdered and frizzed hairstyles went out of fashion, and some women even cut their hair very short. Hats and bonnets became correspondingly smaller but at the same time, as dresses became less elaborate, hats assumed a new importance as part of the ensemble. Headwear was made in an assortment of styles, materials, and colors. In 1798, Josephine du Pont wrote that women were wearing, "Little fantasy bonnets.... no two alike." Two years later, she had a "chapeau nacarat" (geranium colored hat) and "a charming white straw hat garnished with a buckle and a type of steel fringe" (Low 1974, 45, 64, 73). In 1803, Williamina Ridgely purchased "a becoming black plush hat trimmed with feathers" in Philadelphia (de Vallinger and Shaw 1948, 252). Pile fabrics must have been a popular choice for winter. In 1805, Mary Ridgely wrote to her mother, then in Philadelphia, "beavers [probably beaver fur felt, like men's hats] or velvet bonnets are much worn but as to the head there is no fashion about it" (de Vallinger and Shaw 1948, 264). For the March 1809 presidential inauguration of her husband, Dolley Madison wore "a beautiful bonnet of purple velvet, and white satin with white plumes" (Smith 1906/1965, 58). In November 1810, Sylvia Tyler had a "Velvet Bonnet" made. In October 1812, she wrote, "Bought some white Velvet for Cynthia & Nancy some Bonnets" and in November, she made a "Velvet & silk bonnet" (Tyler Diaries 1801–1820).

In 1816, Mary Boardman Crowninshield attended President Madison's New Year's Day afternoon open house, where women wore a variety of bonnets and hats, including a white bonnet with feathers; a black velvet hat turned up in front, with a large bunch of black feathers; and a white hat turned up in front. On social calls, she also saw two "young ladies" wearing "very pretty white satin bonnets" and another in "black straw with feathers." Mrs. Crowninshield herself wore "a new chip bonnet with flowers, that I bought in Baltimore" (Crowninshield 1935, 35–36, 48, 55, 63). As hairstyles were once again growing higher by this time, the crowns of bonnets also extended upward.

Straw hats (and later, bonnets) were originally imported from Livorno, a town in Italy (anglicized as *Leghorn*). In 1805, the Baltimore milliner Miss Hunter advertised "Leghorn, Dunstable, and Chip Hats and Bonnets." (As Italy came under French domination, the British could not import hats from Italy, and began making their own, often called Dunstable straw hats.) Straw hats and bonnets were also being manufactured in the United States by the early 19th century. In his report on American manufacturing, Secretary of the Treasury Albert Gallatin wrote about the industry in Wrentham, Massachusetts:

> This business commenced in this town in the year 1801; at that time the English straw bonnet had become the fashionable out-door head-dress of the ladies in the large towns, who are allowed always to take the lead in the fashions. The prices demanded for them were so great as to prevent the farmer's daughter's purchasing them. (1810, 60)

A cap is a form of indoor headwear that is usually sewn from fabric. It often ties under the chin and may be decorated with ribbons, ruffles, or lace. The wearing of caps had its roots in the ancient Biblical custom of women's covering their heads for modesty, and married women generally wore caps during the day. There were times during the Federal era when fancy caps were also worn for more formal occasions. Jane Austen wrote in 1798, "I have made myself two or three caps to wear of evenings since I came home, and they save me a world of torment as to hair-dressing" (Byrde 1999, 47; Miss Austen never married but, as this indicates, she must have found it practical to wear a cap nonetheless). A woman also sometimes put her hat or bonnet over her cap to go outdoors. Caps were almost always white and were usually made of very fine lightweight linen early in the period. As cotton fabrics became more common, they were also used. Some women had dressy caps made of silk. Abigail Adams wore silk crape dress caps "upon publick Evenings" (Bassett 1999).

Caps, like hats, became larger in the late 1780s as women's hairstyles became more voluminous. Laura Collins Wolcott in her circa 1789 portrait wears an elaborately "pleated, spotted, striped, and starched" cap (Kornhauser 1991, 148–49). In 1792, both Abigail Wolcott Ellsworth and Mary Alsop wear large versions of the mobcap, with the crown section, or caul, gathered onto a ribbon-covered band, and a pleated ruffle around the edge (Kornhauser 1991, 183, 190).

With less hair to cover, caps became smaller by the beginning of the 19th century. In 1800, Margaret Manigault asked for "an organdy pattern of some pretty little biggin" (Low 1974, 57; the biggin, originally a child's cap or nightcap, had been adopted for morning wear. Organdy is a sheer, stiff, cotton fabric). In 1803, Williamina Ridgely wrote that she had made herself several fashionable caps copying French and English models (de Vallinger and Shaw 1948, 242).

Several of the Baltimore women painted by Joshua Johnson before 1820 wear similar sheer caps with narrow lace edgings. These include Elizabeth Henderson McCormick, 1804–1805; Isabella Douglas Millholland, circa 1807; and Laura Winship McCausland, circa 1813 (Weekley and Colwill 1987, 123,137,153). Rachel Cloberg Schumacher, painted 1808–1810, has long ribbon streamers on her cap, which may be a distinctly German feature (Weekley and Colwill 1987, 144). Some younger married women gave up wearing caps by this time, but it seems likely that older women continued to wear them. Rachel Gratz Etting wears an elaborately ruffled cap with a ribbon rosette and ties in her 1810–1812 portrait by John Wesley Jarvis; however, Mrs. Gratz was Jewish and therefore probably more likely to cover her head in public (Maryland ArtSource, http://www.marylandartsource.org). The elderly Rachel Walker (Mrs. Paul) Revere, wears a cap in her 1813 portrait by Gilbert Stuart (Barratt and Miles 2004, 289).

Two new headwear options at the end of the 18th century were the *bandeau,* or band, and the turban. The bandeau may have originated as a ribbon or strip of fabric informally tied around the head. American women wearing bandeaux in portraits include Mary Sydebotham Shaaff, painted by Robert Field in 1800, and Grace Allison McCurdy, painted by Joshua Johnson in 1806–1807 (Maryland ArtSource, http://www.marylandartsource.org; Weekley and Colwill 1987, 135).

The turban shows the exotic influence of the Ottoman Empire. Women probably created early versions by twisting and wrapping pieces of fabric around the head, but by the early 19th century turbans were more structured. Dolley Madison was especially fond of turbans, and they seem to have been a good choice for older women, providing covering for the hair but looking very chic. Mrs. Madison wore a buff colored velvet and white satin turban at her husband's first inaugural ball in 1809 (Smith 1906/1965, 62). In 1815, Mrs. Madison wore "a turban of velour gauze" for a morning call, and a "white lace turban, starred in gold, and white feather" to a ball (Crowinshield 1935, 16, 23). Mrs. Crowninshield observed several women in Washington wearing turbans in the winter of 1815–1816. The wife of then Secretary of State James Monroe, Elizabeth, wore a "black velvet turban close and spangled," and Arabella Maria Dallas wore "a green and white turban helmet front and green feathers waving over" while Ellen Wayles Randolph (a granddaughter of Thomas Jefferson) wore "a pink turban with a black feather" (Crowninshield 1935, 20, 24, 54). Anne Telfair Timothy wears a turban in her circa 1818 portrait by Rembrandt Peale. It appears to be made of sheer tulle or gauze twisted with a shiny pleated fabric (Maryland ArtSource, http://www.marylandartsource.org).

Hats, bonnets, and turbans were decorated in a variety of ways, and women updated their headwear by changing the ribbons and trimmings. Large feathers, or plumes, were fashionable throughout the period, and sometimes a woman wore only feathers for a headdress, as does Esther Boardman, painted in 1789 (Kornhauser 1991, 158). Margaret Manigault described a "very pretty hat" she had in 1800, "Of black satin with steel spots, & a handsome steel button, & loop in front, & a plume of blue, and white feathers" (Low 1974, 72). Ostrich feathers were most common, but women also wore the plumage of other birds. Josephine du Pont wrote from Paris in 1798, "They are also wearing some of those peacock feathers that are so common where you are" (Low 1974, 46; her friend was in Charleston). Dolley Madison's turban for the 1809 inaugural ball was decorated with feathers of the bird of paradise. Artificial flowers and fruit were other alternatives for trimming bonnets. Mrs. Madison asked a friend to shop for her in Philadelphia in 1811, "I will avail myself of your offer to chuse me a *fascinating* Head-dress—I enclose you 20$—my darling & you will add to the Bonit or Turbin some artificial Flower or fruit for the head—" (Shulman 2007).

The *calash* was a form of protective headwear. It was made of silk or glazed cotton on a cane frame. It folded flat when not in use but could expand to cover a voluminous hairdo of the late 18th century. (The name comes from the calêche, a type of carriage that has a similar collapsible cover). There is a green silk calash lined with pink silk in the collection of Colonial Williamsburg (Baumgarten 1986, 42). The calash enjoyed renewed popularity in the second decade of the 19th century, when women wore their hair piled high on the head. Rosalie Stier Calvert wrote in the winter of 1819, "We have a well-closed carriage...large cloaks of silk lined with wadding and with a calash, which don't rumple either our clothes or our coiffures" (Callcott 1991, 346).

In New England, there were garments called *hoods*. Whether these were separate hoods or hoods attached to cape bodies is not known. Separate hoods are known to date to the second decade of the 19th century. A hood was cut to completely cover the head and may have had either a quilted lining or an interlining or wadding for warmth. New England probate inventories include velvet, quilted, silk, silk satin, and wool hoods (M. Miller n.d.). One of Sarah Snell Bryant's diary entries suggests another form of warm headwear, a "furr cap" she made for herself in January 1801 (Nylander n.d.). This would also have been warm in the New England winter.

Veils went in and out of fashion during the period. The ultra-fashionable Josephine du Pont advised her friend, Margaret Manigault, to buy one in 1800, meanwhile commenting on the transience of new styles, "White veils of point de bruxelles [a kind of lace] cost 40 to 50 louis...You must spend 10 to 12 louis for a black one but perhaps this folly can be replaced by another. They were throwing them entirely to one side on the shoulder. That was charming and draped perfectly" (Low 1974, 65; the *louis* was a unit of French currency worth a little less than four American dollars). That same year, Anna Maria Brodeau Thornton and her mother received "Patinet veils from Phila," and later, Mrs. Thornton "began to net a light pink floss silk veil" (Thornton 1907, 109, 139; *patinet* was machine-made silk net, relatively new and regarded as a novelty). In 1803, Williamina Ridgely reported from Philadelphia that a white veil was a "necessity." Later that year, black lace veils were again in style, and Ann Ridgely sent her daughter some lace to be dyed black (de Vallinger and Shaw 1948, 228, 242). In Boston, Gilbert Stuart painted Sarah Bowdoin circa 1805, and Hepzibah Lark Swan, circa 1806, wearing white lace veils (Barratt and Miles 2004, 274, 297). In the fall of 1805, a milliner in Baltimore imported "Black lace Veils" from "London, via Philadelphia," and "Silk Lace Veils" were advertised in Baltimore again in 1815. Veils were also attached to hats or bonnets. In Philadelphia in 1794, Henry Wansey observed "the ladies...in veiled bonnets" (Wansey 1796/1969, 185).

Neckwear and Sleeves

At the beginning of the Federal period, women most often filled in their low necklines with handkerchiefs or, in French, *fichus*. These could be squares of fabric, or the square could be cut in half diagonally to make a triangular-shaped half handkerchief. These handkerchiefs could be plain or very elaborate. A plain white cotton half-handkerchief in the collection of Colonial Williamsburg has hemmed edges (Hersh and Hersh 1995, 149). Woven plaid or checked handkerchiefs were probably also for utilitarian wear. There are two plaid square handkerchiefs in the collection of the Schwenfelder Museum in Pennsylvania. One is brown, blue and white linen, and the other is red cotton and blue and white linen (Gehret 1976, 55). A variety of white and gold, white and blue, and white, gold, and blue checked or plaid handkerchiefs exist in New England (Merrimack Valley 1980, 88–89). Women probably continued to wear these sorts of everyday handkerchiefs throughout the period; a woman in John Lewis Krimmel's 1814 *Blind Man's Bluff* wears a checked handkerchief with a patterned border (Harding 1994, 68).

Very fancy sheer white cotton mull or linen cambric handkerchiefs were at the other end of the spectrum. Handkerchiefs with elaborate embroidered (also called *worked*) borders remained in style until about 1790. Mary Alsop wears a worked handkerchief and apron in her 1792 portrait, although these accessories were going out of style by this time (the straight pins that hold the handkerchief in place can be seen in the painting; Kornhauser 1991, 190).

Several of Ralph Earl's subjects in the 1790s wear sheer neckwear with worked or plain ruffled edges, including the Bradley sisters and Mary Anna Boardman (Kornhauser 1991, 190, 200, 201, 212). These may have been made in a curved shape to wrap around the neck, rather than being square or triangular. As the neckline of the woman's dress became lower in the middle of the 1790s, the handkerchief filling it in had, of necessity, become very large and often "immensely puffed out in front" (Wright 1990, 52). Many women continued to wear plain handkerchiefs as neckwear through the Federal period. These plain handkerchiefs were often white, but, in 1801, Sarah Snell Bryant made a black silk handkerchief for herself, and the woman selling soup in John Lewis Krimmel's *Pepper-Pot: A Scene in the Philadelphia Market* wears an orange-red handkerchief with her white dress (Nylander n.d.; Harding 1994, 17).

***D. P. Madison,* drawn by J. Herring after J. Wood, circa 1820, engraved by J.F.E. Prud'homme. Dolley Madison wears her trademark turban, a white chemisette under her dark dress, and a multi-colored shawl.** Courtesy of Biographical Images.

However, there was a new style of neckwear by the early 19th century. This was sometimes called by the English word *tucker* or the French *chemisette,* meaning a "little shirt." These often featured very full ruffles around the neck, and the ruffles also had various names, such as *Betsy* (because they resembled the ruffs of Queen Elizabeth I), *cherusque* (from the French for mushroom, as the pleats resemble the gills of a mushroom), or *Vandyke* (because they often had pointed edges, similar to the trimmings that were also named for the Flemish painter Van Dyke). Sarah Bryant wrote that she made a "vandike" for herself in 1803 (Nylander n.d.). In 1815, Mary Boardman Crowninshield wrote, "Tell Aunt Priscey nothing I have worn has been more complimented than the ruff she netted for me.... I wish I had some of the old net Van Dykes" (Crowninshield 1935, 21). In the craft of netting, an open-work fabric is produced by twining threads together, and this craft was a pastime for women in the Federal period. (Anna Maria Brodeau Thornton netted shawls and a veil in 1800 [Thornton 1907, 101, 139]). Chemisettes, like caps and undergarments, were almost always white.

In her 1805 portrait, Marcia Burns Van Ness wears a rather plain chemisette (Barratt and Miles 2004, 270). Eliza Schaum, in her 1816 portrait, wears an example of a Van Dyke collar attached to a chemisette. It appears to be made of a lightweight but not sheer white fabric and has a double ruffle with pointed edges (Ryan 2003, 110). During this period, it seems to have been common for chemisettes to be worn tucked into the neckline of the dress, but there is pictorial evidence that they were sometimes worn over the dress. Mary Ann McJimsey Patterson, whose portrait was painted by Jacob Eichholtz sometime before 1810, wears one with a high ruffled collar, for example (Ryan 2003, 99). Neck ruffles could also be made of lace. At a ball in 1815, Dolley Madison wore "fine elegant lace round the neck and lace handkerchief inside and a lace ruff." Mrs. Crowninshield later described a fashionable style of muslin ruff:

> I sent in the bundle a ruff that is much worn here—it is only made for a pattern, but perhaps nothing new. They sell them here worked at the edge with a scollop, or peaked, with a pink ribbon through the collar, for 30 dollars. Sometimes the ruffles are plaited. I made this by Mrs. Porter's made of plain muslin with edging. (Crowninshield 1935, 23, 35)

Another style of neckwear was the tippet, usually in the form of a long strip of fur or swansdown (the soft under feathers of the swan) worn around the neck and hanging down in front like a modern boa. These must have been worn for style as well as warmth, as Eleanor Mae Short Peale wears a fur tippet with a short-sleeved dress that leaves her arms bare in her circa 1811 portrait by her husband, Rembrandt Peale (L. Miller 1996, 37). Ruth Henshaw Bascom made muffs and tippets from fox fur (Fennelly 1961, 12). Sylvia Tyler made a tippet for a neighbor in February 1811 but did not specify the material (Tyler Diaries 1801–1820).

Women sometimes wore separate sleeves in addition to those attached to the dress. Josephine du Pont found that separate knitted sleeves were popular in Paris in the 1790s, perhaps because they allowed a woman's arms to be covered when she was wearing a fashionable short-sleeved dress. In 1800, she wrote:

> I saw announced in the newspaper a case of wigs and knitted silk sleeves just arrived from France. If I were in New York I would surely be greatly tempted to make these two purchases for you. I no longer know how to dress with any other style of sleeve, but I am afraid this miserable case will make them very common. (Low 1974, 67; for more on wigs, see below)

Separate sleeves seem to have continued in style for some time. In 1807, Rosalie Stier Calvert of Maryland sent her sister, Isabelle, a pair of lace sleeves (Callcott 1991, 157). In 1812, Joseph Wheeler & Co. advertised "figured and plain Silk Sleeves," and "figured and plain Cotton Sleeves" in the *Hartford Courant.*

Pockets and Reticules

When full skirts were in style, women wore separate pockets to carry their necessities. These pockets were attached to a tape that tied around the waist and hung down at the side, under the skirt. Both the outer skirt and the petticoat or petticoats underneath had slits to allow the woman to put her hand through and pull out what she needed. Sarah Snell Bryant made a patchwork pocket for herself in 1799, and other pockets in 1803 and 1805. (Nylander n.d.). It appears that, as the waistline of women's dresses rose, they began to make their pockets longer to correspond with the higher waist position.

Pockets became less common, though, as the dresses became so narrow and clinging that the outline of the pocket would be seen. Women then adopted small handbags called *reticules, ridicules,* or *indispensables.* Many of these were simple drawstring bags made at home. White cotton muslin reticules with embroidery and ruffled trim seem to have common, and women sometimes stitched the dates on them. Two in the collection of Old Sturbridge Village are dated 1816 and 1818. One in the collection of American Costume Studies is embroidered "Eunice Staples/of Scarborough/Aged 31 years/1809." Perhaps it was a birthday gift. These plain white bags also sometimes have designs painted or drawn in ink.

Some reticules were netted or knitted, while others were made from silk fabric. In 1802, Eliza Southgate Bowne received a "most elegant Indispensable, white lustring spangled with silver" (Bowne 1887/1980, 143; *lutestring* is a lightweight silk fabric and *spangles* are sequins). Some elaborate ones had leather or tortoiseshell trimming or metal frames

Pocket made of two blue resist dyed cotton prints and white dimity, lined and backed with handwoven white linen, circa 1800–1820. Ties are probably later replacements. Courtesy of American Costume Studies.

and clasps. Sarah Jane Waite holds a reticule with a gold frame and chain handle in her 1819 portrait (Weekley and Colwill 1987, 162). There is a reticule netted from black silk ribbon with an ivory silk lining in a private collection. It resembles the red netted reticule that one of the women is holding in John Lewis Krimmel's *Fourth of July in Centre Square.*

Gloves

A well-bred woman always wore gloves outdoors to protect her hands from the sun and, in cold weather, for warmth. She also wore gloves in the ballroom as it was not thought proper for a woman and man to touch bare hands.

Various kinds of leather were made into gloves. Probably the most common for women was kid skin, from either young goats or lambs. Doe skin was a lightweight deerskin, not necessarily just from the females, while buckskin was heavier. Dress gloves were also knitted from silk or, for summer, linen (often called *thread* gloves). In 1794, there were silk and linen gloves in the probate inventory of Sarah Allen of Carlisle,

Pennsylvania (Hersh and Hersh 1995, 138). In 1799, Williamina Cadwalader reported from Philadelphia that silk gloves were cheaper than leather, and were fashionable (de Vallinger and Shaw 1948, 194).

In her circa 1789 portrait, Laura Collins Woolcott wears elbow length white silk gloves (Kornhauser 1991, 148–49). John Marshall's observation that Anne Bingham's gloves did not reach to her elbows (see above) suggests this was fashionable and fashion plates of the period often show elbow-length or slightly shorter gloves worn for evening. In 1803, Mrs. Calvert reported that, when women were wearing gowns with very short sleeves, they wore "gloves of a kind of lace called 'patinet,' which lets the skin show through" (Callcott 1991, 72).

Women continued to wear both long and short gloves through the end of the Federal era. Alida Livingston Armstrong wears white gloves that end slight above her elbows in her circa 1810 portrait (L. Miller 1996, 53). Joseph Wheeler advertised a wide variety in the *Hartford Courant* in October 1812, "Ladies' long and short white, black, and coloured Silk Gloves, do. long and short white, black, and coloured Kid Gloves."

Women's gloves were made in France, Spain, Italy, and England. Josephine du Pont wrote, "These little things are always prettiest in France" (Low 1974, 71). In 1791, William Bingham ordered luxury goods from French merchants, including "two dozen white gloves (very fine)," no doubt for his wife and female relatives (Alberts 1969, 215). In 1806, J. W. and P. L. Vandervoort advertised that they had "just received from France" "Long and short silk and kid gloves" (Majer 1989, 224). In 1813, Elizabeth Patterson Bonaparte wrote that one could buy French gloves in Baltimore (Shulman 2007). Ann Van Rensselaer, of Albany, New York, had a pair of gloves from England; these are dated 1775 to 1800 (Baumgarten 2002, 91). Women also made their own gloves. Sarah Snell Bryant made white and black silk gloves for herself. We do not know if these were knitted or cut and sewn. However, as she "cut out" and finished a pair of nankeen gloves in 1799, these were definitely not knitted (Nylander n.d.).

Mitts are similar to gloves but leave the fingers and thumb exposed. They can be made with no finger portion, usually with a point coming down on the back of the hand, or they can look like gloves with the fingers cut off, with separate finger and thumb portions. Mitts worn as an alternative to gloves seem to have been going out of style by the end of the 18th century, as long sleeves replaced elbow-length ones. Ralph Earl painted several older women wearing mitts. Tamar Boardman Taylor, circa 1789–1790, wear black silk mitts, Hannah Wright wears black knitted silk mitts in 1792, and Sarah Bostwick Boardman wears fine cotton or silk gauze mitts in 1796 (Kornhauser 1991, 161–62, 187–91, 214–16). In the 19th century, the bride in John Lewis Krimmel's *Country Wedding* wears one white mitt, while her bridesmaid holds the other (Harding 1994, 73).

Fans, Muffs, and Parasols

In the days before air conditioning, fans were functional as well as decorative accessories. Women could carry a simple hand screen (a decorated card mounted on a stick), or a folding fan. (While a fan was certainly an elegant accessory, there is little evidence that women learned an elaborate "language of the fan" to flirtatiously send non-verbal signals to men.) A folding fan had sticks of wood, ivory, mother-of-pearl (the iridescent lining of some seashells), tortoiseshell, or bone, with a leaf of paper, skin, or lace, often elaborately painted or printed on one or both sides. The sticks were also often carved or painted, and the end sticks, called guards, were often more highly decorated, sometimes set with gemstones, so that the fan looked attractive when closed. The *brisé* fan consisted of elaborately carved sticks strung together with ribbon, without a leaf. Henry Wansey observed the women in Philadelphia in 1794, "carrying large fans, like the fashion of last year in England" (Wansey 1796/1969, 185). Several women hold folding fans in portraits painted by Ralph Earl, including Mary Floyd Tallmadge in 1790, Lucy Bradley in 1794, and Apphia Ruggles Lane, Mabel Ruggles Canfield, and Sarah Bostwick Boardman in 1796. An unknown artist painted Deborah Richmond holding a fan in 1797, while Simon Fitch painted Hannah Beach Starr holding one in 1802 (Kornhauser 1991, 174, 201, 205, 209, 214, 246, 248). In about 1813, Sophia Burpee Conant holds a fan in her portrait by an unknown artist (National Gallery of Art, http://www.nga.gov). Most of these women's fans appear to have ivory, bone, or wood sticks with painted or spangled (sequined) leaves, but Mrs. Canfield's is made of black feathers. One of Deborah Richmond's fans descended with her portrait, and is reputed to be the one she was holding.

Most of these women were wealthy and could therefore afford a fancy accessory imported from France. Margaret Manigault, of Charleston, South Carolina, received a Parisian fan from her friend, Josephine du Pont, in 1799, with this note, "I am also sending a fan which, entirely unworthy of its brilliant destiny will perhaps recall me to your mind in the midst of some tumultuous assembly" (Low 1974, 48). Elizabeth Monroe had the opportunity to buy fans in France when her husband was the U.S. minister to that country. During the late 1790s, she bought two fans with pierced mother-of-pearl sticks and painted leaves. During her second stay in Paris, from 1804 to 1807, she added a fan with ivory sticks and a black silk lace leaf (Langston-Harrison 1997, 102, 103, 162). However, the English also made fans. Catharine Reid, of Suffolk, Virginia, had an English fan with bone sticks and engraved and painted paper trimmed with sequins (Baumgarten 2002, 91). An English hand screen style of fan, dated 1785 to 1795, with the moralistic motto, "Keep Within Compass," is in the collection of Colonial Williamsburg

(Baumgarten 1986, 44). Fans were also made in the United States, especially in Boston (White 2005, 123).

Women carried muffs to keep their hands warm but a fur muff was likely also a sign of status. In the 18th century, muffs were small and sometimes made of fabric instead of fur. A muff in the collection of Colonial Williamsburg, dated 1780 to 1790, is cream silk with embroidered trim (Baumgarten 1986, 42; it is probably English). As the waistline of women's dresses rose at the end of the 1790s, muffs became very large and remained so through the end of the Federal period. Popular furs included ermine, seal skin, sable, white fox, and bear. Sarah Snell Bryant made a sable muff for herself in 1801 (Nylander n.d.) and Williamina Ridgely purchased a black bearskin muff in Philadelphia in 1803 (de Vallinger and Shaw 1948, 252). Swansdown was also used for muffs, tippets, and garment trimmings, as it is warm and soft.

Women carried umbrellas for protection from the rain, as men did. (For more on the history of umbrellas, please see chapter 4). Huldah Bradley holds a dark green umbrella on her lap in her 1794 portrait by Ralph Earl. The smaller version of the umbrella called a *parasol* was a fashionable and functional accessory. A parasol or umbrella protected a woman's skin from the sun, keeping it fashionably pale instead of unfashionably tanned. In 1799, Ann Ridgely told her mother that she needed her umbrella, "as the sun is so warm in the Spring" (de Vallinger and Shaw 1938, 197). On a sunny Philadelphia day in 1812, two women in John Lewis Krimmel's painting *Fourth of July in Centre Square* carry parasols. One is open, and one is closed, and both are dark green with gold fringe trim, which seems to have been a popular color combination. Parasols, like umbrellas, were made of oiled silk and had whalebone ribs and wooden handles. Around 1800, a hinge was invented that allowed the top of the parasol to be tilted vertically (Cumming 1998, 75).

Jewelry

Women wore a variety of jewelry during the Federal period, ranging from simple earrings or bead necklaces to elaborate sets with many pieces. While gold set with pearls, diamonds, and other gemstones were traditional choices of the well-to-do, new styles of semi-precious or imitation stones and base metals meant that jewelry did not have to be limited to the very wealthy. Pastes, imitation gems made of glass or crystal, were popular throughout the 18th century. They could be backed with colored foils to imitate other gems, such as rubies or emeralds, or to produce gems of colors not easily found in nature, like pink. Cut steel jewelry, made of individual studs of steel that were faceted and polished, was invented in the 1760s but became more fashionable at the end of the century. Abigail Adams wore a necklace of cut steel beads to a ball in London in 1786, and wrote to her niece that they were "much in fashion and brought to such perfection as to resemble diamonds" (Fales 1995, 119). Pinchbeck, an alloy of copper and zinc, was an inexpensive substitute for gold.

Certainly, well-to-do women did own and wear an array of costly pieces of real gold and gems. Perhaps more heavily adorned than most is Matilda Stoughton de Jaudenes y Nebot, the American wife of a Spanish diplomat, in her 1794 portrait by Gilbert Stuart. She wears golden snowflake pins in her hair; a festoon necklace of small pearls and red gemstones; large pearl and gold earrings; a pair of matching bracelets; a long gold chain with a large pendant (perhaps a miniature portrait); a large pin at the neckline of her dress; an assemblage of a watch and other objects on chains on the right side of her bodice; and what appears to be an *equipage,* or set of sewing tools, at her left waist (Barratt and Miles 2004, 124; Fales 1995, 80–81; White 2005, 129–30; waist-hung assemblages or equipages would come to be called *chatelaines* later in the 19th century, but that term was not used in the Federal period). This mixture of different objects illustrates the fashion of the 18th century, when jewelry pieces were considered more as "mix and match" items. Matched sets, or *parures,* became more popular in the early 19th century (Kamer 1989, 137).

***Louisa Catherine Adams,* engraved by G. F. Storm after a painting by C. R. Leslie, 1816. Mrs. John Quincy Adams wears a red velvet dress with white trim, a comb with coral beads, a twisted red bead necklace, beaded tassel earrings, and white gloves. The comb still exists and has an alternate set of jet beads.** Courtesy of Library of Congress.

Some women chose to wear simple gold jewelry for their portraits. Sally Bullard Crosby wears a short necklace of gold beads in her 1790 portrait (White 2005, 82). Anna Peale wears a simple gold circle pin on the neckline of her dress in her 1805 portrait by James Peale (L. Miller 1996, 220). Mary Anne Jewins Burnett wears gold hoop earrings in her circa 1812 portrait by Joshua Johnson (Weekley and Colwill 1987, 151).

Pearls and diamonds were worn throughout the Federal period. Small seed pearls were made into a variety of jewelry, and Martha Washington owned earrings, a cross, and a bird pin. She may have bought the pin in Philadelphia around 1790, when her husband was president. A seed pearl set, or parure, that Eleanor Coffin wore when she married John Derby in Salem, Massachusetts, in 1801, consists of earrings, bracelets, a necklace, a brooch, and a hair ornament. This ornament, called an *aigrette,* is in the form of a flower. The blossom is mounted on a spring, or *trembler,* so it moves when worn. Decima Cecilia Shubrick Heyward wears a similar seed pearl aigrette in her early 19th century miniature portrait (Fales 1995, 108–9).

Colored stones also became popular as accents to the plain white dresses of the early 19th century. Coral, which is the skeletonal material of particular marine animals, is organic, and, while it comes in several colors, the red-orange variety is best-known, giving its name to that color. While it is often made into either smooth or faceted beads, the natural branch shapes were also used for necklaces, bracelets, and tiaras. In 1815, Mary Boardman Crowninshield observed that Eliza Monroe Hay wore "a dozen strings of coral around her neck" (Crowninshield 1935, 20). Amber, also an organic substance, is fossilized tree resin. A jeweler in Boston advertised "real amber Ear Jewels and Necklaces to match" in 1804 (Fales 1995, 122). Carnelian, an orange-red opaque gemstone, was another fashionable choice. It was often carved into seals and embellishments on watch keys but was also made into other jewelry. Edward Malbone painted a miniature portrait of Sally Foster Otis of Boston in 1804. She wears a carnelian cross suspended from a pearl necklace. The cross has a topaz center surrounded by seed pearls. The cross survives today in the collection of Historic New England with a strand of carnelian beads. It is possible that the cross came with both necklaces; in 1810, the Boston jewelers Fletcher and Gardiner advertised interchangeable sets of carnelians and pearls (Fales 1995, 124).

Yellow topazes, purple amethysts and other colored faceted gemstones were also popular in the first two decades of the 19th century. Elizabeth Monroe had sets of three different colored stones. Her purple amethyst set included a tiara, two bracelets, and a clasp set in yellow gold. She also had a set of yellow citrines. Citrine resembles topaz and was sometimes identified as such. This set includes a tiara, earrings, a necklace, and a pendant. Her parure of aquamarines set in rose gold includes a necklace, cross, bracelet clasps, and earrings. As was often the case, the two bracelet clasps could also be joined together with gold links to form a choker (Langston-Harrison 1997, 152–55). In 1814, New York jeweler Charles Osbourn sold a pair of pearl and topaz earrings and also counted an amethyst finger ring in his inventory (White 2005, 86–87). In 1817, Caroline Calvert of Maryland received a "splendid set of amethyst" from her grandfather in Europe (Callcott 1991, 328).

Cameos became fashionable as part of the craze for all things classical, and Napoleon and Josephine were very fond of them. Antique Roman cameos served as models for contemporary jewelry with the figures often carved to represent scenes from antiquity. Cameos were carved in relief from shells so that the image is a light cream color and the background a darker orange-brown color. The best were made in Italy. Elizabeth Monroe had two cameo brooches among the things she bought in France. One has a design of flowers and the other shows the image of a girl of the late 18th century, rather than a classical figure (Langston-Harrison 1997, 126). In England, Josiah Wedgwood produced ceramic jasperware plaques that resembled cameos, with white figures on blue, lilac, green, or black grounds. Mary Anna Gibbes Garden wears a belt buckle set with a Wedgwood medallion in her 1803 miniature portrait by Adam Buck (Fales 1995, 118).

Jewelry either woven from hair or with hair set under glass was also fashionable. While this type of jewelry is often associated with mourning, with the hair of the deceased given as a memento, it could also be a token of affection using the hair of one's friend or beloved. Elizabeth Salisbury of Worcester, Massachusetts, bought a pearl brooch with her husband's initials and a pair of bracelet clasps set with his hair from London in 1802 (Fales 1995, 105). In 1812, as a sign of friendship, Mercy Otis Warren and John and Abigail Adams exchanged locks of hair when reconciling after years of political differences. Mrs. Adams had the hair set in a ring for Mrs. Warren and a pin for herself (Fales 1995, 106). (Warren and the Adamses were estranged after the publication of Mrs. Warren's history of the American Revolution. See chapter 2.)

Another type of jewelry that was popular throughout the Federal period was the miniature, mounted in a metal frame and worn as a pendant, brooch, or bracelet clasp. Miniature portraits were originally painted on velum or cardboard, but by the 18th century they were most often painted on ivory. By the early 19th century, cut silhouettes were also being mounted in jewelry. Ann Penington in her 1805 portrait by Gilbert Stuart wears a silhouette hung on a gold chain. Stuart also painted Sarah Shippen Lea, who wears a painted miniature of her son, and Sarah McKean, the Marquesa de Casa Yrujo, who wears a painted miniature of her father (Barratt and Miles 2004, 236, 237, 246).

Although a watch was a luxury item, a few women owned one. These were often worn as part of an assemblage either pinned onto the waist of the dress or having a hook or chain that looped over the waistband. In 1818, Stephen Salisbury of Worchester, Massachusetts, ordered a watch and "Seals Keys and trinketts" from a London merchant for his wife, Elizabeth's, 50th birthday (Fales 1995, 130–31).

As the waistline of the dress rose, the watch was often worn on a chain around the neck. In 1816, Mary Bagot's jewelry included "a gold watch chain around her neck" (Crowninshield 1935, 61). Watches were often imported from France or England, although Americans also made them. When Grace Harrison died in Maryland in 1794, her estate included "1 gold french watch" (Gunston Hall). Elizabeth Monroe bought a fancy watch while she was in France in the 1790s (Langston-Harrison 1997, 107).

Footwear—Stockings

Women often knitted their own stockings with very fine needles and linen, worsted wool, or cotton yarns. Linen or flax stockings were sometimes called *thread* stockings, and *yarn* stockings always referred to wool. Through the years of her diary, Sarah Snell Bryant recorded that she knitted many pairs of "linnen" stockings for herself, along with some cotton and white wool worsted ones (Nylander n.d).

However, machine-knitted stockings had been made since the 17th century. Hose were knitted flat on a stocking frame and the center back seam was then sewn by hand. Most machine-knitted stockings were probably imported from Europe, but there were stocking frames in the United States. Frames in Philadelphia and nearby Germantown produced stockings that were advertised as "cheaper and more lasting 'than those of any nation in Europe'" (Farrell 1992, 40), and there were also manufacturers in Connecticut and New York. According to Coxe, cotton had almost entirely replaced flax in manufactured hosiery by 1810 (Coxe 1814, xxix).

By the 1780s, stockings with clocks were fashionable. A clock is a fancy design either knitted in or embroidered by hand after knitting. From time to time, colored clocks would be fleetingly fashionable, but plain white clocks were most common during this period. Clocks went out of fashion as women's skirts became longer in the 1790s and then come back in fashion around 1810, as skirts shortened again.

Other patterns also became fashionable in the second decade of the 19th century, as women's skirts became shorter and the trim around the hem drew attention to the feet. In 1810, Peter Hoffman and Son in Baltimore advertised "Fashionable ribbed Silk Hose" imported from London. Later, lacy openwork stockings came into fashion. In 1816, Rosalie Calvert received some stockings from her sister in Europe, "I have never seen anything as fine as these open-work stockings—surely one should wear very short skirts with these. Do you wear other stockings underneath?" (Callcott 1991, 304; by "very short" Mrs. Calvert meant just above the ankle.)

Plain white stockings were the norm throughout the Federal period, although there was a brief period when pale pink, or flesh-colored, stockings, were in fashion. These gave a nude look under the very sheer dresses in vogue in the early 19th century. While this style originated in France, women in New York had the opportunity to adopt it by 1806, when "a cargo ship from Bordeaux arrived bringing with it, among other goods, '3 [boxes] women's silk stockings, flesh colour and lace clocks;'" and "Ebenezer Stevens advertised for sale '2 bales womens white and flush coloured silk stockings embroidered clocks'" (Majer 1989, 225). Women also wore black stockings. In 1811, Dolley Madison requested both black and white stockings from France (Shulman 2007), and Joseph Wheeler & Co. advertised "Ladies' white and black Silk Hose" in the *Hartford Courant* in 1812.

Stockings had to be held up with garters made from ribbon or narrow braided or woven tape or knitted bands. Garters were tied just above or below the knee, above the swell of the calf. In the early 19th century, so-called elastic garters were developed. These were made with small flexible metal springs, covered with thread, that adjusted to stay snugly in place. Stretchable elastic made with rubber, as it is made today, was not be invented until after 1820.

Footwear—Shoes and Boots

At the beginning of the Federal era, women's dress shoes generally had a heel about two inches high and latchets, or straps, for metal buckle closures. The buckles were not permanently attached and could be used on more than one pair of shoes. The uppers were often made of silk or wool, lined with leather. All-leather uppers became more common by the end of the century. Small, slender, Italian heels, no more than an inch and a half high, was an option in the 1780s. Through the 1790s, the heels shrank until, by the early 19th century, shoes had little or no visible heels at all. As skirts became longer, buckles went out of style, as they were no longer seen (and could also become entangled in the skirt's drapery). After the buckles disappeared, some shoes kept the latchets, now made with holes to accommodate ties. The toe was very pointed at the end of the century but became more round or oval durin the early 19th century. An example of a 1799 wedding shoe, made of green Morocco leather, has a low Italian heel and a very pointed toe, and a blue silk shoe is similar. Both have slender latchets and single ribbon ties (Rexford 2000, pl. 1–2; *Morocco* is a type of tanned goatskin with a grain, finished in black or bright colors, often red, so called because it originated in the North African country of the same name). In 1799, Williamina Ridgely asked her sister in Philadelphia for a "pair of black shoes with heels," and pointed toes. She wanted Morocco leather, but would settle for worsted wool (de Vallinger and Shaw 1948, 320).

In the early 19th century, most women seem to have worn a type of slipper—that is, a shoe with no closures and little or no heel. In an 1805 *American and Commercial Daily Advertiser,* Amos Fitch and Co. in Baltimore advertised the wares in their "Fancy Shoe-store," including "Ladies' Kid Slippers, with heels all colours," "Spring Heel do [ditto]" (a spring heel is just one thickness of leather inserted between the sole and the heel seat [Rexford 2000, 342]), and "Ladies' good Morocco do."

Slippers were often made of lightweight leather, such as kidskin, or silk fabric. Leather slippers with stamped designs or stripes were

White kid leather shoes with silk rosettes and cotton lining, Massachusetts, 1805–1810. These are straights, that is, the left and right shoes were not differentiated. One has a label, "SHOES,/Made and Warranted/ BY/Samuel Brimblecom, /LYNN." Courtesy of American Costume Studies.

fashionable at the turn of the 19th century. In Massachusetts museums, there is a purple shoe with stamped tan rosettes and another of white kid with a black design (Rexford 2000, pl. 2, p. 59). The Museum of Fine Arts, Boston, has a pair of slippers made about 1800, with "Pompeiian red" stripes painted on the cream leather and red Italian heels (Museum of Fine Arts, http://www.mfa.org; the color "Pompeiian red' indicates the influence of the recently discovered frescoes in the excavated Roman city). As skirts became shorter in the 19th century, shoes might have ribbon rosettes or other trims. The Baltimore "Fancy Shoe-store" had "a handsome assortment of silver and ribbon rosettes, of the latest London fashions."

As classical styles came into vogue, women on the cutting edge of fashion adopted Roman or Greek style sandals. Some slippers had criss-crossed ribbons that tied above the ankle to resemble sandals. Philadelphia women in two of John Lewis Krimmel's painting wear shoes with crossed ribbon ties—in the 1812 *Fourth of July in Centre Square* they are pink, while in *Election Day 1815,* they are blue (Harding 1991, 21, 84). Another style of shoe or sandal had ribbons threaded through shaped tabs with eyelets. A white kid shoe in the Peabody Essex Museum, dated

1805 to 1810, is cut this way, and a young woman in Krimmel's 1811 painting, *Pepper-Pot* wears a red pair of this style (Rexford 2000, 73; Harding 1991, 17).

In 1815, Mary Boardman Crowninshield reported that white shoes were worn for formal occasions (Crowninshield 1935, 23). In 1817, Rosalie Stier Calvert requested both white and colored shoes. She asked her sister to buy "three or four pairs of shoes, two white and two of color" for herself, and "six pairs of shoes, four white and two colored" for her daughter. The next year she asked for "two pairs of white for me and six pairs of white dancing shoes for Caroline" in addition to colored shoes for day wear (Callcott 1991, 320, 347).

Leather shoes with a single tie through the narrow latchets would have been more sturdy than the very lightweight slippers and may have been a woman's choice for everyday working and walking wear. English shoes of this type that survive include a brown pair with wedge heels and a black pair with low heels. Both tie on with laces run through a single set of holes (Pratt and Woolley 1999, 60, 67).

Although many shoes were imported from England, they were also manufactured in the United States. Several towns in Massachusetts produced them on a large scale. In 1795, Lynn produced 300,000 pairs of women's shoes, while a pair of shoes worn at an 1812 wedding has a label from a manufacturer in Reading (Rexford 2000, 9, 11). During this period, both shoes in a pair were generally made on straight lasts, that is, there was no differentiation for left and right feet.

Women sometimes wore low boots, often called half boots, for walking outdoors or for horseback riding. However, boots do not seem to have been as common in the United States as in England. A short, plain black leather boot with a low heel, dated 1805 to 1815, is in the collection of the Peabody Essex Museum. This would have been sturdy enough to wear in the snow. Another boot, made of nankeen cotton with a linen lining and green silk trim, is very lightweight and would most likely have been worn in the summer. It was probably worn in Salem about 1805 to 1815 (Rexford 2000, 108).

Women must also have worn some kind of protective footwear in bad weather. It appears that New England women wore thick knitted socks over their shoes in the snow. Sylvia Tyler recorded knitting several pairs of what she called overshoes in her diary (Tyler Diaries 1801–1820). And when Eliza Southgate was getting ready to go to a dance in the middle of a February snowstorm in 1801, she wrote that she "slipt on my socks," probably similar to these knitted overshoes, before going out to the carriage (Bowne 1887/1980, 92). In 1819, Rosalie Calvert wrote that she and her daughter had "specially-made slippers which keep our feet as warm as possible" when traveling in their carriage (Callcott 1991, 146). It is not known how these shoes were made, but perhaps they resemble the fur-lined overshoes that a maid is removing from a lady's foot in Rolinda Sharples's 1817 painting of the Clifton (England) Assembly Rooms (Swann 1982, 33).

Pattens provided protection on wet pavements. Pattens have wooden soles with raised iron rings and leather straps to slip on over the shoes. A pair dated to 1804 is in the Lynn Museum (Rexford 2000, 146). Clogs with wooden soles and leather uppers were common footwear in the English countryside, but do not seem to have been common in the United States.

Hairstyles, Cosmetics, and Bathing

Hairstyles

While the extremely high, lavishly decorated hairstyles fashionable in France in the 1770s were no longer in style, the hairstyles of the 1780s were still very high and full. This effect was achieved with *frizzing* or *frizzling,* or setting the hair in very small curls with a hot curling iron. (The irons in use by this time look very similar to modern ones except, of course, that they had to be heated over a fire. Use of protective curl paper mitigated scorching of the hair.) The volume was often supplemented by combing the natural hair over pads of human hair, horse hair, or wool. Mrs. Tallmadge has frizzed and powdered hair ornamented with feathers, flowers, and jewels (Kornhauser 1991, 38). The hair was set with pomatum, often scented, and usually with some type of grease as the base. It was still fashionable to powder the hair with white or gray powder but as the 1790s progressed, the use of powder decreased, leaving a woman's hair its natural color. Elaborate hairstyles likely required the skill of professional hairdressers or trained ladies' maids. These professionals could also make the preparations from published recipes, but those with European connections could import them. In 1791, William Bingham placed an order with his agent in France for 36 "rouleaux of pommade" and six pounds of powder, both probably for hairdressing (Alberts 1969, 215).

An alternative to tightly frizzed hair was a bunch of large loose curls piled on the head, often with a fall of loose curls hanging down the neck and a long loose ringlet on either side of the face. Sisters Huldah and Lucy Bradley have similar curled hairstyles (Kornhauser 1991, 200–201).

At the time of the French Revolution, women in France adopted short hairstyles. These were partly inspired by statues of ancient Roman women, who often had short hair. However, they were also rather gruesomely sometimes called *à la victime,* for the victims of the guillotine who had their hair cut short before being executed. Josephine du Pont, visiting France in 1798, wrote that women had short haircuts, just as the men did, "and this fashion is extremely convenient." She amplified in 1800 that she could now wash her hair every day (Low 1974, 45, 65).

But these new styles did not catch on immediately in the United States. In 1797, the ultra-fashionable Anne Willing Bingham of Philadelphia sat for her portrait with a full frizzed hairstyle, although unpowdered (Barratt and Miles 2004, 197). And according to Josephine du Pont, the women of New York were slow to accept the new styles. As late as January 1800, she wrote, "the women seem perfectly happy with their antique white-powdered floating chignons, their immense hats., &c. &c., which are dated by at least 10 years" (Low 1974, 52).

Women also began to wear wigs over their own hair, "for the sake of variety," and it was fashionable to wear wigs that were not one's natural hair color (Low 1974, 45). Josephine du Pont continually made efforts to have a wig made in New York for her friend, Margaret Manigault. But finally, in December 1800, she had to admit:

> There is no way to get anything from him. He pretends that the hair he had set aside for us was burned in the oven! What a misfortune! What a calamity for the New York belles. So how do you manage? Can it be that you would still have the courage to use your own hair. Pretty as it is, it seems impossible to me to use now. The revolution is complete here—wigs and no powder at all! But they are for the most part curled and stiff. There are still very few like mine, although mine are pronounced very attractive. (Low 1974, 73; despite the claim that the ladies of New York were 10 years behind the times just a few months earlier, they had evidently caught up)

However, Margaret Manigault did have a wig in June 1800, "You wish to know, my dear friend, whether I wear a wig? I have one, but I do not overwork it. It comes from Philadel—But the hair is too long in the back, &c. You know I did not use much powder, even when you were here. I have not worn any for a century" (Low 1974, 63). Williamina Cadwalader had noted in 1798 that the women in Philadelphia were adopting the fashion, "some ladies here wear wigs....real wigs all over the head." Ann Ridgely wrote the next year that she had her hair cut and arranged to "look like a wig." In 1800 Eliza Southgate, in Massachusetts, also wanted a wig:

> Now Mamma, what do you think I am going to ask for?—a wig. Eleanor has got a new one just like my hair and only 5 dollars, Mrs. Mayo one just like it. I must either cut my hair or have one, I cannot dress it at all *stylish.* Mrs. Coffin bought Eleanor's and says that she will write to Mrs. Sumner to get me one just like it; how much time it will save—in one year we could save it in pins and paper, besides the *trouble.* At the assembly I was quite ashamed of my head, for nobody has long hair. (Bowne 1887/1980, 23)

It appears that not all women cut their hair short (or covered it with a wig) during this period and during the second decade of the 19th century, long hair seems to have become the norm again. It was, however always worn pulled up into a mass of curls, braids, or a bun. This could be worn low on the head, as Lydia Smith does in her portrait, circa 1808–1810; her hair is parted in the middle and there is a ringlet or curl hanging in front of her ear (Barratt and Miles 2005, 299). Catharine Trissler Eichholtz wears her hair in a bun higher on her head, and also has curls in front of her ears, in her 1818 portrait (Ryan 2003, 152). Marie Françoise Trachon de Lorrière Dubocq wears her hair in a high mass of curls on her head, accented with a jeweled ornament, and a row of curls across her forehead (L. Miller 1996, 216). Once again, a hairdresser or a lady's maid would often arrange a woman's hair. In 1804, Rosalie Calvert wrote, "Kitty…is my chambermaid and an excellent one. She is quite skillful and even puts my hair in curl-papers every night" (Callcott 1991, 100).

In 1815, Mrs. Crowninshield was 37 years old and felt she should have been wearing some kind of head covering, perhaps a turban, to the evening parties she was attending in Washington, D.C. But she wrote:

> any one who has tolerable hair does not care to cover it up,—the object is to look as young as you can. The folks here in the house say I must dress my hair, not cover it up, so last eve it was combed up as high on the top as I could get it, braided, and a bunch of flowers pinned in with one of my best ornaments—the green and gold one.

She added later, "I save much expense by not wearing turbans." However, she did have to curl her hair, and that took time (Crowninshield 1935, 24–25, 27).

The elaborate curls massed on the head or hanging in front of the ears may not always have been natural. In November 1812, hairdresser John Scotti paid a visit to Washington and had "a small assortment of" various false hair, including "Frizettes, Kill Beaus, Heart Breakers, Beau Catchers, and a variety of other powerful instruments of love." But in 1817, Margaret Bayard Smith could not find what she needed in Washington, and wrote to her niece, "I went forth on a shopping expedition and procured most of the winter clothing for the family.…One article I could not get,—curls, french curls, parted on the forehead, you know how. You must get them for me either in New York or Phila. Now remember CURLS!" (Smith 1906/1965, 143).

Cosmetics

Many European women in the 18th century unabashedly whitened their faces (often with lead, a dangerous practice, as this toxic heavy metal can be absorbed through the skin) and rouged their cheeks. The common red ingredient in rouge was carmine, made from an infusion of the red dyestuff cochineal, obtained from a small insect. The vegetable dyes alkanet, Brazilwood, camwood, or sanders wood, were also used. "Painting" was not to the taste of many Americans, however, and most women probably adopted what we call today the natural look. The Polish traveler Julian Ursyn Niemcewicz wrote about the women at an assembly in Philadelphia in 1797, "Th[eir] lack of brilliancy may perhaps be attributed to the absence of rouge, which the women in this country never use, unless in stealth, and then so little that one can not notice it" (1965, 35). Englishman John Lambert concurred, "I must not omit to mention, in justice to the American fair, that I saw but very few, who had recourse to *rouge* for the purpose of heightening their charms" (Lambert 1810, 2:197). Abigail Adams disparagingly reported meeting the American, Maria Matilda Bingham, divorced wife of the French Comte de Tilly, in Philadelphia in 1799, who did use rouge, "She has the appearance and dress of a Real French woman. Rouged up to the Ears," and later, "the face, a la mode de Paris, red as a Brick hearth" (Mitchell 1947, 214, 242). However, evidently other American women decided to follow suit and openly use cosmetics. Sara Gales Seaton observed in Washington in 1813 that "it is the fashion for most of the ladies a little advanced in age to rouge and pearl." (Despite its innocent-sounding name, pearl powder was made with bismuth, a toxic heavy metal like lead; rice flour was a safer alternative.) She added, "Mrs. C. and Mrs. G. paint excessively, and think it becoming; but with them it is no deception, only folly, and they speak of it as indispensable to a decent appearance." She added that Elizabeth Monroe "paints very much." However, Mrs. Seaton claimed that Dolley Madison did not use rouge, although others asserted that she did. "I do not think it true, as I

Drawing by Rosalie Stier Calvert in a letter to her mother, Marie Louise Peeters Stier, March 1804, "I am including here a small drawing showing how we do our hair . . . sometimes with a garland of flowers, or the hair is turned up with combs garnished with pearls, or for those who have them, diamonds." Text from Callcott 1991, 80; image courtesy of the Riversdale Historical Society.

am well assured I saw her color come and go at the naval ball" (Seaton 1871, 90–91).

Bathing

Full body bathing was not the norm during this period. Most people probably were content to wash their hands and faces using a basin of water and rubbing briskly with a towel to remove dead skin—soap was not generally used. However, there were advocates of full-body bathing, such as the English Lady of Distinction, who wrote in 1811, "The generality of English ladies seem to be ignorant of the use of any bath larger than a wash-hand bason.... I strongly recommend to every lady to make a bath as indispensable an article in her house as a looking-glass" (1811/1997, 40–41). Philadelphia and New York had public baths by the turn of the 19th century, and some private homes had baths, as well. In 1796, George Tucker of Williamsburg put a copper bathtub in his dairy, with hot water piped in from the laundry (Park 2000, 2). Henry and Elizabeth Drinker of Philadelphia installed a shower box in their backyard in 1798. Their daughter, Nancy on July 29, "went this evening under the Shower bath, talks of repeating it" and did on July 31, when "Nancy pulled the string of the Shower bath again this evening she seems better reconsiled to it—the water has stood some hours in the Yard, which alters the property much, she goes under the bath in a single gown and an Oylcloath cap" (Drinker 1994, 197; the water was probably more tolerable because it was warmer from standing in the sun all day; note that Nancy did not go unclothed into the bath. Oil cloth was made by treating cotton fabric with oil or a resin to make it waterproof. Bathing dress is discussed in the next section).

DRESS FOR SPECIAL ACTIVITIES—RIDING AND BATHING

Riding

The only true sport for women that required special attire was horseback riding. This was limited to those who could afford to own a riding horse or could borrow one. A woman's riding ensemble was called a habit and generally consisted of a separate jacket and skirt. Women rode side-saddle, and the skirts of their habits were cut to accommodate this. The jackets, however, were generally made much like men's tailored coats and were, in fact, often constructed by tailors. Women did also wear a modified form of the riding habit for traveling, even if they were not going by horseback. An article in the 1808 *Lady's Monthly Museum* stated, "Habits are very appropriate for travelling costume." The French called a riding habit *Amazone,* after the mythical Greek female warriors.

In 1797, Rosalie Stier, who lived in Annapolis, wore "a Spencer of nankeen from the Indies a skirt made from the same material" when riding her horse, Brilliant (Callcott 1991, 14). Most tailor-made riding habits were wool, but the natural tan-colored nankeen cotton would have been a cooler alternative for summer wear.

In 1800, Eliza Southgate was going to travel with some friends, and she wrote her mother, "I was very sorry I did not wear my *habit* down as I shall want it when I go to Wiscassett. If you can possibly find an opportunity, I wish you would send it to me." In her next letter, she again lamented, "I shall go on horseback,—How I want my habit,—I wish it had not been so warm when I left home and I should have worn it" (Bowne 1887/1980, 26, 29).

In 1803, Rosalie Stier, who by then was married to George Calvert, described the habits that she and her niece, Eliza Custis Law, had made for their trip to Bath, Virginia, (now Berkeley Springs, West Virginia),

> Hers is Hussar-style; mine is bottle-green [with] a quite short skirt, with two rows of small gold buttons on the pockets and five rows on the jacket all the way up to the shoulders and gold cord [in a criss-cross design] between the buttons. It is most becoming. The hats are velvet, the same color as the habits, turned up on one side à la Henry IV, with a lovely plume and a cord and pendant of gold. (Callcott 1991, 55)

(*Hussar style* referred to various elaborate military-style details, such as braid and metal buttons, inspired by the uniforms of the 12 Hussar regiments in the French empire, that "reflected many novelties of dress borrowed from outside France and provided a pretext for the most dazzling display of military finery. Their regiments.... competed with one another for elegance, resulting in a stunning spectacle for the beholder" [Brunon 1989, 194]. Bottle green is a dark green color so called because many bottles, especially wine bottles, are this color. Henry IV, king of France from 1589 to 1610, gave his name to velvet hats with large plumes that evoked styles of the Renaissance.)

A habit in the collection of the Salsbury Museum in England, dated 1795 to 1810, is made of pale blue wool. It has a short jacket reflecting the fashionable high waist of the period. The very long skirt is mounted onto a silk taffeta bodice that enabled the wearer to keep the skirt in place at the high waist position. Inside the skirt are ties and tabs that could be used to loop the skirt up while the woman was riding or walking (Arnold 1977, 48–49). This was a typical construction for riding habits through the end of the Federal era.

A habit with a known American history and dated 1805 to 1815 is in the collection of the National Museum of American History. It is made of blue camlet. The jacket is double-breasted with large lapels, self-covered buttons, and short pleated tails in back. The skirt, rather than being attached to a bodice, has shoulder straps to hold it in place at the raised waistline position. The skirt is not, however, long enough to be tied up, like the English habit above. It is possible that the habit was made for walking or traveling rather than for horseback riding.

In the United States, James Queen and William Lapsley published *The Taylor's Instructor, or, a Comprehensive Analysis, of the Elements of Cutting Garments of Every Kind* in 1809. This book was based on an earlier English work, *The Taylor's Complete Guide;* however, Queen and Lapsley did update the text for the newer men's and women's styles of the early 19th century. They noted the raised waistline in women's garments:

> What will you think, when informed of the difference and quick transition of fashion, in this particular, between 1791 and 1797? In the former, the waist was cut full nine inches long, from under the arm down to the hip, which by the by, is the proper way of measuring for the length of the waist. In the latter, we have seen, and were frequently obliged to cut them only three inches long, for figures of exactly the same size. (Shep 1998, 100)

Riding accessories included a modified form of shirt called a *habit shirt.* This was cut similarly to a man's shirt (see chapter 4), but was shorter, in order to fit under the short jacket. Early in the era, a waistcoat might have been part of the ensemble. Woman's riding hats often had a masculine look and, like men's hats, were often made of felt. The hat in Mary Anna Boardman's portrait is likely a riding or outdoor hat. It has a high crown similar to a man's top hat, but a feminine blue silk ribbon band (Kornhauser 1991, 212–13). While boots would be practical for riding, some illustrations suggest that women wore low shoes instead. Leather gloves completed the outfit.

Bathing

Women did not generally go swimming during the Federal period, but they did go bathing for medicinal reasons and had special attire for the purpose. Spa resorts were built around hot springs in such places as Bath, Warm Springs, and Sweet Springs, in Virginia and Saratoga and Ballston, in New York. Some women also went bathing in the ocean, in places such as Long Branch, New Jersey. A bathing dress that Martha Washington wore at Bath in 1769 is in the collection of Mount Vernon. It is cut similarly to a woman's shift but with less fullness and is made of two kinds of blue and white checked linen (probably because there was not enough of one fabric) and has lead weights in the hem that would prevent the shift from floating up in the water. Women who took the waters in Bath, England, seem to have worn similar shifts, made of natural tan linen, into the 19th century. It seems likely that women continued to wear similar garments for bathing in the United States through the Federal period. It is also possible that at spas where the sexes bathed separately, women went into the water wearing no clothing. The Drinkers' daughter, Nancy, wore an oilcloth cap in the shower bath in their yard, and women may have worn similar caps for spa bathing.

Rites of Passage—Attire for Weddings, Maternity Wear, and Mourning

Weddings

A bride might have a new dress for her wedding, but she would likely continue to wear it as her best dress for some time after. White, blue, and silver were all popular colors for wedding dresses in the 18th century. As white became generally fashionable in the late 1790s, many wedding dresses of the period were white, although the color had no particular connotation for weddings. The dress Eunice Hooper wore for her wedding to her cousin, John Hooper, in about 1799 is in the collection of the Museum of Fine Arts, Boston. The white silk satin open robe has a raised waist and elbow length sleeves. It is trimmed with folds of silk georgette crêpe, artificial pearls, and fly fringe. The petticoat is white India mull muslin embroidered with silver dots (Museum of Fine Arts, http://www.mfa.org). This is a very formal dress and Mrs. Hooper probably had limited occasions to wear it later. In contrast, the dress Mary E. Oatley wore for her wedding in 1801, while of a moderately sheer white corded muslin, is less elaborate. It has a very high waist, below-elbow-length sleeves and a center front drawstring closure. (This dress was probably originally made in the 1790s and remodeled. The original longer, pointed, bodice back was left hanging inside the dress.) This dress is in the collection of the University of Rhode Island (McMurry 2001, 67–70). The tan silk dress Anne Taylor wore for her 1804 wedding is in the collection of the Daughters of the American Revolution Museum in Washington, D.C. Mrs. Taylor was a Quaker, and her dress is characteristically very plain, but well made of good quality fabric. The bodice closes at the center front with drawstrings, the skirt has a drop front, and the sleeves are very long. The bride in John Lewis Krimmel's 1814 *Country Wedding* wears a fairly simple white dress that could definitely have been worn again for other occasions. It has short sleeves, a pink ribbon around the waist, and a tuck and ruffle around the hem. It is accessorized with a ruffled chemisette, a gold necklace, mitts that end above the elbow, and black slippers. The bride wears no head covering (Harding 1994, 73). A white kid shoe with a black stamped design was worn by a bride in 1806 (Rexford 2000, 110–11). The shoe shows a great deal of wear, indicating that the bride continued to wear her shoes long after the wedding.

Maternity Wear

Married women could expect to be pregnant more than once in their lives. There is little evidence that they made clothes especially for this but probably more often adjusted clothes they already had. Early in the period, a petticoat that had a drawstring casing could be adjusted as needed. The dresses of the late 1790s, with their drawstring closings, could also be easily adjusted. Sarah Snell Bryant, who had seven children, several times made what she called "loos gowns" for herself. She may have used this term to refer to those relatively unfitted styles of the period. As she also made loose gowns for other women, and for herself when she was not pregnant, these were not only for maternity wear, but they would certainly have leant themselves to the size adjustment needed. There is one intriguing example of a dress in the collection of the University of Rhode Island that may have been specifically made for maternity wear. It is a silk damask fabric and shows evidence of having been remade. The back, with loose pleats from the neck to the hem, suggests the style of the late 1780s, while the long tight sleeves are more characteristic of the early 1790s. The front, with a high waistline and drawstring closures at the neck and raised waist, seem more in keeping with the late 1790s. The large amount of fullness in the front seems disproportionate to the small size of the back unless this was designed for maternity wear (McMurry 2001, 51–53). Chloe Smith wears a similar dress in her 1798 portrait. She was painted with her five children, the youngest an infant, and it has been suggested that her brown silk dress with a loose back and high front drawstring waist was also designed for pregnancy (Kornhauser 1991, 220–21). The bib front dresses of the early 19th century would have been functional for nursing an infant.

Mourning

The custom of wearing black for a certain period of time after the death of a family member or friend was common. While white with black trim was sometimes proper mourning attire earlier in the 18th century, by this time all black was the norm. After a suitable time, one could switch to half-mourning, which could be white with black trim or some other variation. When George Washington died in December 1799, the whole country plunged into mourning. Abigail Adams, wife of President John Adams, was in Philadelphia, then the nation's capital, and wrote, "I shall not have occasion now for any thing but Black, untill Spring, then I shall put on half mourning. Mrs. Smith wants her white, as she will after a certain period appear in white trimd with blacke; at present the whole Family are in full mourning." At the next Friday drawing room she held, Mrs. Adams wrote:

> Upwards of a hundred Ladies, and near as many Gentlemen attended, all in mourning—the Ladies Grief did not deprive them of taste in ornamenting their white dresses 2 yds of Black mode [a silk fabric] in length, of the narrow kind, pleated up one Shoulder crossd the Back in the form of a Military sash tyed at the side, crosd the peticoat & hung to

> the bottom of it. were worn by many. others wore black Epulets of Black silk trimd with fring upon each Shoulder, black Ribbon in plaits upon the Gown & coat [petticoat] some plain ribbon, some blacke Snail [chenille] & their Caps were Crape with black plumes or black flowers black Gloves & fans. (Mitchell 1947, 223, 225)

The various draped and applied trims suggest that women altered dresses they already had to suit the occasion. (The custom of rigidly prescribed periods of time to wear the various stages of mourning did not arise until later in the 19th century and may have originated in the English court, when those attending official functions were required to conform with official etiquette. Mrs. Adams said after Washington's death, "the Ladies many of them wanted me to fix the time for wearing mourning. but I decline. and left them to govern themselves by the periods prescribed by the Gentlemen" [Mitchell 1947, 225]—this suggests that the president had made a specific recommendation for a period of mourning among the male government officials.)

There is some evidence that one was not necessarily expected to wear black at the funeral itself, but rather for some period thereafter. (One might already have a stock of black garments, but if one did not, it would take some time to make something appropriate; further, wearing all black to the funeral could suggest that the bereaved had been unduly anticipating the event.) In 1797, Frances Baylor Hill and two of her cousins bought black fabric for dresses after Frances's sister, Polly, died, and it took several days to make them (Botorff and Flannagan 1967, 43). When Ross Wyman died in Shrewsbury in 1808, his will included bequests for his wife, daughters, and granddaughters to buy "decent mourning" clothes. They most likely did not get this money until some time after the funeral. In Joshua Johnson's 1818 portrait of the family of Thomas Everette, his widow, Rebecca Myring, and the three oldest children, two boys and a girl, all wear black. (The toddler John wears red and infant Rebecca wears white). This group portrait was most likely painted sometime in the year after Mr. Everette's death (Weekley and Colwill 1987, 161).

Fabrics for mourning attire included *bombazine,* a blend of silk and wool, that was considered appropriate because it has a dull, rather than a shiny, surface. Barbara Johnson, an Englishwoman who kept an album of swatches of her dress fabrics from 1738 to 1825, had several occasions in her long life to wear mourning clothes. She bought a black and purple calico print and black silk taffeta when one of her brothers died in 1799, and bombazine when another died in 1814 (Rothstein 1987, 94, 123).

Work Clothing

It is difficult to know what women wore while engaged in household or farm work. It does appear that, by the early 19th century, there

Pastoral scene, artist unknown, circa 1809. Watercolor on paper. The woman at the cottage door wears an old-fashioned working ensemble of short gown and petticoat, while the couple in the foreground wear fashionable outfits. Courtesy of the New Hampshire Historical Society.

was probably little differentiation of the dress of hired domestic servants from everyone else. Sometime between 1807 and 1822, Anne-Marguerite-Henriette, the Baroness Hyde de Neuville, painted a picture of an African American cook in what she called "ordinary costume." The woman wears a fashionably cut high-waisted dress with short puffed sleeves. She has a white handkerchief around her neck and wears black shoes with white stockings (New-York Historical Society, http://www.nyhistory.org). John Lewis Krimmel portrayed a woman of color selling soup in a Philadelphia market in 1811. She, too, wears a fashionable high-waisted, short-sleeved dress. The white dress is accented with a red-orange neck handkerchief, but the woman is bare-footed (Harding 1994, 17). Some women, though, do seem to have had distinctive working attire. The simple garment often called a short gown did not require great skill to make and, as it was loose-fitting, it would have been comfortable and functional. As its name implies, it was usually about hip length and was worn with a matching or contrasting skirt or petticoat. The extent to which women in the United States wore short gowns is still being researched. Both documentary evidence and extant examples suggest that they were especially common among Pennsylvania German women, but Pennsylvanians of Scots-Irish and English heritage wore them, too (Hersh and Hersh 1995, 143). Short gowns are also mentioned in records of New England women and enslaved African American women in Virginia and North Carolina. Most women who owned short gowns seem to have owned other clothing as well, suggesting that, for most, short gowns were merely working garments. Englishman John Lambert wrote about the women in New England, "their dress is neat, simple, and genteel; usually consisting of a printed cotton jacket with long sleeves, a petticoat of the same, with a coloured cotton apron or pincloth without sleeves, tied tight, covering the lower part of the bosom" (Lambert 1810, III:105). Whether the "jacket" he described was indeed a tailored, fitted, jacket or the looser fitting short gown is not known.

Sarah Allen, of Carlisle, Pennsylvania, owned both short gowns and petticoats and a variety of long gowns, including a silk one. This suggests that her short gowns were work garments, while she wore her long gowns for more formal occasions. In Vermont, Joel Jones in his 1795 list of his deceased wife's clothing included "one calico short gown." She also had four long gowns, again suggesting she wore the short gown for work (Smith 1925, 50). Likewise, the estates of several New England women who died from 1793 to 1808 include both short and long gowns (M. Miller n.d.) However, Cathrin Weinglar, a prosperous Pennsylvania German, owned only short gowns and petticoats when she died in 1794, indicating that she wore them for all occasions. (Hersh and Hersh 1995, 138, 140). Sarah Snell Bryant of Massachusetts made herself at least one short gown every year from 1796 to 1805. She made her final one in 1808, suggesting that they were going out of style even as working attire by that time (Nylander n.d.). Extant Pennsylvania short gowns include a blue and white linen striped gown in the Schwenkfelder Museum in Pennsburg and 11 short gowns made of a variety of fabrics in the collection of the Chester County Historical Society (Burnston 1998, 4). A Connecticut example is in the Danbury Scott-Fanton Museum and Historical Society. It is an example of *linsey-woolsey,* a mixed linen and wool fabric, in this case with a black and white striped linen warp and a white wool weft (Kidwell 1978, 15).

Women no doubt wore aprons, which could be easily washed, with either their short gowns and petticoats or their long working dresses. White, natural, or blue and white checked linen, or later, cotton, fabrics were common. In the Connecticut Valley of New England, aprons and other utilitarian garments and household items were often made from blue and white checked linen that was grown, spun, dyed, and woven at home. Aprons that tied around the waist were made in two ways. In one method, the upper edge of the fabric was turned down and stitched, forming a narrow casing through which a tape was pulled to form ties, with the fullness adjusted to fit. In another method, the upper edge of the apron fabric was gathered and a fabric or tape band was stitched on. Either the band was left in lengths at each end for the ties or ties were added separately. Some women wore a pincloth style of apron, also sometimes called a smock. This had a sleeveless bodice and skirt cut in a single piece, similar to the coverall garment children wore. Both an apron with a drawstring casing and a pincloth style are in the collection of the Pocumtuck Valley Memorial Association in Deerfield, Massachusetts (M. Miller 2006, 27, pl. 1). Joel Jones's wife had three aprons when she died in 1795, "one white and two checked linin" (Smith 1925, 50). At the beginning of the Federal era, women sometimes wore decorative, rather than functional, aprons, often made of sheer white fabric with white embroidery, but these were going out of style by the last decade of the 18th century. However, Mary Alsop wears such an apron in her 1792 portrait by Ralph Earl (Kornhauser 1991, 45).

Making and Acquiring Clothes

Almost all clothing during the Federal era was produced individually for the wearer, and it was all sewn by hand. Most women and girls could make basic garments such as shifts, short gowns, and petticoats for themselves at home. Some used clothing was available, either given as gifts or bought through second-hand dealers. Some ready-to-wear clothing began to appear in the market at the end of the Federal era, but it was, of course, still entirely sewn by hand. English novelist Jane Austen wrote in 1798, "I cannot determine what to do about my new Gown. I wish such things were to be bought ready-made" (Byrde 1999, 55).

The closely fitting women's styles of the late 18th century were best produced by skilled professionals. The women who made gowns or dresses professionally were called mantua-makers, from the term for an earlier style of dress, the mantua, that was fashionable early in the 18th century. (Gradually, these women would come to be called dressmakers, instead.) It was difficult for a woman to cut and fit her own closely fitting gown bodice, and she often would have that done by a mantua-maker. The client could then have the mantua-maker make the whole gown, or, more economically, just fit and baste it together, allowing a less-skilled (and less expensive) seamstress, the woman herself, or someone in her household to sew the long straight seams of the skirt sections or separate petticoat. Courtney Norton wrote from school in 1791 that she "put out to be made two of my best dresses," as she did not feel confident to make them herself. She did, however, make "all my common apparel" (Baumgarten 2002, 89).

As fashions changed, a woman might need to engage a professional to cut out a new style. Once she had one new garment, though, a skilled home seamstress could replicate it. Rosalie Calvert and her daughter received several gowns from Europe in 1817. These were no doubt custom-made, as they sent old dresses to use as guides. However, for the next social season, Mrs. Calvert wrote, "We have made a dress exactly like the one with the geranium garland, but trimmed in rose instead of flame-color" (Callcott 1991, 346). Women also borrowed ideas from the clothing of others. In 1797, Frances Baylor Hill "began to cut the girls muslins by a new dress of Mrs Legars" (Bottorff and Flannagan 1967, 36). In 1800, Anna Maria Thornton wrote, "I sent 'Joe' to Mrs R. Forrest to borrow a new Gown to look at" (Thornton 1907, 93). Both women at home and professional mantua-makers used European fashion plates for inspiration. Women also often contributed design ideas to their mantua-makers, offering suggestions for styles of sleeves, necklines, or trimmings.

Male tailors often made women's riding habits, since the jackets were cut much like men's coats. Alexander Briggs advertised in Carlisle, Pennsylvania, in 1785–1786 that the "ladies riding dresses" he made were "distinguished not only in this town but distant places by ladies of the first taste in dress—for a peculiar genteel air, neatness of work, and elegance of fitting, which ever adds beauty to the beautiful sex" (Hersh and Hersh 1995, 145). The boned corsets of the 18th century were generally made by professionals who specialized in this trade. These were usually men, as they had the strength to work with baleen and sew through the multiple layers of fabric and leather. In 1792, Mr. Serre, a French immigrant to Philadelphia, advertised that he made both ladies' stays and riding habits (Majer 1989, 218). (As corsets replaced the less structured stays they were probably made either by dressmakers or at home.)

"Curious, & Entertaining, & Astonishing"—Fashion Plates

Fashion plates are hand-colored prints struck from engraved steel plates that were bound into periodicals beginning in the late 18th century. (They were eventually replaced by other forms of illustration and ultimately by photographs.)

These periodicals were not exclusively about fashion, featuring travel, celebrities, poetry, and music. In England, *The Lady's Magazine* included plates intermittently from 1770 on. In 1794, Nicholas Heideloff began the *Gallery of Fashion*, depicting dresses of "Ladies of Rank and Fashion" (Arnold 1970, 18). The French *Journal des Dames et des Modes* began in 1797 with plates showing "Costume[s] Parisien[s]" in each issue. (Pineault 2003, 6–7). American women had access to European plates and doubtless used them as guides for making their clothing. In 1795–1796, Margaret Manigault, of Charleston, South Carolina, subscribed to the *Gallery of Fashion*. New Yorker David Langworth also subscribed and charged a fee for exhibiting the plates to the public (Majer 1989, 220). In 1814, Harriet Manigault wrote that Mrs. Daschkoff, wife of the Russian minister, "brought us a fine collection of 'Belle Assemblies'. . . ; it is a great while since we received any of them before" (Manigault 1976, 23). This was *La Belle Assemblée;* despite its French name, it was published in England.

American women received loose plates from family or friends. Margaret Manigault's friend, Josephine du Pont, sent some "curious, & entertaining, & astonishing, & very acceptable Costumes Parisiens" from Paris in 1799 (Low 1974, 51). Rosalie Calvert's sister sent "little fashion designs" from Antwerp in 1817 that were shown when "friends come to call" (Callcott 1991, 330).

Women had access to a wide array of imported goods in shops in the United States, but those with overseas connections had fashionable items imported directly from Europe. In the early 1790s, William Bingham sent for fashion accessories and cosmetics for his wife (Alberts 1969, 215). After her own return from France, Josephine du Pont made arrangements with a friend "who promised me that whenever I wished she would select them [fashions] at my marchande de modes, who is the best but rather expensive" (Low 1974, 64). In November 1811, Dolley Madison asked Ruth Barlow, wife of the minister to France, to send her "large Headdresses a few Flowers, Feathers, gloves & stockings (Black & White) or any other pritty thing." Unfortunately, the headdresses, when they arrived the next April, were "two tight around.... I shall lay them by for next Winter, & then enlarge & make them fit." In 1816, Hannah Gallatin, the new French minister's wife, bought two caps, a "cambric muslin spencer," and a lace veil for Mrs. Madison. (Shulman 2007; using diplomatic connections was a way to circumvent the trade restrictions of the pre-War of 1812 period, and it could make shipment less risky, as combatants would in theory recognize the neutrality of ships on diplomatic business. Rosalie Calvert wrote in 1811, "My last letter... was entrusted to Mr. Barlow.... I also think he could manage it so that I could get the candelabra, etc., that you bought for me. A large number of articles always come on these government ships—several ladies in Washington recently received a number of things that Mr. Warden [Consul General to France] sent them" [Callcott 1991, 242].)

After the War of 1812, normal trade with Europe resumed. Rosalie Stier Calvert had clothes sent from Antwerp in 1817 as she prepared to introduce her daughter into Washington, D.C., society. Because true ready-to-wear clothing was not yet available, Mrs. Calvert sent her sister "an old ragged dress" to "serve as a measure" for the European dressmaker. Mrs. Calvert observed, "Mrs. Monroe [Elizabeth, wife of President James Monroe], her daughters, and four or five other Washington women receive their clothes from Paris" (Callcott 1991, 320, 348). (As early as 1794, Citizeness Lisfrand offered made-to-measure women's clothing at her Maison Egalité in Paris. Her trade catalogue included instructions for providing measurements and arranging payment [Low 1974, 38, 40–41].)

Women also sent requests to friends and families in the larger cities of the United States. Dolley Madison wrote to Philadelphia, where the shops were superior to those in the new city of Washington. In 1804, she asked her sister, Anna, for "a light shaul a douzn yds. of fashionable handsome broad ribbon a pr or 2 of gloves." In 1809, Mary Elizabeth Latrobe (wife of the architect Benjamin Latrobe, who was helping the Madisons decorate the President's House), sent a wig, a hat, and a turban in addition to household goods. In 1813, Mrs. Madison received an offer from Elizabeth Patterson Bonaparte to shop for "French Gloves

Fashions &c." in Baltimore, and Mrs. Madison responded enthusiastically (Shulman 2007).

Some women were able to go abroad when their husbands went on personal or official business and took advantage of the opportunity to buy European fashions. Elizabeth Monroe accompanied her husband to both Great Britain and France and bought fans, shawls, and other accessories. Sarah Bowdoin's husband, John Bowdoin III, was appointed associate minister to France by Thomas Jefferson from 1805 to 1808. Mrs. Bowdoin returned to the United States with a dress made of fine white cotton mull from India with delicate white embroidered trim. In the latest Paris fashion, it had a very high waist, a gored skirt, and a small train (Nouvel-Kammerer 2007, 126–27).

As the 18th century progressed and styles changed, women often altered older gowns to update them. Fabrics were expensive, and there are examples of fabrics from the 1770s that have been remade into styles of the 1790s, or even later. In the early 1790s, Elizabeth Perkins Wildes re-made an "old camlet gown" after first washing it and taking it apart (Ulrich 2001, 299). In, 1796, Charlotte Sheldon recorded in her diary, "Began to alter my muslin into a robe which is the most fashionable dress in Hartford." She finished the dress the next Tuesday, when she "starched my gown and hung it to dry" (Vanderpoel 1903, 12). Josephine du Pont, who was visiting France at the time, wrote in 1798, "Remaking almost all my dresses without great expenditures,

A. SAWYER

RESPECTFULLY informs the ladies of Washington and Georgetown, that she has just received and is now opening a handsome assortment of Millinery and fancy articles, consisting of silk velvets, satins and ribbands, Ostrich feathers, white, black and other colors garniture and worked muslins, spencers, hhdfs. thread laces, caps and turbans, straw hats, childrens worsted caps, and various other articles, at her new stand in F street, between T. W. Pairo's and the General Land Office.

Nov. 13—

Newspaper advertisement, *Washington National Intelligencer,* November 20, 1817. Milliner A. Sawyer sold hats, trims, fabrics, and ready-made spencers at her shop in Washington, D.C. Courtesy of Library of Congress.

I find myself just about as well dressed as others" (Low 1974, 46). As style changes became more extreme, simple alterations were not adequate and a woman might opt to take a gown completely apart to be remade. For example, Frances Baylor Hill wrote in 1797 that she "rip'd up a gown for Cousin Susan & began to alter it" (Bottorff and Flannagan 1967, 44). Extant garments often offer clues to remaking such as old stitching or fold lines. As waistlines rose, the skirt might be moved up to a higher position on the bodice, but the rest of the original bodice was left inside, no doubt in case waistlines fell again. For example, a green-printed cotton dress in the National Museum of American History reveals a finished back bodice with the current waistline two to three inches above the original level.

When there was enough yardage, as, for example, in a full petticoat from the 1770s, the woman could make herself a new dress. Sometimes a woman would sew small pieces of fabric together in order to have enough yardage for the new garment. This was called *piecing.* A floral print dress in the National Museum of American History has extensive piecing at the top of the skirt, where it is less noticeable because of the folds of the gathers. In all likelihood, the original skirt was not long enough for the new longer skirt length required by the raised waistline of the very end of the 18th century, making the piecing necessary. Anna Payne Cutts wrote to her sister, Dolley Madison, in 1805, "if I make out, to peise one or two of my gowns (for they are all too small and out of shape) by the time we sett of for Washington I shall think myself smart" (Shulman 2007).

Even headwear was re-made. Changing the trimming on a bonnet to update it was easy, but women did more extensive alterations. In May 1811, Sylvia Tyler wrote, "Miss Huldah Norton came here to alter my Straw Bonnet" (Tyler Diaries 1801–1820). In 1817, Rosalie Stier Calvert cut the large brim, which she found unbecoming, off a hat and made it into a turban (Callcott 1991, 329).

How Much in a Wardrobe

Probate inventories can provide valuable information on the types and quantities of garments in a person's wardrobe. The county court appointed local appraisers to visit the estate of a recently deceased person, list the goods, and estimate the value. These inventories sometimes include detailed lists of garments owned by the decedent. (Unfortunately for the modern researcher, some enumerators merely lumped everything together as "the wearing apparel of the deceased" or listed some things individually and put others together in "lots.") A group of probate inventories from Connecticut and Massachusetts provide some information on the composition of women's wardrobes between 1793 and 1808 (M. Miller n.d.), while Hersh and Hersh studied inventories in Cumberland County, Pennsylvania, from 1750 to 1800 (1995). However, probate inventories may not always include all the clothing owned by a person at the time of death. As clothing was highly portable, it is possible that some was disposed of before an inventory was taken. (It was not customary to bury the deceased in regular clothing at this time, but rather in a winding sheet or shroud. Therefore, clothing items that seem to be missing from an inventory cannot be assumed to have been buried with the body.)

Mehitable Price of Wethersfield, Connecticut, had a very limited wardrobe when she died in 1804. She had four gowns, but one was muslin and may therefore have been of the latest fashion. She had three petticoats, one shawl, three pairs of cotton stockings, one linen shift, and two handkerchiefs—one silk and one cotton. (It is puzzling that such seeming necessities as outer wear, headwear, or shoes, are missing.) Ruth Palow of Windsor, Connecticut, who died in 1794, also appears to have had a scanty wardrobe. She had one chintz gown, surely her best, three "loose" gowns and one "short loos gown." To wear with the short gown, she had one linen petticoat and one black petticoat. Two neck handkerchiefs, a camlet hood, two checked aprons, and three caps rounded out her wardrobe. There is a listing for "old linen," which may include such missing items as shifts (M. Miller n.d.). These small wardrobes may be compared with the estimated expense of clothing for a poor woman for a year in England in 1796, which was considered the bare minimum that a woman would need: a wool gown, a petticoat, two shifts, two pairs of shoes, a "coarse apron" and a "check" one, two pairs of stockings, a "coloured neck-handkerchief," and two "common caps." In addition, the woman needed one hat and one cloak every two years, and a pair of stays every six years (Eden 1797/1966, 3:cccxliii).

At the other end of the spectrum, Sarah Chester of Wethersfield, Connecticut, had an extensive wardrobe when she died in 1797. It included 11 silk and cotton gowns, 3 long and 3 short cloaks, 5 pairs of gloves and several pairs of mitts, 10 pairs of stockings, 8 aprons, 18 handkerchiefs, and 18 caps. Even she, however, had only two bonnets, whereas most women had one or none. However, the hood seems to have been a common choice of headwear for these New England women, and she had three of these. She had no short gowns or petticoats, unlike many of her contemporaries (M. Miller n.d.). She had only two shifts, and this seems out of keeping with the number of other items in her wardrobe, but Hersh and Hersh found that most Pennsylvania women had only one (1995, 145).

Sarah Allen, a wealthy widow who died in Carlisle, Pennsylvania in 1794, also had a large wardrobe. It included 7 gowns and 2 gown "patterns" (perhaps fabric waiting to be made into gowns), more than 7 short gowns and 9 petticoats, 6 cloaks, 1 habit (perhaps a riding habit or a matching jacket and skirt ensemble), 3 "deshabilles" (probably loose-fitting informal gowns, or what were called in New England "loos" gowns), 15 shifts, 3 "lots" of caps, 20 aprons, and numerous handkerchiefs. She also had two bonnets, three shawls, nine pairs of gloves, one umbrella, and one lot of stockings (Hersh and Hersh 1995, 138).

A wardrobe in between the two extremes was that of Elizabeth Norton in Suffield, Connecticut, in 1800. She had six gowns, including cotton, wool, and one "old loos" one; four aprons, including one silk and two everyday checked ones; two cloaks; two hoods; one bonnet; two petticoats; one short gown; three shawls; one cap; two pairs of stockings; and one handkerchief. That same year, the widow Abiah Stoughton of Windsor, Connecticut, had seven gowns, including silk, cotton, and wool ones and two "loos" ones; one "jacket"; four aprons; two "riding hoods," one green and one red; one silk cloak; one bonnet; six caps; a pair of silk mitts; and a pair of shoes. She had only one pair of stockings, though, if the list is accurate. Neither of these women was reported to have had shifts, but the enumerators recorded "shirts," and it may be that this term was used instead. (M. Miller n.d.)

One glimpse of the contents of a woman's wardrobe on the frontier is provided by an 1813 list of articles lost on a trip between Worthington and Sudbury, Ohio, that appeared in the newspaper. It is possible that these were most of the unfortunate woman's wardrobe, other than what she was wearing, "one black cambric gown; one dove colored, white and black gown; one green calico gown, one white muslin petticoat, one large leno shawl, two pocket handkerchiefs, one pair of scissors, and several other articles," and they were all wrapped in "a cotton cross-barred handkerchief" (Utter 1942, 403). (The woman was probably wearing a gown or perhaps a habit for traveling, a shift, a bonnet or other headwear, and shoes and stockings.)

AMERICAN INDIANS

There were many different tribes of indigenous peoples native to North America. However, while there were certainly distinctions among tribes, and even among individuals, American Indians living in the same region usually dressed similarly. There was also an active intertribal trade even before Europeans first came to North America; therefore, apparel items typical of one tribe might also be worn by another. For example, hunting tribes traded skins for food raised by agricultural tribes. In this brief and general discussion, the following designations will be used.

Eastern Woodlands has come to be applied to the various tribes in the eastern United States and Canada. Primary among these were the tribes comprising the confederacy of the Six Nations: the Mohawks, Oneidas, Onondagas, Cayugas, Senecas, and Tuscaroras. Indians in the southeastern United States will also be included in this group.

Plains tribes were in the northern area of the Louisiana Purchase, along the Missouri River and beyond. These included the Sioux, the

Missouri, the Osage, the Mandans, the Hidatsa, the Arikara, the Cheyenne, and the Shoshone.

Pacific Northwest tribes inhabited the northwest coast of the Pacific Ocean, including the territory along the Columbia River. Among these tribes were the Chinook and the Umitilla. There were a number of tribes further north along the coast, into what are today British Columbia and Alaska. These tribes traded with each other, primarily traveling by water up and down the coast.

(Because the southwestern region was not part of the United States in the Federal period, tribes in this area will not be discussed.) The published accounts of travelers are one of the best sources for information about what was worn by American Indians in these regions. There are also some extant garments, but only a few that can be positively dated to the Federal period. A few artists have left us painted images.

Eastern Woodland

By this time, the Indians had been in contact with Europeans for two centuries, and they had enthusiastically adopted European manufactured textiles to replace their native clothing made of animal skins, as the skins were valuable trade items. European glass beads also largely supplanted the porcupine quills used in native beadwork.

Both women and men wore a garment generally referred to as a matchcoat, also called by Anglo European observers a blanket or mantle. It was made of wool broadcloth, most often dark blue, red, or white. It was made of about 2 yards of 54-inch-wide fabric (the standard width for broadcloth). Women draped them differently from men, sometimes wearing them as a head covering. Women often decorated their fancy matchcoats with silk ribbons. Robert Hunter, Jr., who traveled through the eastern United States and Canada in 1785 and 1786, observed along the Canadian border that the woman's "blanket" was "covered with spangles and different-colored silk—so many blue ribbons curiously sewed upon it half way down their back, and so many red ones to the rest of the blanket, which reaches to the calf of their leg" (Wright and Tinling 1943, 111).

A type of broadcloth called *stroud* was made in Gloucester, England, especially for the Indian trade (Montgomery, 1984, 252–53). The Indians used the selvage edges, woven with a characteristic pattern of contrasting stripes, as decorative elements. For example, this selvage made a decorative edge on the matchcoat.

American Indian women in the northeast wore shirts similar in cut to a man's garment. A woman fastened her shirt at the neck with a brooch, and, for full dress, she might cover her shirt with a number of small silver brooches.

A woman also draped a length of broadcloth to form a sort of skirt or, in early American terms, a petticoat. This was usually about knee length. Below the skirt, a woman wore close fitting leggings similar to a man's. A tube of fabric was fitted to the leg and sewn with a lapped seam that had the finished selvage on the outside. Some women were, however, giving up native dress by the second decade of the 19th century. Women wore their hair long, and Isaac Weld, traveling from 1795 to 1797, wrote:

> The women do not pluck any of the hair from off their heads [as men did] and pride themselves upon having it as long as possible. They commonly wear it neatly platted up behind, and divided in front on the middle of the forehead. When they wish to appear finer than usual, they paint the small part of the skin, which appears on the separation of the hair, with a streak of vermilion. (1807/1970, 231)

Weld observed that women decorated their hair with ribbons for special occasions. "In full dress they likewise fasten pieces of ribands of various colours to their hair behind, which are suffered to hang down to their very heels." Women also wore jewelry, "silver bracelets when they can procure them." And a woman might wear "silver ear-rings; the latter are in general of a very small size; but it is not merely one pair they wear, but several" (Weld 1807/1970, 235–36). Small metal hawk bells, so called because they were originally placed on European hunting birds, were another favorite decoration. Women also used European thimbles, received as trade goods, for adornment. John Heckewelder wrote that the women "have thimbles and little bells rattling at their ancles" (1876/1971, 203). Travelers saw both women and men wearing elaborately decorated garments, as well as complex hairstyles and body paint; however, such ensembles were most likely reserved for special occasions such as religious rituals and celebrations.

Plains

While various European or white American travelers wrote about Indians in the eastern part of the United States, the members of the Lewis and Clark Expedition were among the first to encounter many of the different tribes of the Great Plains and write detailed descriptions of their clothing. They saw similarities among different tribes of the plains. Unlike the Indians in the eastern United States, these tribes generally still made most of their clothes from animal hides, although some did use European woven fabrics. Lewis and Clark observed that women of the lower Missouri River, including the Ricaras, Mandan, and Minatares, wore a "Shift of the Antelope or a big horn animal, fringed and decerated with Blue Beeds Elk tusks & pieces of red Cloth." The women, like the men, completed their attire with "a Roabe of Buffalow Skin Dressed" (Moulton 1983, 3:488). The "*Cho-pun-nish* or Pierced nose

Indian" women wore a "shirt of Ibex;" "Skins which reach quite down to their anckles with[out] a girdle.... ornamented with quilled Brass, Small peces of Brass Cut into different forms, Beeds, Shells & curios bones etc." (Moulton 1983, 5:259). In other areas, women's dresses were made from antelope hides. A woman could make a dress from one large skin by wrapping it around the body and having only one seam down the side. An armhole would be cut on the opposite side. If the skins were smaller, two were sewn together for a dress. Sometimes the dresses had printed or painted designs. The Cheyenne decorated their dresses with "beeds and Shells & Elk tuskes of which all Indians are very fond of. those dresses are als[o] frequently Printed in various regular figures with hot sticks which are rubed on the leather with Such velosity as to nearly burn it this is very handsom" (Moulton 1983, 8: 319).

The Cheyenne women wore "their hair flowing and are excessively fond of ornimenting their ears with blue beeds" (Moulton 1983, 8: 319). Among the Shoshone, "both men and women wear their hair in a loos lank flow over the sholders and face" (5:121).

Pacific Northwest

Indians of the Pacific Northwest also made clothing from animal skins. A woman sometimes wrapped a short rectangular piece of twisted and woven fur strips around her torso. Women also used another local raw material. They beat the bark of the cedar tree until it was thin and pliable and then wove strands of this into a kind of skirt that covered them from waist to knee. Lewis and Clark wrote, "The womens peticoat is about 15 Inches long made of *arber vita* or the white Cedar bark wove to a String and hanging down in tossles and [t]ied So as to cover from their hips as low as the petticaot will reach and only Covers them when Standing, as in any other position the Tosels Separate" (Moulton 1983, 6:30). As the climate is very rainy, women also wove a sort of poncho from rushes. The Chinooks shaped their infants' heads by flattening them with boards, as the flat head was regarded as a mark of status. The baby was strapped to one board, and another was fastened at the top.

AFRICAN AMERICAN WOMEN

Free women of color likely dressed much as their white counterparts did. Englishman Henry Bradshaw Fearon, visiting New York City in 1817, wrote, "One striking feature consists in the number of blacks, many of whom are finely dressed, the females.... showing a partiality to white muslin dresses, artificial flowers, and pink shoes" (1818/1970, 9). Another Englishman, John Palmer, wrote of African Americans in Philadelphia in 1818, "I have seen several of the *softer sex* with a white muslin, or gay coloured silk gown, modern straw hat, trimmed with artificial flowers, and ridicule [reticule]" (Palmer 1818, 285). Enslaved African Americans, however, did not have the freedom or the means to dress as they wished and were largely dependent on what their masters provided. There were regional variations. Life for enslaved people in the upper South—states such as Delaware, Maryland, and Virginia—was generally less onerous than for those on the large plantations in the Deep South, in the territories that would become the states of Mississippi, Alabama, and Louisiana. The southern climate was milder, too, and owners were not compelled to provide as much warm clothing as those further north.

Many enslaved people did have some disposable income that enabled them to supplement their wardrobes. Slaves grew produce on plots of land allotted to them, raised chickens and hogs, or caught fish. Often, the master bought their excess or allowed the slaves to sell it elsewhere. Slaves almost universally were allowed Sundays off, and, if they opted to work instead, they might be paid wages. In keeping with the general economy, this extra income was generally in the form of credit, rather than cash, and slaves used some of this to buy fabrics or ready-made garments. It was a fairly common practice for masters and mistresses to give house servants, both enslaved and free, cast-off clothing. Sometimes the servants wore these garments themselves, but, as this clothing could be a valuable commodity, sometimes the recipients sold it instead.

In 1794, when a slave named Sall ran away to seek freedom in North Carolina, her master wrote, "she carried away a good many cloaths, and will be able to dress very well" (Parker 1994, 47). In 1805, freedom seeker Else was described, "She will probably appear in a black Silk or white muslin gown, as she has many very good clothes, and is fond of dress" (Meaders 1997, 62). White muslin gowns were very fashionable at this time and, while silk was not as fashionable, it would still have been rather expensive. Fanny, who also called herself Louisa Smith, ran away to Richmond in 1809 wearing "an India cotton frock." Indian cottons varied in quality, so this might not have been a really expensive dress; however, she "left, she says a variety of clothes at different houses where she has been secreted; is very fond of dress, and has been frequently detected in committing daring robberies" (Meaders 1997, 128). It is not clear if she acquired her clothing in these "daring robberies."

It is not usually clear whether lists of clothing over and above what the freedom seekers were wearing were personal belongings or were appropriated. Theft was suspected at least once, however. In 1806, Lucinda's mistress wrote, "Her intention of going off was suspected, and her usual summer cloaths taken from her—she may very probably have stolen others" (Meaders 1997, 70).

In 1786, most enslaved women seem to have been wearing the two-piece working ensemble of short gown and petticoat. The petticoat was often referred to as a "coat" at this time. There are also garments called wrappers or jackets in runaway advertisements. A wrapper was most likely a variant of the short gown. Usually, a jacket was a more fitted garment with separately cut sleeves, but it seems unlikely that enslaved women were issued very elaborate garments, so their jackets may have been more simple variations or may even have been basic short gowns. In 1785, in Georgia, Sall wore "a blue woollen jacket and petticoat," and Candis and Jenny wore wrappers and petticoats of "white negro cloth" (Windley 1983, 4:122,124). Negro cloth was most likely coarsely woven linen or cotton. It could have been locally made on the plantation or purchased. As early as the 1790s, mills in New Hampshire were making "considerable quantities of tow-cloth, some of which is exported to the Southern States, to Clothe the Negroes" (Belknap, 1792, 2:161; tow-cloth is a coarse linen fabric). Also in 1785, Muntilla "had on when she went away an oznabrig coat and wrapper, but she may change her dress, as she carried other cloaths with her" (Windley 1983, 4:129). (Oznabrig, today more commonly called *osnaburg,* was a coarse linen or hemp fabric originally made in Osnabrück, Germany [Montgomery 1984, 312–13].)

In 1786, freedom seeker Rose, in South Carolina, had on "a white negro cloth wrapper and a blue negro cloth petticoat." Two years later, Maria wore "an oznabrig wrapper and green coat" (Windley 1983 3: 394,406). As late as 1807, Jane Murray wore "a redish striped short gown" and "a whitish striped petticoat," and in 1808, Poll wore a "striped country woollen short gown, osnabrigs shift and white roles petticoat" (Meaders 1997, 86,102).

Cotton became a more common fiber for utilitarian garments after the invention of the cotton gin in 1793. In 1799, Kate wore "a plain home spun cotton jacket and coat, dyed purple, shoes, stockings, hat, and blanket" (Parker 1994, 67). In 1808, Nancy wore "a blue cotton and yarn [wool] short gown" and a "white hummums petticoat" (Parker 1994, 111; humhum was a thick plain cotton cloth originally woven in India [Montgomery 1984, 262]; it was probably also being woven locally by this time). Cotton calico could be a solid color or printed; Jenny's "Calico gown" had a printed "running vine flower" (Meaders 1997, 123).

In the upper South, some women wore wool garments. Winnie, or Winny, who "absconded" in 1801, wore a "brown striped calimanco petticoat" in addition to her green and yellow calico short gown (Meaders 1997, 6–7; *calimanco,* a glazed wool, was very common for petticoats in the late 18th century, but it was going out of fashion by this time). In 1801, freedom seeker Amie left Alexandria, Virginia, in "a blue cloth [wool broadcloth] habit," and Betty "had on a blue kersey petticoat and a dark cloth jacket" (Meaders 1997, 3, 6; *kersey* was a "cheap, coarse woolen cloth," not as finely finished as wool broadcloth [Montgomery 1984, 272–73]). In North Carolina, Fanny wore "a blue woollen homespun petticoat and wrapper" when she ran away in 1802 (Parker 1994, 75).

Occasionally, a woman's attire is described as a "suit" or "habit," and these were likely some variation of a two-piece ensemble. Phillis, in 1799, "had on a grey coat and jacket, and took a drab suit with her." In 1811, Clara, in North Carolina, "carried with her two suits of Cloaths, one of grey, the other blue." In 1812, Lydia left in "a white homespun habit made of cotton and tow" (Parker 1994, 69, 546, 360). As late as 1819, Sally Thronton evidently wore a two piece ensemble—"a blue striped country habit" (Meaders 1997, 324).

The two-piece outfit may have remained the usual attire for those who worked in the fields; however, it appears that one-piece long gowns, often of printed cotton, became the more usual attire for enslaved women by the second decade of the 19th century. In 1804, Rachel, "a field negro," "went off with a cotton dress" (Meaders 1997, 29). This is a rare instance where it is certain the woman in question was a field hand. That same year, Matilda had a variety of clothes, taking "two Muslin gowns, one striped, the other checkered." These sound very much like the clothes fashionable free women were wearing. She must have been skilled in the needle arts as, "on her last elopement she dressed herself in mens cloaths, and assumed the possession of a tailor," and may therefore have made her own clothing (Meaders 1997, 33). In 1807, the advertiser specified that Anney took "four long gowns.... one white, or cotton husks [natural cotton], one do. [ditto] blue country cloth, two do. of calico" (Meaders 1997, 81). In 1811, Nancy, on the other hand, took only what she was wearing, "a dark calico frock, which is all the clothes she took with her" (Meaders 1997, 157). Three years later, Fanny had "a number of clothes, some of them pretty good, amongst which there is a silk dress of purple changeable color" (Parker 1994, 250). How Fanny acquired such an elegant dress is unknown: was it purchased, cast-off, or stolen? In 1815, Judy or Juda had several frocks, but nothing so elegant as changeable silk—one was "filled with black yarn and streaked in the warp," and the poor quality suggests this was not professionally woven. Another was "striped with red and blue"; she also took "one pair of blue yarn stockings. "Likewise, in 1817, Tempy wore a utilitarian "striped homespun frock" (Parker 1994, 428,266).

Headwear and Other Accessories

Relatively few advertisements of female freedom seekers mention any head covering, and those that are specified vary from bonnets to hats to handkerchiefs. The handkerchief, worn tied on the head and today more commonly called a headwrap, has come to be regarded as the predominant head covering for African American women. Rather than reflecting an African origin, this seems to have been an innovation of enslaved Africans in the Caribbean that made its way to the United

States. In 1724, the Louisiana Code Noir had mandated that black females cover their heads with handkerchiefs, locally called *tignons,* and the Spanish governor reinforced this law in 1786. But in the eastern part of the United States, wearing a handkerchief on the head seems to have been a matter of choice for women of color, both enslaved and free. (One Philadelphia woman of color in John Lewis Krimmel's *Fourth of July in Centre Square* [Harding 1994, 21], wears a red headwrap, while her companion is bareheaded.) In advertisements for freedom seekers, Nanny in 1787 "had a check handkerchief on her head" (Windley 1983, 151). In 1808, Nancy had "a white handkerchief round her head, and striped with blue and a good deal faded," and Jesse "generally wears a blue handkerchief on her head, which comes down over her eyes on account of their being very weak" (Parker 1994, 111,175).

Advertisements also describe hats or bonnets. Juno, in 1806, wore a "chip or straw bonnet" with her calico dress (Meaders 1997, 71). In 1807, Jane or Jenny Davis wore a "black round hat" that sounds like a man's felt hat (Meaders 1997, 79). In 1810, Nancy had what sounds like a fashionable "green muslin bonnet" (Meaders 1997, 132). Ruth, in 1814, carried away "a black cambric bonnet" (Parker 1994, 119). This may have been similar to the black fabric bonnets that were common for the poor in England at the end of the 18th century.

Those who advertised for the return of their slaves often mentioned physical characteristics such as scars. Betty, in 1805, had "holes made in her ears for the purpose of wearing ear-rings" (Parker 1994, 79).

References

Alberts, Robert C. 1969. *The Golden Voyage.* Boston: Houghton Mifflin Company.

Arnold, Janet. 1971. "The Classical Influence on the Cut, Construction and Decoration of Women's Dress c. 1785–1820." In *The So-Called Age of Elegance: Costume 1785–1820,* 17–23. London: The Costume Society.

Arnold, Janet. 1977. *Patterns of Fashion 1: Englishwomen's Dresses & Their Construction c. 1660–1860.* New York: Drama Book Publishers.

Arnold, Janet. 1990. "The Cut and Construction of Women's Clothes in the 18th Century." In *Revolution in Fashion: European Clothing, 1715–1815,* Kyoto Costume Institute, 126–134. New York: Abbeville Press.

Altman, Saundra Ros. 1997. Past Patterns #031.

Altman, Saundra Ros. 2000. Past Patterns #030.

Baltimore American and Commercial Daily Advertiser. 1805. October 14.

Baltimore American and Commeiical Daily Advertiser. 1805. November 12.

Baltimore American and Commercial Daily Advertiser. 1810. October 17.

Baltimore American and Commercial Daily Advertiser (supplement). 1810. November 2.

Baltimore American and Commercial Daily Advertiser. 1815. November 1.

Banks, William Nathaniel. 1998. "History in Towns: Wiscassett, Maine." *Antiques.* December: 808–17.

Barratt, Carrie Rebora, and Ellen G. Miles. 2004. *Gilbert Stuart.* New York: The Metropolitan Museum of Art.

Bassett, Lynne. 1999. Transcriptions of the Letters of Abigail Adams, Collection of the American Antiquarian Society.

Baumgarten, Linda. 1986. *Eighteenth-Century Clothing at Williamsburg.* Williamsburg, VA: The Colonial Williamsburg Foundation.

Baumgarten, Linda. 2002. *What Clothes Reveal: The Language of Clothing in Colonial and Federal America.* Williamsburg, VA: Colonial Williamsburg Foundation; New Haven, CT: Yale University Press.

Baumgarten, Linda, and John Watson with Florine Carr. 1999. *Costume Close-Up, Clothing Construction and Pattern, 1750–1790.* Williamsburg, VA: Colonial Williamsburg Foundation.

Belknap, Jeremy. 1792. *History of New Hampshire.* Repr. New York: Arno Press, 1972.

Bissonnette, Anne. 2003. *Fashion on the Ohio Frontier 1790–1840.* Kent, OH: Kent State University Museum.

Bottorff, William K., and Roy C. Flannagan, eds. 1967. "The Diary of Frances Baylor Hill of 'Hillsborough' King and Queen County Virginia (1797)." *Early American Literature Newsletter* 2 (Winter): 3–53.

Bowne, Eliza Southgate. 1887. *A Girl's Life Eighty Years Ago: Selections from the Letters of Eliza Southgate Bowne.* Repr., Williamstown, MA: Corner House Publishers, 1980.

Brunon, Raoul. 1989. "Uniforms of the Napoleonic Era." In *The Age of Napoleon: Costume from Revolution to Empire 1789–1815,* ed. Katell le Bourhis, 179–201. New York: Metropolitan Museum of Art.

Buchan, William. 1807. *Advice to Mothers, on the Subject of Their Own Health; and of the Means of Promoting the Health, Strength, and Beauty of Their Offspring.* Charleston, SC: John Hoff.

Burnston, Sharon Ann. 1998. *Fitting & Proper: 18th Century Clothing from the Collection of the Chester County Historical Society.* Texarkana, TX: Scurlock Publishing Co.

Byrde, Penelope. 1999. *Jane Austen Fashion.* Ludlow, England: Excellent Press.

Callcott, Margaret Law, ed. 1991. *Mistress of Riversdale: the Plantation Letters of Rosalie Stier Calvert 1795–1821.* Baltimore: Johns Hopkins University Press.

Coxe, Tench. 1814. *A Statement of the Arts and Manufactures of the United States of America, for the Year 1810.* Philadelphia: A. Cornman, Jr.

Crowninshield, Francis Boardman, ed. 1935. *Letters of Mary Boardman Crowninshield 1815–1816.* Cambridge, MA: Riverside Press.

Cumming, Valerie. 1998. *The Visual History of Costume Accessories.* New York: Costume & Fashion Press.

Drinker, Elizabeth. 1994. *The Diary of Elizabeth Drinker: The Life Cycle of an Eighteenth-Century Woman,* ed. Elaine Forman Chase. Boston: Northeastern University Press.

Eden, Frederic Morton. 1797. *The State of the Poor.* Vol. 3. Repr. London: Frank Cass & Co., 1966.

Fales, Martha Gandy. 1995. *Jewelry in America 1600–1900.* Woodbridge, U.K.: Antique Collectors' Club.

Farrell, Jeremy. 1992. *Socks and Stockings.* London: B. T. Batsford.

Fearon, Henry Bradshaw. 1818. *A Narrative of a Journey of Five Thousand Miles through the Eastern and Western States of America.* Repr., New York: Augustus M. Kelley, 1970.

Fennelly, Catherine. 1961. *Textiles in New England 1790–1840.* Sturbridge, MA: Old Sturbridge Village.

Fennelly, Catherine. 1966. *The Garb of Country New Englanders 1790–1840: Costumes at Old Sturbridge Village.* Sturbridge, MA: Old Sturbridge Village.

Flint, James. 1822. *Letters from America.* Repr., New York: Johnson Reprint Corporation, 1970.

Gallatin, Albert. 1810. *Report of the Secretary of the Treasury on American Manufactures Prepared in Obedience to a Resolution in the House of Representatives.* Boston: Furrand, Mallory, and Co.

Gehret, Ellen J. 1976. *Rural Pennsylvania Clothing.* York, PA: George Shumway.

Gunston Hall Plantation. Probate Inventory Database: Virginia and Maryland Probate Inventories 300+ Transcriptions Recorded Between 1740–1810. http://www.GunstonHall.org/probate/inventory/htm.

Gurewitsch, Matthew. 2008. "True Colors." *Smithsonian* July: 66–72.

Harding, Annaliese. 1994. *John Lewis Krimmel: Genre Artist of the Early Republic.* Winterthur, DE: Henry Francis du Pont Winterthur Museum.

Hartford Courant. 1812. October 27.

Heckewelder, John. 1876. *Account of the History, Manners, and Customs of the Indian Nations Who Once Inhabited Pennsylvania and the Neighbouring States.* Repr., New York: Arno Press, 1971.

Hersh, Tandy, and Charles Hersh. 1995. *Cloth and Costume 1750–1800 Cumberland County, Pennsylvania.* Carlisle, PA: Cumberland County Historical Society.

Hosford, David. 1984. "Exile in Yankeeland: The Journal of Mary Bagot, 1816–1819." *Records of the Columbia Historical Society* 51: 30–50.

Kamer, Martin. 1989. "Brilliant Adornments." In *Revolution in Fashion: European Clothing, 1715–1815,* Kyoto Costume Institute, 135–37. New York: Abbeville Press.

Kidwell, Claudia. 1978. "Short Gowns." *Dress* 4: 30–65.

Krimmel, John Lewis. 1812. *Fourth of July in Centre Square.* Pennsylvania Academy of Fine Arts.

Kornhauser, Elizabeth Mankin. 1991. *Ralph Earl: The Face of the Young Republic.* New Haven, CT: Yale University Press.

Lady of Distinction [pseud.]. 1811. *Regency Etiquette: The Mirror of Graces.* Repr. Mendocino, CA: R. L. Shep, 1997.

Lady's Monthly Museum. 1808. September.

Lambert, John. 1810. *Travels through Lower Canada, and the United States of North America, in the Years 1806, 1807, and 1808.* 3 vols. London: Richard Phillips.

Langston-Harrison, Lee. 1997. *A Presidential Legacy: The Monroe Collection at the James Monroe Museum and Memorial Library.* Fredericksburg, VA: The James Monroe Museum.

Low, Betty-Bright P. 1974. "Of Muslins and Merveilleuses: Excerpts from the Letters of Josephine du Pont and Margaret Manigault" *Winterthur Portfolio* 9: 29–75.

Mackenzie, Althea. 2004. *Hats and Bonnets.* London: The National Trust.

Majer, Michele. 1989. "American Women and French Fashion." In *The Age of Napoleon: Costume from Revolution to Empire 1789–1815,* ed. Katell le Bourhis, 217–37. New York: Metropolitan Museum of Art.

Manigault, Harriet. 1976. *The Diary of Harriet Manigault 1813–1816.* Rockland, ME: Colonial Dames of America, Chapter II.

Mason, Emily V., ed. 1871. *Journal of a Young Lady of Virginia: Lucinda Lee, 1787.* Repr. Richmond, VA: Robert E. Lee Memorial Association, 1976.

Mattern, David B., and Holly C. Shulman, eds. 2003. *The Selected Letters of Dolley Payne Madison.* Charlottesville: University of Virginia Press.

McMurry, Elsie Frost. 2001. *American Dresses 1780–1900: Identification & Significance of 148 Extant Dresses.* CD-ROM. Ithaca, NY: Cornell University.

Meaders, Daniel. 1997. *Advertisements for Runaway Slaves in Virginia, 1801–1820.* New York: Garland Publishing.

Merrimack Valley Textile Museum. 1980. *All Sorts of Good Sufficient Cloth: Linen-Making in New England 1640–1860.* North Andover, MA: Merrimack Valley Textile Museum.

Miller, Lillian B., ed. 1996. *The Peale Family: Creation of a Legacy 1770–1870.* New York: Abbeville Press.

Miller, Marla R. n.d. Unpublished probate inventories from the Connecticut Valley, 1791–1808.

Miller, Marla R. 2006 *The Needle's Eye: Women and Work in the Age of Revolution.* Amherst: University of Massachusetts Press.

Mitchell, Stewart, ed. 1947. *New Letters of Abigail Adams 1788–1801.* Boston: Houghton Mifflin Company.

Mitchill, Catherine Akerly, to Margaret Miller, November 21, 1811, Catherine Akerly Cock Mitchill family papers, Library of Congress Manuscript Division, Washington D.C.

Modert, Jo, ed. 1990. *Jane Austen's Manuscript Letters in Facsimile.* Carbondale: Southern Illinois University Press.

Montgomery, Florence. 1984. *Textiles in America 1650–1870.* New York: W. W. Norton & Company.

Moulton, Gary E., ed. 1983. *The Journals of the Lewis and Clark Expedition.* Vols. 3, 5, 6, 8. Lincoln: University of Nebraska Press.

New-York Herald. 1802. June 26.

Niemcewicz, Julian Ursyn. 1965. *Under Their Vine and Fig Tree,* trans. and ed. Metchie J. E. Budka. Elizabeth, NJ: The Grassmann Publishing Company.

Nouvel-Kammerer, Odile. 2007. *Symbols of Power: Napoleon and the Art of the Empire Style 1800–1815.* New York: Abrams.

Nylander, Jane. n.d. Unpublished notes taken from the Sarah Snell Bryant diaries, 1795–1836; Houghton Library, Harvard University, Cambridge, MA.

O'Brien, Alden. 1998. Unpublished notes on corset, accession no. 2505, Daughters of the American Revolution Museum, Washington, D.C.

Palmer, John. 1818. *Journal of Travels in the United States of North America and in Lower Canada, Performed in the Year 1817.* London: Sherwood, Neely, and Jones.

Park, Edwards. 2000. "To Bathe or Not to Bathe: Coming Clean in Colonial America." *Colonial Williamsburg Journal,* autumn. On-line edition: www.history.org/Foundation/journal/Autumn00/bathe.cfm.

Parker, Freddie L., ed. 1994. *Stealing a Little Freedom: Advertisements for Slave Runaways in North Carolina, 1791–1840.* New York: Garland Publishing.

Pineault, Louisa. 2002. *A Compilation & Index of British Fashion Plate Descriptions: 1798–1819.* CD-ROM.

Pratt, Lucy, and Linda Woolley. 1999. *Shoes.* London: V & A Publications.

Raffel, Marta Cotterell. 2003. *The Laces of Ipswich.* Hanover, NH: University Press of New England.

Ramsay, David. 1809. *The History of South-Carolina: from its First Settlement in 1670, to the Year 1808.* Charleston: David Longworth.

Randolph, Ellen Wayles Coolidge. Family Papers Project, Thomas Jefferson Retirement Series. http://www.monticello.org/papers/index.html.

Rexford, Nancy. 2000. *Women's Shoes in America, 1795–1930.* Kent, OH: Kent State University Press.

Ribeiro, Eileen. 1988. *Fashion in the French Revolution.* London: B. T. Batsford.

Ribeiro, Eileen. 2002. *Dress in Eighteenth-Century Europe 1715–1789.* Rev. ed. New Haven, CT: Yale University Press.

Rothstein, Natalie, ed. 1987. *A Lady of Fashion: Barbara Johnson's Album of Styles and Fabrics.* New York: Thames and Hudson.

Ryan, Thomas R., ed. 2003. *The Worlds of Jacob Eichholtz, Portrait Painter of the Early Republic.* Lancaster, PA: Lancaster County Historical Society.

Seaton, Josephine. 1871. *William Winston Seaton of the "National Intelligencer." A Biographical Sketch.* Boston: J. R. Osgood and Company.

Shep, R. L. 1998. *Federalist & Regency Costume: 1790–1819.* Mendocino, CA: R. L. Shep.

Shulman, Holly C. 2007. *Dolley Madison Digital Edition.* Version 2007.07. http://rotunda.upress.virginia.edu/index.php?page_id = Home.

Smith, Elbert. 1925. *The Descendants of Joel Jones, a Revolutionary Soldier.* Rutland, VT: Tuttle. Online edition at http://www.ancestry.com.

Smith, Margaret Bayard. 1906. *The First Forty Years of Washington Society,* ed. Gaillard Hunt. Repr., New York: Scribner, 1965.

Swann, June. 1982. *Shoes.* New York: Drama Book Publishers.

Thornton, Anna Maria Brodeau. 1907. "Diary of Mrs. William Thornton, 1800." *Records of the Columbia Historical Society* 10: 89–226.

Tyler, Sylvia Lewis. Diaries, 1801–1820, transcribed by Alden O'Brien, Acc. 2889, America Collection, National Society of the Daughters of the American Revolution, Washington D.C.

Ulrich, Laurel Thatcher. 2001. *The Age of Homespun.* New York: Alfred A. Knopf.

Utter, W. T. 1942. *The Frontier State, 1803–25.* Vol. 2 of *The History of the State of Ohio,* ed. Carl Wittke. Columbus: Ohio State Archaeological and Historical Society.

de Vallinger, Leon, Jr., and Virginia E. Shaw. 1948. *A Calendar of Ridgely Family Letters 1742–1899 in the Delaware State Archives.* Vol. 1. Dover: Delaware State Archives.

Vanderpoel, Emily Noyes. 1903. *Chronicles of a Pioneer School, being the History of Miss Sarah Pierce and Her Litchfield School.* Cambridge, MA: University Press.

Virginia Gazette and Alexandria Advertiser. 1787. March 29.

Volney, C. F. 1804. *A View of the Soil and Climate of the United States of America,* trans.

C. B. Brown. New York: Hafner Publishing Company, 1968.

Wallace, Carol McD., Don McDonagh, Jean L. Druesedow, Laurence Libin, and Constance Old. 1986. *Dance: A Very Social History.* New York: Metropolitan Museum of Art.

Wansey, Henry. 1796. *The Journal of an Excursion to the United States of North America in the Summer of 1794.* Repr., New York: Johnson Reprint Corporation, 1969.

Washington National Intelligencer. 1812. November 29.

Weekley, Carolyn J., and Stiles Tuttle Colwill. 1987. *Joshua Johnson: Freeman and Early American Portrait Painter.* Baltimore: Maryland Historical Society.

Weld, Isaac, Jr. 1807. *Travels Through the States of North America and the Provinces of Upper & Lower Canada During the Years 1795, 1796 & 1797.* Vol. 2. Repr., New York: Augustus M. Kelly, 1970.

White, Carolyn. 2005. *American Artifacts of Personal Adornment 1680–1820, a Guide to Identification and Interpretation.* Lanham, MD: Altamira Press.

Windley, Lathan A. 1983. *Runaway Slave Advertisements: a Documentary History from the 1730s to 1790.* 4 vols. Westport, CT: Greenwood Press.

Wright, Louis B., and Marion Tinling, eds. 1943. *Quebec to Carolina in 1785–1786, Being the Travel Diary and Observations of Robert Hunter, Jr., a Young Merchant of London.* San Marino, CA: The Huntington Library.

Wright, Meredith. 1990. *Everyday Dress of Rural America, 1783–1800.* New York: Dover Publications.

CHAPTER 4

Men's Fashions

EVERYDAY AND SPECIAL OCCASION CLOTHES

While American women primarily followed French fashion during the Federal period, American men took their lead from the English. Members of the English aristocracy spent much of the year on their country estates and actively participated in agricultural management, and the men dressed accordingly in plain functional clothes suitable for riding about the countryside. (Thomas William Coke is given credit for bringing country clothes into the city. As a member of the British Parliament in 1782, he exercised his right to appear in public "in his boots," or country clothes, when he was chosen to deliver the results of the vote in favor of American independence to King George III. Contrary to the usual etiquette at the royal court, he wore his "extremely picturesque dress-top-boots with spurs, light leather breeches, a long-tailed coat and a broad-brimmed hat" [Stirling 1908, 1:208–9].) In addition, the growing English middle class of business and professional men tended to wear unostentatious, functional clothing.

In contrast, the French aristocracy spent much of their time at the royal court and so usually dressed in appropriately elaborate styles. But even they, generally acknowledged as the leaders of Western fashion, began to copy Englishmen's fashions, in a wave of *Anglomania,* or craze for English things. This began prior to 1789; however, the onset of the

Made in America—George Washington's Inaugural Suit

George Washington wore a suit of American-made brown wool broadcloth for his April 30, 1789 inauguration as the first president of the United States. By all accounts, he deliberately chose to wear this suit as a symbol of American independence from foreign manufactured goods. American eagles on the buttons reinforced the theme. The fabric for the coat and breeches was made at the Hartford Woollen Manufactory in Connecticut. Washington visited this factory on a tour of New England and chose a piece of its broadcloth for his suit. Jeremiah Wadsworth, the largest shareholder of the company, wrote that this fabric had been chosen "in the hope it will be worn by one whose example will be worth more than any other encouragement that can be given our infant manufactures" (*American Cause,* 2001). Colonel Wadsworth must have had experience with men's suiting fabrics. He had served as both deputy commissary-general and commissary-general in the Continental Army, where one of his responsibilities would have been procuring uniforms.

Despite continuing efforts to promote its products, the Hartford factory was never a success and closed by the mid-1790s. Other factories were established in the United States, however, and in 1809 James Madison wore a suit of black broadcloth from Arthur Schofield's Pittsfield factory (Bagnall 1893/1971, 260). Even so, Americans would continue to buy most of their fine wool fabrics from Great Britain for some time.

French Revolution in that year was a further impetus to the change in men's fashions, as the revolutionaries consciously rejected the trappings of aristocracy.

Of course, Americans had close ties with English fashion; before independence, some well-to-do colonists even ordered clothing directly from English tailors. However, during the Federal period, there were some who consciously began to promote uniquely American styles. But even as late as 1817, Englishman Henry Bradshaw Fearon observed in Philadelphia, "The dress of the gentlemen is copied from the fashions of England" (1818/1970, 172).

Main Garments

The three pieces of coat, waistcoat, and knee breeches were the basic ensemble for men in 1786. Sometimes all three were of the same fabric, or else just the coat and breeches matched, as with modern suits. However, some men had a variety of separate coats and breeches that they combined in different ways. One observer noted that "a poor labouring man" could seldom afford to buy a whole suit of clothes at once, so his coat, waistcoat, and breeches would likely not match, either (*Instructions* 1789, 55). Well-to-do men wore plain woven silk or silk velvet coats for formal occasions early in the period. But the English ideal of quiet elegance dictated rather plain fabrics, in contrast to the fancy silk brocades and patterned and cut velvets of the colonial era. Wool broadcloth, often simply called cloth, was a common fabric choice. (Broadcloth is so called because it is woven on a broader loom than silk, cotton or linen fabrics. Widths of silk fabrics were usually 18 to 21 inches, while cottons and linens were 30 to 45 inches wide.) Broadloomed fabrics are characteristically 54 inches, or a yard and a half, wide, but they could be even wider; in 1795, Ann Ridgely sent her two teen-aged sons some blue superfine broadcloth that was 7 quarters, or 63 inches, wide; therefore, the 3 and 3/4 yards she sent would make coats for both of them (de Vallinger and Shaw 1948, 136). The new English aesthetic also demanded excellent fit. Wool fabrics are more pliable than silk ones and, using cutting, stitching and pressing techniques, tailors molded wool fabrics to the shape of the body.

Rare existing cotton or linen coats suggest that some men chose these cooler fabrics as an alternative in the hot and humid climate of the American South, as well as for summer wear in the northern states. In 1789, a Maryland runaway slave took a white linen coat in addition to a wool one (Windley 1983, 2:395); however, this might have been an inexpensive working garment rather than a fashionably cut summer weight coat. An extant man's coat, probably made in Connecticut, is mixed blue and white cotton with no lining. A fashionably cut tailcoat with a South Carolina provenance is also made of cotton. Both of these coats are in the collection of Colonial Williamsburg (Baumgarten 2002, 103). In 1809, Meriwether Lewis had "One Black Broadcloth coat" and "Two Striped Summer Coats" among his effects when he died (Moore and Haynes 2003, 123); these summer coats may have been cotton or linen. Scotsman John Melish observed in Georgia in the early 19th century that families "spun cotton all the year round, and got the yarn woven into every article necessary for family use," including "pantaloons, vesting, and summer coats for men's use" (1818/1970, 40). The Scottish traveler James Flint, visiting New York in 1818, wrote, "During this season of the year, most people wear light cotton clothes; the jacket is in many cases striped, and the pantaloons of Indian nankin [nankeen]"(1822/1970, 22). However, the use of cotton may also have been in response to the embargo on trade with Great Britain and France, with the resulting scarcity of fine imported wool fabrics, in the years prior to the War of 1812.

Coats; 1786–1800

The frock, the most common style of coat in 1786, was less ornate than its predecessor, and the cut of the coat continued to evolve during the period. (Note: the term *frock* has been applied to different styles of coats over time, including quite different later 19th century styles; however, for the sake of clarity in this volume, the term means the late 18th century style described here, to distinguish it from the later tailcoat.) The skirt was less full than it had been earlier in the century, although it retained side back pleats and a vent—that is, an opening—down the center back from waist to hem. The fronts curved away from the chest, and the curve was so extreme that at most only a couple of the buttons at chest level could actually be fastened, even though the coat had a line of rather large buttons all the way down the front. The corresponding buttonholes, being just for decoration, were stitched but not cut open.

There might be a couple of hooks and eyes fastening the coat edge to edge, that is, with the fronts just meeting instead of overlapping; but, more often, a man wore his coat completely open. The buttons were often wood forms or bone rings covered with the coat fabric. However, plain or fancy metal buttons could add a more decorative element, and such buttons could be quite valuable: they were sometimes bequeathed in wills or given a separate assessed value in probate inventories. The material of buttons was subject to fashion. In 1795, Ann Ridgely wrote that her boys should have fabric covered buttons on their coats, as metal ones were no longer fashionable in Philadelphia. The next year, Williamina Cadwalader wrote her that pearl buttons were the latest style (de Vallinger and Shaw 1948, 136, 148). And in May 1800, the *Lady's Magazine* reported that "all the buttons are of stuff," that is, fabric covered (255).

In contrast to the earlier collarless styles, these coats had turned-down collars. The sleeves had turned-back cuffs at the beginning of the period. In the late 1780s, very narrow sleeves with no cuffs came into fashion. Large shaped flaps covered the slit pocket openings.

In the 1790s, one of the garments of the English country gentleman's attire, the tailcoat, became more common. Not only did Englishmen begin to wear such coats in the city as well as in the country, but the French began to adopt them, as well. This coat was originally designed for horseback riding, with the lower fronts cut away altogether to eliminate the bulk of the front skirts that could get in the way when a man was mounted on a horse. Instead, the front edges were cut horizontally and at waist level. The back was still long, forming the tails. The side back tails retained the pleats of earlier coat styles, while the center back vent, or opening, extending from the waist to the hem, allowed a man to sit on a horse. Instead of having buttons all the way to the neck, these coats had the top front edges folded back to form lapels. The front overlap of the coat became wider, with two vertical rows of buttons; this style was called double-breasted. However, during much of the period, it was not stylish to actually button the coat.

Through the 1790s, the collar became larger and reached higher up on the back of the neck. From the simple notch formed where the collar (called a cape during the period) met the lapel, a new M-shaped lapel developed. This larger collar was most likely an innovation of the French revolutionary youth called the *incroyables* (literally translated as the *unbelievables*). As the young often do, they carried new styles to extremes, exaggerating many of the elements. Eventually these extremes became modified and moved into the mainstream. This extremely large collar reached England by 1800, where in May, the *Lady's Magazine* reported, "The collar of the coat is everyday growing larger" (255).

The coat sleeves became longer, a trend also seen in women's wear. Evidently some men first unfolded the turned-back cuffs of their coat sleeves. Later, the cuffs were no longer intended to be turned back but were made to extend down over the wrists. The pocket flaps, meanwhile, became smaller. It is difficult to determine exactly when the tail-coat reached the United States, but it seems to have appeared sometime during the 1790s. Henry Wansey, an Englishman visiting the United States in 1794, made note of men's clothing in Philadelphia, then the most cosmopolitan city in the country. The men's coats had "high collars and [were] cut quite in the English fashion" (1796/1969, 127).

Josephine du Pont's 1798 letter suggests that young men in the United States were wearing cutting edge fashions such as the tailcoat, as she found that the fashionable men she saw in Paris, had "exactly the same appearance as our American '*merveilleux.*'" (She used the masculine form of *meirveillueuses,* the term for the female extreme trend setters, rather than the term *incroyables,* that today is commonly used to refer to the fashion-forward men of revolutionary France; Low 1974, 45).

Fashion Plate, Costume Parisien, 1809. This fashionable Frenchman wears the ensemble made popular by English country gentlemen in the late 18th century: leather breeches, a double-breasted green tailcoat with M-notch lapels, and top boots, and carries a cane and top hat. He wears a red waistcoat under a white one. Courtesy of Louisa Pineault.

Coats; 1800–1820

While older, more conservative men no doubt continued to wear the old styles, the tailcoat became the norm for men in the United States during the first decade of the 19th century. Portraits from the very early 1800s overwhelmingly show men in tailcoats. In July 1803, an advertisement in the *National Intelligencer* stated that an enslaved blacksmith who ran away from his Virginia master "generally wore a long tail'd coat." If an enslaved worker was wearing a tailcoat in 1803, more fashionable men must have been wearing them for some time before. By 1810, Stephen Powell, a tailor in the small western Massachusetts town of New Marlboro, was evidently making the new style of coat for most of his customers—he recorded that he still made a few "cut the old way" (Rigby 1983, 26).

The tailcoat was the fashionable choice for both day and evening, and the somber colors we today associate with men's wear were becoming the norm. This trend can partially be attributed to the English fashion leader, George "Beau" Brummell, who advocated understated elegance, superb fit, and immaculate grooming. He is said to have worn only navy blue coats for day and black for evening. Most of the coats Powell made were black or dark blue. A few were "bottle green," a dark green (Rigby 1983, 32). There are also occasional references to brown or maroon coats.

Waistcoats/Vests; 1786–1800

The cut of the waistcoat or vest had also changed since the 1770s. It became shorter, settling at hip length. The fronts angled away from the center below the waist. There was a row of buttons from waist to neck, but sometimes the top buttons were left undone to show the shirt frill. (In the United States, the term *vest* eventually supplanted the term *waistcoat.* In England, however, the garment is still called a waistcoat, whereas *vest* is the term for an undershirt.) Earlier in the 18th century, waistcoats sometimes had long sleeves, but, by the 1780s, they were primarily sleeveless garments. The term *jacket,* while generally referring to a short outer coat, sometimes during the late 18th century meant a type of waistcoat, instead.

Some waistcoats were double-breasted. Usually, only one of the two sets of buttons on a double-breasted vest or coat was functional. However, an English tailoring guide recommended "the making of holes down both sides for the advantage of the wearer, lest any unforeseen accident should happen from dirt, and the wearer's day's pleasure should be spoiled, by not having an opportunity of changing the other side of the breast" (Shep 1998, 59). This meant that, In case of a spill, the man could re-button his vest the other way, exposing the clean side. This also illustrates that the modern convention of lapping the left front of a man's garment over the right had not yet been established.

Throughout the era, waistcoats were made of a variety of fabrics. They could be made of plain wool; however, as the fashion changed such that the coat was frequently worn unbuttoned, more of the waistcoat was on view, and so it might be made of a more elaborate fabric. One such fabric choice was Marseilles, a woven fabric made to look like hand quilting. A Connecticut merchant advertised in 1798 "a variety of fashionable Mersailles and muslinet Vesting" (Bassett and Larkin 1998, 82). Another practical fabric choice, especially for summer, was the natural tan cotton called nankeen. In 1799, Thomas Hill packed three nankeen waistcoats for a trip by horseback from New Jersey to Pennsylvania (Hill 1890, 189).

Throughout the period, embroidered waistcoats were fashionable for more formal occasions. These were frequently made from pre-embroidered panels of fabric (these were sometimes called *patterns*). These patterns were generally embroidered by professionals, who stitched the design on a flat piece of fabric, outlining the shapes of the waistcoat fronts, pocket flaps, collar, and button covers. The embroidery was

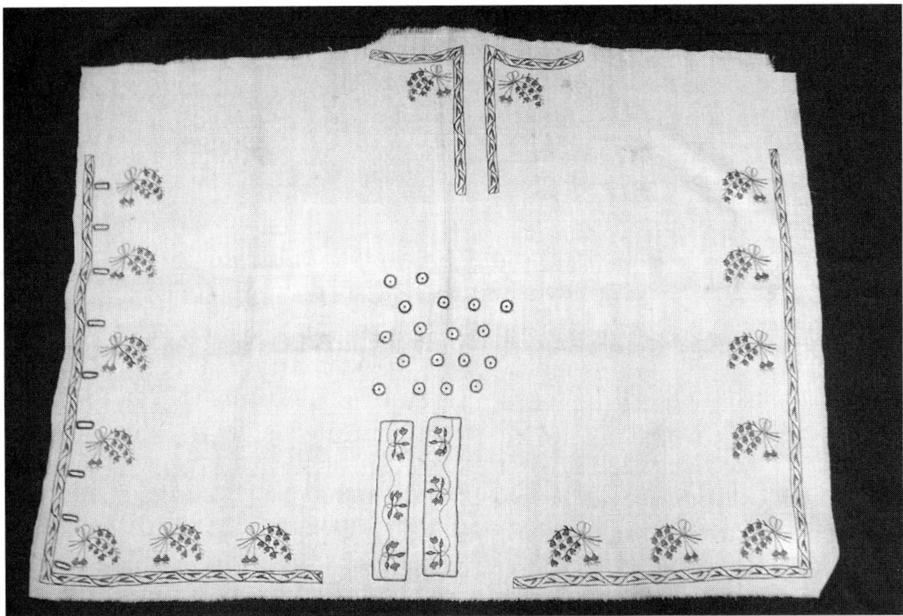

Embroidered Waistcoat Pattern, circa 1790–1800. White cotton with silk tambour work embroidery. This is an example of fabric that was pre-embroidered to be made into a waistcoat. The embroidery is in purple, two shades of pink, yellow, and blue-green. Courtesy of Mary Doering.

usually done with silk thread, and sometimes had accents of metallic thread or sequins. Sometimes the pattern was done in tambour work, a technique using a hook to make chain stitches on the surface of the fabric. In 1797, Stanilslaw Boone's store in Maryland included "13 Tamboured Waistcoat patterns" (Gunston Hall).

Embroidery was also done at home. Williamina Ridgely wrote in 1796 that her sons' waistcoats were finished, "worked [embroidered] from patterns Mamma drew, and made up by Mr. Barry according to the latest style" (de Vallinger and Shaw 1948, 302). Some waistcoats had the design woven, printed or drawn with ink in imitation of embroidery. A tailor, or, less often, a home seamstress, would cut out the pieces and put them together with a plainer, less expensive fabric, often linen, for the back. Since it was rare for a man to be seen without his coat, it would have been a needless expense to use fine fabric for the back.

Waistcoats/Vests; 1800–1820

As the tailcoat evolved, the cut of the waistcoat or vest also changed. It became shorter, usually reaching to just below the waist, and the lower front edges were no longer slanted away from the center. It was often slightly longer than the front edges of the coat and, as the lower edge would be visible, many embellished waistcoats of this period have elaborate decoration below the pocket flaps. The large ornamental pocket flaps of the earlier style became narrow oblongs, today called welts. A high standing collar was often attached, echoing the lines of the high collar of the coat. Occasionally, though, a waistcoat had lapels that turned back and a turned-down collar. The front edges usually had a line of buttons and buttonholes from neck to hem, even though by this time it was almost universal to button only the bottom half, from chest level to the waist. This allowed the fine shirt frill to be seen.

At this time, colored, horizontally striped fabrics came into style for waistcoats. Massachusetts tailor Stephen Powell made one waistcoat of toilenette, a fabric with a silk and cotton warp and wool filling, often woven in stripes, specifically to be made into waistcoats (Montgomery 1984, 367). He also made several velvet vests, as well as one of "marsalla," or Marseilles quilting, between 1810 and 1814 (Rigby 1983, 38–39).

There are extant embroidered waistcoats that appear to have been creatively re-cut using the fancy embroidery from older styles as the shape changed in the early 19th century. These might have been remade from earlier garments or cut from flat embroidered patterns that had never been assembled. For example, the longer lower edge of an older style might have been cut off and made into a standing collar, or the large pocket flaps removed and replaced with smaller ones. As men's attire in general became more restrained and sober, the waistcoat remained the one item of clothing that tended to be colorful or embellished.

Leg Wear—Breeches, Trousers, and Pantaloons; 1786–1800

At the beginning of the era, most men were wearing knee breeches with their coats and waistcoats. Breeches were sometimes called small clothes. Breeches typically had a buttoned front flap opening, called a fall, and usually had either drawstrings or straps and buckles at the center back waist to allow for some size adjustment. Openings in the lower outside leg seams closed with buckles, buttons, or ties. Breeches might match the coat or contrast. Leather breeches were practical for heavy labor and for horseback riding, as leather is both durable and pliable. However, many men adopted this sporting look even if their most energetic activity was walking around the city. Breeches of buff-colored cassimere, a soft twill-woven wool fabric, or of nankeen cotton could substitute for leather, especially in summer, when cooler material was called-for. Nankeen had the added advantage of easy washing. Gentlemen wore breeches made of velveteen, a cotton fabric with a short pile, but working men such as grooms and coachmen also wore them, perhaps because the pile fabric provided some warmth and was also fairly durable. Wealthy men sometimes wore silk satin breeches for formal wear.

Knee Breeches, circa 1780–1810. Cotton velveteen. The brown breeches have a fall front. The knee bands probably fastened with removable buckles. The back waistband has lacing to allow for size adjustment. Courtesy of American Costume Studies.

Farmers and sailors had traditionally worn ankle-length, loose fitting trousers, and little boys began wearing them in the 1780s. In the 1790s, the French revolutionaries adopted long trousers (the spelling *trowsers* is often used in period documents) to symbolize that they were the *sans culottes,* (those "without knee breeches"), the culottes or breeches being the garb of the hated aristocracy. The fashion spread through the ranks of men until, by the early 1800s, they were common for everyone. Fabrics used for trousers seem to have been similar to those used for knee breeches.

Another type of longer leg wear were form-fitting pantaloons. These were often knitted, rather than woven, to achieve the close fit. Pantaloons seem to have first been mid-calf length, reaching just inside new shorter boot styles. Later they were ankle-length or sometimes made to slip over the foot.

Like the oversized, exaggerated tailcoats, these extra-tight pantaloons may first have been an affectation of young French radicals. The French revolutionary government promoted new styles of republican dress and encouraged artists to submit designs. One of the most famous of these artists was Jacques Louis David, whose rather theatrical designs drew from a variety of sources, including the classical sculptures of Greece and Rome. His tight pantaloons in pale colors suggested the nude look of these statues, and it appears that men adopted the pantaloons, if not the rest of the ensembles he designed (Ribeiro 1988, 102–4). The snug fit of the pantaloons was also adopted for knee breeches. An article in the English *Lady's Magazine* in September 1798 reported that, in France, men's "breeches, less tight, are more decent than before" (420), suggesting that they had been worn very tight indeed. By the next year, French men were varying the look, wearing their "pantalons" either tight or "large," that is, loose fitting (Delpierre 1990, 23–24).

Englishmen and Americans also began to wear long pantaloons and trousers, which were especially suited for wear with the new tailcoats. Wansey observed Philadelphians wearing pantaloons in 1794 (1796/1969, 185). Architect Benjamin Henry Latrobe observed in 1796 that "a tight pair of Pantaloons" was essential wear for a "beau" in Virginia (Carter 1977 1:129). Thomas Hill, on his trip by horseback in 1799, lamented that the combination of "rough fustian trousers" and "a hard trotting horse" were giving him blisters. Fustian was a coarse fabric of cotton, linen, or blended cotton and wool that could have abraded sensitive skin. Hill switched to his linen trousers for some relief (1890, 189–90). Sarah Bryant of Massachusetts, who recorded her household sewing in her diary, made her husband, Peter, both breeches and "trowsers" in the late 1790s (Nylander n.d.). Despite the popularity of long leg wear in England and France, many men in the United States continued to wear knee breeches through the end of the 18th century.

Leg Wear—Breeches, Trousers, and Pantaloons; 1800–1820

Pantaloons became more common in the United States after 1800. The October 3, 1801, issue of the Philadelphia weekly *Port Folio* reported, "All our young men of fashion wear a short frock [tailcoat] of dark blue cloth, dark green, or dark brown, with metal buttons, a little convex, a round hat, with a broad brim, short breeches and white stockings, or large pantaloons, with Russian boots high upon the leg" (465). Mary Ridgely wrote from Philadelphia the next year, "Tell him [Henry, her brother] pantaloons and half boots are all the Ton [the latest fashion],...and when dressed [that is, in formal wear], blue or black coat, white waistcoat, black smalls [knee breeches]" (de Vallinger and Shaw 1948, 217).

In 1806, Samuel Copp had a New York tailor cut out a pair of pantaloons and then sent the pieces to his sisters in Stonington, Connecticut to sew. It appears these were tight as they had slits at the ankles with ties to "make them tye snugg." Unfortunately, when he received the finished pantaloons, he found "the Taylor cut them too short by 2 or 3 inches but they will answer with boots" (Murray 1974, 26–27). The fabric was wool "Kersimere" or cassimere, which would have been pliable enough to fit snugly. The British periodical *Ackermann's Repository* described cassimere pantaloons in 1809 (Montgomery 1984, 192–93). Queen and Lapsey included diagrams for snug-fitting pantaloons to be made either ankle-length or with attached feet, much like modern tights, in the *Taylors' Instructor,* published in Philadelphia in 1807 (Shep 1998, 27). Fashionable men were wearing snugly fitting pantaloons in Philadelphia in 1812, when John Lewis Krimmel painted several men who could have stepped out of the pages of a French fashion plate in his *Fourth of July in Centre Square.*

Pantaloons were generally pale colors, such as off-white or buff, to emphasize the nude look. They were sometimes knitted rather than woven, to allow a very close fit, while woven fabrics were often cut on the bias to achieve the desired snug fit. An English example in the Victoria and Albert museum was machine-knitted from white cotton (Murray 1974, 23). By the second decade of the 19th century, black pantaloons were an evening alternative to knee breeches. A satirical poem published in *Dress and Address* described "Tight evening pantaloons of black, and hose/Of the same colour, cover *legs* like crow's" (1819, 76). There is a pair of black knitted pantaloons in the collection of the Museum of the City of New York that are dated 1800–1815 (*Of Men Only* 1975, 11).

The article in the *Port Folio* describing "large pantaloons" suggests that the modern definition of pantaloons as tight-fitting was not necessarily the norm during the period; rather, the term *pantaloons* might refer to any long leg wear. David Ramsay used the word this way when he described the dress of men in Charleston, South Carolina, in 1808;

> About the year 1800 pantaloons, which had been fashionable in England some centuries past, were generally worn in Carolina; but in the lapse of the eight years which followed, they were generally laid aside and breeches are again in common use. The former are much more suitable to the climate than the latter.... The climate requires that suspenders, deep crowned hats with double bottoms, as well as *loose flowing pantaloons,* should be continued. (emphasis added; Ramsay 1809, 409)

Ramsay was clearly not writing about snug-fitting leg wear here. We can only guess why men switched back to knee breeches, if indeed they really did. Perhaps they felt encumbered by the long loose garments.

The looser garments more generally called *trowsers* seem to have become the norm by the second decade of the century. While Queen and Lapsey's 1807 tailoring manual does not mention them at all, Englishman Henry Bradshaw Fearon found in New York City in 1817 that "trowsers

A "Uniform for our Ministers Abroad"—Diplomatic or Court Dress

Elaborately embroidered suits with knee breeches were passing out of fashion by the end of the 18th century. However, they remained required dress for men attending official functions at the royal courts of Europe, and a sword, the mark of a gentleman, was an essential accessory.

This presented a dilemma for diplomats from the United States. Such finery was at odds with republican principles. But, if the Americans were to be effective, they were expected to dress the part. In 1813, Secretary of State James Monroe defined a "uniform for our ministers abroad" as a blue wool coat with a standing collar, lined with white or buff silk, with gold or silver embroidery and matching buttons. Senator James A. Bayard of Delaware wore this ensemble in the Russian capital of St. Petersburg in 1813, where he was sent to negotiate an end to the War of 1812. At a dinner, he wrote, "[the Americans] appeared sufficiently fine for republicans.... but they were quite plain when they came alongside of the Chancellor's guests" (Davis, 1968, 169–70). The negotiations shifted to Ghent, and the peace commissioners were instructed to wear this "uniform."

Further regulations in 1817 even prescribed the hat: "a three-cornered chapeau-bras, not so large as those used by the French, nor so small as those of the English" (Davis, 1968, 170). The chapeau-bras, so-called because it was generally carried under the arm (*bras* is French for arm) rather than worn on the head, was by this time relegated to such ritualized use. Diplomats representing the United States in Europe would continue to wear some form of court dress through the middle of the 19th century.

were universal" (1818/1970, 6). In 1818, a French fashion plate described a pair of loose, ankle-length trousers as "pantalon américain" (Delpierre 1990, 32), suggesting that this style was particularly associated with the United States. Trousers could match the coat or be a contrasting color. In the 1817 probate inventory of John Campbell, of Washington, D.C., two matching ensembles were listed—"1 Coat & Pantaloons Superfine blue (new); 1 ditto brown." Since these were made of superfine wool broadcloth, these "pantaloons" were almost certainly the looser trousers and were made to match the coats.

It appears that American men continued to wear both short and long leg wear, no doubt according to the occasion, at least through the first decade of the 19th century. Etiquette required men to wear breeches for very formal occasions. In rural Pennsylvania, George Schwenk's 1803 probate inventory included both breeches and trousers; John Nyce in 1806 also had both breeches and trousers; and Michael Krause in 1807 had breeches, trousers, and pantaloons (Gehret 1976, 125). In 1807, the probate inventory of Richard Cramplin of Maryland had "6 Pair of Pantaloons and 6 Small Cloth[e]s" (Gunston Hall). He probably wore pantaloons during the day and small clothes, or breeches, for formal evenings. Sarah Bryant made breeches for her husband as late as 1806, but she never made any after that. (He must, however, have continued to wear these breeches for several more years, as she recorded altering a pair of "small clothes" in 1812.) However, she was also making him pantaloons, rather than what she called trowsers, by 1802 (Nylander 1998, 109; Nylander n.d.).

Older or more conservative men were more likely to retain the older styles of their youth and some continued to wear knee breeches for all occasions. English traveler John Palmer observed in New London,

Connecticut, in 1817, "What is singular in the United States, many of the elderly men have retained as part of their dress, small-clothes, instead of the universal American fashion of open pantaloons, or trowsers" (1818, 178). Many noted that President James Madison retained the old-fashioned ensemble of knee-breeches and frock coat, despite the fact that his wife, Dolley, enthusiastically embraced the latest European fashions. Members of the Society of Friends, commonly called Quakers, also retained the older styles. A Quaker man in the center of Krimmel's painting *Fourth of July in Centre Square,* for example, wears a dark coat, waistcoat, and knee breeches. And in 1818, James Flint described the men in Philadelphia; "pantaloons are almost universal: the shorter small-clothes are used only by Quakers" (1822/1970, 39).

***Joseph Slade,* by Ammi Phillips, 1816. Oil on canvas. This prosperous New York State farmer wears a dark blue double-breasted tailcoat with M-notch lapels and fabric-covered buttons, matching long trousers, and a waistcoat with gold metal buttons.** Courtesy of the Trustees of the National Gallery of Art, Gift of Edgar William and Bernice Chrysler Garbisch.

Undergarments

Shirts

A man's primary undergarment was his shirt. The pieces of the shirt were simple rectangles and triangles, very similar to the woman's shift. (The similarity of the man's shirt and woman's shift, in both appearance and function, is indicated by the fact that the French used the same word, *chemise,* for both.) It was very long, reaching to about mid-thigh, and was tucked into the leg wear to serve as an under layer. While the sleeve cuff, collar, and part of the front were visible when he wore his coat, a man would not be seen in public wearing his shirt with no waistcoat or coat, as it was his underwear. Therefore, laboring men may have removed their coats to work but almost always kept on their waistcoats.

Shirts were most often made of fine white linen at the beginning of the period, but as mass production of cotton fabrics made them less expensive, cotton became more common. A working man's shirt most likely would not have a ruffle framing the front slit. A more formal shirt would have a ruffle, sometimes referred to as the chitterlings. This evolved from a gathered ruffle, often lace-trimmed, to a finely pleated one. The ruffles were sometimes made from finer fabrics than the shirts themselves.

Early in the period, the shirt collar, fastened with a single button, was turned down over the neckwear. The buttons were often of a type called dorset buttons that were made out of knotted thread. As the larger, high-standing coat collar came into style in the 1790s, a man began to wear his heavily starched shirt collar standing up instead of folded over. In its most exaggerated form, it came up to his cheek bones. This remained in style through the end of the Federal period.

In the 18th century, the cuff of the shirt was narrow and fastened with shirt links—two buttons attached to each other—through a buttonhole on each end. Fancy shirts had fine ruffles on the cuffs to match the ruffles down the front. In the 1790s the cuff became wider, reflecting

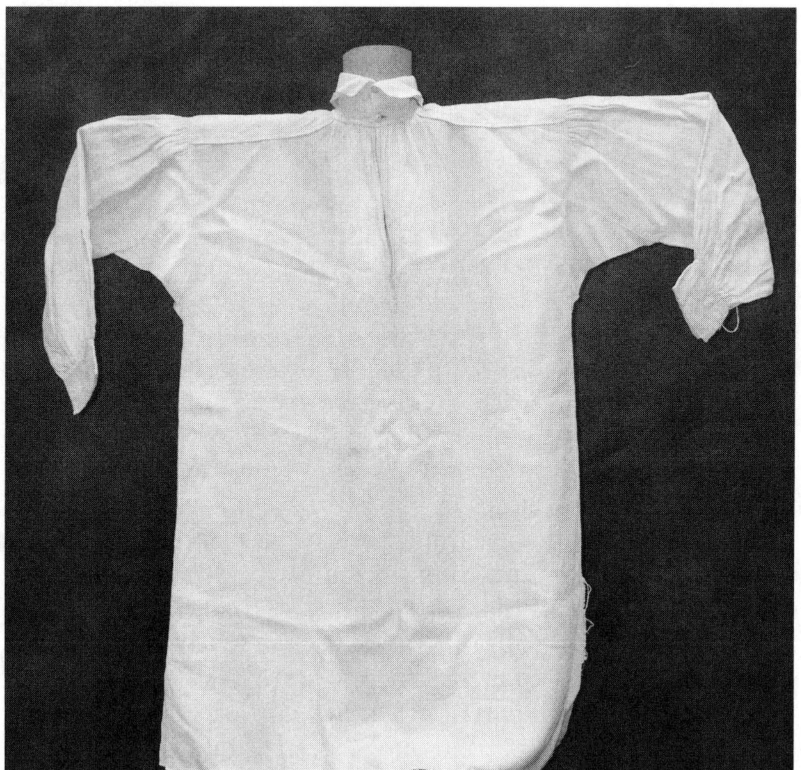

Man's Shirt, 1790–1815. Linen. This is made in a transitional style: the sleeves were made to fasten with sleeve links, a characteristic of late 18th century shirts, but the cuffs are longer, to match the longer coat sleeves of the turn of the century. Shirts do not survive in great numbers and they are difficult to date precisely. Courtesy of William L. Brown III.

the longer sleeve length of the man's coat. The cuff now closed with a button and buttonhole. This was not in the center of the cuff, but rather towards the sleeve seam to enable a man to fold his shirt cuff back over his coat sleeve to protect it. The cuff ruffle disappeared, as it would not have been visible under the longer coat sleeve.

Drawers

At the beginning of the period, men generally did not wear underdrawers; instead, the long shirt tail served that function. Extant examples of knitted wool drawers suggest that they served as an extra under layer for additional warmth, rather than for sanitary reasons. Thomas Jefferson, who complained of the cold winters in Virginia, bought wool flannel drawers, no doubt to help keep him warm (Baumgarten 1992, 5, 13). In 1800, Benjamin Harrison of Virginia had five pairs of drawers, but the fabric is not specified (Gunston Hall). However, by 1807, Queen and Lapsey, in the *Taylor's Instructor,* recommended drawers for cleanliness as they could be washed, whereas the outer leg wear, if made of wool, silk plush, or leather, could not. In the section on making breeches and pantaloons, they wrote, "if the party must have linings (we always recommend drawers, as they can be occasionally washed....)" (Shep 1998, 44). Drawers were cut much like outer leg wear. A waistband fastened with buttons and the crotch seam was left open. Fabrics were likely woven linen, wool, or cotton, though were occasionally knitted wool or silk.

Under-Waistcoats

Men sometimes wore under-waistcoats for warmth. These were made from wool flannel or shammy (chamois, a soft leather), or knitted from wool yarn. Some examples have long sleeves. There seem to have been two types of under-waistcoats (Baumgarten 1992). One type had a decorative collar and must, then, have been worn under the outer waistcoat but over the shirt, so that the decorative collar would be visible, and may have been more for style than warmth. Another, plainer type was most likely worn under the shirt, next to the skin. John May wrote in Ohio in 1789 that he had to get his flannel under-waistcoat washed as it was in "high repute" from continuous wearing, suggesting that he wore it under his shirt (Shine 1993, 50). Massachusetts doctor Peter Bryant wore both drawers and wool flannel under-waistcoats in his later years, when he suffered from consumption (Nylander 1998, 110).

Banyans

Federal era men continued to wear loose robes or dressing gowns for informal wear, as had their predecessors. The robe or gown was often called a banyan, from the name of Hindu traders in India, and it resembled types of garments that men wore in the Orient. Early banyans were cut rather simply and might be made from luxurious fabrics such as hand-painted Indian chintz or silk or wool damask. There were also more utilitarian ones made of printed or striped cotton or linen or plain wool flannel. In 1795, William Sydebothom's wardrobe included "1 flannel gown" (Gunston Hall). Elbridge Gerry, Jr. remembered that, during his introduction to President James Madison in 1813, the president "had a flannel, but handsome loose gown on and rested on pillows" (1927, 178). Pennsylvania merchant John Caldwell had a "calico morning gown" in 1787 (Hersh and Hersh 1995, 108). Banyans were sometimes lined either to finish the inside or to add extra warmth. They also sometimes had matching separate waistcoats or false vest fronts sewn in to give the appearance of two garments. According to the American physician, Benjamin Rush, a man proclaimed that he was a scholar as well as a gentleman by wearing a banyan or gown to sit for his portrait. He wrote in 1790, "we find studious men are always painted in gowns, when they are seated in their libraries," and he wore a coral-colored silk or wool gown for his portrait by Charles Willson Peale (Fortune 2002, 33, 35–36). The Reverend Nehemiah Strong wore a lilac silk gown when he was painted by Ralph Earl in 1790. Strong also had the credentials of a scholar: he had taught mathematics at Yale, was a lawyer, founded a school for young men, and was considered one of the most skillful astronomers in New England (Kornhauser 1991, 170–71). By the early 19th century, the banyan or morning gown evolved into a more tailored, fitted garment, cut much like a man's coat, but with longer skirts.

Man's coat, ca. 1814, wool with silk lining and gold embroidery. Henry Clay of Kentucky wore this coat in Ghent while negotiating with the British for an end to the War of 1812. It follows the specifications of the Secretary of State's directive for dress of American diplomats in Europe. Courtesy of Ashland, The Henry Clay Estate, Lexington, Kentucky.

Outerwear

Men of all classes wore overcoats, called greatcoats or surtouts, in very cold or wet weather. A greatcoat usually had a collar and two or more shoulder capes. It was the occupational dress of the coachman. As he was perched on the box of a coach in the wind and rain, the multiple capes provided him with some protection from the elements. Similarly, such a coat protected a man riding horseback in inclement weather. The greatcoat was made from heavily fulled wool fabric. According to her diary, Sarah Bryant made her husband, Peter, a great coat in 1799. He wore it for 17 years, so it must have been very durable. He finally replaced it with a "Drab [yellowish-brown] Great Coat" that he left to his son when he died in 1820 (Nylander 1998, 109). Dr. William Thornton of Washington, D.C., got a new great coat in 1800, "drab Cloth, cut steel Buttons & white velvet Cape" (Thornton 1907, 102). During the period, there may have been a distinction between what was called a greatcoat and what was called a surtout (also the French term for such a coat); however, today it is not clear what the difference may have been.

Accessories

Headwear

In 1786, most men wore round felt hats with cocked brims. This had been the most common style for some time. The tricorne had the brim cocked, or turned up, in three places, making a triangular shape. In the 1790s, however, the top hat, with a higher crown and narrower brim, came into fashion and continued to be the primary style through the rest of the period. The top hat emphasized the overall vertical silhouette that was coming into fashion. While even working men sometimes wore top hats, the standard working man's hat was called a flapped hat, with a low crown and soft brim. Most hats were made of beaver fur felt, and good hats were expensive. George Wingate Chase, writing about the hat industry in Haverhill, Massachusetts, said, "The best fur [that is, fur felt] hats cost about seven dollars each, and were intended to last a lifetime" (1861, 541).

A summer alternative was the straw hat. Probably these were more prevalent in the hot and humid South, but Henry Bradshaw Fearon, visiting New York City in August, observed that "large straw hats prevailed" (1818/1970, 6). James Flint also visited New York in August 1818 and noted, "A broad-brimmed straw-hat is commonly used, to prevent the face from being scorched by the rays of the sun" (1822/1970, 22). Thomas Hill wore a chip hat, made of thin strips of wood, on his summer 1799 trip through Pennsylvania (Hill 1890, 189). In cold weather, northern men sometimes wore hats made of fur pelts. One of the sleigh drivers in John Lewis Krimmel's 1820 *The Sleighing Frolic* wears a fur hat (Harding 1994, 182).

Early in the Federal era, military officers wore the bicorne, a round-crowned hat with the brim turned up on both sides. Navy officers wore their hats "fore and aft"—that is, with the points at front and back, while Army officers usually wore them sideways on the head.

Men often wore some kind of cap at home with their informal banyans. Such caps were especially popular while wigs were in fashion, when men had to keep their own hair cut very short, and a cap kept the head warm in a drafty interior. Such caps might be home-sewn needlework. Some resembled turbans, emphasizing the exotic oriental effect of a banyan. Pennsylvania merchant John Caldwell, who died in 1787, had two caps, one calico (that may have matched his calico banyan), and one linen (Hersh and Hersh 1995, 108). Listed in Isaac Walker's probate inventory when he died in 1797 was "1 oil Cloth bathing Cap" (Gunston Hall). Walker likely wore this cap for taking mineral baths at a spa or resort, although he may also have worn it for bathing at home.

Neckwear

The most common neckwear was the cravat, a long piece of linen, usually heavily starched, that was tied around the neck over the base of the shirt collar. The cravat was originally a square folded in half and then re-folded into a rectangular shape. A later version was a very long isosceles triangle, about 10 inches wide at the center and 50 to 60 inches long (Hill and Bucknell 1967, 146). By the early 19th century, elegant gentlemen developed different methods or wrapping and tying the cravat, turning it into an art form. The look became extreme, with the heavily starched shirt collar and cravat rising up to the chin, or even beyond, and the shirt points touching the cheekbones. A man might wear a cardboard stiffener underneath, further exaggerating this effect, or he may have worn more than one cravat to produce the desired height and stiffness. Juliana Gales Seaton wrote in 1812, as her brother and another man were going to President and Mrs. Madison's "first drawing-room of the season," "Joseph and R. started in fine style, the latter sporting *five* cravats, Joseph contenting himself with *three*" (Seaton 1871, 83).

For formal wear, only plain white cravats were considered proper. For everyday wear, however, either white on white patterns or colors were permissible. For a more casual look, a man might knot a long, colored silk handkerchief around his neck. Thomas Hill took three silk neck handkerchiefs on his 1799 journey (Hill 1890, 189). In 1803 a slave named Frederick wore "a yellow silk handkerchief around his neck" (Meaders 1997, 17).

The stock was another form of neckwear, more commonly worn in the 18th century. However, military men and older men continued to wear stocks into the 19th century. The stock was a shaped band, stiffened with whalebone or horsehair, usually black or white, that was worn around the neck and buckled, tied, or buttoned in the back. In 1795, William Sydebothom's probate inventory included two stocks as well as two black and two white cravats (Gunston Hall). The black military stock was sometimes made of leather to provide some protection for the neck. After his accession to the English throne in 1822, the former Prince Regent, King George IV, brought the stock back into general fashion (Hart 1998, 46).

Footwear

A man could own a wardrobe of stockings made of different materials in different colors. At a minimum, a man would most likely have wool stockings for winter (often called *yarn* in period sources) and linen (called *thread*) or, later, cotton stockings for summer. Pennsylvania merchant John Caldwell had worsted wool, white cotton, and thread pairs in 1787 (Hersh and Hersh 1995, xvii). For more formal occasions, men wore silk stockings just as women did. Blends of silk and cotton were also used. There was even variety in the types of wool used—worsted wool stockings looked different from those knitted of fine lambs wool, which were soft and warm. Minimally treated wool with the natural oils still present was knitted into water-repellent stockings (Farrell 1992, 40). In October 1812, Joseph Wheeler had "Men's white and mixed Lambs Wool Hose" and "mixed and coloured Worsted Hose" in his shop in Hartford, Connecticut.

White was the usual color for stockings and the only proper color for formal wear. For example, the rules of the 1794 Philadelphia Assembly, where formal dances were held, prohibited colored stockings (Wansey 1796/1969, 134). Clergymen traditionally wore black stockings (Woodforde 1924, 4:108), while various speckled mixtures and striped patterns, some quite elaborate, seem to have enjoyed brief popularity at various times (Farrell 1992, 40). In 1789, a runaway slave from Maryland had "stockings of a clouded colour, of cotton and silk mixed" (Windley 1983, 2: 393). In 1804, another runaway had "a pair of striped cotton stockings" (Meaders 1997, 38).

While knee breeches were in fashion, men's stockings might be decorated with clocks, embroidered or knitted in designs on both the inside and outside of the lower leg. Men could also use the bands of the knee breeches, instead of garters, to keep their stockings in place.

When long trousers came into style, plain stockings became the norm, and sometimes shorter hose were worn. Period sources mention both half stockings, probably mid-calf length, and shorter socks. Just how common they were is not known. In 1795, William Sydebothom had "1 pr Woolen Socks" in addition to "7 pr worsted Stockings 2 pr Cotton do [ditto]" (Gunston Hall).

Men's shoes in 1786 were generally dark brown or black with moderately pointed toes. The heel was about one inch high, and the shoes fastened with buckles. However, a new style that fastened with ties was evolving and would become dominant by about 1800. As with women's shoes, the heel also shrank to little or nothing. The change in shoe styles reflected the generally narrower silhouette of men's wear. In addition, as men wore long trousers or pantaloons, elaborate shoe buckles were no longer a fashion feature, and tie closures replaced them. Shoes were generally made as straights, that is, with no differentiation between the right and the left foot. As the narrower, lighter weight style evolved, however, it became practical to make shaped rights and lefts, and the Philadelphia bootmaker William Young was said to have introduced rights and lefts into the United States in 1800 (Swann 1982, 33). Still, it was not be common to make shaped shoes until later in the 19th century.

Men wore boots for riding or walking. Fashionable men with an interest in horse racing adopted the style commonly worn by jockeys. The top of the dark boot was turned down below the knee, showing the lighter brown lining and the straps for pulling on the boots. This style, also called the top boot, originated earlier in the 18th century but was still worn in the 1780s and remained one of the fashionable boot styles throughout the period. Spurs were often worn with boots. These were functional if a man was riding a horse and could use them to urge his horse forward, but may have been strictly decorative if he was not actually going riding. Mary Boardman Crowninshield's dress "got entangled" in General Brown's spurs at a ball in 1816 (Crowninshield 1935, 57). While the General may have ridden a horse to the ball, it is more likely that he wore the spurs as accessories to his uniform.

As men adopted long pantaloons, they also turned to a new style of boots. The Hessian was shorter than the top boot, with a heart-shaped front, often trimmed with contrasting binding and tassels. As boots became very fashionable, there were occasional complaints that men were wearing them everywhere, even though they were not thought appropriate for formal occasions. The 1794 Philadelphia Assembly rules prohibited boots (Wansey 1796/1969, 134). In 1816, Margaret Bayard Smith of Washington recorded the following conversation when the Presbyterian minister Robert Finley proposed going to an evening reception at the President's House wearing his boots:

> "But," said I, "what are you to do with your boots?" "Why, certainly, a clergyman may go in boots." "I don't know," said I, "but I should be afraid a clergyman's boots would tear the ladies' dresses as much as many other." "Well," said Mrs. Caldwell, "There is a shoe store near, and he can get a pair of shoes."

Finley, we are told, did find a pair of shoes that fit and wore them to the reception (Smith 1906, 130–31). However, when she attended a presidential reception in 1816, Mary Bagot, wife of the British minister, found that many of the men did "come in boots & perfectly undone & with dirty hands & dirty linen" (Hosford 1984, 35).

For leisure at home, men wore mules, backless slippers generally made of colored leather. Red Morocco leather was a frequent choice.

Other Accessories

A man carried his money, bills, and perhaps a memo book and pencil in a pocketbook. These opened flat, with two or more pockets, and, when folded shut, fit inside the coat or breeches/trousers pocket. Ready-made pocketbooks were available in leather or fabric. Women also made them as gifts, embroidering wool or silk yarns in flame stitch, often adding the man's name or initials and date. An existing pocketbook is known to have been made by a girl attending a boarding school in Litchfield, Connecticut, in 1815. This gift for her father was made of wool Irish stitched embroidery on linen canvas with wool binding and linen, cotton, and leather linings. (Baumgarten 1988, 261). The style of these items seems to have changed very little from late colonial times through the early 19th century.

The pocket watch was another common accessory. It was fastened to a chain and often had seals, engraved devices for stamping sealing wax on a letter or document, fastened to the other end of the chain. (Letters were sent by folding up the paper and sealing it with wax, as envelopes had not yet been invented.) A gentleman might sport more than one seal. The watch had to be wound with a key, and the key was also placed on the chain. In October 1812, Jacob Sargeant advertised in the *Hartford Courant* that he had "A large assortment of English and French Watches, gold watch Chaines, Seals, Carnelian set Keys, with almost ever article in the watch line." (The fact that the United States was at war with Great Britain does not seem to have kept him from having English goods in his shop; of course, he may have imported them before the start of hostilities the previous June.) Carnelian, an orange-red opaque gemstone, was also carved into seals that were set in gold or other metals. The watch itself was placed in a special small pocket at the waist of the breeches or trousers. (This pocket was called the fob pocket; the term fob was only later transferred to the items hung on the end of the chain.) These early watches did not have metal covers over the glass faces and therefore were more protected in the pocket, while the seal or seals hung down decoratively outside.

Another item a man might carry in a pocket was a snuff box. Throughout the 18th and 19th centuries, men consumed tobacco in the form of snuff, finely ground tobacco that was inhaled through the nose. Taking the small pinch and placing it in the nose was known as *dipping*. Small boxes to carry the snuff became fashionable accessories. James Monroe owned a variety of wood and metal (tin, copper, brass, and pewter) snuff boxes, some no doubt acquired while he lived in Europe (Langston-Harrison 1997, 134–35). Taking snuff may actually have been more popular than smoking or chewing tobacco until later in the 19th century. (Women dipped snuff, too, although the habit seems to have been going out of style among them in the early 1800s. The 1815 *Farmer's Almanack* suggested that women "pray put your snuff box aside when you are working over your butter" [Larkin 1988, 168]).

Just as a well-bred lady would not appear on the street without gloves, so a gentleman wore them outside. They were also a necessity on the dance floor. As shirt and coat cuffs became longer, the gloves became wrist length, in contrast to the long gloves with gauntlets, or cuffs, of earlier periods. There were functional natural buff or brown leather versions for riding, carriage driving, or other outdoor activities. For evening, choices were fine white kidskin or knitted silk. William Sydebothom had both leather gloves and knitted thread, or linen, ones, that were most likely for summer wear (Gunston Hall). Joseph Wheeler advertised in October 1812 that he had "Men's Beaver, Buck-skin, Silk, and Cotton Gloves" in his Hartford, Connecticut, shop. (*Beaver* gloves were actually made from a washable sheepskin.) James Monroe had a pair of doe skin riding gloves (Langston-Harrison 1997, 179). Men wore knitted wool mittens (like today's mittens) for warmth. David Shultze, a Pennsylvania farmer, had a pair of mittens in 1797 (Gehret 1976, 93). In 1816, Sylvia Lewis Tyler, in Connecticut, wrote in her diary that she knitted a pair of blue and white mittens for her husband and a black and red pair for another man (Tyler Diaries; she had first spun and dyed the wool herself.) In 1803, Ruth Henshaw Bascom made "a pair of shag mittens, that is a pair all over fringed, which is the new mode of knitting mittens" and two pairs of shag mittens survive in the collection of Old Sturbridge Village (Fennelly 1961, 12). Not only would these mittens be thicker, the air trapped by the fringe would provide more insulation in a cold New England winter.

As the front waistline of the coat and the waistcoat rose, the waistline of the trousers, pantaloons, or breeches did likewise, and braces or suspenders were developed to hold them up. These were originally two separate strips of woven or knitted fabric with buttonholes to attach to buttons on the outside of the front and back of the garment waistband. Later in the 19th century the two strips became attached in the back, as we know them today. They also became a medium for a woman's fancy needlework.

Men often owned sets of buckles that could be placed on different garments. Shoe buckles were most common. Knee buckles fastened the knee bands of breeches, while stock buckles held neck stocks in place. These were made of a variety of metals, including silver or silver plate. For mourning, men might have another set of buckles with a dull finish. Fancy shoe buckles trimmed with paste, or artificial stones, seem to have been going out of style by this period. And, as noted earlier, as shoes fastened with ties came into style, there was no longer a need for shoe buckles at all. Similarly, as knee breeches went out of style, knee buckles disappeared.

Men seem to have worn other types of jewelry only rarely. Occasionally, a man in a portrait wears a ring. The signet ring, with an engraved seal to use for stamping wax on letters or documents, seems to have been replaced by the separate hanging seal, usually attached to the watch chain, during this period. Rarely, a man is shown with a decorative pin closing the slit of his shirt. During the early 1800s, these pins seem to have been worn for informal occasions when the shirt had no ruffle.

The walking stick was a fashionable man's outdoor accessory. It had long been the practice in Europe for noble gentlemen to carry swords, but this was another practice frowned upon in revolutionary France, where it could actually be dangerous to appear aristocratic. Even in England, walking sticks were replacing swords, no doubt because they actually could assist a man in walking over rough country terrain or uneven city streets. In the United States, swords were considered appropriate only for military men. Mary Boardman Crowninshield reported in 1816 being escorted to supper at a ball, where, not only did her dress get entangled in General Brown's spurs (see above), but, "I fell over his sword going upstairs, but arrived safe at the table" (Crowninshield 1935, 58). American civilians carried walking sticks. Daniel Boardman holds one in his 1789 portrait (Kornhauser 1991, 152). In 1794, Wansey said that the men of Philadelphia had 'short canes in their hands" (1796/1969, 185).

Another practical accessory, the umbrella, most probably originated in the Far East as protection from the sun. It eventually spread to Italy, Spain, and France. Englishmen were slow to adopt it, as it was regarded as effeminate or a French affectation. However, by the end of the 18th century, a few pioneering men in England brought umbrellas back from continental Europe and others recognized their practicality for protection from the rain (Sangster 1871/2004). These rain umbrellas were heavy, with frames of wood and whalebone, while the fabric cover was oiled silk or waxed canvas. Umbrellas were also available in the United States in the Federal period. They were originally imported, but were later made in the United States, and Baltimore became the center of the industry. In 1794, William Cummins advertised in a Baltimore paper that he made and repaired umbrellas (Kahn 1989, 37), and George Savage advertised his "Umbrella and Oil Cloth Manufactury" in Baltimore's *American and Commercial Daily Advertiser* in 1802. In 1817, English traveler John Palmer described his view of President James Monroe on a passing steamboat, "he appeared a plain middle sized man, it rained, and he stood on deck with an umbrella" (1818, 25).

While the term handkerchief as used during this period more often refers to a triangle or square of fabric worn around the neck, men did also carry "pocket handkerchiefs" for practical purposes. John Caldwell had three pocket handkerchiefs in 1787 (Hersh and Hersch 1995, 108), and Thomas Hill took three pocket handkerchiefs on his 1799 trip (Hill 1890, 189).

Hairstyles and Grooming

In 1786, men generally still wore the wigs that had been fashionable in the colonial period, and a man who wore a wig kept his own hair cut very short of necessity. Distinctive styles of wigs developed for some professions, such as medicine, the law, and the clergy. Some men did not wear wigs, but rather had their own long hair styled and powdered. Ralph Earl painted powder on the collar of sitter Dr. David Rogers's coat in 1788, indicating that the doctor powdered his own hair (Kornhauser 1991, 145). The long hair, natural or artificial, was tied back with a black ribbon or placed in a small bag. As clothing styles became less elaborate in the 1780s, so did hairstyles. Men began to put aside their wigs, long hair, and powder and adopted short haircuts. Both the informality of English country life and the French revolutionary rejection of all things aristocratic contributed to the change. Powder became less fashionable when a tax was levied on it in England, and the London *Times* of April 14, 1795 reported on "the *Crop Club,*" where men cut their hair short "for the purpose of opposing, or rather evading, the tax on powdered heads" (Ashton 1885/1969, 61). The shorter styles showed a classical influence, resembling the hair on ancient Roman statues, and they were given names such as the "Titus" or "Brutus." Men in the United States adopted these shorter styles. On arriving in Paris from the United States in 1798, Josephine du Pont noted that her husband fit right in with his "short Titus haircut" (Low 1974, 45). Shorter hair required more frequent cutting and some men also had their hair curled and styled in various ways. The shorter hair complemented the change in headgear from the cocked to the top hat.

Older or more conservative men did not always adopt the newer styles. When Isaac Walker of Maryland died in 1797, among his possessions was "1 Powder Bag with Puff" (Gunston Hall); however, it is not known if he had still been powdering his hair or had just not disposed of the bag. In keeping with his all-around old-fashioned style of dress, President James Madison (1809–1817) also powdered his hair. Mrs. Bagot described him in 1816, "he is a very little wizen old man wearing a powdered head a thick club tail platted & tied up" (Hosford 1984, 35).

A few men still wore wigs, especially those in professions closely identified with them, such as the clergy and the law, but these do not seem to have been as common in the United States as in England. In 1790, James Peale painted Presbyterian minister George Duffield wearing the traditional style of wig for an English clergyman (L. Miller 1996, 252).

In 1794, Wansey traveled with "a very reverend looking old gentleman," an elder in the Presbyterian Church, "with a tremendous full-bottomed wig of the cut of the last century" (1796/1969, 62). In 1797 and 1798, Latrobe's sketches of Virginia courtroom interiors show judges in wigs (Carter, Van Horne, and Brownell 1985, 124–25, 142–42), but these must have been uncommon, as he wrote that he saw primarily, "judges without Wigs or Robes, in the plain dress of farmers, and Council without Wigs or Gowns" (Carter 1977 129). As late as 1801, Margaret Bayard Smith described a dancing partner she had at a ball in Washington, "Genl. Van Courtland, who with his powdered wig, made a most conspicuous figure in the room" (1965, 18). Both Smith and her companion thought the general's old-fashioned manners and appearance made him appear rather ridiculous.

Beards and mustaches were never in style during the Federal period. Most men remained clean-shaven, although they likely did not shave every day, as most do now. Men did wear facial hair that is now called sideburns with the Roman-inspired hairstyles. (The name *sideburns,* however, dates to the mid-19th century.)

The Hazards of Shaving

A clean-shaven face was the norm in the Federal period, but shaving was not a pleasant task. The folding straight razor, dating to 1680, did not change a great deal until later in the 19th century. A 1740 improvement did produce harder steel that would hold a sharp edge, and Michael Faraday's 1820 addition of a small amount of silver to the steel made further design improvements possible.

In cities, men often went to a barber for a shave. But barbers also performed blood letting and pulled teeth, so the barber shop was probably not the male sanctuary it was to become later. "Barber's itch," no doubt transmitted by dirty brushes and tools, was a hazard.

An alternative to visiting the barber, especially for men who lived outside the city, was self-shaving. Benjamin Franklin wrote, "If you teach a poor young man to shave himself and keep his razor in order, you may contribute more to the happiness of his life than in giving him a thousand guineas" (Pinfold, 1999, 30). The English dandy George "Beau" Brummell, known for his impeccable grooming, shaved several times a day and plucked out stray hairs with tweezers. Some wealthy men were shaved by their personal servants.

WORKING CLOTHES

Many working men wore waist length coats called roundabouts, round jackets, or jackets. These generally were cut like a tailcoat but without the tails. Such a garment would be practical for many jobs where long skirts or tails would get in the way. Robert Roberts, who wrote a guide for house servants, advised them to wear "a round-a-bout jacket of a dark color" as they did dirty household chores such as cleaning lamps and shining boots (Roberts 1827/1997, 4).

Farmers and other laborers, such as teamsters (those who drove teams of animals) often wore fuller, longer versions of a shirt, called smocks or frocks, over their other clothes. James Flint, visiting New York in 1818, wrote, "Draymen [a dray is a cart or sled without wheels used for heavy hauling], and other labouring people, wear a sort of frock or hunting shirt of tow-cloth, that hangs down to the knees" (1822/1970, 22). In England, these garments frequently included decorative stitches to control the fullness at the top, giving rise to the term "smocking" for this type of stitching. These shirts seem to have been made of white or unbleached linen, cotton, or a wool and cotton blend, generally woven in a sturdy twill. In New England, such shirts were often made of a distinctive blue and white or brown and white striped or checked wool fabric (Bassett 2001, 32; Wright 1990, 79). A surviving example from Maryland is made of brown and white checked linen (Brown 1999, 111).

There were shirts made of colored wool flannel, rather than white linen or cotton, that were also most likely working garments. They provided needed warmth for men working outside in cold weather. The Pennsylvania merchant John Caldwell had two white flannel shirts, along with 11 (presumably linen) ones, in his extensive clothing inventory in 1787 (Hersh and Hersh 1995, 108). Perhaps he wore them for warmth. Luther Edgerton made five red flannel shirts for the Woodbridge store in Marietta, Ohio, in 1817 (Saint-Pierre 1999, 218), and Sylvia Lewis Tyler wrote in her diary that she made red flannel shirts for her husband in 1820. Shirts made of woven stripes or checks were another working alternative, particularly common among sailors.

Another variation, the hunting shirt, was distinctly American. As its name implies, men wore these to hunt. They were made out of linen and, later, cotton, and often had strips of fringe made from cut or unraveled fabric. These were worn not only to hunt, but were also the uniform of special militia units of riflemen (that is, those who carried rifles instead of muskets). Their green hunting shirts with red trim served much the same purpose as later camouflage, helping the men blend into the terrain. Images of the frontier suggest that men habitually wore hunting shirts and other Indian-inspired clothing. This is most likely a romaticized view; however, Englishman John Palmer did write that men in Kentucky in 1818 wore "either a home manufactured cotton coat, or a hunting shirt and pair of trowsers, with seldom any handkerchief round their necks" (1818, 128).

Working men wore buckskin breeches before they became fashionable men's wear. Buckskin made practical working garments that lasted a long time, and the pliable leather allowed for some give with a man's movements. Another form of leg wear, called overalls, was developed to protect the working man's legs. These were probably first worn by soldiers during the Revolutionary War, when knee-length breeches were fashionable. Overalls had long legs with pieces of fabric extending to cover the shoe tops, much like later spats (Moore and Haynes 2003, 94–95). These not only protected the legs but also kept sticks and stones out of the shoes. Overalls were generally regarded as military garments, but civilian working men also wore them. Sarah Bryant frequently recorded making her doctor husband overalls. She often made more than one pair a year, suggesting that he was subjecting them to rough wear. Some were nankeen, while once she made a pair of "heavy cloth" (Nylander n.d.).

Sherryvallies were similar to overalls. The outer seam was open from waist to hem and fastened with a row of buttons all the way down the leg. These were originally intended to be worn over other leg wear, especially for protection while riding a horse, but may have become the sole leg wear in some instances (Murray 1974, 102). The pair of "chiverliers" that Sarah Bryant made her husband in February 1799 was probably such a garment (Nylander n.d.).

Many working men protected their clothing with some type of apron. Men doing dirty work such as butchering wore bib-fronted leather aprons. Roberts, in his servants' guide, recommended a green baize apron for doing household chores. (Baize is a heavily fulled fabric almost like felt.) To serve the family at the table, he suggested that the servant change to a white linen apron (1827/1997, 4). Waiters in restaurants and workers in shops selling food probably also wore white linen aprons.

It is likely that some working men, especially poor ones, wore cut and sewn stockings made of bias-cut fabric, rather than knitted ones. They did not fit as smoothly as knitted ones but were more durable, as they did not snag and run.

Working men often wore handkerchiefs around their necks in place of more formal stiff stocks or starched cravats. Such handkerchiefs might have printed or woven designs and were made of silk, linen, cotton, or cotton and silk blends. Ben, a slave in Alexandria in 1801, wore a "blue handkerchief, checked with red, round his neck" (Meaders 1997, 7). One distinctive style of handkerchief, the bandanna, was made in India. Bandannas were tie-dyed, that is, areas of the fabric were wrapped or tied in knots before the fabric was dipped in the dye bath. These areas remained undyed, forming a white design on a colored ground. Bandannas were dyed with madder, which produces a very long-lasting orange-red color. (Modern cotton bandannas reflect their Indian origins in both their red color and their Indian-inspired paisley print designs.)

Far from such rough and ready working clothes, some American house servants, both enslaved and free, wore livery. These very elaborate suits, consisting of the old-fashioned style frock coat, waistcoat, and breeches, were heavily embellished with a specially made braid trim called livery lace. Livery often echoed the family colors from a coat of arms. Rosalie Calvert's postilions, who rode alongside her carriage, wore the Calvert family colors of black and gold, in the form of "yellow jackets, leather pantaloons, and black velvet caps with gold lace trim" (Callcott 1991, 63). George Washington specified red and off-white for his servants' livery and Thomas Jefferson's servants wore blue and red livery with silver lace (Baumgarten, 2002, 130–31). John Tayloe, who lived in Washington, D.C. from 1801 until his death in 1828, dressed his servants in "Blue Quaker Cut Coats Turned up with Red–Red Vests–Collers & Pockets Gold laced–Breeches, Whitest long stockings, Shoes & Buckles–The full Costume Shoulder straps or Small Epaulettes" (Carson 1990, 94–95).

Tayloe's livery was typical with the old 18th-century style ("Quaker cut") of the coat, elaborate trimming, old-fashioned knee breeches and stockings, and shoes with buckles. This remained the style for livery in England throughout the 19th century, and is still occasionally seen there even today; however, in the United States, livery seems to have been common only in the South, where masters could insist that their enslaved servants wear it. (All of the people mentioned above had enslaved servants.) Englishman Willam Cobbett observed that a free servant "will not wear *a livery,* any more than he will wear a halter round his neck. This is no great matter; for, as your neighbours' men are of the same taste, you expose yourself to no humiliation on this score" (Cobbett 1818/1964, 187). However, the Polish traveler Julian Ursyn Niemcewicz observed that the servants of John Livingston, in New York, and William Bingham, in Philadelphia, did wear livery (Neimcewicz 1965, 13, 37).

Making and Acquiring Clothes

It required skill to cut and fit men's coats and leg wear; therefore, professional tailors usually made, or at least cut out, these garments, and they were generally made to order for a particular client. As with other trades, young men (and a few women) learned this craft through apprenticeships. Measuring and cutting were the crucial elements in this process. Before tailors adopted the tape measure, around 1820, a client's measurements were marked with cut notches on a strip of paper. As a cost-saving measure, a client could have a tailor measure him and cut out his garment and then have a hired seamstress or, more rarely, a woman in his own household, sew it together. In 1799, the Massachusetts tailor Silas Wells advertised that he would cut out a coat for one shilling sixpence, or, for nine more shillings, both cut it out and sew it together (M. Miller 2006, 66).

As we have seen with women's wear, mending, altering, and remaking clothing was very common, as textiles were valuable. Some tailors, such as New Englanders Asa Talcott and Catherine Phelps Parsons, seem to have earned most of their income doing these sorts of things, rather than cutting out new tailored garments. Their records describe turning garments (M. Miller 2006, 171–72), that is, taking apart a garment, turning the pieces over to expose the less worn side to the outside, and putting it back together. The life of wool garments could be extended in this way, as the original surface of the wool became too worn and soiled to look presentable. Sarah Bryant "finished turning a coat" for her husband in 1798, and turned a surtout in 1806 (Nylander n.d.)

The construction of leather breeches was a separate trade with its own specialists. From 1790 to 1811, Pennsylvanian Jacob Underkoffler, who was both a tailor and a shoemaker, combined the two sets of skills to make leather breeches. (Gehret 1976, 127).

Men's shirts were usually made at home. Even in wealthy families, wives and daughters did much of this sewing themselves rather than leave it to their servants. As there was less wasted fabric when several were cut at once, shirts were usually made in quantity. In 1796 and 1797, Elizabeth Phelps of Hadley, Massachusetts, made shirts for her brother, Charles, in Boston.

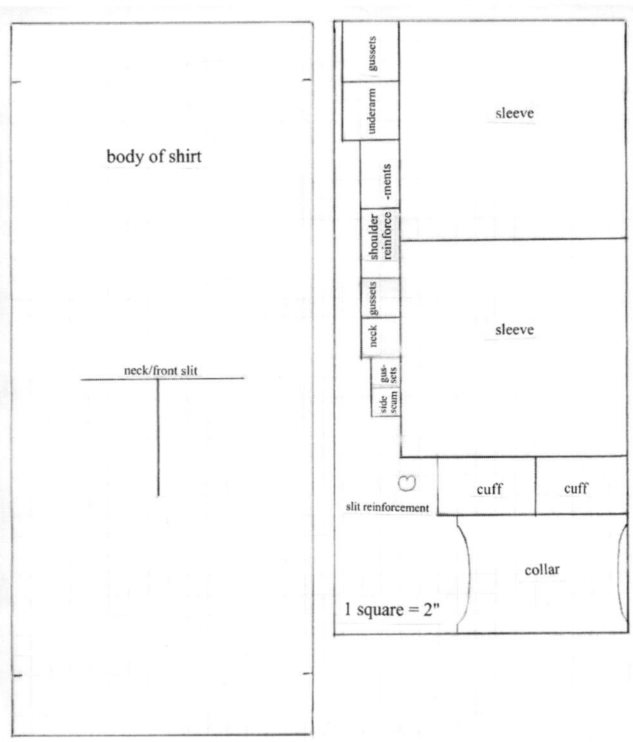

Shirt Cutting Diagram. Shirt pieces were primarily simple geometric shapes until the mid-19th century. Drawn by the author.

> Mr. Hopkins is so obliging as to take charge of two shirts, your finest . . . they are not wash'd for we had to finish making them this morning—we have made up all your fine Holland and cambric–& sometime if you will get more we will make them up for you—we have not made your others but shall soon and send them by the first safe opportunity.

Charles evidently bought the fabric in Boston and sent it home to be made into shirts. The next spring, Elizabeth sent more shirts, writing, "I have made your shirts, with my own hand" (Nylander 1993, 151). Sandra Bryant made her husband an average of five shirts a year (Nylander 1998, 109), and in 1819 and 1820, Harriet Bradley recorded in her diary that she made shirts for two of her brothers.

Unlike coats, waistcoats did not require an exact fit, so they could also be made at home, but more often were constructed by tailors. In 1807, Rosalie Calvert of Maryland wrote, "I rarely do the sewing [hired or enslaved seamstresses did that], but I cut and piece . . . all my husband's linen [shirts] and even his waistcoats" (Callcott 1991, 177).

Providing clothing for a large number of enslaved workers presented a special challenge. On some plantations, lengths of fabric were issued to the slaves and they were expected to make their own clothing. However, on others, the mistress seems to have at least supervised the making of all the clothing, and may even have helped with the actual sewing. Ann Cocke, in Virginia, wrote in 1811, "The sewing of the clothes is worse than weaving them, we have nearly a hundred shirts to make besides other parts of dress—these I am teaching some of the women of the crop to make" (Clinton 1982, 27).

There were some ready-made clothes available. Both unclaimed custom-made garments and second hand garments could be purchased. Frederick M. Eden wrote that the working people in London "content themselves with a cast-off coat, which may usually be purchased for about 5s. [shillings, about 50 cents] and second-hand waistcoats and breeches. Their wives seldom make up any article of dress, except making and mending cloaths for the children" (1797/1966, 554). It is possible that the same was true in the larger American cities, such as New York, Philadelphia, and Boston, where there could be quantities of second-hand clothes in the market.

In addition, there were shops that sold inexpensive pre-made garments called slops. As shirts did not require precise fitting, they were among the first items of clothing to be sold in slop shops. However, as early as 1797, the stock of Boone's store in Maryland included "3 Round ready made jacketts," along with six other jackets and four pairs of trousers (Gunston Hall). Slops were especially appealing to sailors, who might not be in port long enough to have garments custom made, and slop shops were often near the water. Single men who lived alone and had no one to sew for them also bought slops.

Men who traveled to the edge of the frontier in advance of their families also needed access to ready-made clothing. The Woodbridge store in Marietta, Ohio, for example, sold ready-made shirts, vests, and pantaloons in the second decade of the 19th century (Saint-Pierre 1999, 218). However, it must be remembered that, as the sewing machine had not yet been invented, even ready-made clothes were sewn by hand. Women working at home could supplement the family income by doing this kind of work.

By the second decade of the 19th century, tailors branched out to provide a wider assortment of clothes intended to be sold ready-made, such as coats and trousers. Tailoring was a largely seasonal business, with the greatest demand in the fall and winter months. Entrepreneurs found that they could keep their employees busy during slack times by having them sew a stock of ready-made garments. New York merchant John Williams opened the Gentlemen's Fashionable Wearing Apparel Warehouse in 1816, and Henry Brooks joined his brother, David, in the clothing business in 1817. Henry opened his own store in 1818, in the old slops district, where he sold coats, jackets, trousers, and smocks (Zakim 2003, 43–44). (Brooks Brothers continues today as a men's wear chain.) In November 1820, the American Ready made Clothing Store in Baltimore advertised "Cloaks of all descriptions," as well as "a complete assortment of ready made CLOTHING for the present season" (*Baltimore American and Commercial Daily Advertiser* 1820).

Slops had a negative connotation as they were perceived as cheap and poorly fitting. But as ready-to-wear clothing became more prevalent and the quality improved, Americans gradually accepted it.

Composition of a Wardrobe

Probate inventories from a variety of sources are valuable for ascertaining the composition of men's wardrobes during the period. The Gunston Hall Plantation database of inventories from Virginia and Maryland is a particularly good source for men's estates. The researchers not only transcribed the inventories but also classified the decedents according to economic status as elite, aspiring, decent, or old-fashioned, thereby providing a reference point for their level of wealth. (Very few women are included in this database and there are no detailed lists of clothing for them.)

As might be expected, probate inventories show that the contents of men's wardrobes varied widely. Farmer John Milholland, who died in Franklin County, Indiana in 1814, must have owned a bare minimum of garments. He had one coat and vest, one pair of overalls, and two shirts (University of Mary Washington). Evidently Milholland owned only working clothes, with no better clothes at all. It seems rather unusual for him to have only one pair of overalls, which provided no change of leg wear.

At the other end of the spectrum, enumerators recorded the extensive wardrobe of Richard Cramplin, of Maryland, in 1807. Included are 18 coats, 10 wool and 8 for summer, likely either linen or cotton, and 24 waistcoats, likewise in both winter and summer fabrics. He had eight pairs of the then-fashionable pantaloons and six pairs of more old-fashioned breeches. Only seven shirts are enumerated, three of them flannel, and this does not seem in keeping with the large number of other items; however, one item on the inventory is "all other articles of wearing apparel," so perhaps this included more shirts (Gunston Hall).

An inventory like Abraham Sell's, from late 18th century Pennsylvania, is hard to decipher. His 7 coats and 10 pairs of pants (the word used in the reference) sound reasonable, but the figure of 51 shirts seems excessive. And why did Leonard Schnieder of Pennsylvania own two great coats, when most men had one or none, but no regular coats (Gehret, 1976, 93–94)?

Benjamin Harrison, who died in 1799 in Virginia, had 5 coats and one "almost new" suit (matching coat and breeches) with "perl" buttons; 15 pairs of breeches, including 12 pairs of linen or nankeen cotton and three pairs of "corduroy &c;" and 14 assorted waistcoats. Evidently he had not adopted long pantaloons or trousers. Harrison had 11 pairs of stockings but they were all cotton or linen, with no silk ones—a rather odd circumstance given his wealth. On the other hand, the appraisers counted 22 pairs of stockings, including 13 of silk, when they inventoried Virginian David Finlay's estate in 1794 (Gunston Hall).

William Sydebothom's 1795 appraisers were particularly detail-oriented. He had 7 coats; 6 pairs of breeches; 1 pair of overalls; 10 waistcoats; 13 shirts, 1 of them flannel; 1 flannel gown, or banyan; 6 pieces of neckwear: 2 black cravats, 2 white cravats, and 2 stocks; 10 pairs of stockings: 7 worsted, 2 cotton, and 1 buckskin; 1 pair of woolen socks; 1 hat; 2 linen and 2 silk handkerchiefs; 2 pairs of leather gloves and 1 pair of yarn (knitted linen) gloves; and 2 pairs of "Ruffells." These ruffles would have been attached to shirts. Also listed along with the clothing were one yard of new linen and one yard of muslin, perhaps waiting to be made into small clothing items (Gunston Hall).

Wardrobes in the Federal period, then, ranged from those of poor frontier farmers with the bare minimum needed for survival to those of wealthy gentlemen with numerous items for different seasons and various occasions. On the whole, though, even the wealthy had fewer clothes than would become common later in the 19th century, when mass production made fabrics much less expensive.

AMERICAN INDIAN CLOTHING

There were many different tribes of Indians in North America, and there were differences in dress from one tribe to the next. However, contemporary descriptions of clothing suggest that there were similarities among tribes that inhabited the same geographic areas. This general discussion focuses on the general groups of the Eastern Woodlands, Plains, and Pacific Northwest.

Eastern Woodlands

Men of the Eastern Woodlands, especially the Six Nations, had, like the women, almost totally given up garments made of animal skins by this period, as it was more profitable for them to sell or trade the skins and buy manufactured fabrics. Traveler Isaac Weld, who visited the northeastern United States and Canada from 1795 to 1797, wrote, "The Indians, who have any dealings with the English or American traders, and all of them have that live in the neighbourhood, and to the east of the Mississippi, and in the neighborhood of the great lakes to the north-west, have now totally laid aside the use of furs and skins in their dress, except for their shoes or moccasins, and sometimes for their leggings, as they find they can exchange them to advantage for blankets and woolen cloths, etc." (1807/1970, 2:231). Some travelers described the Indians they encountered as "nearly naked," but the number and types of garments most Indians wore seems to have varied with the climate as well as the occasion. Some of their more elaborate garments were reserved for ceremonial use.

Many Indian men went bare-chested in warm weather, but when it was cooler, they wore European-style shirts as tunics. They hung down to mid-thigh and were often belted at the waist. Some men wore solid white linen shirts with or without ruffles, just as Anglo European men did, while others favored bright solid colors or vividly patterned linen or cotton fabrics. Weld wrote that the shirt was "loose at the neck and wrists, generally made of coarse figured cotton or calico, of some gaudy pattern, not unlike what would be used for window or bed curtains at a common inn in England" (1807/1970, 2:234).

A man's breech cloth was a 9-inch strip of 54 inch wide wool broadcloth. He pulled it between the legs and fastened it at the waist with a cord or tie, with the long hanging ends forming flaps in front and back. Some fancy breech cloths had decorated flaps.

Men's leggings were similar to women's leggings. They had pairs of strings that tied to another string around the waist to keep them in place. Leggings were often made of stroud, a wool fabric with a striped selvage. The maker placed the selvage on the outside of the lapped seam, where it formed a decorative element and also served a practical function, as it would not ravel. The leggings could be decorated with beadwork or ribbons, as well. Weld described them as follows, "They are commonly made of blue or scarlet cloth, and are formed so as to sit close to the limbs, like the modern pantaloons; but the edges of the cloth annexed to the seam, instead of being turned in, are left on the outside, and are ornamented with beads, ribands, etc. when the leggings are intended for dress" (1807/1970, 2:233).

Men's matchcoats were similar to those that women wore. Popular colors were dark blue, red, dark green, or white. They were sometimes decorated with braid, fringe, or small bells. A man draped his matchcoat by tying one end around the waist with a belt, then drawing it over the shoulders and either pinning it shut over the chest or holding the corners together. When carrying a gun, the man kept his right arm free. As with women's garments, the striped selvage of stroud was used for decorative effect.

Moccasins were the one item of attire that continued to be made from animal skins. Everyday moccasins were plain, while finer ones were decorated with beadwork.

Indians of the southeastern United States seem to have dressed similarly to those in the Northeast, although it appears that, given the warmer climate, they did not wear as many clothes. Shirts of any kind, all elaborately decorated clothes, and body decoration were reserved for ceremonial occasions. It also appears that some of the Chippewa, one of the tribes in this area, continued to wear animal skin leggings, whereas Indians further north had totally replaced skins with wool. A distinctive garment of the southeastern Indians, according to naturalist traveler William Bartram, "was a short cloak...usually of the scarlet feathers of the flamingo, or others of the gayest colour" (1791/1996, 400).

Many travelers noted that American Indians had very little body hair. Men plucked or otherwise removed most facial and body hair, even the eyebrows. This process was made easier by European-manufactured tweezers. Some Indians later adopted razors and shaved off the hair.

While hairstyles varied, it was common in the east for men to remove all the hair on the head except for a small topknot. Weld wrote, "It is well known, indeed, that the Indians have a great dislike to hair, and that such of the men as are ambitious of appearing gayer than the rest, pluck it not only from their eye-brows and eye-lashes, but also from every part of the head, except one spot on the back of the crown, where they leave a long lock." He added later, "They ornament this solitary lock of hair with beads, silver trinkets, etc. and on grand occasions with feathers" (1807/1970, 2:229,231).

At the beginning of the Federal period, men were described with slit ears, "Their ears are lacerated, separating the border or cartilaginous limb, which at first is bound round very close and tight with leather strings or thongs...the weight of the lead, extends the cartilage an incredible length...decorated with soft white plumes of heron feathers" (Bartram 1791/1996, 399). However, this piercing seems to have been going out of style by the end of the 18th century.

Some men pierced their noses and hung pendants from them. Men of high status wore breast plates made of silver or sea shells. Another sign of distinction was a silver cuff, decorated with scarlet buffalo hair, worn on the upper arm. Men in some areas decorated the shoulders of their shirts with multiple silver brooches.

Men painted their faces for ceremonies; black, red, and white were the usual colors. For battle, they often painted the whole body. Different tribes had different styles of painting. In the Southeast, Indians might have colored designs permanently tattooed into their skin.

Plains

There were differences between the Indians of the plains and the eastern tribes. Many of these tribes still made the majority of their clothing from animal skins, although they did wear some European-style clothes for special occasions. There were similarities of dress among the many tribes of this area. The first Indians explorers Meriwether Lewis and William Clark encountered were on the lower Missouri River, and they found:

> The Indians low down the Missouri dress in Skins & what clothes and trinkets they can procure from the whites–The Sioux dress in leather except a Breach Cloth, except on first days that those who have them put on better Clothes–The Ricaras & Mandans men, Dress in Leather Leagens & mockasons a flap of Blanket Generally before & a Roabe of Buffalow Skin Dressed. (Moulton 1983, 3:488)z

Among the Shoshone, Clark wrote, "the robe is formed most commonly of the skins of Antelope, Bighorn, or deer, dressed with the skin on, tho' they prefer the buffaloe when they can procure them. I have also observed some robes among them of beaver, moonax [probably a groundhog or woodchuck], and small wolves" (Moulton 5:126). Many men in this region wore shirts made of deer, antelope, bighorn, or elk skin, especially in colder weather.

Some tribes wore breech cloths of woven fabric, but others made them from small animal skins. One tribe "conseal[ed] their parts of generation with the Skins of the Fox or Some other Small animal drawn under neath a girdle and hanging loosely in front of them like a narrow apron" (Moulton 1983, 7:125). Further up the Missouri, the male "*Cho-pun-nish* or Pierced nose Indians" did not wear breech cloths, but rather "expose those parts which are generally kept from view by other nations" (Moulton 1983, 5:259). The Shoshone did not wear breech cloths, either. Instead, their leggings were made from whole antelope skins long enough to conceal the pelvic area:

> Their legings are most usually formed of the skins of the Antelope dressed without the har. In the men they are very long and full each leging being formed of a skin nearly entire. The legs, tail and neck are also left on these, and the tail woarn upwards; and the neck deeply fringed and ornimented with porcupine qulls drags or trails on the ground behind the heel. The skin is sewn in such manner as to fit the leg and thye closely; the upper part being left open a sufficient distance to permit the legs of the skin to be dran underneath a girdle both before and behind, and the wide part of the skin to cover the buttock and lap before in such manner that a breechcloth is unnecessary. They are much more decent in concealing those parts than any nation on the Missouri the sides of the legings are deeply fringed and ornamented. (Moulton 1983, 5:127)

Lewis and Clark wrote of the Cheyenne; "their dress in Sumner is Simpelly a roab of a light buffalow Skin with or without the hair and a

Breach cloute & mockerson Some ware leagins and mockersons, their ornaments are but fiew and those composed principally of Such articles as they precure from other indians Such as blue beeds, Shell, red paint rings of brass broaches &c" (Moulton 1983, 8:318).

The Indians decorated their garments with quills or glass beads, animal tusks, and small pieces of wool cloth. The Snake Indians wore ornamental neck pieces made of strips of otter fur. The nose, eyes, and tail were left intact, and small rolls of ermine skin added. Other Indians sometimes used "little fassicles of the hair of an enimy they have slain in battle" as ornamentation (Moulton 1983, 5:127).

For the most part, Plains Indians let their hair grow long rather than removing most of it, as did the eastern Indians. The Shoshone "wear their hair in a loos lank flow over the sholders and face; tho' I observed some few men who confined their hair in two equal cues hanging over each ear and drawnn in front of the body. The cue is formed with throngs of dressed lather or Otterskin alternately crossing each other" (Moulton 1983, 5:121). For special occasions some men decorated their hair with eagle or other feathers. Some Plains Indians slit their ears in a similar manner to those in the east; Lewis and Clark observed of the Cheyenne: "their ears are cut in the lower part, but fiew of them were [wear] ornements in them" (Moulton 1983, 8:318).

For other ornamentation, the Cheyenne "ware Bears Claws about their necks, Strips of otter Skin (which they as well as the ricaras are excessively fond of) around their neck falling back behind" (Moulton 1983, 8:318). The Mandans liked brass finger rings.

Pacific Northwest

Many men of the Pacific Northwest went without clothing most of the time. This was certainly practical in warm wet weather, or while the men were fishing. When a man did wear a garment, it was a simple wrapped robe. Lewis and Clark described them, "Sea otter, Beaver, Elk, Deer, fox and Cat," or, obtained from Indians farther north along the coast, "the Skins of a Small animal about the Size of a Cat, which is light and dureable" (Moulton 1983, 6:76). Smaller skins were sewn together, while larger ones were used intact. Men's robes could also be made of the blue wool yardage common in other areas. However, the Hudson's Bay Company had been supplying ready-made trade blankets since the late 18th century, and Indians also wore these as robes. Lewis and Clark wrote, "maney of the men have blankets of red blue or Spotted Cloth or the common three & 2 1/2 point blankets" (Moulton 1983, 6:75). It is not surprising that, given the very wet climate, the Indians of this area were especially skilled at making waterproof hats. The Indians made these conical hats of cedar bark, spruce root, and bear-grass using the same twining technique they used to make baskets. Men and women also wore woven rush ponchos for protection from the rain.

AFRICAN AMERICAN MEN'S CLOTHING

Like free African American women, free black men most likely dressed just as their white counterparts did. Those who could afford it wore whatever was in fashion at the time. However, enslaved African Americans did not have the freedom or means to wear what they wished. They were, for the most part, dependent on what was provided for them. There may have been a difference, though, between what the field hands were given and what house servants wore. House servants generally were given more formal clothes, and in some households wore the formal, highly decorated suits called livery (see above). House servants might also receive cast-off clothing from their owners. Charles Ball was hired out to be a cook on a U. S. Navy ship, whose crew members gave him "a half-worn coat," "an old shirt," and "a cast off waistcoat and pantaloons" (Ball 1837/1969, 27). Because conditions varied according to time and place, as well as the practices of the individual slave owners, it is difficult to give a general picture of the clothing of enslaved African Americans. Surviving evidence suggests some variety among wardrobes, although perhaps not as much as among free white men.

A common yearly allotment for field hands in the upper South, according to Charles Ball, who was born into slavery in Maryland in the 1780s, was "one wool hat, one pair of shoes, two shirts, two pair of trousers—one pair of tow cloth and one of woollen—and one woollen jacket" (Ball 1837/1969, 41). Mordecai, who sought freedom by running away from his North Carolina master in 1806, took "last winter's black woolen jacket and breeches" (Parker 1994, 82). The allotment of field hands in the Deep South may not have included either shirts or coats. While men did not generally wear long trousers at the beginning of the period, they were common working apparel, and it appears that many slaves wore them. One 1785 freedom seeker in Georgia wore "brown corduroy trowsers, that tied at the ankles," and another in 1786 wore "oznabrig trowsers" (Windley 1983, 4:134–42). However, in the 1780s, some enslaved men did wear the then-fashionable knee breeches. In 1786, a man in South Carolina "had on when escaped, a short Negro cloth jacket and breeches" (Windley 1983, 3:397). A Georgia man had both "white negro cloth breeches, dyed an olive colour," and "Oznaburg trowsers" (Windley 1983, 4:396).

Advertisements for runaways suggest that common fabrics included coarse linen osnaburg and tow cloth. Other fabrics were *country cloth* or *Negro cloth,* probably locally woven cotton; and *Virginia cloth,* locally woven of either cotton or a cotton and wool blend. When Richard Duckett died in Maryland in 1788, his estate included "54 yds Welch plain" and "51 yds Blue Cotton" (Gunston Hall). It seems likely that, in these quantities, these fabrics were intended for slave clothing. (*Welch* is probably the fabric called *Welsh Cotton,* a loosely woven woolen fabric resembling flannel [Montgomery 1983, 373].) Shirts were often brown (natural, unbleached) linen. York, who sought freedom in 1789, had "white, brown, and check shirts" (Windley 1983, 2:394).

Other inexpensive goods were produced especially for slave clothing. George Wingate Chase reported that hatters in Haverhill, Massachusetts, made "the common quality of hats, which were called 'Negro hats'" (1861, 541). The contents of Stanislaw Boone's store in Prince George's County, Maryland, in 1797 included "12 pair Negro Hose," which were much less expensive than other types of hose in the inventory (Gunston Hall). In 1788, Eager took "one pair of coarse gray Negro stockings, one pair of blue ditto, one pair of clouded blue and white ditto" (Windley 1983, 2:384).

Enslaved men as well as women sometimes had opportunities to earn income through hunting and fishing, raising produce, or hiring out their labor. If their masters allowed them to keep this money, the slaves often spent it on clothes. Charles Ball wrote, "The slaves were permitted to work for themselves at night, and on Sunday.... if the men are industrious and *employ themselves well on Sundays and holydays,* they can always keep themselves in comfortable clothes" (1837/1969, 41). In 1785, Will took a substantial wardrobe when he left to seek freedom, and, as the garments were called "his own," it seems he did not steal them. Among his "several suits" were "a pair of black velveret breeches and waistcoat, a pair

TEN DOLLARS REWARD.

RUN away from the ſubſcriber, on Tueſday the 27th September, a very likely negro man by the name of TOM, ſometimes he calls himſelf Tom Smith, and at other times Smith—he is about 5 feet 7 or 8 inches high; he generally wears a brown broadcloth coat, a ſwanſdown waiſtcoat, brown corduroy pantaloons, and ſhirt ruffled at the boſom, though he may change his dreſs, as he has a variety of cloaths. He is a black, ſlick, likely, well made fellow, with a very good ſet of white teeth, and as well as I remember, has a ſmall ſcar on one ſide of his face, looks like it was the ſtroke of a whip; he is a proud, artful, cunning fellow, and has a very ſmooth diſſembling tongue. Any perſon that will bring him home to me, living in Eſſex county, ſhall receive *Ten Dollars* reward, if taken out of the county, and if taken in the county, *Six.* All maſters of veſſels and others are hereby forwarned from harbouring or carrying the ſaid negro away.

W. GATEWOOD.

Eſſex, Nov. 30, 1804.

Advertisement, *Richmond Enquirer,* December 13, 1804. Tom Smith, the slave who sought freedom, had clothing beyond the basic garments masters provided to enslaved African Americans. His shirt had a ruffle, and his swansdown waistcoat was probably a wool and silk blend fancy patterned fabric. Courtesy of Library of Congress.

of white corded dimity breeches, and two or three silk waistcoats, two or three pair of linen overalls; a cinnamon coloured broadcloth coat, with a double row of white [silver colored] plated buttons on the breast; a saxon green superfine broadcloth coat, almost as good as new, with white plated buttons; a small round hat, with a black band and plated buckkle; a pair of boots, [and] a drab coloured great coat with white plated buttons" (Windley 1983, 4:122). In 1818, William Smith ran away. He was a waiter in an urban household, which may account for his wide assortment of fashionable apparel. It included, "a London brown surtout coat, with a velvet cape of the same color, a close bodied bottle green coat, both of broad cloth and half worn, one pair of grey stockinet [knitted] pantaloons, one pair of fawn color, figured at the flaps, one pair of green cloth, new and rather coarse, also one new livery surtout of grey cloth, and cape trimmed with black velvet, which he will probably rip off" (Meaders 1997, 311). Since the coat was livery, he might rip off the distinctive velvet collar to make it less conspicuous. We do not know if he bought his clothes with extra earnings, was given cast-offs, or stole some of them; certainly his master gave him the livery coat. In 1785, Nace, from Maryland, did steal some of his finery. His own clothing included "a coat of red halfthick, negro cotton breeches, gray yarn stockings," and "he carried with him a silk jacket which he stole" (Windley 1983, 2:150).

Certainly, though, not all freedom-seeking slaves were so well-attired. In 1787, Adam, in Gerogia, had merely "a brown jacket and oznabrig overalls," and Simon had "a pair of oznabrig trowsers, sailor's jacket, and check shirt" (Windley 1983, 4:148–49).

References

The American Cause. 2001. Helms Plays Hardball. July 23. http://www.theamericancause.org.

Ashton, John. 1885. *Old Times; a Picture of Social Life at the End of the 18th Century.* Repr., Detroit: Singing Tree Press, 1969.

Bagnall, William R. 1893. *The Textile Industries of the United States.* Repr., New York: A. M. Kelley, 1971.

Ball, Charles. 1837. *Slavery in the United States: a Narrative of the Life and Adventures of Charles Ball, a Black Man.* Repr., New York: Negro Universities Press, 1969.

Baltimore American Commercial and Daily Advertiser, 1802. April 16.

Baltimore American and Commercial Daily Advertiser. 1820. November 20.

Bartram, William. 1791. *Travels through North and South Carolina, Georgia, East and West Florida.* In *Travels and Other Writings,* ed. Thomas P. Slaughter, 3–426. New York: The Library of America, 1996.

Bassett, Lynne Zacek. 2001. *Textiles for Clothing of the Early Republic, 1800–1850: A Workbook of Swatches and Information.* Arlington, VA: Q Graphics Production Company.

Bassett, Lynne Z. and Jack Larkin. 1998. *Northern Comfort: New England's Early Quilts, 1780–1850: from the Collection of Old Sturbridge Village.* Nashville, TN: Rutledge Hill Press.

Baumgarten, Linda. 1988. "Costumes and Textiles in the Collection of Cora Ginsburg." *Antiques.* August: 261–77.

Baumgarten, Linda. 1992. "Under Waistcoats and Drawers." *Dress* 19: 5–16.

Baumgarten, Linda. 2002. *What Clothes Reveal: The Language of Clothing in Colonial and Federal America.* Williamsburg, VA: Colonial Williamsburg Foundation; New Haven, CT: Yale University Press.

Bradley, Harriet P. 1819–1820. Diary. In Museum Education Department, Old Sturbridge Village, Sturbridge, MA, resource packet of teaching documents, "Life Cycle: Youth," 1978.

Brown, William L. III. 1999. *Thoughts on Men's Shirts in America 1750–1900.* Gettysburg, PA: Thomas Publications.

Callcott, Margaret Law, ed. 1991. *Mistress of Riversdale: the Plantation Letters of Rosalie Stier Calvert 1795–1821.* Baltimore: Johns Hopkins University Press.

Carson, Barbara G. 1990. *Ambitious Appetites: Dining, Behavior, and Patterns of Consumption in Federal Washington.* Washington, D.C.: American Institute of Architects Press.

Carter, Edward C. II, ed. 1977. *The Virginia Journals of Benjamin Henry Latrobe 1795–1798.* Vol. 1, *1795–1797.* New Haven, CT: Yale University Press.

Carter, Edward C. II, John C. Van Horne, and Charles E. Brownell, eds. 1985. *Labtrobe's View of America, 1795–1820.* New Haven, CT: Yale University Press.

Chase, George Wingate. 1861. *The History of Haverhill, Massachusetts.* Haverill, MA: published by author.

Chotner, Deborah. 1992. *American Naive Paintings.* Washington, D.C.: National Gallery of Art.

Clinton, Catherine. 1982. *The Plantation Mistress: Woman's World in the Old South.* New York: Pantheon Books.

Cobbett, William. 1818. *A Year's Residence in the United States of America.* Repr. Carbondale: Southern Illinois University Press, 1964.

Crowninshield, Francis Boardman, ed. 1935. *Letters of Mary Boardman Crowninshield 1815–1816.* Cambridge, MA: Riverside Press.

Davis, Robert Ralph Jr. 1968. "Diplomatic Plumage: American Court Dress in the Early National Period." *American Quarterly,* 20 (2, pt. 1): 164–79.

Delpierre, Madeleine. 1990. *Le Costume: Consulat-Empire.* Paris: Flammarion.

Dress and Address. 1819. London: J.J. Stockdale.

Eden, Frederic Morton. 1797. *The State of the Poor.* Vol. 1. Repr., London: Frank Cass & Co., 1966.

Farrell, Jeremy. 1992. *Socks and Stockings.* London: B. T. Batsford.

Fearon, Henry Bradshaw. 1818. *A Narrative of a Journey of Five Thousand Miles through the Eastern and Western States of America.* Repr., New York: Augustus M. Kelley, 1970.

Fennelly, Catherine. 1961. *Textiles in New England 1790–1840.* Sturbridge, MA: Old Sturbridge Village.

Fennelly, Catherine. 1966. *The Garb of Country New Englanders 1790–1840: Costumes at Old Sturbridge Village.* Sturbridge, MA: Old Sturbridge Village.

Flint, James. 1822. *Letters from America.* Repr., New York: Johnson Reprint Corporation, 1970.

Fortune, Brandon Brame. 2002. "'Studious Men are Always Painted in Gowns': Charles Willson Peale's *Benjamin Rush* and the Question of Banyans in 18th-Century Anglo-American Portraiture." *Dress,* 29: 27–40.

Gehret, Ellen J. 1976. *Rural Pennsylvania Clothing.* York, PA: George Shumway.

Gerry, Elbridge, Jr. 1927. *The Diary of Elbridge Gerry, Jr.* New York: Brentano's.

Gunston Hall Plantation. Probate Inventory Database: Virginia and Maryland Probate Inventories 300+ Transcriptions Recorded Between 1740–1810. www.GunstonHall.org/probate/inventory/htm.

Harding, Annaliese. 1994. *John Lewis Krimmel: Genre Artist of the Early Republic.* Winterthur, DE: Henry Francis du Pont Winterthur Museum.

Hart, Avril. 1998. *Ties.* New York: Costume & Fashion Press.

Hartford Courant. 1812. October 27.

Hersh, Tandy, and Charles Hersh. 1995. *Cloth and Costume 1750–1800 Cumberland County, Pennsylvania.* Carlisle, PA: Cumberland County Historical Society.

Hill, Margot Hamilton, and Peter A. Bucknell. 1967. *The Evolution of Fashion: Pattern and Cut from 1066 to 1930.* New York: Drama Book Publishers.

Hill, Thomas. 1890. "A Journey on Horseback from New Brunswick, New Jersey, to Lycoming County, Pennsylvania, in 1799." *Pennsylvania Magazine of History and Biography,* 14: 189–98.

Hosford, David. 1984. "Exile in Yankeeland: The Journal of Mary Bagot, 1816–1819." *Records of the Columbia Historical Society* 51: 30–50.

Instructions for Cutting Out Apparel for the Poor; Principally Intended for the Assistance of the Patronesses of Sunday Schools, and Other Charitable Institutions, but Useful in All Families. London: J. Walter.

Inventory of John Campbell. Inventories and Sales, Vol. J.H. 3, p. 122. U.S. District Court for the District of Columbia. National Archives, Record Group 21, Entry 119.

Kahn, Philip, Jr. 1989. *A Stitch in Time: The Four Seasons of Baltimore's Needle Trades.* Baltimore: The Maryland Historical Society.

Kornhauser, Elizabeth Mankin. 1991. *Ralph Earl: The Face of the Young Republic.* New Haven, CT: Yale University Press.

Krimmel, John Lewis. 1812. *Fourth of July in Centre Square.* Pennsylvania Academy of Fine Arts.

Lady's Magazine. 1798. September.

Lady's Magazine. 1800. May.

Langston-Harrison, Lee. 1997. *A Presidential Legacy: The Monroe Collection at the James Monroe Museum and Memorial Library.* Fredericksburg, VA: The James Monroe Museum.

Larkin, Jack. 1988. *The Reshaping of Everyday Life 1790–1840.* New York: HarperPerennial.

Low, Betty-Bright P. 1974. "Of Muslins and Merveilleuses: Excerpts from the Letters of Josephine du Pont and Margaret Manigault." *Winterthur Portfolio* 9: 29–75.

Mattern, David B., and Holly C. Shulman, eds. 2003. *The Selected Letters of Dolley Payne Madison.* Charlottesville: University of Virginia Press.

Meaders, Daniel. 1997. *Advertisements for Runaway Slaves in Virginia, 1801–1820.* New York: Garland Publishing.

Melish, John. 1818. *Travels through the United States of America.* Repr., New York: Johnson Reprint Corporation, 1970.

Miller, Lillian B., ed. 1996. *The Peale Family: Creation of a Legacy 1770–1870.* New York: Abbeville Press.

Miller, Marla R. 2006 *The Needle's Eye: Women and Work in the Age of Revolution.* Amherst: University of Massachusetts Press.

Montgomery, Florence. 1984. *Textiles in America 1650–1870.* New York: W. W. Norton & Company.

Moore, Robert J., Jr., and Michael Haynes. 2003. *Tailor Made, Trail Worn: Army Life, Clothing & Weapons of the Corps of Discovery.* Helena, MT: Farcountry Press.

Moulton, Gary E., ed. 1983. *The Journals of the Lewis and Clark Expedition.* Vols. 3, 5, 6, 7, 8. Lincoln: University of Nebraska Press.

Murray, Anne Wood. 1974. "Breeches and Sherrivallies." *Wafen-und Kostümkunde* 16: 87–106.

Niemcewicz, Julian Ursyn. 1965. *Under Their Vine and Fig Tree,* trans. and ed. Metchie J. E. Budka. Elizabeth, NJ: The Grassmann Publishing Company.

Nylander, Jane. n.d. Unpublished notes taken from the Sarah Snell Bryant diaries, 1795–1836; Houghton Library, Harvard University, Cambridge MA.

Nylander, Jane. 1993. *Our Own Snug Fireside: Images of the New England Home 1760–1860.* New Haven, CT: Yale University Press.

Nylander, Jane. 1998. "Everyday Life on a Berkshire County Hill Farm." In *The American Home: Material Culture, Domestic space, and Family Life,* ed. Eleanor McD. Thompson, 95–117. Winterthur, DE: Henry Francis du Pont Winterthur Museum.

Of Men Only: A Review of Men's and Boys' Fashions, 1750–1975. 1975. New York: The Brooklyn Museum.

Palmer, John. 1818. *Journal of Travels in the United States of North America and in Lower Canada, Performed in the Year 1817.* London: Sherwood, Neely, and Jones.

Parker, Freddie L., ed. 1994. *Stealing a Little Freedom: Advertisements for Slave Runaways in North Carolina, 1791–1840.* New York: Garland Publishing.

Pinfold, Wallace G. 1999. *A Closer Shave: Man's Daily Search for Perfection.* New York: Artisan.

Port Folio, October 3, 1801.

Ramsay, David. 1809. *The History of South-Carolina: from its First Settlement in 1670, to the Year 1808.* Charleston, SC: David Longworth.

Ribeiro, Aileen. 1988. *Fashion in the French Revolution.* London: B. T. Batsford.

Rigby, Janet Low. 1983. The Life of a Rural Tailor, Stephen Powell, (1771–1844). Cooperstown, NY: Cooperstown Graduate Program.

Roberts, Robert. 1827. *The House Servant's Directory: or A Monitor for Private Families: Comprising Hints on the Arrangement and Performance of Servants' Work,* ed. Graham Russell Hodges. Repr., Armonk, NY: M. E. Sharpe, 1997.

Saint-Pierre, Adrienne E. 1999. "Luther Edgerton's 'Cloathing Books': A Record of Men's Ready-to-Wear from the Early Nineteenth Century." In *Textiles in Early New England: Design, Production, and Consumption,* ed. Peter Benes, 212–32. Boston: Boston University Scholarly Publications.

Sangster, William. 1871. *Umbrellas and Their History.* Project Gutenburg, 2004. http://www.gutenberg.org/dirs/etext04/mbrll10.txt.

Seaton, Josephine. 1871. *William Winston Seaton of the "National Intelligencer." A Biographical Sketch.* Boston: J. R. Osgood and Company.

Shep, R. L. 1998. *Federalist & Regency Costume: 1790–1819.* Mendocino, CA: R. L. Shep.

Shine. 1993. "Dress for the Ohio Pioneers." In *Dress in American Culture,* eds. Patricia A. Cunningham and Susan Voso Lab, 42–65. Bowling Green, OH: Bowling Green State University Popular Press.

Smith, Margaret Bayard. 1906. *The First Forty Years of Washington Society,* ed. Gaillard Hunt. New York: Scribner.

Stirling, A.M.W., 1908. *Coke of Norfolk and His Friends.* Vol. 1. New York: John Lane Company.

Swann, June. 1982. *Shoes.* New York: Drama Book Publishers.

Thornton, Anna Maria Brodeau. 1907. "Diary of Mrs. William Thornton, 1800." *Records of the Columbia Historical Society* 10: 89–226.

Tyler, Sylvia Lewis. Diaries, 1801–1820, transcribed by Alden O'Brien. Acc 2899, Americana Collection, National Society of the Daughters of the American Revolution, Washington, D.C.

University of Mary Washington. "Franklin County Indiana Transcribed Probate Inventories." http://departments.umw.edu/hipr/www/inventories/Franklin/19cinfra.htm.

de Vallinger, Leon, Jr., and Virginia E. Shaw. 1948. *A Calendar of Ridgely Family Letters 1742–1899 in the Delaware State Archives.* Vol. 1. Dover: Delaware State Archives.

Wansey, Henry. 1796. *The Journal of an Excursion to the United States of North America in the Summer of 1794.* Repr., New York: Johnson Reprint Corporation, 1969.

Washington National Intelligencer. 1803. July 20.

Weld, Isaac, Jr. 1807. *Travels through the States of North America and the Provinces of Upper & Lower Canada During the Years 1795, 1796 & 1797.* Vol. 2. Repr., New York: Augustus M. Kelly, 1970.

Windley, Lathan A. 1983. *Runaway Slave Advertisements: a Documentary History from the 1730s to 1790.* 4 vols. Westport, CT: Greenwood Press.

Woodforde, James. 1924. *Diary of a Country Parson,* ed. John Beresford. Vols. 2–5. London: H. Milford.

Wright, Meredith. 1990. *Everyday Dress of Rural America, 1783–1800.* New York: Dover Publications.

Zakim, Michael. 2003. *Ready-Made Democracy: A History of Men's Dress in the American Republic, 1760–1860.* Chicago: University of Chicago Press.

CHAPTER 5

Children's Fashions

The distinctive style of clothing for children that had developed by the Federal era reflected the influence of the Englishman John Locke, a philosopher of the Age of Enlightenment, who advocated that children's clothes should not be "too warm or strait" (1692/1997, sec. 30). In the next century, Jean-Jacques Rousseau advocated in his book *Emile* that boys' clothing should not be too tight or closely fitted. He wrote, "the limbs of a growing child should be free to move easily in his clothing; nothing should cramp their growth or movement; there should be nothing tight, nothing fitting closely to the body, no belts of any kind" (1762/1972, 91). There was also a new realization that children were not just small adults. Parents began to recognize that children went through stages of development and that their clothing should change accordingly as they grew older. Because the new styles evolved throughout the three and a half decades of the period, the following discussion will consider the era as a whole.

MAIN GARMENTS

Infants

Infants of both sexes wore some form of dress or gown. (Gender differentiation did not occur until the children were older, when boys began to wear breeches or trousers.) The dress was often of the style called a frock, opening all the way down the back. An alternative was a front-opening gown, called a bedgown, that the infant most likely wore for sleeping. Before children were old enough to walk, their dresses were very long, extending past the feet. A November 1799 article in the *Lady's Monthly Museum* suggested that infants' garments should be "two or three inches longer than the child's feet," to allow "the legs may be got at with ease, in order to have them often rubbed in the day with a warm hand or flannel" (390–91). (While the *Lady's Monthly Museum* published this advice in 1799, it is copied from a 1762 publication, Hannah Glasse's *Servants Directory*. This illustrates a frequent problem with 18th and early 19th century documentary sources in that publications often borrowed freely from other sources with no attribution.)

The 1789 guide to charity sewing, *Instructions for Cutting Out Apparel for the Poor* (later referred to as *Instructions for Cutting Out Apparel),* describes how to cut an infant's frock with the bodice and skirt cut separately and sewn together at the waist. However, infants' garments were often cut in a single piece without a waist seam. This type of dress was sometimes called a cooler. Earlier in the period, the bodice of such frocks was fitted with small pleats that ended at the waist position, allowing the skirt's fullness to fan out. Later, the frock may have been fitted with drawstrings at the neckline and waist position. The strings tied in back, providing the closure. The waistline of children's clothes, like that of women's dresses, rose to a higher level through the last decade of the 18th century and remained at a raised position into the early 19th century.

Infants' dresses were often made of white linen or cotton. Mrs. Roger Smith and her infant son, Edward Nutt Smith, of Charleston, South Carolina, were painted by George Romney while visiting England in 1786. Edward wears a long white dress with a ruffle around the neck and a blue cord or sash around the waist (McInnis 1999, 133). The infant in the 1800 portrait of the Sargent family, from Boston, also wears a long white dress (National Gallery of Art, http://www.nga.gov; artist unknown). Portraits of several Baltimore families by Joshua Johnson illustrate that the long white dress continued to be the norm through 1820, at least for dress-up occasions. Infants pictured with their families include William McCormick in 1804–1805, Andrew Kennedy Long in 1805, James McCausland in 1813, and Rebecca Everett in 1818 (Weekley and Colwill 1987, 123,131,152–53,161). There are three extant white infants' dresses in the collection of Colonial Williamsburg. One, dated 1800–1815, is cotton with a design woven in linen thread; another, of plain white cotton, is dated 1790–1815, and the third, dated 1810–1825, probably from Maine, is elaborately embroidered around the hem, back opening, and sleeves (Baumgarten 2002, 174).

The *Instructions for Cutting Out Apparel* recommended printed linen for front-opening bedgowns and printed cotton, with linen bodice linings, for back-opening frocks (1789, 74, 79). The *Lady's Economical Assistant,* an 1808 instruction book, suggested "fine jaconet muslin," a fabric slightly heavier than regular muslin, for frocks. The *Assistant* also recommended for bedgowns or night gowns, "any warm light material:—That which is striped, and called muslinette, is very good for the purpose" (1808/1998, 1–2). In 1797, Frances Baylor Hill made several frocks for her newborn niece. Three were flannel, a soft wool; two were calico, printed or solid cotton; and one was Virginia cloth, probably a locally woven fabric of either cotton or a cotton and wool blend (Bottorff and Flannagan, 1967, 43).

***Mrs. Benjamin Tallmadge and Son Henry Floyd and Daughter Maria Jones,* by Ralph Earl, 1790. Infant Maria wears a frock of a sheer patterned white fabric with an elaborately decorated cap. Henry, about age three, wears a white frock with a dark green sash.** The Litchfield Historical Society, Litchfield, Connecticut.

Because these long infants' dresses were often white, extant garments today may be identified as christening gowns when they were not. However, wealthy Christian families who had their infants baptized did sometimes dress them in elaborately decorated white ensembles for the occasion. Unlike today, there was no gender significance attached to the color of infants' or toddlers' garments. Infants and toddlers of both sexes wore pink, blue, or other pastel sashes around their waists, often matching the pastel slips under their sheer white dresses. In 1811, Sylvia Tyler made her infant son a "Pink Calico frock," while in 1813 she made her infant daughter a "Blue factory cloth" one (Tyler Diaries).

Toddlers

At the age of six months to a year, children would be "put into short coats," also called three-quarters clothing. This shortened version of a frock, about ankle length, allowed the toddler to walk unencumbered. Charlotte Louise Papendiek said one of her children was weaned (switched from breast milk to solid food) and put into short coats at the same time (1887, 1:220; while Mrs. Papendiek lived in England, her recollections provide details that most likely can also be applied to the United States). Early in the period, the frock had a full skirt and fitted bodice, with the waist nearly at the natural position, while a wide colored sash gave the illusion of a raised waistline. Mrs. Papendiek described her "babes" in 1786 "in clean white frocks, and blue satin sashes" (1887, 1:249). By the early 19th century, children's frocks reflected the same slender silhouette as women's fashionable attire. As the waistline rose to a higher position, the sash was often eliminated. The frock, which opened at the back, often had drawstrings around the neck and across the center of the bodice, as well as at the waist position. This construction allowed for extra fullness in the garment so that the girth could be expanded as the child grew. A child's frock in the collection of Colonial Williamsburg is made this way, with drawstrings at the neck, mid-chest, and waist (Baumgarten 2002, 161).

A toddler's or child's dress generally had a wide hem and a row of tucks around the lower hem edge as well as tucks on the sleeves. These tucks, sewn folds of fabric, were decorative as well as practical, as they could be let out, thus lengthening the garment, as the child grew. Mrs. Papendiek described her daughter's first short coats, "We made her four white frocks and two coloured ones, with the skirts full and three tucks and a hem; the bodies plain, cut cross-ways, and the sleeves plain, with a cuff turned up" (1887, 1:221). A boy's dress from the 1790s in the collection of the Chester County Historical Society shows stitching marks where a growth tuck was let down in the skirt, while a bodice tuck is still intact (Burnston 1998, 79–81).

These toddlers' garments were made out of a variety of fabrics including lightweight white linen or cotton and colored or printed linen or cotton. Toward the end of the 18th century, fine white cotton fabrics were sometimes embellished with small woven or embroidered designs.

For everyday wear, printed fabrics, particularly those with dark backgrounds, or darker solid color fabrics were more practical. In the late 1780s, Mrs. Papendiek's husband "brought home four gown pieces, one of a very pretty green, with a small pattern of a dark shade, another with a white ground and small bunches of convolvulus over it, and two dark ones" (Papendiek 1887, 2:120). The young daughter of Martha Tennent Rogers, painted by Ralph Earl in 1788, wears a pink or peach dress with a blue sash (Kornhauser 1991, 144). The Chester County dress referred to above is white cotton printed with small flowers in pink, green, and brown (Burnston 1998, 79–81). There is a back-opening frock in the collection of the Massillon Museum (Ohio) that is made of a dark floral printed fabric. While the fabric is dated circa 1775–1785, the frock was probably made circa 1810–1811, and is known to have belonged to a boy (Bissonnette 2003, 133). The frock in the Colonial Williamsburg collection referred to above is made of an English white cotton fabric block-printed with brown. Another toddler's or child's frock in that collection is made from white cotton block-printed in reddish brown. It is dated circa 1810 and is possibly from Pennsylvania (Baumgarten 2002,

161,173). Toddlers also wore solid colors, as Eliza White O'Donnell, who was two or three when Joshua Johnson painted her portrait, wears a bright blue dress (Weekley and Colwill 1987, 128,111). Stuff, a worsted wool fabric, or grosgram, a wool and silk blend fabric, were recommended in England, where they would provide warmth in the chilly climate (*Instructions* 1789, 16). Children also sometimes wore wool fabrics in the colder regions of the United States.

Under a sheer white fabric, a child might wear a colored silk slip or underdress. Two-year-old Daniel Taylor, painted by Ralph Earl in 1790, wears a very sheer white dress with lace edging on the neck and cuffs over a pink slip. His sash is a wide, fancy patterned ribbon with blue edging (Kornhauser 1991, 165). Nearly transparent fine cotton fabrics with separate slips continued to be fashionable into the early 19th century, although such ensembles were probably reserved for dress up occasions. In the circa 1805 portrait by Joshua Johnson, a young child identified as Emma Van Name wears a very elaborate sheer white dress with

Child's frock, blue and buff striped cotton, circa 1810–1825. This dress bodice and sleeves are cut on the bias, and there are drawstrings at the waist and neckline and a tuck around the lower edge of the skirt. Courtesy of American Costume Studies.

tucks and embroidered trim over a pink underdress. The sleeves are embellished with strands of beads.

By the early 19th century, toddler boys began to wear long pantaloons or trousers under their frocks or dresses. These outfits were sometimes made of the fashionable white cotton of the day. In 1807, George Ridgely, not quite three years old, had a frock over "trowsers" made of white dimity (a heavy ribbed cotton fabric) with green ribbon ties. He was "so delighted with its trowsers" that his mother could "scarcely get them off again" (de Vallinger and Shaw 1948, 277). Nankeen, a naturally tan-colored cotton, was a more practical choice, as it would not show dirt as readily. The 1808 *Lady's Economical Assistant* suggested that, "the prettiest dress for a little boy [about two years of age], is a nankeen frock and pantaloons" (1808/1998, 10). In 1816, Mrs. Crowninshield inquired about her son, George, who was about four years old, "I think you must have got George new clothes,—I long to see him with his trousers. I suppose he despises frocks and trousers" (Crowninshield 1935, 50).

Toddlers of both sexes wore coveralls called pincloths to protect their other clothing. These were back-opening, sleeveless garments. They would come to be called pinafores and would remain a common garment of childhood for decades. Either checked or natural brown linen were the recommended fabrics for the strictly utilitarian pincloth, or "thick brown Holland, or a cloth called Duck, which answers very well for boys" (*Instructions* 1789, 26–27). Fancier versions were made of fine white linen or cotton.

Childhood—Girls

Girls continued to wear simple frocks throughout childhood, although the style evolved much as women's fashions did. In the 1780s, the dress had a tight fitting bodice with a seam at the natural waist position and a broad colored sash, similar to the dresses of toddlers. And, like toddlers' dresses, the child's dress often had growth tucks above the hem of the skirt. Catherine Brower, who was painted by MacKay in 1791 when she was six years old, wears a white dress with the waistline at the natural position, a neck ruffle, elbow-length sleeves with cuffs, and a full skirt with six tucks. Her turquoise waist sash has elaborately fringed ends (National Gallery of Art, http://www.nga.gov).

Before 1800, girls sometimes wore silk dresses. An unknown girl, probably about 10 years old, painted about 1790, wears a full-skirted dress that appears to be bright peach silk with an ivory sash (National Gallery of Art, http://www.nga.gov). White cotton and linen were popular for girls' dresses as well as for infants' and toddlers' clothing through the whole Federal era, especially for dress-up clothes, and many children wore white when they had their portraits painted. Anna Maria

Cumpston, painted circa 1790 by Charles Peale Polk, wears a full-skirted white dress with what appears to be a peach underdress (National Gallery of Art, http://www.nga.gov). The dress is tied with a peach sash and there are three tucks in the skirt. In their 1796 portrait by Ralph Earl, sisters Elizabeth Hannah and Julia E. Canfield wear nearly identical white dresses (Fields and Kightlinger 1990, 16). All three daughters in the 1800 portrait of the Sargent family, in Boston, wear white dresses. Two-year-old Eliza's has a dark pink sash tied in a bow on the side; four-year-old Maria and five-year-old Martha "Patty" Hills, have peach or off-white sashes (Chotner 1992, 588–89).

However, white was certainly not practical for active little girls. Mrs. Crowninshield's daughters had red dresses for everyday (Crowninshield 1935, 38). The unknown girl in *Feeding the Bird,* by an anonymous artist, wears a bright yellow dress with black lace trim around the neck and a black ribbon around the high waist; while the date of this painting is not known, the style of the dress places it sometime in the first decade of the 19th century (National Gallery of Art 1994, #3). In a group portrait of the Budd family, painted about 1818, the seven- or eight-year-old daughter wears a pale blue dress (Chotner 1992, 480).

Around 1815, plaid wool fabrics became popular for both girls and boys. When Mary Boardman Crowninshield dined with Elizabeth Monroe, wife of Secretary of State James Monroe, in December 1815, Mrs. Monroe's six-year-old granddaughter was "dressed in plaid" (Crowninshield 1935, 20), and that same year, Auben S. Lewis's dry goods store in Washington advertised in the *National Intelligencer* "a beautiful assortment of Tartan plaids for children's clothes, etc." (Tartan plaids, associated with the clans of Scotland, would be fashionable several times during the 19th century. This first wave of popularity may be attributed to the Scottish regiments at the 1815 Battle of Waterloo, who

"Such Sights When They Got Home"

Mary Boardman Crowninshield brought her daughters, 12-year-old Elizabeth and 10-year-old Mary, to Washington to spend the winter of 1815–1816 with her husband, Secretary of the Navy Benjamin Crowninshield. They lived in a boarding house, as most transient Washington residents did. She wrote her mother, who was back home in Salem, Massachusetts caring for the younger children, about her daily life, including the challenge of keeping her girls presentable. She had to send her laundry out, and it took several days to get it back, and she lamented, "the girls dirty their white aprons very soon." She added, "Mrs. [Stephen] Decatur and others wonder I do not let the girls wear black silk aprons," which were fashionable in New York and Philadelphia. She decided that was a good idea, and asked her mother to send some black silk. She also had to make new everyday dresses for the girls out of bombazet, a wool fabric, because, "their red ones are worn out. They sometimes put on white, which is not a day's wear." Later, Mary "put on her new [gown] yesterday, but she dirted it so much I won't let her wear it any more, for she must keep a best one." She also had problems buying sufficient numbers of stockings, as "they want clean ones every day." When she took the girls to a ball, they wore "new white kid shoes. Gave five dollars for both, and new gloves, but such sights when they got home,—so dirty, and yet they did not dance" (Crowninshield 1935).

were noted for their bravery as well as their distinctive plaid kilts [Susan North, pers. comm. 2006].)

Older girls wore aprons to protect their clothes while playing or working. They may have worn the capacious pincloth style, as younger children did, if they had dirty work to do. A simple tie-on style of apron, sometimes called a *tyer,* made of white linen or cotton, was another option. Mrs. Bryant made her daughters tyers from infancy through childhood (Nylander n.d.). Blue and white checked linen, often woven at home, was common for those in rural areas, especially in New England, or the poor. The *Instructions for Cutting Out Apparel* recommended "Check, exactly three quarters wide [27 inches]" with tape to make the ties (*Instructions* 1789, 4). The 12- and 6-year-old daughters of a runaway slave in 1818 were wearing "blue domestic frocks and check aprons" (Meaders 1997, 316; *domestic* here probably means home-woven fabric). From about 1812 to 1816, black silk aprons were stylish, and these,

***Alexander Spotswood Payne and His Brother, John Robert Dandridge Payne, with their Nurse,* by the Payne Limner, 1790–1800. Oil on canvas. On their Virginia plantation, Alexander wears a full suit, his brother wears only a shirt, and the enslaved nurse wears a short gown and petticoat. Also see chapter 3, "African American Women."** Courtesy Virginia Museum of Fine Arts Collection, gift of Dorothy Payne.

while difficult to wash, would not readily show dirt. Mrs. Crowninshield had been told they were fashionable in both Philadelphia and New York. In fact, Rachel Jackson, wife of General Andrew Jackson, who had recently been in New Orleans, said even grown women were wearing black aprons in that city (Crowninshield 1935, 37–38). A girl in John Lewis Krimmel's 1812 painting, *Fourth of July in Centre Square,* in Philadelphia, wears a black apron over a red dress.

As girls entered adolescence, they would no longer wear frocks that were open all the way down the back but would switch to closed gowns in more grown up styles. Of course, by the early 19th century, "grown up" dresses had evolved from the elaborate styles of the 1780s and 1790s to a simpler style that had some resemblance to children's garments.

Childhood—Boys

It was a significant milestone in a boy's life when he traded his toddler's frock for leg wear like his father's. This rite of passage was called *breeching* and signified that the boy was moving out of the household world of women and into the wider world of men. At the beginning of the era, a boy's first leg wear, when he was formally breeched, was actually a pair of knee breeches. He then wore the ensemble of breeches, waistcoat, and coat much like his father's. Costume scholars have suggested that breeching occurred when a boy was three to six years old. While mothers began dressing their toddlers in "frocks and trousers" by the early 19th century, it was still significant when the boy put aside the frock to wear his trousers with a shirt and jacket or coat.

In the 1780s, boys began to trade knee breeches for long, rather loose trousers that may have been adapted from farmers' and sailors' attire. With the new long trousers a boy wore a shorter jacket, often without tails. The trousers must have been more comfortable for an active little boy than breeches that buckled at the knee. There have been several explanations of the origin of the new boys' clothing. One credits Marie Antoinette, queen of France, with first dressing her young son in such an outfit in the 1780s, as part of the so-called simple rural lifestyle she led at the Petit Trianon (Weber 2006, 173). However, the idea may actually have been of English origin. When Thomas Gainsborough painted King George III, his wife, and their 13 children in 1782, four of the younger sons were wearing variations of the new outfit. And in 1787, the German magazine *Journal des Luxus und der Moden* showed children in the "comfortable and functional clothing for children based on the theories of John Locke" (Rose 1989, 50). But it is certain that boys led the way with a new style that would be adopted by fashionable men, just as the new style of girls' clothes was later adopted by grown women.

As the boy's jacket got shorter, the waistline of the trousers got higher. Another innovation was to fasten this shorter jacket to the waistband of the trousers with buttons. This ensemble, called a skeleton suit, became the primary garment for pre-teen boys through the rest of the era. An active little boy would maintain a neater appearance in such a suit, as there would not be an unsightly gap, with the shirt hanging out, between the pants and jacket. The buttons must have must have made it rather difficult to get in and out of, though, and some examples have a small functional slit in the crotch seam of the trousers. As the jacket was usually buttoned, there was no longer the need for a separate waistcoat underneath. However, an existing jacket in the collection of Historic Deerfield was made with a false waistcoat front and tails in the back to simulate the look of a man's suit.

The skeleton suit provided a transitional outfit from the toddler's frock to the man's ensemble. The suits were made from a variety of fabrics, including wool, solid or printed cotton, or linen. There are a scarlet calamanco wool suit and an indigo-blue dyed cotton suit in the collection of Old Sturbridge Village (Fennelly 1961, 40; 1966, 38; calimanco is a wool fabric with a glazed surface). The wool plaid fabrics that appeared for girls around 1815 were also used for boys' skeleton suits and the collection of the Litchfield Historical Society includes a red and blue plaid one. In some pictures, the pants of the skeleton suits appear very form-fitting, like men's snug-fitting pantaloons. Such tight-fitting garments would have to be knitted or bias-cut, and there is not enough existing evidence to suggest that skeleton suits were actually made this way.

It appears that, with the development of this new outfit, parents may have been breeching their sons at an earlier age. Sarah Snell Bryant, of Massachusetts, made coats and trousers for her sons before they were three years old. Austin, born in 1793, was 28 months old. His brother, Cullen, born in 1794, made the transition at 31 months, while Cyrus, born in 1799, was 29 months old (Nylander 1998, 108). In 1812 Sylvia Tyler "cut out a Coat and trowsers for Lewis," her son, and finished constructing them just a month before his second birthday (Tyler Diaries).

However, in 1799, Philadelphia Quaker Elizabeth Drinker reported that her grandson, Henry, was not breeched until after he was four years old. Mrs. Drinker wrote in her diary on September 19, "Sally [Henry's mother] has a Young Woman at work,... making a little man of Henry—he is very pleas'd." The outfit was completed by September 22, as "littel Henry was Yesterday put in Jacket and trowsers, one of the happiest days of his life" (Drinker 1994, 214–15). Nylander speculates that breeching occurred when the boy was toilet trained. Of course, then, as now, some boys may have lagged behind in being toilet trained, or some parents may have delayed breeching for other reasons.

Existing child-sized waistcoats and tailcoats indicate that not all little boys wore skeleton suits but rather continued to wear totally separate pieces. For example, the very young brothers John and Edward Anderson, painted by Joshua Johnson in 1812–1815, wear matching double-breasted tailcoats that are unbuttoned, revealing white waistcoats (Weekley and Colwill 1987, 152).

Sometime in later childhood (suggested ages vary from 7 to 12), all boys graduated to separate jackets, waistcoats, and trousers. The jacket was often the style called a round jacket, that was waist length and without tails, but sometimes boys wore tailcoats just like their fathers. Basil Brown, of Baltimore, was painted by Joshua Johnson in 1813, when he was eight or nine. He wears a double-breasted tailcoat with a large collar, a horizontally striped waistcoat, shirt with high collar and cravat, and buff or tan leg wear—although his lower legs aren't visible, it is likely he is wearing pantaloons (Weekley and Colwell 1987, 154). Perhaps this was his first grown-up outfit, newly made for him to wear for his portrait.

Instead of trousers, boys might wear buckskin breeches like their fathers when more sturdy garments were required. Very poor boys likely wore just trousers and shirts, perhaps with coats for warmth or for "Sunday best."

***The Westwood Children,* by Joshua Johnson, ca. 1807. The three sons of John and Margaret Westwood are, left to right, Henry, born in 1801 or 1802, George Washington, born in 1804, and John H., born in 1798. They wear nearly identical dark green skeleton suits and black boots.** Courtesy of the Board of Trustees, National Gallery of Art, gift of Edgar William and Bernice Chrysler Garbisch.

Sarah Bryant made her sons garments she called *frocks* when they were seven or eight years old (Nylander n.d.). As she put her boys into breeches very early, these must not have been children's frock-style dresses, but were rather worn over the other clothing for protection, similar to the smocks or frocks of working men. They were probably cut like oversized shirts and made of utilitarian fabrics.

UNDERGARMENTS

The infant wore several layers of undergarments. First and most essential was the diaper. At night, the baby wore a pilch over the diaper to keep the outer clothes dry. The early pilch was probably a simple square of fabric folded in half like the diaper. The fabric of choice was the same dense wool flannel that was used for men's overcoats, as it was naturally water repellent. A later version was shaped much like modern waterproof pants.

A baby also wore a shirt. It was cut like a man's shirt, but opened all the way down the front. The round neck might be trimmed with narrow lace. The elbow-length sleeves were left plain or gathered into a band. Shirts were made of fine lightweight linen, such as cambric, or, later, fine cotton muslin.

The infant often wore a long strip of fabric called a belly band or roller, wound two or three times around the body to support the navel. This might be made of wool, linen, or cotton. It is variously described as being worn next to the skin or over the shirt, where it would help to keep the shirt closed. This band was a vestige of the practice of swaddling, or wrapping the baby completely in long lengths of fabric, a practice that had virtually disappeared in the United States and western Europe by this time.

At the beginning of the period, the baby was still put into stays to encourage the development of proper

From Clouts to Diapers

Babies wore diapers before being toilet trained, as they do now. Such utilitarian textiles almost never survive, so we have to rely on other sources to give us information about their appearance. The recommended size was 22-1/2 by 45 inches, folded in half to make a square double layer (Hale 1838/2002, 29).

The recommended fabric was *diaper,* a linen or linen/cotton blend fabric with a small woven design, because this weave structure made it more absorbent. The best diaper came from Flanders, in Europe. Those who could not afford to buy new imported fabric made do with old linen sheets or tablecloths that, being softened by repeated laundering, were comfortable next to the skin. There is an 1800 reference in *The Pennsylvania Gazette* to a diaper of "old Marseilles." Marseilles was woven to look like a hand-quilted fabric and would be very absorbent. Diapers were fastened with straight pins or, more safely for the baby, with sewn-on tape ties (safety pins would not be invented until 1849).

During the Federal period, these items was not called *diapers;* that term first appeared in the United States after 1837. Through the 18th century, they were *clouts, tailclouts,* or *squares of diaper.* (Sylvia Tyler wrote in her diary on October 30, 1810, that she "washed some Clouts," no doubt for her infant son, Lewis [Tyler Diaries].) By sometime in the 19th century, they were often called *napkins,* later changed to *nappies* in Great Britain.

posture. While there are examples of small-sized fully boned stays, it seems more likely that most infant stays were very lightly boned with reeds. As a woman's stays became less rigidly constructed, so the infant's evolved into just a band, or surcingle, of firmly woven fabric, such as corded dimity or buckram, a heavily stiffened linen fabric.

An under-petticoat was the next layer. In England, the stays and petticoat might be combined into a single garment with a skirt made of wool flannel attached to a dimity top. Over this was still another layer of a second linen or cotton petticoat (*Lady's Economical Assistant,* 1808/1998, 4, 29). It is difficult to know how many children actually wore so many layers. In the United States, Mary Palmer Tyler suggested that a child wear only one petticoat, with the weight of the fabric suiting the season (1818, 24).

Toddlers traded shirts for shifts or chemises similar to those women wore while continuing to wear petticoats. In England, two petticoats, one of cotton or linen and one of wool, were suggested. This would add warmth and also provide some support for the fuller skirt in fashion in the 1780s and early 1790s.

We have seen that male toddlers began to wear new bifurcated undergarments (pantaloons or trousers) in the 19th century. Young girls also began to wear ankle-length pantaloons, showing beneath their mid-calf length skirts, early in the century. These were constructed with the two legs attached separately to a waistband and were likely part of the trend towards allowing children more freedom at play. Girls' pantaloons were regarded with some trepidation, as they were so reminiscent of male trousers, and grown women would not adopt them until later. Pantaloons, like the rest of the underwear, were made of white linen or cotton, sometimes with a simple decoration at the ankle-length hem. The young Adelia Ellender, painted by Joshua Johnson in Baltimore circa 1803–1805, wears white pantaloons with ruffles around the hems peeking out from under her gray-blue dress (Weekley and Colwill 1987, 119). When James Monroe's family returned from England in 1807, daughter Maria, who was then about four years old, wore "a short frock, that reach'd half way between her knees and ancles—under which she display'd a pair of loose pantaloons" (Ammon 1971, 279). These girls' undergarments came to be called pantalettes later in the 19th century.

After a young boy was breeched, he, like a grown man, wore a shirt as his primary undergarment. The basic cut was similar to a man's, but the boy's shirt had a distinct style of collar that folded down and was usually edged with a ruffle. A simple shirt, without the ruffled collar, may have been a young enslaved African American boy's (or girl's) only garment. Frederick Douglass remembered that, on the plantation in Talbot County, Maryland, when he was a boy:

> The children unable to work in the field had neither shoes, stockings, jackets, nor trousers, given to them; their clothing consisted of two coarse

Paper doll clothes. These are two outfits for the first commercially produced paper doll, *The History of Little Fanny,* published in 1810. On the left, a white dress with high waist, red sash, and tucked skirt is worn over pantaloons; on the right a red hooded cloak covers a dress and blue checked apron. The doll accompanied a book that told a moral tale. Courtesy of Emily Fanning and the Riversdale Historical Society.

> linen shirts per year. When these failed them, they went naked until the next allowance-day. Children from seven to ten years old, of both sexes, almost naked, might be seen at all seasons of the year. (1845/1993, 44)

OUTERWEAR

Early in the period, girls wore wool cloaks or capes, often red, like their mothers. The *Instructions for Apparel* recommended the heavy wool fabric known as "Duffeild," or duffel, of a more utilitarian gray color, as a relatively inexpensive alternative. These cloaks were not to be lined, and the edges, if the fabric tended to ravel, were to be bound with ferret, a type of woven tape (*Instructions* 1789, 12).

As the silhouette of the female dress became less full, girls, as well as women, adopted the pelisse, a front-opening outer garment with sleeves. A common fabric choice was wool; if silk was used, it might be wadded or interlined with wool batting for warmth. Like their mothers, by the early 1800s girls adopted the short jackets called spencers.

Extant examples are made of silk and nankeen cotton. Other outerwear garments were short wool or fur capes. The accessory called a tippet, also worn by women, was a long straight piece of fur, much like what is today called a boa, worn draped around the neck or shoulders. By the end of the period, the term was also used for a separate shaped fabric piece, rather like a short cape, usually worn over a coat or pelisse for extra warmth.

Boys wore greatcoats of heavy wool with multiple capes, similar to men's garments. Austin Bryant's mother made him a great coat when he was four or five, and another, of blue broadcloth, when he was six or seven (Nylander, n.d. As Austin likely outgrew them before they wore out, they were probably handed down to his two younger brothers).

ACCESSORIES

Headwear and Hairstyles

Babies wore caps, with both plain undercaps and more decorative overcaps prescribed early in the period. The *Lady's Monthly Museum* in

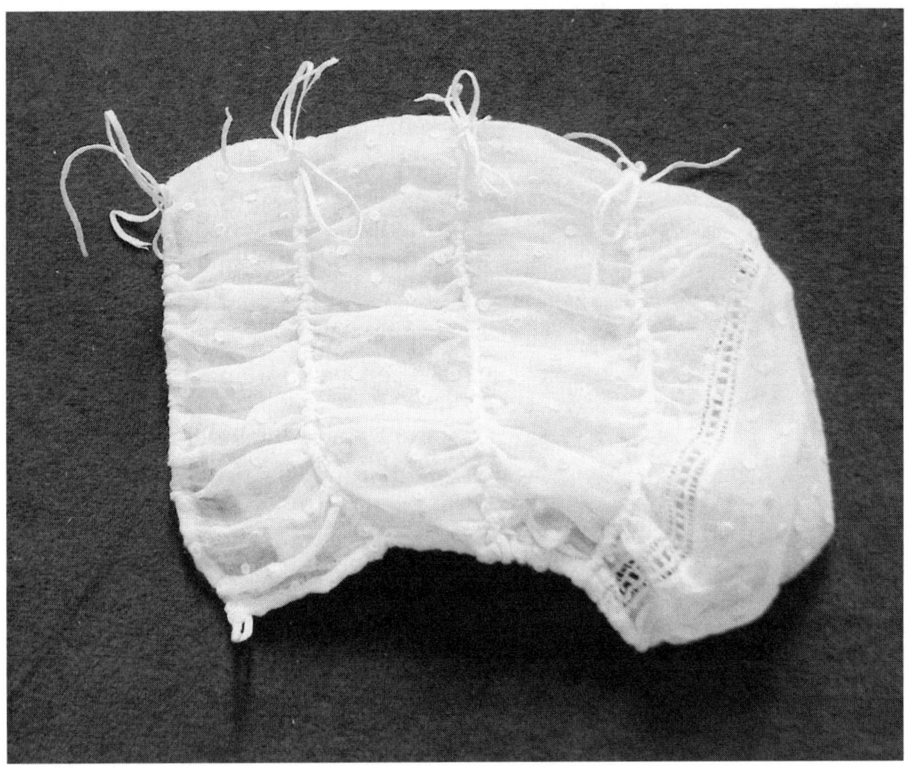

Infant's cap of white cotton mull with tamboured dots and needle lace beading, circa 1790–1800. Courtesy of American Costume Studies.

November 1799 stated, "Two caps should be put on the head till the child has got most of its teeth" (391). The two layers may have been thought to provide some extra protection for the head, much as the padded headgear called a pudding, common in the earlier 18th century, had done. Some caps were constructed with rows of drawstrings that allowed for size adjustment. The infant Hannah Williams Pitt wears such a cap, similar to her mother's, in their circa 1801 portrait by Joshua Johnson (Weekley and Colwill, 1987, 108). Caps were commonly trimmed with lace. In 1816, Rosalie Calvert asked her sister in Antwerp, a center of lace-making, to send her "16 aunes [a measurement of 45 inches] of the smallest or next smallest for children's bonnets [caps] in four different pieces and designs" (Callcott 1991, 299). Even caps for poor infants were decorated with lace; the 1789 *Instructions for Cutting Out Apparel* specified "three quarters of long lawn" for the fabric and "five yards and a half of *Hanover* lace" for trimming to make six caps; "one piece of *Hanover* lace trims six caps and six shirts" (*Instructions* 1789, 76–77; unfortunately, what was meant by *Hanover* lace has not been determined). Older girls continued to wear caps into the 1790s. These were often trimmed with a pastel ribbon to match the waist sash. Later on, toddlers and older girls generally abandoned caps and went bareheaded indoors.

***The Ragan Sisters,* by Jacob Eichholtz, 1818. Elizabeth Barbara, on the left, was about 9 and her sister Mary was about 11 in this portrait. Their straw bonnets with pink ribbons and pink and white flowers and their white dresses are nearly identical.** Courtesy of the Board of Trustees, National Gallery of Art, gift of Mrs. Cooper R. Drewry.

Toddlers of both sexes wore hats outdoors. Little boys wore broad-brimmed, low-crowned hats made of straw or felt. Some boys also wore fitted peaked caps. Early in the period, the jockey cap was fashionable. Older boys wore felt hats. By the early 1800s, these took the form of either round hats, with short crowns and wide brims, or top hats similar to men's styles. John Lewis Krimmel painted two boys in *Cherry Woman with Children,* 1813–1815. The one who can afford to buy cherries is putting them into his felt top hat, while the other (penniless) boy wears a straw top hat (Harding 1994, 77–78).

Girls of all ages wore fabric or straw hats. In the late 1780s, soft hats with very large crowns were in fashion. These resembled the oversized headgear that women were wearing. As women began to wear straw or fabric bonnets in the early 19th century, girls followed suit.

Hairstyles became more natural during the period. Boys wore their hair no longer than shoulder length. By the 1790s, girls wore their hair either long or shoulder length. If it was artificially curled, the curls were soft and loose. In the early 19th century, boys wore their hair cut short and so did girls, again following women's fashions. For example, in Cephas Thompson's circa 1805 painting, the *Girl with Dove* has very short hair and her ears are visible. Several young children painted by Joshua Johnson also had short hair. Among them are two- or three-year old Eliza White O'Donnell, three- to five-year-old Mary Ann West, and two-year-old Sarah Ann Rutter (Weekley and Colwill 1987, 11,120,122). Mary Palmer Tyler's reminder in her 1818 advice manual to comb a baby's hair regularly (28) suggests that this may not have been common practice.

Footwear

As babies wore dresses covering their feet, they were usually barefoot. The 1799 *Lady's Monthly Museum* advocated that "after six months the child may wear shoes and stockings—the shoes must be quite large enough, and broad at the toes, that the feet may not be cramped" (391). Stockings were made of linen or cotton for summer and wool for winter. The Scottish physician William Buchan suggested wool socks in cold or wet weather (1811, 54). Eliza Southgate Bowne in 1806 requested socks for her son, "I whish you to get me 3 pr. of Mr. Smith's little white worsted socks, such as I bo't for Walter, only two or three sizes larger, big enough for him next winter,—don't neglect it, for I wish for them very much. Let them be full large for a child 3 years old" (Bowne 1887/1980, 209–10). In 1811, Sylvia Tyler knitted her one-year-old son both cotton and wool stockings (Tyler Diaries). For formal occasions, boys and girls might wear silk stockings. However, in 1794, when Williamina Cadwalader went shopping for boys' stockings, she bought cotton, which she "thought satisfactory for year-round wear" and "the genteelest" available, suggesting she also thought they were suitable for all occasions. She bought 10 pairs in large, medium, and small sizes, and added that "Four pr lasts a year" (de Vallinger and Shaw 1948, 115). It seems likely that boys wore shorter socks, also called half hose, rather than long stockings, when they switched to long trousers.

Two men who did farm work as boys at the turn of the 19th century remembered wearing old cut off stocking tops over their trousers in cold weather. Daniel Drake wrote, "My equipments were a substantial suit of butternut linsey, a wool hat, a pair of mittens, and a pair of old stocking-legs, drawn down like gaiters over my shoes, to keep out the snow" (Mansfield 1855/1975, 18). Asa Sheldon wrote, "mother Parker would make me leggings from his [Mr. Parker's] old stocking legs" (Sheldon 1862/1988, 27).

Youth's shoes of dark brown or black leather with cotton lining, circa 1805–1815. These straight-lasted shoes have a split vamp with a single set of holes for the ties (the ties are modern replacements). Courtesy of American Costume Studies.

Dr. Buchan advocated shoes shaped to the feet, rather than the unshaped shoes that were common at the time (Buchan 1811, 554). Children in portraits often wear red tie-on shoes, so these must have been common, especially for younger children. A single red shoe with a wool fabric upper stitched to a leather sole exists in the collection of the Western Reserve Historical Society. For boys, shoes that buckled were replaced by ones that tied early in the period. Girls wore slippers like their mothers as they passed out of toddlerhood. Boys sometimes wore boots, especially for active sports. Like their mothers, girls may have worn ankle-length boots for walking or riding. In 1807, toddler George Ridgely wore "green sandles" with his white dimity frock and trousers (de Vallinger and Shaw 1948, 278); however, sandals do not seem to have been a common style for children.

Jewelry, Pockets, and Bibs

The red-orange gemstone coral has been regarded since ancient times as a protection against both evil spirits and disease, and children of the

Federal era often wore strands of coral beads. Many of the small children painted by Joshua Johnson wear either a string of coral beads or a necklace of coral beads with a small metal plaque in the center (Weekley and Colwill, 114, 131, 135, 142). A silver baby rattle with a coral charm was also common. The young girl identified as Emma Van Name wears a necklace of coral beads and a silver and coral rattle on a cord or chain around her neck. Infant Andrew Kennedy Long, painted about 1805, wears a similar rattle tied to a narrow green ribbon around the waist of his dress (Weekley and Colwill 1987, 128, 131).

Occasionally, other types of jewelry are mentioned or appear in paintings. The girl in *Feeding the Bird* wears coral pendant earrings with her coral necklace, as well as a bracelet of black beads and a black and gold comb (NGA 1994, #3). Miss Daggett, of Connecticut, painted circa 1795, wears a miniature portrait on a ribbon tied in a bow pinned to the neckline of her white dress (National Gallery of Art, http://www.nga.gov; artist unknown). In 1816, Mrs. Crowninshield had "been shopping all the morning with the girls. Bought them new rings with which they are much delighted" (Crowninshield 1935, 44).

Portrait of a Boy from the Taylor Family, by Rembrandt Peale, c. 1812. This boy, name and age unknown, wears a black coat and pantaloons with a black-trimmed red vest and red-trimmed black boots. His shirt has a fold-over collar with a ruffle. His black top hat and gloves lie on the floor. Courtesy of the Brooklyn Museum, New York; Gift of the Estate of Eliza Herriman Griffith.

Like their mothers, children wore tie-on pockets. While boys wore dresses, they wore pockets, too. When the small purses or handbags called reticules came into fashion for women, girls also carried them. For arm covering, babies wore long mitts that tied on above the elbow. Girls and boys would be expected to wear gloves outdoors or when dressed up. In 1800, 12-year-old Miranda Southgate was preparing to go away to school, and needed "a pair of cotton gloves to wear to school; she had 3 pairs of white mitts and I have given her another pair" (Bowne 1887/1980, 41). John Spear Smith, painted by Joshua Johnson in 1797–1798, when he was about 12 years old, holds both a pair of dark gloves and a cane

(Weekley and Colwill 1987, 99). Children wore utilitarian knitted mittens to keep them warm in the winter. In February 1816, Sylvia Tyler knitted her six-year-old son a pair (Tyler Diaries). Girls of means carried fans and fur muffs as their mothers did. Eliza Southgate Bowne sent her young sisters "two little fans" in 1803 (Bowne 1887/1980, 171).

It does not appear that mothers used bibs for their infants. While there are extant examples of fancy bibs as part of elaborate christening ensembles, especially in the 18th century, they do not seem to have been common everyday wear. Burnston (2005) observed that, because there are so few period descriptions of bibs, they probably were not regularly used.

ACQUIRING CLOTHES AND HOW MUCH IN A WARDROBE

Children's clothes were generally made at home or other family members might lovingly sew garments as gifts. In 1804, Rosalie Calvert wrote her sister, "I am sending you a little baby dress of the latest style which I made myself. I made it with pleasure, hoping it would remind you of me every time your little darling wears it" (she was in Maryland, while her sister was in Antwerp). Meanwhile, Mrs. Calvert's nieces were making "pretty little bonnets [caps] and baby frocks" for a child she was expecting herself (Callcott 1991, 100, 83).

Since most families had several children, clothes would most likely be handed down. This economical practice was made easier because children's styles did not change rapidly. In addition, as infants and toddlers of both sexes wore the same types of garments, either boys or girls could inherit a sibling's outgrown clothes. For example, Sylvia Tyler's daughter, Ruth, evidently wore hand-me-downs from her brother, Lewis. In 1814, Mrs. Tyler wrote in her diary that she "a[l]tered a striped slip for Ruth." This was probably one of the two striped slips she had made Lewis in 1812, when he was not quite two years old (Tyler Diaries).

Adult clothes could also be cut down for children: in 1795, Ann Ridgely sent her son at school a coat that her adult brother could not wear, with instructions to have a tailor remake it for him (de Vallinger and Shaw 1948, 135). Asa Sheldon, while apprenticed to farmer David Parker, described his "winter habiliments," "striped blue and white woollen trowsers, fulled cloth vest and jacket. They were commonly made of Parker's or Dave's old ones" (1862/1988, 26). In 1816, Mrs. Tyler wrote that she made her young daughter "a frock out of Hannah's" and in 1820, she made her son a "Coat out of his Pa's" (Tyler Diaries). The dark floral print boy's dress from Ohio (see above) was made around 1810 from a fabric that is dated 1775–1785. This might have been made from fabric left over from another, earlier garment, or a long-out-of-style woman's dress might have been taken apart and some of the pieces re-used.

Some details on the composition of infants' and children's wardrobes are provided in both the 1789 *Instructions for Cutting Out Apparel for the Poor* and the 1808 *Lady's Economical Assistant.* These books recommended the practice of buying fabric in quantity and cutting many garments at once, resulting in less waste. (As such bulk purchasing would be beyond the means of most poor women, this was often a charitable endeavor by the more well-to-do, and there were a number of charity sewing groups that provided clothing for the poor in the United Kingdom. It is not known how common such efforts were in the United States. Further, the 1789 book recommended that, as the daughters of poor families got older, they could sew much of the clothing themselves and learn a valuable skill in the process.)

Both of these books list the contents for a box to be provided to a poor mother as she was about to give birth. (Included are sheets and pillowcases and clothing for the mother, as well as the infant.) These suggest what was regarded as a minimum number of garments for a newborn. In 1789, the box was to include: "2 frocks, 2 bedgowns, 6 shirts, 6 caps, 6 under caps, 24 squares of double diaper [diapers], 2 robe blankets, and 2 squares of white flannel [for pilches]" (*Instructions* 1789, 85). The 1808 list was similar: "4 shirts, 4 caps, 2 frocks, 2 bedgowns, 2 flannel blankets, 2 rollers, 2 pair of stays and flannel coats [petticoats], 2 upper petticoats, and 24 napkins [diapers]" (*Lady's Economical Assistant* p. 25).

In these lists, infants had at least two of each garment. The 1789 lists for older children indicate only one of each type of garment, but it does seem that at least two sets of undergarments and two frocks or dresses would be required to allow for laundering. Evidently even children in better-off families did not have extensive wardrobes. Mrs. Crowninshield's (1935) letters to her mother suggest that, in the winter of 1815–1816, each of her girls had only two dresses, a white one for "best," and a red one for everyday.

Both Sylvia Lewis Tyler's (Tyler Diaries) and Sarah Snell Bryant's diaries (Nylander n.d.) provide some information on the number of garments they made for their children. These entries do not seem complete, and it is possible that the children received some garments from others in addition, particularly in the Bryant household, where others may have been sewing for the children. Mrs. Tyler's son, Lewis, was born September 26, 1810. Before he was born, she made a "little frock," probably for him. After his birth, she made a petticoat, a slip, a flannel slip, and a nightgown. In 1811, she made him a petticoat, two shirts, a "loosegown," a frock, two white aprons, and four slips. One of the slips was "bombasette" [bombazet], and this was evidently from the "gowns cloth for myself and Lewis" that she bought, as she first made herself a gown out of bombasette and then made his slip. On March 2, 1813, Mrs. Tyler's daughter, Ruth, was born. Later that month, she cut and "worked" a cambric frock. The "work" was probably embroidery to embellish the plain white linen garment. In May, she was again sewing a white frock (it is not possible to tell if this is the same or another one), and she finished it in June, along with a "Blue factory cloth" one. She made two more frocks later that year, for a total of four or five new frocks in all (Tyler Diaries).

Mrs. Bryant's sewing for her three oldest sons gives an idea of the size of their wardrobes from the age of breeching (see above). Each boy generally had two to four new jackets and trousers of some kind each year until age 10. The youngest of the three, Cyrus, only had one of each the year he was five. He may have been able to wear hand-me-downs that year, or someone else may have made garments for him. It does not appear, though, that the brothers were routinely wearing hand-me-downs. Perhaps they were subjecting their clothes to hard wear, as Mrs. Crowninshield wrote that her son, Francis, did, in 1816, "Does Francis wear his knees out as fast as he did?" (Crowninshield 1935, 50).

On the other hand, Sally, the oldest daughter in the Bryant family, did not have even one new frock every year. She was born in 1802 and did not have new frocks or gowns in 1806, 1809, or 1811. Of course, frocks were usually cut to allow for growth (see above) and could have been adjusted as she grew, while the boys' jackets and trousers would have been difficult to alter. And she, too, may have had clothes made by other members of the household.

References

Ammon, Harry. 1971. *James Monroe: The Quest for National Identity.* New York: McGraw-Hill.

Baumgarten, Linda. 2002. *What Clothes Reveal: The Language of Clothing in Colonial and Federal America.* Williamsburg, VA: Colonial Williamsburg Foundation; New Haven, CT: Yale University Press.

Bissonnette, Anne. 2003. *Fashion on the Ohio Frontier 1790–1840.* Kent, OH: Kent State University Museum.

Bottorff, William K., and Roy C. Flannagan, eds. 1967. "The Diary of Frances Baylor Hill of 'Hillsborough' King and Queen County Virginia (1797)." *Early American Literature Newsletter* 2 (Winter): 3–53.

Bowne, Eliza Southgate. 1887. *A Girl's Life Eighty Years Ago: Selections from the Letters of Eliza Southgate Bowne.* Repr., Williamstown, MA: Corner House Publishers, 1980.

Buchan, William. 1811. *Advice to Mothers, on the Subject of Their Own Health; and of the Means of Promoting the Health, Strength, and Beauty of Their Offspring.* Boston: Joseph Rumstead.

Burnston, Sharon Ann. 1998. *Fitting & Proper: 18th Century Clothing from the Collection of the Chester County Historical Society.* Texarkana, TX: Scurlock Publishing Co.

Burnston, Sharon Ann. 2005. "Baby Linen or How to Make a Basic Essential Layette for Eighteenth Century Re-enactor Infants," http://www.sharonburnston.com/baby_linen/index.html.

Callcott, Margaret Law, ed. 1991. *Mistress of Riversdale: the Plantation Letters of Rosalie Stier Calvert 1795–1821.* Baltimore: Johns Hopkins University Press.

Calvert, Karin. 1992. *Children in the House: The Material Culture of Early Childhood, 1600–1900.* Boston: Northeastern University Press.

Chotner, Deborah. 1992. *American Naive Paintings.* Washington, D.C.: National Gallery of Art.

Crowninshield, Francis Boardman, ed. 1935. *Letters of Mary Boardman Crowninshield 1815–1816.* Cambridge, MA: Riverside Press.

Douglass, Frederick. 1845. *Narrative of the Life of Frederick Douglass, an American Slave, Written by Himself,* ed. David W. Blight. Repr., Boston: Bedford Books, 1993.

Drinker, Elizabeth. 1994. *The Diary of Elizabeth Drinker: The Life Cycle of an 18th-Century Woman,* ed. Elaine Forman Chase. Boston: Northeastern University Press.

Ewing, Elizabeth. 1977. *History of Children's Costume.* New York: Charles Scribner's Sons.

Fennelly, Catherine. 1961. *Textiles in New England 1790–1840.* Sturbridge, MA: Old Sturbridge Village.

Fennelly, Catherine. 1966. *The Garb of Country New Englanders 1790–1840: Costumes at Old Sturbridge Village.* Sturbridge, MA: Old Sturbridge Village.

Fields, Catherine Keene, and Lisa C. Kightlinger. 1990. *"Though Inanimate They Speak": Ralph Earl Portraits in the Collection of the Litchfield Historical Society.* Litchfield, CT: The Litchfield Historical Society.

[Hale, Sarah Josepha Buell]. 1838. *Workwoman's Guide.* Repr., Easton, CT: Piper Publishing, 2002.

Harding, Annaliese. 1994. *John Lewis Krimmel: Genre Artist of the Early Republic.* Winterthur, DE: Henry Francis du Pont Winterthur Museum.

Instructions for Cutting Out Apparel for the Poor; Principally Intended for the Assistance of the Patronesses of Sunday Schools, and Other Charitable Institutions, but Useful in All Families. London: J. Walter.

Kelly, Franklin, Nicolai Cikovsky, Jr., Deborah Chotner, and John Davis. 1996. *American Paintings of the 19th Century,* Part I. Washington, D.C.: National Gallery of Art.

Kornhauser, Elizabeth Mankin. 1991. *Ralph Earl: The Face of the Young Republic.* New Haven, CT: Yale University Press.

Krimmel, John Lewis. 1812. *Fourth of July in Centre Square.* Pennsylvania Academy of Fine Arts.

Lady's Economical Assistant. 1808. Repr., Springfield, OH: Kannik's Corner, 1998.

Lady's Monthly Museum, November 1799.

Locke, John. 1692. *Some Thoughts Concerning Education.* Repr., Internet Modern History Sourcebook. New York City: Fordham University, 1997. http://www.fordham.edu/halsall/mod/1692locke-education.html.

Mansfield, Edward D. 1855. *Memoirs of the Life and Services of Daniel Drake, M.D.* Repr., New York: Arno Press, 1975.

McInnis, Maurie D. 1999. *In Pursuit of Refinement: Charlestonians Abroad, 1740–1860.* Columbia: University of South Carolina Press.

Meaders, Daniel. 1997. *Advertisements for Runaway Slaves in Virginia, 1801–1820.* New York: Garland Publishing.

Miller, Lillian B., ed. 1996. *The Peale Family: Creation of a Legacy 1770–1870.* New York: Abbeville Press.

National Gallery of Art. 1994. *Children from Another Time: American Naive Paintings.* San Francisco: Pomegranate Art Books.

Nylander, Jane. n.d. Unpublished notes taken from the Sarah Snell Bryant diaries, 1795–1836; Houghton Library, Harvard University, Cambridge, MA.

Nylander, Jane. 1998. "Everyday Life on a Berkshire County Hill Farm", in *The American Home: Material Culture, Domestic space, and Family Life.* Ed. Eleanor McD. Thompson, 95–117. Winterthur, DE: Henry Francis du Pont Winterthur Museum.

Papendiek, Charlotte Louise Henrietta. 1887. *Court and Private Life in the Time of Queen Charlotte: Being the Journals of Mrs. Papendiek, Assistant Keeper of the Wardrobe and Reader to Her Majesty.* 2 vols. London: R. Bentley & Son.

Pennsylvania Gazette. 1800. December 24.

"Proper Manner of Nursing Children." 1799. *Lady's Monthly Museum.* November.

Rose, Claire. 1989. *Children's Clothes Since 1750.* London: B. T. Batsford.

Rousseau, Jean Jacques. 1762. *Emile.* Trans. Barbara Foxley. Repr., New York City: Dutton, 1972.

Sheldon, Asa. 1862. *Yankee Drover: Being the Unpretending Life of Asa Sheldon, Farmer, Trader, and Working Man.* Repr., Hanover, NH: University Press of New England, 1988.

Thompson, Cephas. ca. 1805. *Girl with Dove.* Abby Aldrich Rockefeller Folk Art Museum, Williamsburg, VA.

[Tyler, Mary Palmer]. 1818. *The Maternal Physician; A Treatise on the Nurture and Management of Infants, from the Birth Until Two Years Old: Being the Result of Sixteen Years' Experience in the Nursery: Illustrated by Extracts from the Most approved Medical Authors.* Philadelphia: Lewis Adams.

Tyler, Sylvia Lewis. Diaries, 1801–1820, transcribed by Alden O'Brien. Acc. 2889, Americana Collection, National Society of the Daughters of the American Revolution, Washington, D.C.

de Vallinger, Leon, Jr., and Virginia E. Shaw. 1948. *A Calendar of Ridgely Family Letters 1742–1899 in the Delaware State Archives.* Vol. 1. Dover: Delaware State Archives.

Weber, Caroline. 2006. *Queen of Fashion: What Marie Antoinette Wore to the Revolution.* New York: H. Holt.

Weekley, Carolyn J., and Stiles Tuttle Colwill. 1987. *Joshua Johnson: Freeman and Early American Portrait Painter.* Baltimore: Maryland Historical Society.

Glossary: The Federal Period

aigrette: 1. A tuft of feathers. 2. A jeweled hair ornament that stands out from the head, sometimes mounted on a spring or *trembler,* so it will move when worn.

Amazone: The French term for a woman's riding *habit,* named for the mythical race of Greek female warriors.

amber: A yellow translucent fossil resin used as a gemstone.

amethyst: A light purple semi-precious gemstone.

baize: A densely woven wool fabric that has an appearance similar to felt.

bandanna: A square of cotton, silk, or blended fabric that has a pattern formed by tying areas of the fabric in a design (tie-dyeing, a type of resist dyeing) and then dyeing with the red dye madder, forming a white pattern on the red ground. The name is from the Hindustani word for the dyeing process.

bandeau: A narrow strip of fabric worn around the head, or a narrow jeweled headpiece.

banyan: A robe for informal wear, usually worn by men; the name derives from the name of Hindu traders in India, as it resembled types of garments that men wore in the Orient.

bed gown: 1. A woman's short garment, about thigh-length, mainly for working wear. 2. An infant's long garment, opening all the way down the front.

bias (true): The forty-five degree angle to the lengthwise and crosswise threads of a woven fabric. Pieces cut on the bias have more give and can therefore be close-fitting yet comfortable.

bombasette, bombazet: Worsted wool cloth resembling bombazine, which could be twill or plain weave.

bombazine: Twill weave fabric made with silk *warp* and worsted wool *weft* often dyed black for mourning.

bonnet: Structured woman's headgear, worn outdoors, that ties on the head. Different from a hat, which does not tie and usually has a brim all the way around.

bottle green: A dark green color, so called because many glass bottles, especially wine bottles, were this color.

braces: A pair of narrow strips of woven or knitted fabric or leather that fasten to the waistband of men's leg wear to keep them from sliding below the waist. Later, the strips were joined together and are today called suspenders.

breech cloth: A long strip of either wool fabric or animal skins worn by Native American men to cover the pelvic area.

breeches: Male knee-length leg wear, with a waistband, a button fall front or fly opening, and knee bands.

breeching: A rite of passage when a toddler boy is switched from wearing a dress or frock to either knee breeches or trousers, depending on what was in fashion. The age of breeching seems to have varied from just over two years old to about six years old.

brisé: A style of fan made of carved sticks, with no paper or fabric leaf.

broadcloth, cloth: A wool fabric woven on a broader loom than silk, cotton or linen fabrics. Broadcloth was at least 54 inches wide but could be wider.

brocade: A fabric with an elaborate woven pattern, often floral, created by inserting extra *filling* yarns, usually multi-colored, to make the pattern. The yarns were usually silk, and sometimes metallic yarns were incorporated into the design.

buckram: A loosely woven linen fabric heavily stiffened with a starch or sizing, often used as a supporting fabric.

bum roll: A pad, often made of cork, that tied on around the waist under the skirt to emphasize the fullness in the back, also called a *false rump.*

busk: A long, straight or curved piece of wood, metal, or whalebone inserted down the front of a corset to stiffen it and support the body. Later applied to a continuous metal hook closure down the front of a corset.

calash, calêche: A form of protective headwear, made of fabric on a frame made of cane, that can be folded flat when not in use but expands to cover a voluminous hairdo.

calico, calicoe, callico: Medium weight cotton fabric, usually a plain weave, originally from Calicut (known today as Kozhikode), in India. Calico could be dyed a solid color, printed, or have a woven checked or striped design.

calimanco: Wool fabric with a *glazed* finish.

cambric, cambrick: Fine plain-weave linen fabric.

camblet, camlet: *Glazed* wool or wool and mohair blend fabric; sometimes has a *watered* finish.

canezou: French term for a short jacket made of a lightweight fabric for summer use. A canezou is different from a spencer, which was usually made in a dark color and from a heavier fabric, such as silk velvet or wool.

cap: A close-fitting type of headwear, usually made of fine fabric or lace, worn by women and infants.

carnelian: An opaque red gemstone.

chapeau bras: A small three-cornered man's hat, so called because it was usually carried under the arm (*bras* in French) rather than worn on the head; an accessory for formal court or diplomatic attire.

chemise: In French, a man's shirt or a woman's shift. In English, used only as an alternate term for the woman's shift.

chemise gown: A dress made of full widths of fine white linen or cotton fabric shaped to the body with drawstrings. While the body had no shaping, a neckline and armholes were cut to shape and separate sleeves were set in.

chintz: Originally, a multi-colored painted or printed cotton fabric made in India, often with a glazed finish. Later applied to hand- or machine-printed imitations made in Europe.

chip: Thin strips of wood woven to shape to make a woman's hat or bonnet, a less expensive alternative to braided or plaited straw. Also called *willow.*

christening gown: The dress an infant wears to be baptized in a Christian church.

citrine: A yellow semi-precious gemstone; it resembles topaz and sometimes is misidentified as such.

clout: The square of fabric that today is called a baby's diaper in the United States. Before the use of the word "diaper" it was sometimes called a "napkin" and today is called a "nappie" in Great Britain.

clouded: An indistinct color or pattern. Often used to refer to the fabric made by the ikat, or *warp*-dyeing, process, where a pattern is dyed on the *warp* yarns before the fabric is woven, or where the pattern is printed on the warp yarns before weaving. May also refer to objects knitted with yarn of mixed colors.

cocked hat: A round hat with a broad brim, where the brim is folded up against the crown. A bicorne has the brim folded up in two places, while a tricorne, or three-cornered hat, has it folded up in three.

coral: A semi-precious gem made of the skeletons of certain marine animals, often red-orange in color.

corset: The French term for *stays.* In the 19th century, the term was applied to the foundation garments that replaced the heavily boned stays of the 18th century.

cotton: Fibers attached to the seeds of plants in the genus *Gossypium.*

cravat: A long strip of fabric, either rectangular or triangular, worn knotted around the neck, usually heavily stiffened with starch.

crape, crêpe: Lightweight, fluid silk fabric, made with highly twisted yarns to give a crinkled surface. The natural gums of the silk are not washed out, giving the fabric a different feel from other silks.

damask: Fabric with an elaborate woven pattern, usually with alternating plain and satin weave areas, and usually all one color, made of linen, wool, or cotton.

douilette: A French term for a woman's *pelisse* that is *wadded,* with an extra inner layer of wool or cotton batting for warmth.

drab: A dull, light yellowish-brown color.

drawers: Knee-length leg wear worn as an undergarment.

dress, gown: A woman's outer garment with the bodice and skirt in one piece.

duck: Heavy fabric, usually a twill weave and made of linen.

duffel, Duffield, duffle: Heavy, napped (raised fibers on the surface) woolen fabric.

English back, en fourreau: A gown with the back fitted to the body with stitched-down pleats; also called *robe à l'Anglaise.*

equipage: A set of metal articles, usually including small sewing tools, worn on a chain or pinned to the clothing as an accessory.

ferret: Woven narrow tape trim.

fiber: The raw material from which yarns are spun—the yarns are then made into fabric by weaving, knitting, or other processes. The only fibers in the Federal Era were from natural sources, and ones used primarily for clothing were *cotton, linen, silk,* and *wool.* Cotton, linen, and wool are *staple* fibers, that is, they are in short lengths that must be spun together into long yarns. Silk is a *filament* fiber, that is, the strands are very long (1,000 to 3,000 yards); however, because they are so fine, they, too, are spun together into yarns.

filling: The crosswise yarns on a loom, also called the *weft.*

flannel: Soft, spongy wool fabric, often bleached white.

flapped hat: A felt hat with a soft, rather than a stiffened, brim.

flax: A plant, *Linum usitatissimum,* that is the source for *linen* fibers. The fibers are in bundles in the stem of the plant. In processing, the fibers are separated from the woody parts of the plant. The long smooth fibers, sometimes called *line,* are woven into linen fabrics. The shorter fibers that are left are called *tow* and are spun and woven into more coarse fabrics. Plants with the fibers in bundles in the stem are called *bast* plants, and hemp is another example of a bast fiber.

fob: The pocket in a man's leg wear designed to hold a watch. In the late 19th century, the word was also used to describe the watch chain or the items hanging off of it.

frock: 1. The characteristic man's coat of the last half of the 18th century. 2. A man's oversized shirt, worn over the other clothes for protection when working, also called a *smock.* 3. An infant's or child's dress that is open all the way up the back.

fulling: The process of treating a wool fabric so that the fabric shrinks up, causing it to become more water- and wind-resistant. It was often done by agitating the fabric in hot soapy water.

fustian: Heavy, coarse fabric of linen, cotton, wool, or a blend of these fibers.

glaze: To give a textile a polished or shiny surface. It can be done mechanically, using heat and friction, or through applying a finish such as a beeswax solution.

gore: A triangular shaped piece of fabric inserted to add width, often inserted into an otherwise straight skirt to add fullness at the hem.

greatcoat, great coat: A man's or boy's long overcoat, usually made of heavily fulled wool, often with multiple shoulder capes that helped protect the wearer from the elements. Occasionally also used for a woman's man-tailored dress or coat.

gusset: A square or triangular shaped piece of fabric inserted to allow extra fullness for movement; for example, square gussets were inserted in the underarm of men's shirts and women's shifts.

habit: A woman's two-piece ensemble. Also, a woman's tailored outfit specially designed for riding horseback.

handkerchief: A large square or triangle, usually of cotton or linen, often worn by women to fill in a low neckline. They could be decorated with embroidery or printed. See also *pocket handkerchief.*

Hessians: Boots, slightly below knee length, with a heart-shaped front.

Holland: General name for linen fabrics, often denoting a high quality fabric.

hunting shirt: A man's overshirt usually with strips of the same fabric unraveled to make a fringe trim, often brown or green to blend in with a forest background; the style may have been influenced by American Indian dress and was often associated with those living on the frontier.

Hussar style: Various elaborate military-style details, such as braid and metal buttons, inspired by the heavily embellished uniforms of the 12 Hussar regiments in the French empire; usually applied to women's garments.

Italian heel: On a shoe, a small slender heel with a wedge-like extension under the instep.

jacket: 1. A waist-length man's coat. 2. A woman's fitted bodice, worn with a separate skirt. 3. A man's waistcoat or vest.

jean: Heavy, twill weave cotton fabric, often used for corsets.

jockey boots: Dark boots with a lighter lining, above knee length, but worn with the top folded down so the lining shows as a contrasting band. Also called a top boot.

kersey: Inexpensive, coarse, woolen fabric, not as finely finished as broadcloth.

latchets: On a shoe, the top front quarters extended into straps to which buckles for fastening could be attached; later, the latchets had holes for laces.

leggings: Protective leg wear that cover the calves and comes down over the tops of the shoes.

Leghorn: The anglicized name for a hat or bonnet made of high-quality braided straw, originally from the Italian city of Livorno.

linen: Fabric made from the *flax* plant.

linsey-woolsey: Fabric with both linen and wool fibers; often made with linen threads in the *warp* and wool threads in the *weft.*

livery: Suit of clothes worn by servants, usually decorated with a type of woven braid called livery lace, and often made in a family's distinctive colors.

lustring, lutestring: Thin, crisp, shiny silk fabric.

Mameluke: One of a class of warriors of the Ottoman Empire, known for being fierce fighters. Napoleon formed his own detachment of Mamelukes in France, and their uniforms, with Egyptian, Turkish, and Middle Eastern elements, inspired women's fashion.

mantua-maker: One who made women's gowns or dresses; from the term *mantua,* which was a style of loose-fitting gown popular in the early 18th century. The term continued to be used after the mantua was out of style.

Marseilles quilting, marsalla: Loom woven double cloth with an extra heavy cording *weft,* made to imitate hand quilting; named for its city of origin in France.

matchcoat: A piece of wool broadcloth, about 54 inches wide and 72 inches long, worn by Eastern Woodland Indians as an outer wrap. Also called a blanket or mantle by European Americans.

milliner: One who sold a wide range of trimmings, fabrics, and accessories, primarily for women, and also made and decorated hats and bonnets. Named for the Italian city of Milan, which had earlier been the source of many of these types of goods.

mitts: Coverings for the hands that leave the fingers and thumb bare.

mittens: Covering for the hands with one undivided portion for the fingers and a separate portion for the thumb.

moccasins: American Indian footwear made entirely from the hide of an animal, with a hide sole and no heel.

Morocco leather: Type of leather from the northwest African country of Morocco, made from goat skin, treated to show the pattern of the grain, and often dyed red.

muslin: Fine cotton fabric first made in India. Not the same as modern muslin, which is a rather coarse, often unbleached, cotton fabric. Muslin with a small printed pattern was called sprigged muslin.

nankeen: Fabric made from cotton fibers that grow a natural tan or yellow color; originally from China.

oil cloth: Fabric treated with oil or resin to make it waterproof.

open robe: A gown that is open all the way down the front, with the bodice opening filled in by a stomacher and worn with a separate petticoat underneath. An open robe may also have a bodice that meets at the front edges, but has the open skirt.

overalls: A type of long men's protective leg wear, cut like trousers but with extra pieces of fabric to cover the ankles and tops of the shoes.

oznabrig, oznaburg: Coarse linen or hemp fabric originally made in Osnabrück, Germany.

paste: An artificial gemstone made from glass or crystal, often backed with colored foil or paper.

pantaloons: Long leg wear, often knitted for a snug fit; however, sometimes pantaloons were described as loose-fitting.

parure: A matched set of several pieces of jewelry.

pattens: Wooden overshoes with raised platforms that strap onto the regular shoes to protect the feet from moisture and mud.

pelisse: A woman's long outer coat.

pelisse robe: A dress that has a button closure all the way down the front like a coat. Later sometimes called a pelisse dress.

peplum: A short skirt attached to a bodice. It could go all the way around the waist or just hang down in back.

petticoat: A skirt, often worn as the outer layer with a short bodice or jacket or under an open robe, where it would show through the split front. Sometimes called a *coat* in the 18th century. If worn as an undergarment, it would be called an *under-petticoat.*

piecing: Sewing small sections of fabric together to make a section large enough for the intended purpose.

pilch: Covering for a *clout* or diaper, often made of heavily fulled wool, which was water resistant.

pinafore: An apron with a bib that was pinned in place, worn by children to protect their clothing.

pincloth: A sleeveless apron-like overgarment worn by children to protect their clothing; later applied to an apron with a bib that was pinned in place. This type of garment was also called a *pinafore.*

plaid: Twill weave woolen fabric, often, but not always, with a woven tartan pattern—that is, one with regular stripes of color crossing at right angles.

plush: Silk pile fabric with a fuzzy surface that resembles fur.

pocket: A separate fabric sack tied around the waist under a woman's skirt, used to hold small objects.

pocket handkerchief: A small square of cotton or linen, like a modern handerchief.

pocketbook: A small folding case to hold money and other necessities; usually for men. Often made of leather or needleworked fabric.

polonaise: A style of looping up the back of the skirt of a robe or gown so it forms decorative puffs and reveals the petticoat underneath.

probate inventory: A record of a deceased person's property, often required by the county court where the person resided as part of the process of settling the person's estate. The court usually appointed two or more persons, sometimes called enumerators, who listed the items in the estate and assigned values to them.

redingote: French term, derived from "riding coat," usually designating either an overcoat or coat-like dress with a large turned-back collar and long sleeves.

reticule, ridicule: A small woman's handbag, usually with handles for carrying on the arm. Also called "indispensable."

robe à l'Anglaise: See *English back.*

robe à la Française: A gown with large, unstitched pleats that flow down the back. Also called *sack back.*

rouleau: The French term for a tube of fabric stuffed with padding, used for decoration and to add body or structure, for example, around the hem of a skirt.

roundabout, round jacket: A man's short waist length coat with tails, often worn by working men.

russel: Wool *damask.*

sack back: See *robe à la Française.*

seal: An intaglio engraved device for leaving an impression on melted sealing wax, often hung from a watch chain for decoration.

sherryvallies: Man's long protective leg wear that fastened with buttons and buttonholes all the way up the outer side seams, allowing them to be easily put on over another pair of pantaloons or trousers.

shift: A woman's undergarment, worn next to the skin, with sleeves and a round neck, usually about knee length, usually made of linen. The shape did change somewhat as the silhouette of the outer garments changed. Also called *chemise* in French and sometimes a *smock.*

short coats: A dress for a toddler that was mid-calf to ankle-length, allowing the child freedom to walk, so called because it was shorter than the infant's dress, which extended past the feet. Also called *three-quarters clothing.*

short gown: A long-sleeved bodice with a front opening and a *peplum,* cut from one piece of fabric so that the sleeves were cut in one with the bodice and there was no shoulder seam; sometimes fitted to the body with pleats or drawstrings. The front fastened with drawstrings at the neck and waist or was pinned; there were no other fastenings. The short gown was worn over a *petticoat.*

silhouette: The overall shape or outline of a garment.

silk: Long, lustrous fibers from the cocoons spun by the silkworm, the larval stage of the *Bombyx mori* moth.

skeleton suit: A boy's two piece outfit consisting of long trousers that are buttoned to a short jacket. The jacket and trousers were usually of matching fabric during the Federal period.

slip: An underdress worn under a sheer outer dress and usually cut along similar lines. It provided an opaque layer and might be flesh-toned, to suggest a nude look, or colored to match the trim on the outer dress.

slipper: A type of shoe that has no closures and little or no heel.

slops: Inexpensive ready-made clothing, often bought by sailors on port visits.

smock: 1. An oversized shirt worn by working men to protect the clothing, sometimes made with decorative stitching controlling the extra fullness around the neck and shoulders. 2. An alternate term for a woman's shift, common in rural England. 3. A child's coverall.

snail: Also called chenille, a kind of cord having short threads of silk or wool standing out at right angles from a core of thread, stitched onto garments as embellishment.

spangle: A small metal disk used as decoration; a sequin.

spencer: A short jacket worn by women or girls, usually with long sleeves, and usually made of a heavy, dark-colored fabric.

stays: Also known as a *corset.* A shaping foundation garment, made with boning encased between two layers of fabric; the plural is used because the garment was originally made in two pieces laced together in front and back.

stock: A shaped band, stiffened with whalebone or horsehair, usually black or white, worn around the neck over the shirt collar and buckled, tied, or buttoned in the back.

stroud, strouding: Type of wool *broadcloth* made in Gloucester, England, especially for trading to American Indians. It had decorative stripes in the selvages (finished woven edges) that the Indians used as decorative elements in making finished garments.

stuff: General term for *worsted* wool fabrics.

surcingle: A stiffened band placed around an infant's abdomen for support.

surtout: French term for an overcoat or *greatcoat.* It is not clear if a surtout was made differently from a greatcoat or was identical.

swaddling: (verb) Wrapping bands of fabric around an infant to prevent free movement of the limbs.

swansdown: 1. The soft warm under-plumage of the swan, used for muffs and garment trimmings. 2. Fancy wool, or wool and cotton fabric, used for men's vests.

tambour work: Decorative needlework in which a special hook is used to form chain stitches of thread that lay on the surface of the fabric; so called because the fabric was stretched tight in a hoop, resembling a tambour or drum.

tippet: 1. A long strip of fur or feathers worn around the neck and hanging down the front, much like a modern boa. 2. A short cloak, just covering the shoulders and ending at the elbow; may have been made to match a dress or in heavy wool fabric to wear over a coat for warmth in winter.

three-quarters clothing: Dress for a toddler that is mid-calf to ankle-length, also called *short coats.*

toilenette: Fabric made with a silk and cotton *warp* and wool *filling* yarns, often woven in fancy stripes and used for men's waistcoats.

tow: The short coarse fibers left from the processing of flax after the long smooth fibers (called line) have been separated out.

trousers, trowsers: Male long, usually loose-fitting, leg wear.

tuck: A stitched fold to take out length or fullness, or for decorative effect.

turban: A draped fabric headdress; in the early 19th century, the turban was often constructed permanently on a base rather than being draped with each wearing

turning: Taking a garment apart and flipping the pieces over to use the less worn and soiled inside surface as the outside.

tyer: A sleeveless coverall that ties in the back.

Vandyke: Trim with pointed edges; often refers to a neck ruffle made this way; named for the 17th century Flemish painter Anthony Vandyke or van Dyck, whose subjects often wore pointed lace trim.

Virginia cloth: Coarse fabric from yarns spun and woven in a home or plantation setting, made from cotton, or a blend of wool and cotton or *tow* and cotton.

wadded: Having an extra layer of cotton or wool batting between the outer fabric and the lining of a garment for warmth; today often called *interlined.*

waist: A woman's undergarment for the top part of the body, often made of wool for warmth.

waistcoat: The sleeveless garment, usually worn by men, over the shirt and under the outer coat, also called a vest in the United States; some earlier examples, however, may have sleeves.

warp: The lengthwise threads on a loom. Because they are under tension, they must be stronger than the *filling* or *weft* yarns.

watered: An impressed wavy design on the surface of a fabric, causing areas to reflect light differently, giving the effect that the surface is wet.

weave constructions: The *warp* and *filling* yarns on the loom may be interlaced in a variety of different ways. Below are three of the most common weave constructions. The simplest weave is the plain or tabby weave, with the *filling* going over one *warp* and under the next throughout the fabric. In the twill weave, the *filling* threads pass over two or more *warp* yarns and under one in a successive pattern that forms diagonal lines on the surface. Because this structure allows the yarns to be packed more tightly, twill weave fabrics are more durable than plain

Left to right, plain weave, twill (2×1) weave, satin weave. Drawn by the author.

weave fabrics. In the satin weave, the *warp* threads float over several *filling* threads in an irregular pattern. (Or the *filling* threads may float over the *warp* threads.) Traditionally, lustrous silk yarns were used and the luster, combined with the weave structure, created a fabric with a very smooth surface. Satin is one such fabric. (Today, yarns of lustrous synthetic filament fibers may be used instead of silk.)

weft: The crosswise threads on a loom, also called *filling.*

wool: Fibers from the fleece of the domestic sheep, *Ovis aries.*

worked: Decorated with embroidery.

worsted: Lightweight fabric made of fine quality, long wool fibers that have been combed before spinning to make them very smooth.

Portrait of Mrs. Richard Tilghman (Mary Gibson) and Sons William Gibson Tilghman and John Lloyd Tilghman, by Charles Willson Peale, 1789. Oil on canvas. A fichu, or handkerchief, fills in the neckline of Mrs. Tilghman's gown. Both boys and girls wore long white dresses and red shoes like John Lloyd's. See chapter 3, "Neckwear and Sleeves," and chapter 5, "Main Garments, Infants." Courtesy of the Maryland Historical Society.

***Mariann Woolcott,* by Ralph Earl, 1789. Oil on canvas. Miss Woolcott's white dress with full skirt and long tight sleeves is the latest fashion, as is her full curled hair. Her sash is blue, the white kid gloves have scalloped trim, and she has a dark green umbrella.** Courtesy of the Litchfield Historical Society, Litchfield, Connecticut.

Colonel Benjamin Tallmadge and Son William Tallmadge, **by Ralph Earl, 1790. Oil on canvas. This prosperous merchant wears a pale green silk coat, buff knee breeches, a white embroidered waistcoat, and silk stockings with clocks. His own hair or wig is powdered. Five-year-old William wears a dark green skeleton suit with his hair loose and flowing.** Courtesy of the Litchfield Historical Society, Litchfield, Connecticut.

The Squire's Door, **by Benjamin Duterreau after a painting by George Morland, 1790. Stiple-engraving. The English squire's lady wears a tailored redingote, masculine-inspired top hat, and brown leather gloves. See chapter 3, "Outerwear."** Collection of the author.

Fashion Plate #1272, ***Journal des Dames et des Modes,*** **November 25, 1812. "Costume Parisien/ Spangled velvet hat. Merino redingote trimmed with silk plush." American women used fashion illustrations like these for inspiration to create their own fashionable garments. See chapter 3, sidebar "'Curious, & Entertaining, & Astonishing'—Fashion Plates."** Collection of the author.

Columbia teaching John Bull his new lesson, **S Kennedy, del.; Wm Charles, Sculp., 1813. The United States, as Columbia, asks for respect from England, as John Bull, a personification for England in caricatures, while France, as Napoleon, looks on. Columbia holds a Phrygian cap, a symbol of liberty to the ancient Romans adopted by American and French revolutionaries. See chapter 1, "James Madison's Administration and the War of 1812."** Courtesy of Library of Congress.

***Woman Wearing a Bonnet and Shawl,* watercolor on paper, by Anna Maria von Phul, 1817. Miss von Phul painted scenes of life in Saint Louis, Missouri, including this woman wearing a straw bonnet and brown shawl with her white dress.** Courtesy Missouri Historical Society.

Portrait of Mrs. Thomas Everette (Rebecca Myring) and Her Children, by Joshua Johnson, 1818. Oil on canvas. Thomas Everette, a successful Baltimore merchant, died shortly before this family portrait was painted, and all but the two youngest family members are dressed in mourning. See chapter 3, "Rites of Passage—Attire for Weddings, Maternity Wear, and Mourning, Mourning." Courtesy of the Maryland Historical Society, gift of Miss M. Augusta Clarke.

The elongated waistline of 1840s women's fashion is shown in this plate from *Graham's Magazine,* dated 1841. Courtesy The New York Public Library.

Identified as "Americanised Paris Fashions" from *Godey's Lady's Book* of 1848, the silhouettes of both women's and girls' fashion are similar. Courtesy The New York Public Library.

An elaborate ball dress, illustrated in an 1857 issue of *Harper's Magazine*.

Resource Guide: The Federal Period

PRINT RESOURCES

Arnold, Janet. 1977. *Patterns of Fashion 1: Englishwomen's Dresses & Their Construction c. 1660–1860.* New York: Drama Book Publishers.

Barratt, Carrie Rebora, and Ellen G. Miles. 2004. *Gilbert Stuart.* New York: The Metropolitan Museum of Art.

Bassett, Lynne Zacek. 2001. *Textiles for Clothing of the Early Republic, 1800–1850: A Workbook of Swatches and Information.* Arlington VA: Q Graphics Production Company.

Baumgarten, Linda. 2002. *What Clothes Reveal: The Language of Clothing in Colonial and Federal America.* Williamsburg VA: Colonial Williamsburg Foundation; New Haven CT: Yale University Press.

Baumgarten, Linda, John Watson, and Florine Carr. 1999. *Costume Close-Up: Clothing Construction and Pattern 1750–1790.* Williamsburg, VA: Colonial Williamsburg Foundation; New York: Quite Specific Media Group.

Bissonnette, Anne. 2003. *Fashion on the Ohio Frontier 1790–1840.* Kent OH: Kent State University Museum.

Brown, William L. III. 1999. *Thoughts on Men's Shirts in America 1750–1900.* Gettysburg, PA: Thomas Publications.

Burnston, Sharon Ann. 1998. *Fitting & Proper: 18th Century Clothing from the Collection of the Chester County Historical Society.* Texarkana TX: Scurlock Publishing Co.

Cumming, Valerie. 1998. *The Visual History of Costume Accessories.* New York: Costume & Fashion Press.

Fales, Martha Gandy. 1995. *Jewelry in America 1600–1900.* Woodbridge, U.K.: Antique Collectors' Club.

Gehret, Ellen J. 1976. *Rural Pennsylvania Clothing.* York PA: George Shumway.

Harding, Annaliese. 1994. *John Lewis Krimmel: Genre Artist of the Early Republic.* Winterthur, DE: Henry Francis du Pont Winterthur Museum.

Hersh, Tandy, and Charles Hersh. 1995. *Cloth and Costume 1750–1800 Cumberland County, Pennsylvania.* Carlisle, PA: Cumberland County Historical Society.

Kornhauser, Elizabeth Mankin. 1991. *Ralph Earl: The Face of the Young Republic.* New Haven, CT: Yale University Press.

Kyoto Costume Institute. 1990. *Revolution in Fashion: European Clothing, 1715–1815.* New York: Abbeville Press.

Lady's Economical Assistant. 1808. Repr., Springfield, OH: Kannik's Corner, 1998.

Low, Betty-Bright P. 1974. "Of Muslins and Merveilleuses: Excerpts from the Letters of Josephine du Pont and Margaret Manigault." *Winterthur Portfolio* 9: 29–75.

McMurry, Elsie Frost. 2001. *American Dresses 1780–1900 Identification & Significance of 148 Extant Dresses.* CD-ROM. Ithaca, NY: Cornell University.

Mackenzie, Althea. 2004. *Hats and Bonnets.* London: The National Trust.

Miller, Lillian B., ed. 1996. *The Peale Family: Creation of a Legacy 1770–1870.* New York: Abbeville Press.

Miller, Marla R. 2006. *The Needle's Eye: Women and Work in the Age of Revolution.* Amherst: University of Massachusetts Press.

Montgomery, Florence. 1984. *Textiles in America 1650–1870.* New York: W. W. Norton & Company.

Moore, Robert J., Jr., and Michael Haynes. 2003. *Tailor Made, Trail Worn: Army Life, Clothing & Weapons of the Corps of Discovery.* Helena MT: Farcountry Press.

Moulton, Gary E., ed. 1983. *The Journals of the Lewis and Clark Expedition.* 13 vols. Lincoln: University of Nebraska Press.

Nylander, Jane. 1993. *Our Own Snug Fireside: Images of the New England Home 1760–1860.* New Haven, CT: Yale University Press.

Nylander, Jane. 1998. "Everyday Life on a Berkshire County Hill Farm," in *The American Home: Material Culture, Domestic Space, and Family Life,* ed. Eleanor McD. Thompson, 95–117. Winterthur, DE: Henry Francis du Pont Winterthur Museum.

Pineault, Louisa. 2002. *A Compilation & Index of British Fashion Plate Descriptions: 1798–1819.* CD-ROM.

Pineault, Louisa. 2003. *French Fashions 1799–1820.* CD-ROM.

Queen, Sally, and Vicki L. Berger, eds. 2006. *Clothing and Textile Collections in the United States: a CSA Guide.* Lubbock: Texas Tech University Press.

Rexford, Nancy. 2000. *Women's Shoes in America, 1795–1930.* Kent, OH: Kent State University Press.

Ribeiro, Aileen. 1988. *Fashion in the French Revolution.* London: B. T. Batsford, Ltd.

Rothstein, Natalie, ed. 1987. *A Lady of Fashion: Barbara Johnson's Album of Styles and Fabrics.* New York: Thames and Hudson.

Ryan, Thomas R., ed. 2003. *The Worlds of Jacob Eichholtz, Portrait Painter of the Early Republic.* Lancaster, PA: Lancaster County Historical Society.

Shep, R. L. 1998. *Federalist & Regency Costume: 1790–1819.* Mendocino CA: R. L. Shep.

Weekley, Carolyn J., and Stiles Tuttle Colwill. 1987. *Joshua Johnson: Freeman and Early American Portrait Painter.* Baltimore: Maryland Historical Society.

White, Carolyn. 2005. *American Artifacts of Personal Adornment 1680–1820, a Guide to Identification and Interpretation.* Lanham, MD: Altamira Press.

Wright, Meredith. 1990. *Everyday Dress of Rural America, 1783–1800.* New York: Dover Publications.

MUSEUMS, ORGANIZATIONS, AND USEFUL WEB SITES

Colonial Williamsburg
PO Box 1776
Williamsburg, VA 23187-1776
1-800-HISTORY
www.history.org

While the Historic Area is interpreted in the Colonial period, the collection of artifacts includes objects through the 19th century, and some of these are periodically featured in exhibits at the DeWitt Wallace Decorative Arts Museum and in Colonial Williamsburg publications.

Daughters of the American Revolution Museum
1776 D Street, NW
Washington D.C. 20006
202-628-1776
www.dar.org/museum/

Exhibits and programs periodically feature items from the DAR's extensive collection of American clothing. The Web site has highlights of past exhibits that include clothing. Qualified scholars may contact the costume curator for special appointments to view items in the collection.

Historic Deerfield
PO Box 321
84B Old Main Street
Deerfield, MA 01342
413-775-7214
http://www.historic-deerfield.org/

The museum includes 13 houses built between 1730 and 1850. Items from the collection are on view in the houses and in rotating exhibits in the Flynt Center of Early New England Life, which also features items on view in visible storage in the Museum Attic.

A searchable database of objects from Deerfield and other museums in western Massachusetts is at http://museums.fivecolleges.edu/

Kent State University Museum
PO Box 5190
Rockwell Hall
Kent, OH 44242-0001
330-672-3450
www.kent.edu/museum

The Kent State Museum contains important collections of fashion and decorative arts that are featured in rotating exhibits. The online "Visual Dictionary of Fashion" features clothing from the collection including items from 1800 to 1829. The Web site also has highlights of past exhibitions that included clothing items from the Federal era. Interested researchers may request an appointment to visit the collection.

Los Angeles County Museum of Art
5905 Wilshire Blvd.
Los Angeles, CA 90036
1-323-857-6000
www.lacma.org
http://collectionsonline.lacma.org

At press time, the Costume and Textiles permanent collection was temporarily not on view.

The Costume and Textiles section on the Collections On-Line feature a large assortment of early 19th century fashion plates.

Metropolitan Museum of Art
1000 Fifth Ave. at 82nd St.
New York City, NY 10028-7710
212-535-7710
www.metmuseum.org

The Costume Institute houses one of the preeminent collections of costume in the world. Rotating exhibits are mounted in the Costume Institute's gallery space within the museum and are often accompanied by informative printed catalogues. However, at press time, the Costume Institute is closed for several years to conduct a survey to address conservation and storage issues.

The on-line Works of Art Collection Database includes a section for the Costume Institute that features several Federal-era garments. The large collection of American portraits can be helpful in the study of dress and fashion.

Missouri History Museum
Lindell Blvd. and DeBaliviere Ave. in Forest Park
PO Box 11940
St. Louis, MO 63112
314-746-4599
www.mohistory.org

The museum has clothing items from the late 18th and early 19th centuries with an emphasis on objects that document everyday life, as well as special occasions, in and around St. Louis. The library and research center are in a separate location, and researchers may access the collection by appointment.

Museum of Fine Arts, Boston
Avenue of the Arts
465 Huntington Avenue
Boston, MA 02115-5597
617-267-9300
www.mfa.org

The museum has an outstanding collection of textile and fashion arts, and objects are featured in period exhibits. The online collection database has interactive exhibits and provides access to photographs of many objects in the collection.

National Society of the Colonial Dames of America
William Hickling Prescott House
55 Beacon Street
Boston MA 02108
617-742-3190
http://www.nscda.org/ma/william_hickling_prescott_house.htm

This is one of several properties around the country owned by the National Society of the Colonial Dames of America. The Federal era house houses extensive collections of furniture and the decorative arts. The costume collection has items dating from the 18th through the 20th centuries. Selections are on continuous display, and the collection is available to researchers by appointment.

Old Sturbridge Village
1 Old Sturbridge Village Road
Sturbridge, MA 01566
1-800-733-1830
www.osv.org

Old Sturbridge Village re-creates a New England country town of the 1830s. However, the collection encompasses items from 1790 to 1840, thus including the Federal period. The gallery has rotating exhibits that may incorporate clothing items. The searchable online collection includes 423 clothing and textile items.

The Smithsonian Institution
National Museum of American History
Kenneth E. Behring Center
14th Street and Constitution Ave., NW
Washington D.C.
202-633-1000
www.americanhistory.si.edu

The museum, newly re-opened in fall 2008, features a re-installed exhibit on the First Ladies. The online collection includes a group of women's dresses with some from the Federal era, as well as early American items in "History Wired."

OTHER USEFUL WEB SITES

The Costumer's Manifesto: Regency and Empire Fashion Costume Links. Ed. Tara Maginnis. http://www.costumes.org/history/100pages/regencylinks.htm
Individual Web sites change frequently. This site seems to keep most links up to date.

Digital Gallery. New York Public Library.
http://digitalgallery.nypl.org/nypldigital/index.cfm
Searchable database includes English and French fashion plates from the early 19th century.

Fashion Plate Collection. University of Washington Libraries, Digital Collections.
http://content.lib.washington.edu/costumehistweb/
Searchable database includes plates from Empire (1806–1813), Georgian (1806–1836), and Regency (1811–1820) periods.

The Regency Fashion Page. Ed. Catherine Decker.
http://locutus.ucr.edu/~cathy/reg3.html
http://regencyfashion.org/ (In progress)
As the name indicates, this site features primarily British sources from 1790 to 1829. A wide variety of primary source materials are posted on the site and others are linked. At press time, Dr. Decker was in the process of moving the page contents to the regencyfashion.org site.

FILMS

The Works of Jane Austen

There have been many film and television adaptations of Jane Austen's novels through the years. The following are among the best for representations of early 19th century fashions. Though the novels are set in England, the fashions are for the most part true of middle class and wealthy people in the United States of the same period.

Emma, DVD. 1996. Directed by Douglas McGrath. Distributed by Miramax. Rated PG.

Persuasion, DVD. 1995. Directed by Roger Michell. Distributed by Sony Pictures. Rated PG.

Pride and Prejudice (mini series), DVD. 1996. Directed by Simon Langton. Distributed by Image Entertainment. Not rated.

Sense and Sensibility, DVD. 1995. Directed by Ang Lee. Distributed by Sony Pictures. Rated PG.

OTHER PERIOD FILMS

Affair of the Necklace, DVD. 2002. Directed by Charles Shyer. Distributed by Warner Home Video. Rated R. Based on the true story of a plot to implicate Queen Marie Antoinette in pre-revolutionary France.

Amazing Grace, DVD. 2006. Directed by Michael Apted. Distributed by Fox Home Entertainment and Bristol Bay Productions. Rated PG. Recounts William Wilburforce's crusade to outlaw slavery in the British Empire.

Hornblower, 8 episodes. DVD. 1998–2003. Directed by Andrew Grieve. Distributed by A & E Home Video. Not rated. Based on the C.S. Forester books that track the career of a British naval officer through the wars with France in the late 18th and early 19th centuries.

Jefferson in Paris, DVD. 1995. Directed by James Ivory. Distributed by Walt Disney Video. Rated PG-13. Chronicles Thomas Jefferson's years as the American minister to France on the eve of the French revolution.

John Adams (miniseries), DVD. 2008. Directed by Tom Hooper. Distributed by HBO Films. Not rated. Traces the career of John Adams from the Colonial era through the early Federal era, including his term as the second president.

Scarlet Pimpernel (6 episodes), DVD. 1999. Directed by Edward Bennett, Simon Langton, Patrick Lau, Graham Theakston. Distributed by A & E Home Video. Not rated. Based on the early 20th century play and novel by Baroness Emuska Orczy about British fop Sir Percy Blakeney, who, in his secret identity as the Scarlet Pimpernel, saves victims of the French Reign of Terror.

About the Author

ANN BUERMANN WASS has a PhD in costume and textile history from the University of Maryland and is the historian at Riversdale, a Federal era house museum, where she coordinates programs and exhibits. She has lectured on a wide variety of topics as well as presenting juried papers and research exhibits and is a member of the Costume Society of America.

PART TWO

The Antebellum Era, 1821–1860

Michelle Webb Fandrich

Introduction

It is difficult to discuss antebellum America, America before the Civil War, without certain images coming to mind. Patriotic revolutionary war heroes and statesmen dressed in the elegance of a bygone era. The sweeping veranda of the southern plantation, its dainty mistress dressed in silks and laces with a bell-shaped skirt swaying gently as she walks may come to mind. Or images of the dungaree-wearing millionaires who struck it rich in the early days of the gold rush might be entertained. These often romanticized views of pre-Civil War United States must be balanced with the realities most Americans faced during this period. The United States was at war with itself long before the war began. The federalist views of the early political climate were being challenged by advocates for states-rights. The labor that built the elegant southern plantations was provided by those forced to work against their will, enslaved African Americans who were treated as property and stripped of their rights as human beings. The successes of the gold rush were shared among the few, not the many.

This period in America saw the transformation of a series of colonies into a nation. But even as concepts of nationalism were being forged, the political and philosophical differences of the American people began to tear the country apart. Economic strains, rising immigration, the growing cause of abolitionism—these would all play a part in stoking the growing storm of war.

As America began to carve out its national identity, so too did fashion seek out a style that would be uniquely American. Though a truly American style was nearly a century away from being created, many of the instruments that would help shape this American look were put in place during the antebellum period. The ready-made garment industry rose to prominence during this time, with the majority of men's and boys' clothing being mass-produced. Fashion periodicals with an American slant were put into circulation starting in the 1830s. Although Paris and London would continue to call the shots until World War II, New York had secured its place as a capitol of fashion by the end of the era. The antebellum period saw a number of innovations in the area of dress, for both sexes, but these are frequently overlooked by the casual observer. The student of fashion must delve deeper to better understand this period and the silhouettes that shaped the dress of its people.

For many, a discussion of antebellum fashion centers around only one silhouette—the large, bell-shaped hoopskirt. So much attention is paid to this silhouette probably due to its almost inhuman proportions. Spectacular stories of women burned alive or nearly so due to the sheer circumference of their skirts and their unknowing proximity to open flame help to draw further attention to this fashion oddity. It is perhaps unfortunate that the hoopskirt, or more properly, the crinoline silhouette, commands the spotlight of antebellum fashion history for the general population. In fact, the Antebellum Era in American fashion saw very little of the crinoline as it was only introduced in the last four years of the period. The majority of the era was consumed by fashion's forward motion into the fast-paced phenomenon contemporary observers will recognize as modern fashion. The silhouettes that preceded the crinoline were no less spectacular in their attempts to mold and reshape the human form. While women's fashions were changing with greater rapidity, men's clothing became more static, with only subtle changes to distinguish one decade from the next, and indeed, one class from another.

In this volume, the dress of Americans is defined in terms of what was worn by individuals across the economic and class spectrum. Primary sources such as extant objects with well-documented American provenances were used to form the base of opinion about what was worn and by whom. Printed materials of the period, from fashion periodicals to social commentary, provided the context in which to view these objects. With an encyclopedic intent, this volume is also built upon the research of others. For the purposes of this volume, the antebellum period in America is defined as spanning from 1820 to 1860, however, fashion is rarely insular. The effects of styles of preceding years are felt and seen—this is reflected in the text when necessary.

This work is by no means a complete reflection of life in the Antebellum Era. The information about the politics, economics and other aspects of American life is provided to serve as a backdrop to the fashions discussed in this volume. Just as fashion is rarely not self-reflective, it also rarely exists without influence by the culture in which it is worn. Instances where politics or economics played a very significant role in the shaping of fashion have received particular attention, as have those in which fashion has played a role in shaping the political or economical history of the country during this period.

Like Part 1, Part 2 presents a timeline highlighting significant historical dates, in order to put the clothing history into more context. Chapter 6 provides a brief overview of the political and economic history of the country during the antebellum period. Chapter 7 discusses social and cultural events that influenced how Americans dressed. Chapter 8 surveys women's fashions, including different social classes and people; and chapter 9, men's fashions, also with consideration of all social classes, urban and rural inhabitants, enslaved African Americans, and American Indians. Chapter 10 discusses children's fashions. Illustrations provide visual images of many of the styles of clothing of the era. A glossary defines unfamiliar terms. The resource guide includes not only books, but also museum collections and Web sites where the reader can look for further information, and a list of films featuring authentic clothing of the period.

Acknowledgments

The writing of history should never be a solitary pursuit. Along the way, fellow travelers are met and ideas are exchanged. I thank Barbara C. Cox and Myra Walker for helping me take my first steps into the field of costume history and Heather Vaughan for starting me on the journey of this book. As I prepared to write, the ever helpful and accommodating staff of the Los Angeles County Museum of Art's Department of Costume and Textiles made research in their collection and archives a pleasure. This book would not have been possible without the guidance and support of others such as Ann B. Wass, Mary-Beth Brophy, Brigette Ginter, Melinda Webber Kerstein, and Kaye Spilker. Above all, I'd like to thank the editor, Anne Thompson, and Chris and Xander for their patience and understanding as I completed this manuscript.

Timeline

THE ANTEBELLUM ERA, 1821–1860

1812 War erupts between United States and Britain.

1817 James Monroe is elected President. Mississippi is admitted to the United States. New York state legislature decrees that all slaves be emancipated by July 4, 1827. The New York Stock Exchange is founded.

1818 The first American sewing machine is invented by John A. Doge and John Knowles. Illinois is admitted to the United States.

1819 The Panic of 1819 begins.

1820 The Missouri Compromise is enacted. Alabama is admitted to the United States, Maine is admitted to the United States as a free state.

1821 Missouri is admitted to the United States as a slave state.

1823 The Monroe Doctrine announces that the Western hemisphere is no longer open to colonization. Water-powered equipment is used in Massachusetts cotton mills to produce cloth.

1825 John Quincy Adams is elected President.

1828 The "Tariff of Abominations" is enacted on all imports.

1829 Andrew Jackson is elected President.

1830 *Godey's Lady Book* begins publication and distribution in the United States, becoming the first American fashion magazine. The first fully functional sewing machine is produced in France by Barthelemy Thimonnier.

1831 The first national conventions are held by political parties to select a presidential candidate (the Antimason party would lead the way).

1832 The Nullification Crisis of 1832 begins.

1834 A hand-cranked sewing machine is produced by American Walter Hunt.

1836 Arkansas is admitted to the United States as a slave state.

1837 Martin Van Buren is elected President. The Panic of 1837, a general economic depression, begins. William Proctor and James Gamble form a partnership to make soap, marking the first instance of a mass consumer product replacing one that was formerly made within the home. Michigan is admitted to the United States as a free state.

1838 The Underground Railroad is developed to transport slaves to free states.

1839 Daguerre announces he has invented a method for making photographic images.

1840 William Henry Harrison wins the presidential election.

1841 John Tyler becomes president when William Henry Harrison suddenly dies.

1842 *Peterson's* magazine begins publication and distribution, becoming the 2nd American fashion magazine.

1845 James K. Polk is elected President. Texas and Florida are admitted to the United States as slave states.

1846 Elias Howe patents the lock stitch sewing machine. Iowa is admitted to the United States as a free state.

1847 The immigration of Irish amounts to over 100,000 in a single year following the Potato Famine of 1845.

1848 The first Women's Rights Convention is held in Seneca Falls, NY. Wisconsin is admitted to the United States as a free state.

1849 Zachary Taylor is elected President. The Gold Rush begins with the discovery of gold at Sutter's Mill in California.

A cholera epidemic spreads throughout the southern United States.

1850 California is admitted to the United States as a free state. The Compromise of 1850 is enacted.

1851 Isaac M. Singer patents the continuous stitch sewing machine. The "Bloomer Costume" is published in *The Lily,* reflecting the growing Dress Reform Movement.

1852 Franklin Pierce wins the presidential election. Harriet Beecher Stowe publishes *Uncle Tom's Cabin.*

1857 James Buchanan is elected president. Cage crinoline is introduced. The Panic of 1857 begins. The Dred Scott decision is made.

1858 The leather sewing machine is patented by Lyman Blake, increasing the ease and speed with which shoes can be manufactured. Minnesota is admitted to the United States. The Lincoln-Douglas debates take place.

1859 Cotton production reaches nearly two billion pounds a year in the United States. Oregon is admitted to the United States. The Harpers Ferry Raid occurs.

1860 Abraham Lincoln wins the presidential election. South Carolina secedes from the Union, starting the secessionist trend. Charles Frederick Worth begins working with Empress Eugenie.

1861 Kansas is admitted to the United States. Civil War begins with the first major battle at Bull Run in Manassas, Virginia.

CHAPTER 6

The United States in the Antebellum Era

> Scarlett O'Hara was not beautiful, but men seldom realized it...Her new green flowered-muslin dress spread its twelve yards of billowing material over her hoops and exactly matched the flat-heeled green morocco slippers her father had recently brought her from Atlanta. The dress set off to perfection the seventeen-inch waist, the smallest in three counties, and the basque showed breasts well matured for her sixteen years. But for all the modesty of her spreading skirts, the demureness of hair netted smoothly into a chignon and the quietness of small white hands folded in her lap, her true self was poorly concealed. The green eyes in the carefully sweet face were turbulent, willful, lusty with life, distinctly in variance with her decorous demeanor.
>
> —Excerpted from *Gone with the Wind,* originally published in 1936 (Mitchell 2007, 25)

It is only fitting that Margaret Mitchell would use the language of fashion to help describe the variances in outward and inward character of her antebellum heroine in *Gone with the Wind,* her Pulitzer Prize–winning novel of 1936. In many ways, her description exemplifies the romantic view taken by many in the 20th century of the clothing, as well as the people, of the antebellum period. From the material of Scarlett's gown to the body on which it was worn, we are presented with an idealized southern lady in the years immediately preceding the Civil War. We are even presented with a picture of how and where Mitchell thought fine clothing would have been bought by the upper classes in the South during this period. It is not from Paris or even London that Scarlett's perfectly matched slippers were bought but from Atlanta, one of the most metropolitan cities in the south. A description of Scarlett's ensemble is aptly used by Mitchell to place her within the correct social strata of the world in which she lived. The wealth and prominence of her family is broadcast for future suitors through the quality, type and amount of material used for the construction of her gown for a day of picnicking on the family's plantation. All of these details paint a picture of a paradoxically proper yet rebellious young lady of the Antebellum Era.

For many people, whether from the North or the South, a discussion of the Antebellum Era conjures just these kinds of images of a genteel age in America's history, a time before the push of industry changed the face of America's communities and lifestyles. In *Gone with the Wind,* Mitchell takes us back to the age of lordly plantation owners and southern society before the Civil War, projected, of course, through the romanticized vision of a southerner. Upon further examination, however, the reality of life and, indeed, the clothing worn in the Antebellum Era is hardly as romantic as Margaret Mitchell and so many others have envisioned. The clothing worn by antebellum Americans was shaped by geography, politics, social movements, invention, industry, and religion. In order to understand the fashion of the Antebellum Era, it is important to first set it in its proper context.

EXPANSION AND CONFLICT

Economic, Geographic, Political, Social, and Technological Issues in 1820–1860

Between 1820 and 1860, the United States experienced the growing pains common to any young nation. After all, its collection of states and territories resembled what might be referred to more as a third-world country today than a fully formed nation. Having finally won complete independence from the British in 1783, America was witness to a period of great growth and change during the Federal Era. The period after the Federal Era but before the Civil War has been defined by later historians as the Antebellum Era, taking its name from the Latin *ante bellum* meaning "before the war." This name serves to emphasize the place of these four decades within American history as more of a precursor to the Civil War than a period unto itself. Ultimately, the years that make up this antebellum period, 1820–1860, were witness to so much more than the growing unrest between the North and South, which would lead to the greatest schism in American history.

The United States was once a series of 13 colonies clinging to 900,000 square miles along the coast of the Atlantic Ocean. By the end of the Antebellum Era, it became a nation of 31 states covering almost three million miles, reaching to both the Pacific Ocean and the Gulf of Mexico. Alongside this expansion, the population grew as well, with as few as four million residents immediately following the Revolutionary War blossoming into nearly 23 million by 1850. A rise in birth rates and decrease in infant mortality led, in part, to this increase. By 1820, the population had increased by nearly 100 percent, with 80 percent of this increase the product of native births (Johnson 1999). An influx of immigrants from European countries such as Ireland, Germany, Great Britain, and others was also at the root of this surge in population (Volo and Volo 2004). By 1850, nearly 1 in every 10 Americans was foreign-born.

The growing nation was faced with issues such as how to provide services to its citizens, including protection, public health and resources such as water. The creation and funding of a public education system became essential to the development of literacy among its growing populace. With the push for industrialization that would follow, antebellum America would also define decent labor conditions as well as help to resolve land conflicts between the growing populace and indigenous populations (Howe 2007). The Antebellum Era was a time in which the nation would experience rapid development—geographically, politically, and, with its first baby steps towards an industrialized economy, technologically—as well as great internal conflict.

A Nation Dividing: The Growing Conflict Between North and South

At the heart of the Antebellum Era was the growing conflict between America's northern and southern populations just as the nation was beginning to create concepts of its identity. Though the term "nationalism" was not in full usage until sometime in the 1830s, concepts of a national identity were already forming before the beginning of the Antebellum Era. Celebrations of national festivals such as the Fourth of July as well as international policies formed following the War of 1812 helped to shape the identity of the growing nation as a whole (Howe 2007). However, the United States was hardly as unified in character as this nationalistic intention might imply. As the nation grew through westward expansion, migrating populations from the South and the North would begin to settle together in communities, where their cultural differences, both real and imagined, would be shown in the greatest contrast. In his history of Illinois published in 1857, Thomas Ford records a contemporary settler's observation regarding the tense relationship between the two populations: "Southerners believed the 'Yankee was a close, miserly, dishonest, selfish getter of money, void of generosity, hospitality, or any of the kindlier feelings of human nature'; northerners saw the [southerner] as 'a long, lank, lean, and ignorant animal, but little in advance of the savage state; one who was content to squat in a log-cabin, with a large family of ill-fed and ill-clothed, idle, ignorant children.'" (Howe 2007, 139). These contemporary opinions, as negative and overblown as they may seem, would have been based on some very real differences in the way northerners and southerners approached their day.

In the North, a growing industrial economy encouraged more men to work outside of the home, seeking an hourly wage and allowing their days to be governed by the clock. A day's work was consistently begun at the same time each day and typically ended between 12 and 14 hours later. This governance by the clock was at odds with the Southern manner of organization. Life in the South was centered on the passage of the seasons, not the hands of a clock. Labor was primarily performed by slaves or, in some cases, free white men who were paid on a per-task basis. Visitors from the North often marveled at the manner in which the southern economy was run. In a letter dating to the 1850s, Emily Burke, a Northern woman working as a teacher in the South stood in wonder as she observed the amount of labor that went into the harvesting and packing of cotton, which was then sold at a staggeringly low price. "In packing the cotton, the sack is suspended from strong spikes, and while one colored person stands in it to tread the cotton down, others throw it into the sack. I have often wondered how the cotton could be sold so cheap when it required so much labor to get it ready for the market, and certainly it could not be if all their help was hired at the rate of northern labor" (Burke 2003, 199). With agriculture the primary form of enterprise in this region, it was only natural to continue in a lifestyle dictated by the needs of the crops they planted and harvested each season. And with the need to keep prices low and competitive, slave labor was seen as a necessity to remain in competition with overseas markets.

Most historians note that the South was bound to folk traditions and this is partly true. It was also a society built on a hierarchical social structure with plantation owners at the top, followed by the working classes with the slave class at the bottom. It can be seen as a culture that, in many ways, was the antithesis of the "American dream." The planter class arrived at their station largely through birth, not necessarily by individual industry. This class liked to present itself as an aristocratic people, with a lineage tracing back to the European aristocracy. More often than not, this was not the case. In fact, many of the South's social elite were mere *parvenus,* having only recently acquired their aristocratic pretensions upon arriving on American soil. People of little means or social ties in the South had little hope of rising up in this society, which was based on artificial hierarchies. It was only the select few, namely white males, who could rise up through their own achievements and monetary gain. These individuals, like those in the elitist planter class, would also engage in behaviors often contradictory to the long-term maintenance of their way of life. As is often the case with the *nouveaux riches,* many of the South's planter class spent well beyond their means in order to maintain the conspicuous consumption required to keep up the façade of a sophisticated and aristocratic society. Many times, this pattern of behavior led to the accumulation of great debt—ironically, often owed to wealthy investors from the North (Howe 2007, 60).

In this light, it is not difficult to recognize the South's resistance to a more modern, more "northern" way of life. In the North, the South was viewed by some as "backwards," "lazy" and resistant to technological progress. In the South, the North was a force threatening to change their entire way of life, pushing for the adoption of a culture based on the "slavery" of the hourly wage and robbing the South of what was perceived as a more dignified and "polite" society based on everyone knowing and keeping his place within it.

THE END OF AN ERA OF GOOD FEELINGS

Following the War of 1812, the international outlook of America changed. Before and during the antebellum period, an attitude of neutrality towards the conflicts of Europe was adopted. This allowed the focus of America's statesmen to turn inwards, and it was during this period that the political system with which modern America is most familiar was formed. Though there was great change in the political arena with the formation and dissolution of many factions from the Democratic-Republican party to the Whig party, the foundation of the American government remained fairly unchanged. The Constitution had been written in 1787 and ratified in 1789 and though it was amended several times before 1804, it remained unchanged throughout the entirety of the antebellum period. It was not until the Civil War that this important document would be amended again.

The factors that would contribute to this war would appear again and again within the forum of antebellum politics. Among these hot-button issues were the conflict of states' rights versus the role the federal government might play in the day-to-day business of the states, the abolition of slavery across the growing nation and its territories, and an ongoing economical struggle faced by those in both the North and the South.

When James Monroe was inaugurated as the fifth president of the United States in 1817, a brief period of peace between the prevailing political parties reigned. Dubbed the "Era of Good Feelings," Monroe's presidency was marked by the dissolution of the Federalist Party and the slow decline of the Democratic-Republican party in its wake. Like most of the presidents before him, James Monroe descended from a well-established family (in this case, from Virginia) and like most of the early presidents, he too was a slave owner. Despite his family history and position as slaveholder, it was the compromise struck over the admission of slave states and free states with Missouri and Maine in the early 1820s that would bring an end to the political "good feelings" the Monroe presidency had introduced.

In spite of this, the Monroe presidency would be most well-remembered for a document delivered to Congress in 1823. In what would become known as the Monroe Doctrine, President Monroe set forth the proclamation that the Americas were no longer open for colonization and interference by European countries. Additionally, he set forth a national policy of neutrality towards European wars as well as an attitude of hostility towards European interventions or interferences with independent countries in the Americas. In its time, the Monroe Doctrine was less important than it would become in years to come. It would not be until after the Civil War that the Monroe Doctrine would be seriously invoked by the United States—most notably, the Monroe Doctrine would be cited in American interventions in Pacific and South America throughout the 20th century (Howe 2007, 116). Serving as Monroe's secretary of state, it was John Quincy Adams who drafted the Monroe Doctrine and, as the next president, Adams would turn the focus of the growing nation inwards by setting forth policies designed to support national growth over international diplomacy.

Hard Times Begin: The Panic of 1819

Within two years of James Monroe's inauguration, the citizens of the growing nation were witness to the first widespread financial crisis in its history—the Panic of 1819. This economic depression was caused not only by the unchecked accumulation of debt as the country expanded at an increasingly rapid pace, but by the largely unsupervised system of state banks that replaced the First Bank of the United States before the War of 1812. As more and more states chartered greater numbers of banks, allowing them to issue tender up to 300 percent of their existing capital, the financial security of the nation began to slip. Though a Second Bank of the United States was created by Congress in 1816, it was a case of the remedy worsening the existing economic illness. The banks leaders injudiciously allowed for easy credit during the growing land boom of the late 1810s, providing terms that allowed purchasers to finance as much as 80 percent of the total cost of property as well as allowing them to cover the second installment through further financing (like a second mortgage) (Johnson 1999). A thoroughly corrupt institution, the Second Bank of the United States compounded America's debt problem through easy-credit policies that were extended even to the bank's regional managers. As more unsecured loans circulated greater and greater sums of soft money, inflation soared. Then in 1819, the market fell out in American-produced cotton overseas (the driving force behind so much of the nation's expansion in this period). State banks were ruined and the cotton industry, one of the largest industrial and agricultural industries in America at the time, crumbled. Thousands lost their jobs, and though news traveled to Europe of America's big economic bust, it did not travel fast enough. Immigrants by the thousands continued to arrive upon American shores, only to find less opportunity than in their home countries and a growing contempt for them from the native population.

The ease with which immigration could occur before the Panic of 1819 was staggering. Paul Johnson reports that "an Englishman, without passport, health certificate or documentation of any kind—without luggage for that matter—could hand over £10 at a Liverpool shipping counter and go aboard," with luck he would disembark on the shores of America with his life and health intact (Johnson 1999). However, the Panic of 1819 was a "traumatic awakening to the capitalist reality of boom-and-bust"—the first time that Americans as a whole would experience a "sharp downward swing of the business cycle" (Howe 2007, 143). With this new universal catastrophe of a bank crash, the tide of immigration was checked—but in a fashion that truly exemplified the country's *laissez-faire* attitude of the time. While the individual citizen may have regarded the arrival of more competition for fewer jobs with contempt, the government's official stance was one of ambivalence. John Quincy Adams declared on behalf of the State Department in an issue of the *Niles's Weekly Register* that: "The American Republic invites nobody to come. We will keep out nobody. Arrivals will suffer no disadvantages as aliens. But they can expect no advantages either. Native-born and foreign-born face equal opportunities" (Johnson 1999, 288).

The equal opportunity to improve oneself in the New World, as embraced and advertised by Adams in his statement, would be a driving force in the second great revolution the nation would participate in—the Transportation Revolution. But not all people living in the United States during this period were afforded this opportunity, despite the benefits created through the Transportation Revolution. Slavery—the primary issue over which the nation would divide and war with itself—was already a festering point of contention in the early years of the antebellum period.

The Missouri Compromise and the Issue of Slavery

At the beginning of the Antebellum Era it seemed that America was gradually moving away from slavery as a practice. The emancipation of slaves had begun in the early 1800s and 1810s in many of the Northern states including New York, New Jersey and elsewhere. However, soon after the period began the "apologetic attitude toward slavery" present in the late 1810s would be challenged by new arguments for the continuation of the practice. Among these rationalizations on the part of slave owners was a need to provide a paternalistic guidance for these people, the "negroes as a race...were childlike" in their estimation and it was only fitting and proper that the white male slave owner should play the role of father. This attitude, however, did not extend to the overseer responsible for the day-to-day production and output of slaves. His charge was simply to bring in as much produce as possible without causing undo or permanent harm to the master's investment (Howe 2007). This charge was especially imperative in the case of female slaves, whose value was measured not only in their daily output but in the offspring they might produce. With the dissolution of the Atlantic slave trade in the early part of the century, the primary resource for new slaves was the natural production of existing ones. One Virginia planter is noted as admonishing his overseer to practice caution when working with a "breeding woman" slave; he must remember that "her healthy baby was worth more money than her extra labor would represent" (Howe 2007, 59).

"America's free land had promoted slavery," historian Daniel Walker Howe indicates (2007, 52). With the burgeoning profitability of short-staple cotton in the years after 1815 encouraging expansion as well as the employment of slave labor, it seemed that the Southern economy was inextricably tied to the practice. "The key factor in explaining...the perpetuation of slavery in the United States was profitability. In the South when a yeoman farmer purchased his first slave it usually signaled a resolve to emphasize production for the market, that is for profit as opposed to family subsistence. Had short-staple cotton not emerged in the years after 1815 as an extremely profitable employment for slave labor, finding a peaceful, acceptable resolution to the problem of emancipation might not have been so difficult" (Howe 2007, 56).

The nightmare of slave insurrection was an ever-present fear in the South. This extended to the whole of the white population, not just the slave holders who relied on their labor for the cheap production of cotton. All white males, whether slave holders or not, were enlisted into the service of enforcing existing slave laws. This fear of eminent uprising helped the institution to endure. Even the promise of financial restitution upon the emancipation of their slaves held no solace for those who feared rebellion by African Americans.

The tension over whether slavery would continue as a practice in the United States first came to a head when Missouri applied for statehood in the 1820s. Under Monroe's leadership, the Missouri Compromise allowed Missouri to enter the United States as a slave state under the condition that Maine was admitted as a free state and essentially prohibiting slavery as a practice from spreading into the emerging western territories. As much as this policy expressed interest in divorcing the nation from the practice of slavery gradually, the crux of the conflict over this piece of legislature could be found in the issue of states' rights. With this Compromise a new era of political animosity arose between the pro-state sovereignty Democratic-Republicans and the emerging nationalistic Whig party.

As the economy in the South began to incorporate industrial production, enslaved Africans were bought and sold based on the skills they had acquired in their lifetimes. The acquisition of these skills was viewed by many southerners as the slave's way of bettering himself through achievement. This argument lobbied against abolitionists naturally ignored the fact that the "enslaved pursued personal achievement in spite, not because of, slavery" (Lakwete 2003, 111). By the 1830s, slavery had declined in most American metropolitan or largely populated cities, most of which were located in the North. "Urban life proved less congenial to slavery than rural largely because masters found it difficult to control every aspect of the slave's life in the city. Urban slaves were far more likely to make successful escapes. The shrewdest contemporaries came to regard the growth of cities as one of the factors undermining the persistence of slavery" (Howe 2007, 54).

The issue of slavery in America was far from resolved with the Missouri Compromise. It would continue to be a bone of contention for both the emerging political parties as well as individual citizens throughout the nation for some time to come.

TECHNOLOGY SHAPES THE GROWING NATION: THE TRANSPORTATION REVOLUTION

The landscape of America was changing with the slow transition from an agricultural, subsistence-based economy to one in which the home was no longer the focus of economic production. The populations in cities throughout America grew, with many more individuals working outside of the home and buying the goods that they needed instead of producing them themselves. At the heart of this transition can be seen the touch of new and advanced technologies that affected more and more Americans in every facet of their lives, including how they moved.

"The Transportation Revolution," as historians have dubbed it, was begun out of a growing need for a better transportation system. "The Great Migration [westward from the original colonies] had increased the number of agricultural producers wanting to get their crops from the interior to national or international markets," historian Daniel Howe has observed (2007, 211). There were hurdles to overcome, however, before the wishes of the citizens of America could

Eli Whitney and the Era of Invention

Eli Whitney has often been cited as the inventor of the cotton gin, perhaps one of the most revolutionary inventions of the antebellum period. While he certainly contributed to its development and innovation, another of his endeavors would ultimately contribute more meaningfully to the industrial age in America. In a small factory near the dam in Whitneyville, Connecticut, Eli Whitney spent the better part of the first two decades of the 19th century trying to apply the concept of standardized machine parts that could be easily interchanged to a contract he held for the production of muskets for the federal government. In doing so, he had put his finger on the technique that would "transform the world" (Howe 2007, 532). The revolution in invention that would ensue was centered primarily in the North, most prominently among those in New England. Here a culture of innovation was built, which caused one British visitor to observe, "Every workman seems to be continually devising some new thing to assist him in his work, there being a strong desire both with masters and workmen, throughout the New England states, to be 'posted up,' in every new improvement" (Howe 2007, 534).

be realized. The greatest obstacle against the improvement of transportation nationwide was the controversy over whether the federal government should be involved in internal improvements at all. This issue divided people along party lines—Democrats stood against internal improvements (states should take care of themselves), while those in the Whig party were for federally funded internal improvements (and other forms of "big government"). Federal government intervention into transportation improvements was also seen by many as a threat to the "peculiar institution" of slavery, which was at the core of life in the south. If the government could step in on issues such as canal development and dictate traffic patterns, what would stop it from challenging slave holder's rights to continue in a practice that was largely regarded as inhumane throughout most of the North, as well as parts of Europe? As northern states pushed for more improvements, politicians in the south sought to check them in their progress, in case they "stretch the Constitution" so far that emancipation would become imminent (Howe 2007, 221).

But progress occurred despite the concerns of the South and the Democrats, though it was not widely funded by the federal government. Among the most important innovations in the Transportation Revolution was the introduction of steam technology into its realm. "The invention of the steamboat enhanced the comparative advantages of water transportation [over land-based forms]" (Howe 2007, 214). The wheels of the Transportation Revolution had been set in motion in the previous century, with the first American steamer built in 1787 by John Fitch followed by the first commercially successful steamboat, the *Clermont,* put in motion by Robert Fulton along the Hudson in 1807. State-funded improvements, such as New York's Eerie Canal, were also largely responsible for the growing success of water-based transport of goods throughout the growing nation. And with the introduction of trans-Atlantic steam ships in the 1840s, commerce exported from the United States saw a significant rise.

The Transportation Revolution impacted not only the economics of the expanding United States, its impact was also seen in the daily lives of those living in rural America. The selling of surplus crops was made easier through these improvements and the amount and diversity of products available for purchase in these often isolated areas increased. This phenomenon is best illustrated in terms of fashion history when observing the growing number of ads placed in papers in even the most remote rural areas, which advertised a large variety of "Calicoes, Ginghams, Muslins, Cambricks, Laces, and Ribbands" for sale (Howe 2007, 220).

JOHN QUINCY ADAMS AND "THE AMERICAN SYSTEM"

John Quincy Adams was elected among feelings of great animosity between the two preeminent political parties. The election had been close—a majority of popular and electoral college votes could not be reached, throwing the deciding vote of the election into the House of Representatives where, with the support of former presidential candidate Henry Clay, Adams was elected as the country's sixth president. This was seen as a corruption of the election system by Andrew Jackson and his party as he had won a plurality of both popular and electoral votes and would herald in four years of political "bad blood" between the parties as Adams's attempts to shape the growing country through high tariffs disenfranchised Jackson's supporters even further. At the heart of the Adams administration was an approach based on the ideas of Alexander Hamilton, one of the country's founding fathers and an early American economist. Referred to as the American System, Adams planned to put Hamilton's ideas into action by creating a protective tariff against the importation of European goods, through the promotion of a single national currency (instead of tender created and protected on the state level) and by focusing the country's economic powers on building a better infrastructure for the creation and maintenance of roads and transportation systems. The tariff of 1828, which was introduced to this purpose, quickly became known as the "Tariff of Abominations," particularly in the southern states. With a high tariff levied on the importation of European goods, southern planters experienced a significant loss in the export of cotton, particularly to Great Britain. Coupled with this loss of income, they were then forced to buy products from manufacturers in the North whose prices far exceeded those of the previously imported goods.

Immigrants Coming to America

Even with the economic hardships of the Panic of 1819 and the later Tariff of Abominations, many were still drawn to America in the hopes of a new and better life. The cheap manner in which transportation could be procured coupled with the ease with which land might be acquired was a strong draw to the shores of the new nation. Many immigrants were also escaping hardships faced in their countries of origin, such as massive food shortages and the burden of taxes, far worse than the Tariff of 1828 that had been levied by their native countries, often on those least capable of paying them, following the War of 1812. Hardships at home were incomparable to the promise America held for their futures.

It was in 1821 when the Irish potato crop first failed that the British government hatched a scheme to transport a large portion of the starving Irish population to Canada. At virtually no cost to the passengers, passage was made to Canada. Once there, those arriving could easily slip across the border to the promise of cheap land and opportunity in the United States. It is here that the mass exodus of Southern Ireland's population to America began, resulting in nearly one-third of the population finding their way to America's shores. Later the surge of Irish immigrants continued as the Great Hunger took hold of Ireland between 1845 and 1849. Before this time, the majority of farmers in Ireland had switched their crops to potatoes in response to dwindling land resources and rising rent prices. Potatoes were primarily a subsistence crop and when the worst outbreak of blight occurred in 1846, farmers and their families were forced to consume most of their seed potatoes for the next season. The next crop was thus depleted and just as subject to blight as previous ones. Very little was done by the English government to ease the suffering of the starving Irish people, leading many to immigrate and risk death on the high seas than stay and surely starve (Daniels 2003, 264). "The census of 1851 showed clearly the results of natural disaster and human mismanagement; there were about two and a half million fewer people in Ireland than there would have been under normal conditions. About half, 1,000,000 to 1,500,000 human beings—perhaps a sixth of the population—died from a combination of hunger and disease. An equal number emigrated, most to America . . . All told, in the famine years something more than two million Irish went overseas" (Daniels 2003, 265–66).

Even as the economy recovered following the bank disasters of 1819, the large numbers of Irish immigrants were still made to feel unwelcome by the native population of America. Typically, the Irish would find themselves on the lowest rung of the economic ladder, particularly in the urban areas of America (centered primarily in the North). Those who could find work were most likely to be found performing unskilled labor or in the role of domestic servant. Many more could be found in municipal institutions such as jails, charity hospitals, and, most frequently, poor houses (Daniels 2003). In the south, the recently immigrated might find work performing those tasks that were deemed too dangerous and life-threatening to be performed by enslaved African Americans. The loss of a valuable investment—the enslaved worker—was weighed as heavier than the loss of a contracted immigrant laborer. However, with westward expansion and the promises of the Gold Rush, some Irish immigrants did find the better life they sought in coming to America.

JACKSONIAN DEMOCRACY

As the next presidential election approached, a radical change had occurred in who would be allowed to vote. Since 1810, six states had entered the union with constitutions allowing for the privilege of voting to be extended to white males who did not own property. This shift in suffrage encouraged other states to liberalize their voting practices—by the time the 1828 election rolled around there were nearly 1.16 million voters compared to under 355,000 in 1824.

After failing to win the 1824 election, the Andrew Jackson campaign was determined to win in 1828. Andrew Jackson campaigned as a man of humble origins. In this way, he appealed to the new constituency of first-time voters and was poised for victory. But his campaign was not limited to appealing to the masses as a "man of the people". His drive to become president, and that of his party to see their man in office, also meant that attacking the character of the incumbent president was not out-of-bounds in his campaign. The campaign set off the trend for mud-slinging politics that endures today in America when they leaked allegations that Adams had turned the inner sanctum of the White House into a gaming house, complete with "gaming tables and gambling furniture" (Findling and Thackeray 2003, 150). But the Jackson camp was not alone in its descent into dirty politicking—the Adams campaign retaliated by spreading tales about Jackson's wife and her alleged act of bigamy with Jackson when with her first husband. When the dust settled, the voters were swayed by Jackson's heroism in the military and his campaign as the "common man" and he entered the office of the President in 1829. The two-party system was now firmly in place in the world of American politics.

The period from 1824 to 1840 is often referred to as the era of Jacksonian Democracy despite the fact that Jackson's term ended in 1837. The concept of Jacksonian Democracy was built upon the idea of the president's responsibility to the voting public. This concept, along with Jackson's concerns over Indian Removal, was carried over into the next presidency, that of Jackson's vice president, Martin Van Buren. Andrew Jackson and Van Buren, unlike their predecessors, were not content in merely administering the legislation put forth by Congress. Jackson, in particular, felt he should play an active role in shaping that legislation, largely through his veto power. But perhaps the most lasting effect of

Jackson's tenure as president from 1829 to 1837 was the introduction of the spoils system. When Jackson took office in 1829, he was the first president to dismiss bureaucratic officials on a large scale, replacing them with "deserving" members of his own party, regardless of their experience or efficacy. The outcome of these replacements was often disastrous, such as the case of Samuel Swartout, who was appointed to the position of collector of customs at the port of New York. This disreputable Jacksonian was able to embezzle more than $1 million before he was finally brought to justice (Findling and Thackeray 2003). Despite ushering in an era of corrupt and often inept bureaucrats, Jackson firmly believed that the office of president must be used to create a "plain system" of government "protecting all and granting favors to none" (Findling and Thackeray 2003, 153). His would be a presidency in which the aristocratic establishments of early America would be challenged, making way for the era of the "common man."

Exemplifying this belief, the campaign for presidency in 1832 was largely won over the issue of the legitimacy of the Bank of the United States. Initially in favor of this institution, which sought to regulate currency throughout the nation and provide economic support for enterprise through financing, Jackson came to believe that it was another tool of the aristocratic monopolies that he sought to destroy. When he vetoed the renewal of this institution in 1832, the battle between the bank (under the guidance of Nicholas Biddle) and the president began. This war, coupled with the Nullification Crisis of 1832 in which Jackson failed to lower the tariffs on European goods, would result in the worst economic crisis of the century. It would be Jackson's vice-president and successor, however, Martin Van Buren, who would bear the brunt of this crisis—the public would largely blame Martin "Van Ruin" for the economic crisis when he took office in 1837.

HARD TIMES UNDER MARTIN VAN BUREN

Martin Van Buren wasn't in office long before the Panic of 1837 overcame the United States. Though Jackson had succeeded in eliminating the national debt, his opposition to and destruction of the Bank of the United States made it more difficult to control the supply of money domestically. This widespread economic depression would last for nearly seven years. Van Buren sought to combat it by lowering the tariffs Jackson had failed to act upon and introducing a proposal for the Independent Treasury System in 1837. This system of converting all legal tender to federally controlled funds was not formally put into place until 1840, however. Within a year, it was repealed and the United States sank further into economic despair. The fall in cotton prices in 1839 didn't serve to help economic matters, either. The repercussions following the glut in the cotton market were felt throughout the economy. Domestic productivity slowed and a condition of high unemployment resulted.

Van Buren's presidency is also significant for his continuation of Jackson's primary concern—the removal of American Indians.

The Trail of Tears: Indian Removal Policy in Antebellum America

Van Buren's role in the "Trail of Tears" in 1838, or the forced expulsion of Cherokee peoples from their homelands in Georgia, Alabama, South Carolina, and Tennessee, resulted in the relocation of these indigenous people to the territory of Oklahoma, which would not formally join the union until 1907. The expulsion of tribes from their native lands had begun early in Jackson's tenure with the Indian Removal Bill of 1830. This move was seen by many as essential to the continued growth of the United States. Jackson saw American Indian tribes such as the Cherokee and the Seminole as a threat to U.S. sovereignty and white supremacy. In his inaugural address, Jackson had called for the voluntary removal of Indian populations from their tribal lands but his Indian Removal policy was anything but—bribery, treachery, and underhandedness would all be employed to ensure the removal of the native people from the fertile lands so envied by Americans like Jackson. But not all Americans were behind Jackson's policy—particularly strong voices in the outcry against the Indian Removal Bill came from the Protestant clergy and women. Catherine Beecher, the sister of author Harriet Beecher Stowe, mounted a petition drive, one of the few devices left to women to have their voices heard in the Antebellum Era. It was not successful.

In 1829, gold was discovered on the lands of the Cherokee tribe in Georgia. What should have been a great windfall for this tribe turned out to be their greatest liability. This discovery was a driving force behind the Bill of 1830. White prospectors didn't wait for the Bill to take effect, however, and rushed into the area to begin looting the land before it was even put in place. But the native people were not without a voice. In 1831, the Cherokee Nation turned to the highest court in the country for protection. They presented existing treaties and agreements as evidence that the Removal Bill was in direct conflict with prior arrangements. The issue, unfortunately, was sidestepped by the court. It was only a matter of time before Jackson turned his gaze to other tribes throughout the southern states. With the ball rolling for the Cherokee removal, Jackson wasted no time in seeking the removal of the Choctaw and Chickasaw tribes in Mississippi and the Creeks in Alabama. These actions were not without their own repercussions, of course. The massive scale of deception and fraud perpetrated against the Creek Nation resulted in the Second Creek War of 1836. And even those tribes that were compliant with Jackson's policy received no better treatment.

The Chickasaws, perhaps the most compliant of all the tribes, were rewarded for their trouble by having to purchase their own land in Oklahoma upon their arrival following removal. This was due to the government's short-sighted negligence in identifying a new settlement area for the tribe. In Florida, the Seminoles proved particularly troublesome to those intent upon Indian Removal—their resistance would cost the government more than 10 times the estimated budget for the removal of all tribes. And tribes in the south were not the only peoples affected. The tribes of the Northwest were also routed out of their native lands. Before the end of Jackson's term as president, nearly 46,000 American Indians had been dispossessed with an equal amount awaiting transportation to new land. By 1840, most American Indians would be removed to areas west of the Mississippi (Mintz 2003).

While the greatest tragedy of this period may seem to be that existing treaties with the American Indian tribes were largely ignored, it may ultimately be found in the cruel manner in which Jackson's Indian Removal Bill was carried out during both his tenure and that of Van Buren. Many of the government and military officials put in charge of Indian Removal were more interested in pocketing funds reserved for the safe transport of the tribespeople than in ensuring that they arrived at their destinations safely. Despite the best efforts of individuals such as General John Ellis Wool, who attempted to prepare properly for the removal of the Cherokee peoples to Oklahoma, the Trail of Tears westward during the fall of 1838 and continuing into the winter of 1839 resulted in a shockingly high death rate amongst the native people—estimated at 4,000 (Mintz 2003). The Indian Removal Bill and the manner in which it was carried out reveals not only the inherent racism felt by the U.S. government at the time but also the growing nation's imperialistic intentions.

Westward Ho!

With the lands of the uprooted Indians now empty, Jackson's vision of American farming families settling and building a life on this fertile soil could be realized. Unfortunately, Jackson's vision was not initially realized. Instead of independent farmers settling in the new lands, the former Indian territories were overrun with land speculators, looking to make a profit off of the cheap and plentiful acreage. Still, the farming families of Jackson's vision did find their way to these lands eventually, joining others in the growing expansion of the United States into the West.

Life in the former Indian territories offered great promise for some, but not all. "Westward migration meant different things to different people," states Howe, "For a white man eager to raise cotton, it could mean a welcome fresh start in life and even a chance at quick wealth...For white female participants, the move might be less attractive...For African Americans, the move across the mountains constituted a second giant disruption in the generation following the end of forced migration across the ocean" (2007, 130). Historian Ira Berlin has aptly named this migration of enslaved African Americans a "Second Middle Passage." Like their first forced passage from Africa, living and working conditions were worse in the new lands than in those that they had left behind. Slaves were often overworked in conditions similar to the worst of the Caribbean sugar plantations of the 18th century. For women, westward migration meant the loss of family connections and a disruption of the social network they had built among their neighbors. Very few women traveled west initially, making for a life of further isolation in the new territories for those that did once they arrived.

The ever-growing population of the United States was enough, however, to encourage an increasing wave of "pioneers" into these lands. The census of 1800 had only identified a mere third of a million people living beyond the Appalachians. By 1820, the number had increased to well over two million occupants (Howe 2007). These individuals lived up to their legendary name. They were "pioneers" in a very real sense. Like the advance guard of an army, they too occupied land that wasn't theirs. And it was their role to prepare that land for future generations through settlement and construction.

"TIPPECANOE AND TYLER TOO"

By the election of 1840, the Whig party had caught on to the powerful imagery of the "common man" as used by the Democratic party in the Jackson campaign. The candidate they placed on the ballot would be a simple man that would appeal to the masses. William Henry Harrison was a hero of the American Indian wars and his campaign slogan of "Tippecanoe and Tyler Too" reflected this. It was near the Tippecanoe River that Harrison was victorious over the Shawnee Indians in Indiana. Ironically, it was the Democrats portrayal of Harrison as an out-of-touch old man disengaged with American politics sitting in his log cabin and drinking hard cider that would provide the most effective campaign propaganda for this candidate. The Whigs turned this seemingly negative slur to their benefit, with Harrison and his running mate John Tyler adopting the symbols of the log cabin and hard cider as a kind of heraldry. After his election, Harrison would become the first president to sit for a photographic portrait. However, his was to be one of the most short-lived presidencies in U.S. history. He was dead within a month of his inauguration and John Tyler stepped into the uneasy role of accidental president.

Ruefully dubbed "his accidency" or the "acting president," John Tyler abandoned the Whig party upon rising to the seat of president following Harrison's death in 1841. A strong supporter of states' rights and small government, Tyler struggled with his former party throughout his presidency. It was during his tenure, in fact, that the Whig party became intrinsically identified with the North and the Democrats with the South. This division would color American politics throughout the next decade.

Tyler's abandonment of the Whig party upon his inauguration led the way for the election of another Democrat to the office of president in 1845. Though James K. Polk was an ardent supported of Jackson, his policies would not reflect those of his predecessor. Polk entered the office with four clearly defined goals in mind: first to re-establish the Independent Treasury System, second to reduce tariffs and encourage trade, third to acquire some or all of the territory involved in the Oregon boundary dispute and fourth to purchase the California territory from Mexico. Polk's intention was to serve only one term as president and with this resolution in mind, he managed to achieve all four of his goals with that single term.

The Whig party would once again possess the presidential office when Zachary Taylor or "Old Rough and Ready" as he was called took office in 1849. A military leader with a long and distinguished career, Taylor was a paradoxical figure in American politics. At once a slaveholder and opposed to the spread of slavery into the new territories of the United States, it would not be until after his death just 16 months into his term that the issues over slavery in the new territories following the Mexican-American War would be settled with the Compromise of 1850. Taylor's successor, Millard Fillmore, was a strong supporter of the Compromise, which sought to tamper growing political contention regarding the issue of slavery in states entering the Union. Unlike Taylor, Fillmore supported slavery in new territories. Included within the Compromise of 1850 was legislation that was meant to enforce the rights of slaveholders. The Fugitive Slave Act of 1850 imposed penalties upon law enforcement if "run-away" slaves were not sought and returned and rewarded individuals who returned fugitive slaves to the service of their masters. One of the most contentious outcomes of the Compromise of 1850, many states responded by setting up laws of their own allowing for the freedom and security of fugitive slaves within their borders. The bitterness surrounding these laws in response to the Compromise of 1850 would be cited in the case for secession by the state of South Carolina. Fillmore would be the last of the Whig presidents, as the party quickly dissolved following the ineffectual nomination of General Winfield Scott as its candidate for president in 1852. Many of the party's members went on to join the Republican party.

THE COMMUNICATIONS REVOLUTION

Just as improvements in transportation had changed the way the American people moved through their ever-growing country, changes in the

U.S. Post Office in the 1840s affected the way Americans communicated with each other. This desire to communicate over long distances was only reinforced by the patterns of migration that occurred in antebellum America as the country expanded and new lands and prospects opened up to its citizens. According to historian David M. Henkin, "During the middle decades of the nineteenth century, ordinary Americans began participating in a regular network of long-distance communication, engaging in relationships with people they did not see" (2006, 2). With technological advances in the printing industry, news traveled more quickly from one part of the country to another, affecting everything from the decisions made by America's biggest businesses to the way everyday people made decisions about what to wear. As early as 1811, the German Friedrich Koenig had invented a steam-driven cylinder press. With this innovation, the production of printed materials became mechanized. "After about 1830, these improvements [steam-power, stereotyping, etc.] had reached the point where a national market for published material existed" (Howe 2007, 227). Even before these innovations had occurred, the U.S. Post Office had been designed to serve the founding fathers' desire to spread news, particularly that of a political nature, around the country. With subsidized postage for newspapers, the highest postage rates were charged on individual mail such as letters and packages, whether it was of a personal or business nature. Naturally, consumers of the early postal system found ways around paying the high price for personal communication in the form of letters (typically charged by the sheet rather than by weight) by taking advantage of the subsidized postage rates of newspapers. Inventive individuals created a system of marks or simply modified the newspapers they sent to others in order to communicate their ideas. These methods were crude, however, and the full communication potential of the postal service in the United States was not realized until postal reforms occurred between 1845 and 1851. It was then that letter rates were lowered and a system of postage based on weight was put in place. The effect was palpable—between 1840 and 1860, the U.S. Postal Service saw the number of letters put into their care increase nearly six-fold, to almost 161 million by 1860 (Henkin 2006).

The largest group of consumers of the reformed mail system continued to be free white men (as it had been before the postage reforms), but this communications revolution was not limited to their consumption (Henkin 2006). Women, slaves and free blacks, literate and illiterate, all used the mail system as well though their efforts may have been met with more resistance than those of the white male contingency. The communications of slaves could be interrupted at any point in their journey, whether it was in the process of reaching the post office or by the postmaster himself, at which point it might be summarily returned to his or her master. And those who received mail, particularly the illiterate among the slave class in the South, were equally in jeopardy of having their mail communications interrupted. Their mail might only be delivered into the hands of their master, since many would not delegate the responsibility of picking up mail to their slaves for fear of its use in rebellion. Without knowledge of the contents of a letter, an illiterate slave whose mail did make it into the right hands might choose poorly when selecting his or her reader, often exposing the escape plots and attempts to achieve freedom by their friends or family to individuals who would take every action to thwart their endeavors.

While the concept of letter-writing may seem feminine in nature, a notion supported through the numerous magazine articles and writing guides of the period, many women were met with great resistance when trying to engage in the communication revolution that was the U.S. mails. Post offices were primarily masculine places throughout most of the antebellum period, often housed within bars or other places of business perceived as unsuitable for an upstanding lady. The duty for mail retrieval almost fell entirely upon one of the males of the household, and in particularly patriarchal families, the mail sent and received for wives and daughters might be subject to close scrutiny and censure by the head of the house. As more men traveled west without their families, however, women venturing into the postal arena became a necessity. The presence of women in the postal environment ultimately evolved into a standardized architecture where separate entrances and claim windows were reserved for female customers, in order to help protect them from the more raucous and uncivilized male portion of the post office.

But it is perhaps the kinds of things sent through the mails, and not necessarily the users of the service, that is most revelatory to the modern historian and student of fashion. Among the most popular items was the Daguerrotype image, invented by Louis-Jacques-Mandé Daguerre in France and introduced to the world in the summer of 1839 (Library of Congress). By that fall, agents had arrived in New York City to sell the rights, and the equipment, needed to capture images using this new process. Their popularity spread like wildfire throughout the United States such that within a couple of years there were daguerrotype studios in even the smallest and most remote towns and villages (Severa 1997, 1). "The numerous Daguerreotypes of that period [circa 1841] furnish us with many accurate details of dress," Elizabeth McClellan observed in her book on American dress, including how the hair was worn in contrast (or similarity) to earlier periods and that hairstyles were similar in countries far removed from America, such as England (by comparing Daguerreotypes with portraits of Queen Victoria from the same period) (McClellan 1969, 438). As a means of personal contact, particularly to those participating in the Western Gold Rush, the daguerrotype was perfectly suited to the reformed post office of antebellum America. Studies of extant daguerrotypes, such as that found in *Dressed for the Photographer: Ordinary Americans and Fashion, 1840–1900* (Severa 1997) have been made within the field of fashion history and it is interesting to note that many of these images may have been taken not just as a record of what was worn but as a surrogate for the original individual or individuals pictured for relatives and loved ones separated by great distances during America's western expansion.

In a time when most mail was sent postage due and delivered to a general post office, not a private residence or place of business, the advertisements for the "dead letters" left by unknowing recipients that appear frequently in local and regional newspapers of the period offer a window into additional types of objects sent through the mail. It should be noted that among the items regularly listed in these roll calls were items that help to paint a picture of how fashion information, outside of that conveyed through pre-printed materials, was dispersed among individual consumers. For example, the *Overland Monthly* informed its readers that actual items of dress such as kid gloves, gaiters, and lace might be found among the "dead letter" roster as well as "no end of dress samples" (Henkin 2006, 163). A similar list appeared in the *Albany Register* in 1852, where we find "patterns for silk, good for city cousins to match for country friends" included in the roll call (Henkin 2006, 163).

The proliferation of magazines and books in the Antebellum Era was a result of the same technological advances that affected the newspaper industry. Of particular interest to the student of fashion is the appearance of America's first fashion journal in 1830, *Godey's Lady's Book*. This publication, founded by Louis Godey of Philadelphia, Pennsylvania, quickly grew to a wide circulation. Modeled after European publications, *Godey's Lady's Book* contained serials, prose, and poetry, along with fashion commentary, updating its readers of the latest fashions in literature, art, and dress. It also offered practical advice, especially under the editorship of Sarah Hale, who joined the publication in the late 1830s (Oberholtzer 1906, 230). Women were instructed on how to keep house, how to clothe their children, as well as provided with plates and diagrams for creating the latest fashions. This was followed 12 years later by the publication and distribution of *Peterson's Magazine* in 1842 and soon a proliferation of publications marketed directly to American women consumers of fashion followed. These publications offered advice on all things, not just the latest fashions. For example, as the engagement in correspondence through the mails increased among women in the United States, readers of *Godey's Lady's Book* were advised in 1852, "Remember the mail is always open," a reassurance to its readers that "a prompt response to a letter was better than a complete one" (Henkin 2006, 5).

KING COTTON AND THE AMERICAN INDUSTRIAL REVOLUTION

Early in America's history, a variety of endeavors contributed to America's economy. In New England at ports such as New Bedford, Massachusetts, there was whaling and by the time of the antebellum period, the majority of whaling ships on the ocean were American. Whale-based products such as oil for lamps rose in demand as the population of the country increased throughout the period. An additional industry that contributed to the American economy before the beginning of the Antebellum Era was the fur trade. This was one of the fastest growing endeavors of the late 18th and 19th centuries and it involved the participation of both the American Indian population and citizens from the United States and Canada as well as the British and Russians. Beaver pelts were long the most sought after fur in the trade but their reign declined as men's fur hats passed out of fashion in the 1840s. Perhaps one of the most important industries in antebellum America, however, was cotton. Produced in the South and processed in the North, cotton would become king of the American economy by the start of the Antebellum Era. It would also become the driving force behind the industrial revolution in the United States.

In Great Britain, the Industrial Revolution had begun in the mid-18th century. There, as it would be in America in the 1810s, it was driven by textile manufacturing. As more efficient machinery was developed (such as the power loom) home-based production was replaced by large factories, creating an industry where the majority of output was produced outside of the home. Unlike Great Britain, America was a bit slow to enter this revolution in manufacturing. It would take strong economic tools and the ingenuity of a handful of American inventors and innovators before America would truly enter the industrial age.

At the core of any successful business endeavor must be the ability to raise capital. Around 1810, American merchants and bankers in the North developed the "corporation" as a legal device to help raise funds through the selling of stock. In New York, the Stock Exchange was founded in 1817, making it even easier for entrepreneurs and corporations to raise capital. And with the deregulation of American banking following the Panic of 1819, the number of banks grew from around 30 at the beginning of the 19th century to well over 800 by 1850 (Howe 2007). Through the introduction of protective tariffs, the U.S. government also helped to encourage industrial innovations and allowed the revolution that began around the textile industry to flourish.

The Growth of the Cotton Economy

Short-staple cotton was the golden crop of the south. The ease with which it was grown was hampered only by the labor-intensive practices required to process it into a usable raw good. These difficulties were largely overcome by the invention of the cotton gin and the innovations in its mechanics that followed. By 1820 the South "was the domain of King Cotton" (Dudley 2003, 22). Production of the fiber had outgrown that of India by leaps and bounds and exports of raw cotton from the Southern United States quickly outgrew those from the south Asian country.

With the success of cotton agriculture in the South, it was only natural that industry related to the processing of this fiber might follow. And in fact, the expanding agricultural economy of the South was complemented by a rise in an industrial economy, particularly in regions where cotton was most highly produced. This industry naturally centered around the development, production and maintenance of cotton gins. In *Inventing the Cotton Gin,* Angela Lakwete notes the impact of this agricultural field, its new technology and the industry it sparked on expansion and the southern economic structure. "During the 1830s cotton was the primary factor [in the expanding agricultural economy]. As a response to increased demand, production accelerated westward migration and capital formation, dominating interregional and foreign trade. The gin industry complemented the cotton economy and demonstrated that predominance in agriculture did not preclude investment in manufacturing" (2003, 98). However, many in the South felt at a disadvantage to the North, especially following the Tariff of 1828, which had levied a large tax on goods imported from overseas and forced many southerners to rely on high-priced goods from the North. Despite the creation of local gin manufacturies, by the late 1840s, many were still complaining about the South's continued reliance on northern industrial goods. William S. Figures, an editor of a paper based in Huntsville, Alabama, complained in 1849, "Let the South learn to live at home! At present, the North fattens and grows rich upon the South. We depend upon it for our entire supplies...In northern vessels products are carried to market—his cotton is ginned with northern gins" (Lakwete 2003, 101). There is evidence that might seem to contradict Figures's opinion, according to a study of the gin industry performed by Angela Lakwete. "Demographic data taken from the population schedules confirm that most gin makers not only lived in the South but were born there as well" (2003, 101). The gin industry was dominated in sheer numbers by small southern proprietors and partners. However, Lakwete (2003) does go on to note that of the largest of the cotton gin manufacturers in the South, the majority were in fact headed by northern-born industrialists.

The growth of King Cotton in the South wrought an incredible transformation. Cotton would help to expand and transform the U.S. economy in both the South and the North. As southern plantations were growing and processing the raw fiber, textile mills in the North were weaving the cloth of the American industrial revolution.

The Mill Girls of Lowell, Massachusetts

Before Francis Cabot Lowell died in 1817, he had set in motion the technology that would change the U.S. textile industry forever. During his travels in England, he had meticulously memorized the most closely guarded secret of that country's powerful textile industry—the construction of the power loom. He brought this technology back with him, the plans neatly smuggled in the one place where British customs inspectors could never look—his mind. With the help of several partners, he set about creating three successful mills in Massachusetts. The success of these mills was followed by the creation in 1826 of a town bearing his name, built around another mill in Lowell, Massachusetts. While other towns had sprung up around industrial centers throughout the United States during this period, Lowell was different. This planned community was designed to suit the needs of the mill's labor force, drawn from the surplus of young, unmarried women in rural New England. "Unlike most parts of the United states, New England had a surplus of women over men because so many of the males had migrated west, while the region received at that time few immigrants from overseas.... young women left home, recruited by company-owned boarding houses in Lowell. There they put in long hours under unhealthy conditions and contracted not to leave until they had worked at least a year" (Howe 2007, 133). These "mill girls" as they became known, felt their wages were good at 12 to 14 dollars a month and found plenty to attract them to the mill town of Lowell—shops, churches, social and educational facilities. The fears of those who dreaded the introduction of industrialized labor were assuaged by the Lowell experience, due largely in part to the limited time most "mill girls" would spend in service before they were married. The planned community and its "mill girls" were a success—before the Civil War began, Lowell would boast the largest concentration of the cotton textile industry in the United States.

Textile Mills

Economic historian Eric Hobsbawm has observed, "Whoever says industrial revolution says cotton" (Howe 2007, 132). The effect of cotton on the industrial economy was staggering. Organization of the cotton industry occurred at any size. Like the cotton gin industry in both the North and South, small entrepreneurs might start out without the help of a corporation. It was a particularly popular endeavor among those who emigrated from countries such as Scotland or England, where they had gained skills and knowledge in the field. With little upfront capital, they were able to start their own mills in the United States. These small textile companies grew into large corporations. In fact, by the early 1830s, nearly 90 percent of the largest corporations in the United States were textile companies (Howe 2007).

Textile mills found a natural home in the northern United States, where water power was plentiful. This left the production of the raw materials entirely to the South, allowing the North to focus on the production of inexpensive, and often coarse, cotton products. The majority of textiles produced in the northern United States were sold back to the plantation owners of the South in the form of slave cloth. This coarse fabric of blended cotton and wool was the primary material used by slave owners to clothe their slaves.

COUNTDOWN TO THE CIVIL WAR

In the next two elections, the Southern-sympathizing Democratic party would support the winning candidates. Franklin Pierce was elected to office in 1852. While in office, he would nullify the Missouri Compromise with the Kansas-Nebraska Act of 1854. With the creation of the Kansas and Nebraska territories, popular sovereignty was restored to settlers, allowing them the final decision regarding the acceptance of slavery in their territory. This act was seen by many in the North, particularly those who supported abolitionism, as a concession to the South and the "Slave Power." In essence, the prohibition of slavery north of the 36° 30′ latitude was repealed and the stage was set for the landmark Lincoln-Douglas debates. For his part, Pierce would go on to support the Southern Confederate states during the ensuing Civil War.

The divisive Kansas-Nebraska Act would lead the Democratic Party to nominate a seemingly neutral candidate for the 1856 election. James Buchanan had been absent for the vote on the Act and was perceived as "untainted" by either side of this contentious issue. His sympathies, however, were clearly expressed throughout his tenure. As several southern states moved towards secession, Buchanan would stand by as the nation divided. Even before his inauguration, he corresponded with Supreme Court justices regarding the Dred Scott case in which a slave had sought to purchase his freedom following his master's death. His hope was that the decision in this controversial case would be handed down before his inauguration in March, taking the issue of slavery out of political debate and placing it within the realm of the legislature. Ultimately, Buchanan's hope was not attained, even though a decision was reached in early March—the verdict in the Scott case (that neither Scott nor any person of African descent brought onto the shores of the United States as slave could ever rightfully attain freedom, either through purchase or transportation to a "free state") was a divisive milestone on the road to the Civil War. By the end of his presidency, seven southern states would desert the union to form the Confederate States of America.

THE END OF AN ERA

Abraham Lincoln had begun his political career at the age of 23 as a member of the Whig Party in the General Assembly of his home state of Illinois. In the fallout of the dissolution of that party following the election of 1852, Lincoln was one of many members who abandoned politics altogether. It wasn't until the Kansas-Nebraska Act and the violence of "Bleeding Kansas" that followed that Lincoln returned to politics, this time as a member of the new Republican Party.

States throughout the South expressed their contempt for his impending election by firmly warning Lincoln against the invasion of their lands for the purposes of furthering abolition. Having run on a platform that extolled the virtues of free labor versus slave labor, slave states throughout the United States felt threatened by their president-elect.

The Civil War, which erupted in 1861 with the battle of Bull Run in Virginia, brought the Antebellum Era to a devastating end.

References

Burke, Emily P. 2003. "Life on a Southern Plantation." In *Antebellum America: 1784–1850,* ed. William Dudley, 197–201. San Diego: Greenhaven Press.

Daniels, Roger. 2003. "The Irish Potato Famine and Migration of the Irish to America." In *Antebellum America: 1784–1850,* ed. William Dudley, 263–71. San Diego: Greenhaven Press.

Dudley, William, ed. 2003. *Antebellum America: 1784–1850.* San Diego: Greenhaven Press.

Findling, John E. and Frank W. Thackeray. 2003. "Andrew Jackson and Jacksonian Democracy, 1828–1840" In *Antebellum America: 1784–1850,* ed. William Dudley, 149–55. San Diego: Greenhaven Press.

Henkin, David M. 2006. *The Postal Age: The Emergence of Modern Communications in Nineteenth-Century America.* Chicago: The University of Chicago Press.

Howe, Daniel Walker. 2007. *What Hath God Wrought: The Transformation of America, 1815–1848.* New York: Oxford University Press.

Johnson, Paul M. 1999. *A History of the American People.* New York: Harper Perennial.

Lakwete, Angela. 2003. *Inventing the Cotton Gin: Machine and Myth in Antebellum America.* Baltimore: The Johns Hopkins University Press.

Library of Congress, Prints and Photographs Division, American Memory. "America's First Look into the Camera: Daguerrotype Portraits and Views, 1839–1864." http://lcweb2.loc.gov/ammem/daghtml/daghome.html.

McClellan, Elizabeth. 1969. *History of American Costume.* New York: Tudor Publishing Company.

Mintz, Steven. 2003 "Jackson's Removal of Native Americans" In *Antebellum America: 1784–1850,* ed. William Dudley, 165–69. San Diego: Greenhaven Press.

Mitchell, Margaret. 2007. *Gone with the Wind.* Scribner: New York.

Oberholtzer, Ellis Paxson. 1906. *The Literary History of Philadelphia.* Philadelphia: George W. Jacobs & Co.

Severa, Joan. 1997. *Dressed for the Photographer: Ordinary Americans and Fashion, 1840–1900.* Kent, OH: Kent State University Press.

Volo, James M. and Dorothy Denneen Volo. 2004. *The Antebellum Period.* Westport, Connecticut: Greenwood Press.

CHAPTER 7

Society, Culture, and Dress

OVERVIEW

Following the heady days of the American Revolution, the democratic ideal was reinforced by the adaptation of existing etiquette, resulting in the relinquishing of class distinctions. The changing social dynamics of the antebellum period, however, demanded a return to a more codified social structure. This demand was brought on by a growing marketplace and emerging consumer culture, both products of the steady rise of the middle class. This new effort to impose a subtle distinction in class came complete with etiquette and advice books that risked little to the reader's own interpretation. Over a hundred new works appeared during the decades of the antebellum period and each offered advice on all areas of conduct to a variety of audiences (Hemphill 1999, 131). Most social, and even fashion, choices (from greeting a friend on the street to the proper color of costume to wear while shopping) were laid out in black and white within their pages. The audience of these manuals was no longer the elite or upper class but instead the middle class, though some addressed the lowest serving classes of American society. These advice manuals differed from prior works not only in audience but in their authorship as well. They were most frequently written, not by members of America's elite, but by members of the middle class. As C. Dallet Hemphill observed, "No longer, then, was the upper class a major force in the instruction of proper behavior; the middle class had completely taken over" (Hemphill 1999, 131). Expectations of proper deportment, and proper dress, were particularly high for women. While men were only expected to have the *ambition* to adopt correct manners, "Certainly every woman should have the manners of a lady" (Hemphill 1999, 133). These rules of etiquette (and indeed dress) were intended to provide demarcation between the classes in a seemingly fluid democratic society where there were meant to be no pre-defined social roles.

A variety of factors affected what clothing was deemed appropriate for the emerging social groups of antebellum America. There were commonalities present within each gender, despite membership in disparate socio-economic groups. Regulating factors for women appear to be more plentiful when considered in this manner. Not only did their gender determine the basic type of garments worn by antebellum women, but their age, marital status and economic standing all played a role in shaping their dress. Religion was also key in determining not only a woman's role in American society but how she might consume fashion and still live up to the predominantly Christian ideal for womanhood in America. For men, the factors appear to have been less numerous. As with women, economic standing played a role in determining what a man might wear. However, the difference between the appearances of men of different economic standing was often a subtle one. The silhouette that emerged for men in the antebellum period became so standardized that it was difficult to tell men of higher means from those just scraping by. Only a close inspection of material and construction would reveal who might have the economic means to consume fashion at a more customized, and therefore higher, level and whose meager means relegated them as consumers of the growing market for mass-produced goods. A man's line of employment was really the most obvious regulating factor in antebellum dress. Except in his best dress, the clothes of a man who worked in the fields was strikingly different from his contemporary in the emerging white collar industries. The clothing of children was regulated by both gender and economic status. But there were other factors that dictated dress worn by other members of society—enslaved African Americans might have their clothing thrust upon them by their masters and even "free blacks" might find their clothing choices limited by legislation or more commonly, social codes that were embedded into the culture during the previous century.

The growing urban culture of antebellum America was a motivating force behind many of these factors influencing dress. As more Americans moved away from rural, agrarian lifestyles, visible symbols of social standing became more essential but, in many ways, more difficult to read. Contrasting this new urban experience was the expansion of American territories and the call to the west that was heeded by so many during the Antebellum Era. On the frontier, clothing was also an essential form of communication of economic and social standing.

Fashion in America was further affected by a number of advances in the production and care of clothing. The repercussions of many of these inventions were to be felt throughout the nation, from the largest metropolitan areas to the most remote frontier settlements. Innovative thought in other arenas also affected the way Americans dressed. Americans of the Antebellum Era sought to improve themselves and their surroundings. These impulses were most clearly expressed through the numerous reform movements founded during this period. Among them, the fight for women's rights had the most profound effect on fashion, both during this period and for a century afterwards. Finally, this chapter concludes with an overview of the art and culture that were to be experienced alongside the popular fashion of the antebellum period.

America's Urban Revolution

The America of the founding fathers had been a primarily agrarian one. The notion of the "gentleman farmer" was one that continued to be cherished by many of them, including Thomas Jefferson, despite its lineage as a tradition among the English aristocracy. However, a shift occurred when America entered a new kind of revolution—industry. While a primarily agrarian lifestyle was still maintained throughout most of the South, the North became the center for urban life and industrialization. Though industrial production did exist on a limited basis in the South, the manner of business tended to be on a small scale. In the North, however, the trend in business was towards incorporation; growing bigger and bigger companies that operated on a larger scale than a family run farm or manufacturing firm could imagine. At the center of this urban, industrial revolution was New York. By the end of the Antebellum Era, New York would be one of the three largest cities in the world.

New York became one of the most attractive places to do big business for a number of reasons. The draw of the stock exchange brought investors to the city while the opening of the Erie Canal, once seen as a folly, enabled the expedient transfer of goods. "Jobs multiplied, and as a result the city grew in population from 125,000 in 1820 to over half a million by 1850. New York had redrawn the economic map of the United States and put itself at the center," observed historian Daniel Howe (2007, 120). New York also made a name for itself internationally, becoming the most notable city in America. To foreign observers such as Frances Trollope, the architecture and street life rivaled the cultural capitals of Europe. During her visit in the 1820s, Trollope observed, "the city of New York...the splendid Broadway...This noble street may vie with any I ever saw, for its length and breadth, its handsome shops, neat awnings, excellent *trottoir,* and well-dressed pedestrians...The dwelling houses

> ***Brooks Brothers and the New Man of Business***
>
> The city abounded with the new American man. Instead of laboring in the fields and measuring his success by the bounty of his harvest, this man worked over half his day in one of the city's many office buildings, getting his hands dirty with ink and not soil. This new working man required a new wardrobe, different from those of his agrarian past. To satisfy this need, a new kind of merchant, and indeed industry, sprung up—the merchant tailor. Preeminent among these was the firm of Brooks Brothers, originally established in 1818 by Henry Sands Brooks and his brother as H. & D.H. Brooks & Co. (Brooks Brothers). In a company history written to celebrate its centennial anniversary, both Henry Brooks and his brother are credited with possessing the skills of master-trained tailors (Zakin 2003, 70). While this presents an idyllic beginning to one of America's most long-lived clothing firms, it underestimates the true nature and significance of the Brooks Brothers. For Henry, his brother and his sons that followed were in fact a new breed of tailor—one that entirely lacked the skills or knowledge to make a suit. What they possessed instead was a keen business sense, enabling them to translate the growing ready-made men's clothing industry into a viable and successful business model, appealing to a wide range of clientele. They helped to transform ready-made clothing into a staple of polite society, shaping the way Americans experience shopping even today. The luxurious store they opened on Broadway and Grand Street in 1857 was a far cry from the cheap workshop and warehouse used at the company's founding and helped to create great expectations for American shoppers in the decades that followed (Zakin 2003, 64).

of the higher classes are extremely handsome and very richly furnished" (Trollope 1832, 2: 190–91). The draw of New York was felt internationally and on a more local level. Recent arrivals from overseas, along with hopeful transplants from the nation's pastoral farm lands, fed the industrial machine. The work supply for the nation's factories would be drawn from these populations, among them children, young women, and the growing number of immigrants seeking a better life.

The changing landscape of the North, shifting from agrarian to industrial, threw into sharp contrast the differences between its states and those in the South. Everything, it seemed, was different. The South had come to rely upon its "peculiar" institution of slavery while the abolition of slavery had already made great headway in the North by the dawn of the Antebellum Era. Visitors to both the northern and southern United States remarked on the growing presence of "freed" African Americans in the North. Frances Trollope commented upon the fashionable *beaux* seen in New York, "There are a great number of negroes in New York, all free; their emancipation having been completed in 1827. Not even in Philadelphia, where the anti-slavery opinions have been the most active and violent, do the blacks appear to wear an air of so much consequence as they do at New York" (Trollope 1832, 2:210) She goes on to observe the excellent manners of African Americans she encountered, in contrast to the somewhat less appropriate etiquette of whites in the same neighborhoods. She had "met groups of negroes, elegantly dressed; and have been sometimes amused by observing the very superior air of gallantry assumed by the men, when in attendance on their belles, to that of the whites in similar circumstances. On one occasion we met in Broadway a young negress in the extreme of fashion, and accompanied by a black beau, whose toilet was equally studied; eye-glass, guard-chain, nothing was omitted...he walked...with an air of the most tender devotion [compared to the white gentlemen attending a lady a few doors down who were without hats and smoking!]" (Trollope 1832, 2:211) More than an air of condescension can be detected in Mrs. Trollope's speech but it is helpful nonetheless in demonstrating the extent to which this segment of the population actively participated in the growing consumer culture of the big city.

Alongside the free black population was the growing middle class. Within this new social group, a different definition of what a proper household was emerged. In the North, a proper middle class household was one where the husband worked in one of a number of growing white collar professions. In the North, the middle class were defined not by the number of servants or slaves they possessed but by the fact that the man of the house was the primary bread-winner, leaving his wife without the need to earn money. Men began to insist on "family wages" not only to eliminate the need for their wives to work, but to resist the infiltration of their industries by lower paid women workers. And so, a masculine-centered workplace was put firmly in place.

Despite her condescending tone in describing the fashionable African American beaux of the new urbane America, Frances Trollope correctly identified one of the emerging markets for fashionable clothing in antebellum America. UCLA Charles E. Young Research Library Dep. of Special Collection, SAD Michael Sadleir Collection of 19th Centrury Fiction.

The city was also home to another emerging class of immigrants. Promises of cheap land and plenty drew many away from the hard times of their homelands. Their dreams, however, were often met with the harsh reality of life in antebellum America. The American dream was not so easy to attain. Many immigrants, in fact, did not make it beyond their port of arrival, which in most cases was New York. They formed the bulk of the working class, providing the labor behind the North's new industrial machine. The North, with its promises of an hourly wage in an industrialized economy, was attractive to the poor immigrants arriving in America. In the South, landless whites had little to call their own and lived a somewhat migratory life, following task-oriented jobs that were felt to be too short-term to justify slave labor. With their frequent moves, these otherwise free individuals were unable to establish credit to purchase land for an enterprise of their own.

The North was characterized by large cities with "well-defined and established business districts…there was also an enormous growth in slums, tenements, and ethnically segregated residential areas filled with the poor and uneducated" (Volo and Volo 2004, 5). Life in the city, and particularly in the highly populated tenements, was often harder than what these new arrivals might have found on the frontier. Hygiene and proper sanitation were absent. Water was not provided by the city; instead individuals and families dug wells—often adjacent to their outhouses. Contamination ran rampant. It is no surprise then that male children from the cities tended to grow up to be shorter than those from farming communities. The death rate in the cities exceeded the birth rate—it was only due to the massive waves of immigration and the arrival of new tenants that city life did not perish entirely.

A large segment of the poor population in the North was made up of the immigrated Catholic Irish. These seekers of the American dream experienced prejudice at the hands of the Protestant majority in antebellum America. They had difficulty finding work due to this prejudice (ironically at the hands of those most ardently against slavery and active in the popular social reform movements of the North). Historian Roger Daniels observed, "When relatively large numbers of Irish and German Catholic immigrants, many of them desperately poor, began to arrive in the late 1820s and early 1830s, what had been a largely rhetorical anti-Catholicism became a major social and political force in American life…in eastern cities…anti-Catholicism turned violent" (Daniels 2003, 270). Concerns over the increasing influx of immigrants found expression in the creation of organizations to support blockages on immigration. These were often backed by large political parties such as the Whigs. In New Orleans a "Native American Association" was formed with this intent—it "denounced the immigration to the United States of 'the outcast and offal of society, the vagrant and the convict—transported in myriads to our shores, reeking with the accumulated crimes of the whole civilized world'" (Daniels 2003, 271).

On the Plantation

The promise of cheap land drew many to the shores of America. The reality of inhumane, cheap labor helped to divide the country. In the South, where slavery continued despite growing abolitionist sentiments throughout the rest of the country, the North was viewed as place where men sold their souls in the name of the hourly wage, a dishonorable way of living. The primarily agrarian nature of the Southern economy was tied to the land; work was measured by tasks rather than hours. From this agriculture-based economy rose a unique social class—the planter class. Their grand style of living was often supported by large loans of money. Although this indebtedness was rarely a cause for embarrassment, hurt pride from other causes could be the source of violence. Matters of personal pride were often settled with duels or fisticuffs. "A virile man was expected to fight if insulted, an expectation shared by southern women as well as southern men," notes Daniel Howe (2007, 435), "Some historians have traced this penchant for violence to the folk culture of the Celtic clans…from which so many southern whites descended. Inherited rural folkways changed more slowly in the South, as the effects of the transportation and communications revolutions were felt more slowly there." The American frontier, growing as the United States took more and more land from American Indian tribes and other countries through war and treaty, offered opportunities that could not be found in either the old South or the modern North. People from all economic levels, white, black, free and slave, immigrant and native migrated to frontier settlements in hopes of finding financial success.

Westward

Viewing antebellum life against the backdrop of a nationally felt expansionist attitude is intrinsic to understanding the clothing of the period. At first individuals and then whole families migrated into the new open territories of the West. With them, they took the cultural standards for life in America that had developed since the dawn of the 19th century. These included expectations regarding family responsibilities, etiquette, and dress. Their experience in this new environment saw many of these expectations tested. Family roles were altered to meet the demands of settling in uncharted territory. Etiquette was often brushed aside in order survive in difficult conditions. And fashionable clothing was modified or, in many instances, given up altogether in favor of more practical and economical choices. In the new frontier regions, fashion was often viewed mainly as a source of entertainment or a novelty unto itself. Though community members might not have been participating in fashion in the same way that their city cousins did, there was still widespread discussion and display when the opportunity arose (Helvenston 1991, 144). As communities developed in these frontier settlements and the transportation and communication revolutions brought more of the conveniences of the homes they had left behind, the frontier lifestyle slowly began to resemble more closely that of those in the rest of the United States. The ways in which clothing was adapted to suit the needs of the frontier is discussed in more detail in each of the following chapters.

Family Life and Dress in Antebellum America

Family life in antebellum America revolved around the home, and at the core of the home was the wife and mother. She was the moral center of the home and as such was expected to provide the spiritual and moral example for both her children and her husband. In Sally Helvenston's study of advice books and domestic manuals for women in the 19th century, she sums up the role of a wife and/or mother thus: "As proprietress of the household, she was expected to remain true to her domestic responsibilities, be submissive to her husband, uphold high religious principles, and dress appropriately for this role" (Helvenston 1980, 32). The fashionable ideal of woman as a fragile ornament of conspicuous consumption for her husband was ultimately deemed incongruous with this concept. The realm of fashion itself was deemed almost an entirely feminine one in antebellum America. Concerns about dress were seen as more suited for women due to their innate sense of style and taste. Yet the realm of fashion was seen as frivolous in nature. Men, therefore, were above the consumption of fashion due to their "good sense" and "practical natures." These attitudes towards fashion and its consumption reveal the underlying expectation of woman as ornament that the reformers worked so diligently to dismiss. "This not only pertained to her everyday activities, but extended to her appearance as well. She was likened to a flower 'beautifying, smiling, diffusing grace around the home' while the male stood as 'the firm protecting tree in the garden of life.' Since the lifestyle of each woman was defined primarily by her husband (or father) her duty was to accede to his desires in her manner of dress" (Helvenston 1980, 33).

Reformers, whether of women's health or the American domestic norm, sought to bring these expectations in line with her "moral superiority, power, and responsibility within the home." These reformers did not seek to change the overall role of women within society but "strove to give her the health and strength she needed to guide her family's moral development" (Helvenston 1980, 32). This served as the impetus behind many forms of dress reform that will be discussed later in the chapter.

Fashion consumption within the family was dictated not only by gender but by economic standing as well. Those with the least means, existing at or below poverty level, did not consume fashion at all. For the poorest in America, daily life was consumed with achieving food and shelter. Clothing the body fashionably was not a possibility. Clothing was most often second-hand or, in some cases, lacking. In the south, the poorest whites would wear the same or worse clothing than that worn by enslaved African Americans.

The growing lower middle class of America consumed fashion on a limited basis. The fashionable silhouette might be followed at a removed distance from its original introduction. Information about the latest fashions would have reached these consumers slower than the wealthiest people in the country and therefore may have been diluted by removal from the original source. For women, this might mean a dress constructed in a less exaggerated line than the fashion plate and lacking the excessive decoration. Dresses might be remade from year to year or season to season to follow the latest skirt width or hemline and sleeve style, but the consumption of the latest fabrics or trims would be limited. The wealthy in America had access to travel, and with that, access to more first-hand information about the fashionable styles out of Paris and London. They were able to import the latest fashions, and therefore consumed fashion at a higher rate and followed all the subtle style changes that new fashions might bring. These women would have worn clothing that was made both in the United States and overseas.

The ability for some but not all women in America to achieve the most fashionable looks created an interesting contrast between genders. In menswear, class was no longer as easily read in the way one dressed. As Caroline Rennolds Milbank observed, "First the frock coat and long trousers and then the lounge suit (precursor of the business suit) became a uniform that had an equalizing effect [in men's wear]." Where fashionably dressed men and women had once consumed decoration and excess equally, there was now a disparity between the staid masculine uniform and the overtly decorative female silhouette. Milbank continues, "In the previous century both sexes had worn powdered wigs, colorful brocaded and embroidered silks, shoes with heels and elaborate buckles. As a definite masculine style emerged that was tailored and somber [at the end of the 18th century], women's clothes became far more feminine by comparison, particularly in silhouette and degree of decoration" (2000, 251).

CLOTHING IN ANTEBELLUM AMERICA

Making Clothes

> The history of woman is the history of the improvements in the world. Some twenty or thirty years ago, when manual labour performed all the drudgery, some five, six, or seven yards of silk or muslin or gingham would suffice for the flitting and flirting of the most gay and volatile of the sex. But as soon as the powers of steam are applied, and labour is changed from physical to intellectual, the ladies, in their charitable regard for the operative class of the community, begin to devise means for their continued employment, and as the material is produced with half the labour, the equilibrium must be sustained by consuming a double quantity.
>
> —From the "National Recorder" in 1829 (McClellan 1969, 406)

Though the cynicism about the frivolity of women felt by this oft-quoted author is nearly palpable, his observation does serve to set the stage for a discussion of the materials and means of production of clothing in the Antebellum Era. In an age in which the amount of material consumed by some women in a single dress might have sufficed for the production of five in another time, speed of production was a key factor in the changing pace of fashion and its consumption in the 19th century. The clothing industry became one in which machine-power began to outrank manpower.

How the clothing of any one period was made shares equal importance with the way it was worn. At the most basic level, the material of clothing—namely, cloth—can serve to explain the level of technology available to a civilization. As the means of processing fiber and the looms on which it is woven become more technologically advanced, so too do other areas of technology. A wide variety of materials was used in the construction of clothing during the antebellum period. From animal skins to imported silk, the materials used in clothing production should be familiar to most modern consumers.

Animal skin and fibers from their pelts or hair form the primary type of materials used in clothing production. At the most unprocessed level was wild animal fur and skins. These were used in the construction of clothing for every level of consumption, from indigenous people to slaves to town gentlemen. The fur trade, particularly in beaver pelts, was fed by the fashion for beaver skin hats while other furs were used as linings, trim, tippets and other accessories for both men and women. At a lower level, skins (when they were not traded) were used by American Indians in the production of their dress. Skins were also used in the production of work clothing and the clothing and accessories of enslaved African Americans, particularly in the frontier regions. Domestic leather production for use in clothing increased in the second quarter of the 19th century, right as the Antebellum Era was beginning to bloom (Foster 1997, 87). Domesticated animals were naturally a source of material for clothing construction. Wool was processed from sheep raised in both the North and the South. At-home processing, i.e. carding and spinning, might be performed on wool gathered from one's own flock or purchased from another farmer. Fabrics produced from wool could also be bought as commercially produced goods. This was, in fact, the most frequent means of consumption of this clothing staple by the time of the Antebellum Era in America. The homespun traditions of Revolutionary America were not entirely absent, however, just reduced. Silk was another fiber that might be produced domestically but was more frequently bought as a commercial product. Fabrics made of this fiber were used almost exclusively for special occasion dress, especially in clothes for those who were enslaved. In this case, the silk clothing might be given to them as hand-me-downs or purchased with money made by hiring themselves out. It was also more rarely worn by most of the general population but there is evidence to suggest that it could be acquired fairly easily. Silk was produced on a limited level in the South. Helen Bradley Foster cites examples of silk production in the South in her work on antebellum African American clothing. One particular area in Georgia was known for its mulberry trees grown to support the sericulture there, and she goes on to cite the remembrances of an enslaved African American who noted that silk was also produced in places as far west as Texas. This particular example identifies the mistress as the sole participant in its creation (1997, 86). The majority of silk used in the production of clothing in America was imported.

Vegetable fibers played a more prominent role in the production of cloth in America. Preeminent among them was cotton. A staple of the Southern economy (and the Northern industrial complex), cotton was the driving force behind many of the industrial advances seen in the Antebellum Era. From processing equipment to looms, the production of cotton cloth in America was an essential part of both the inventive and business spirit of the age. Flax was also produced in the United States, both for domestic and commercial use. Roughly processed flax, called "tow," was used for the construction of work clothes, while finer grades of linen were reserved for the construction of linen dresses. Sack cloth, the most humble of textiles, was made from a variety of vegetable fibers including hemp, jute (burlap), and cotton and used in the production of clothing for enslaved African Americans and others along the lowest ends of the economic scale (Foster 1997, 91). There were several commercially made fabrics that were specifically marketed for use in the production of slave clothing. These included a variety of weaves and fiber combinations, including "kerseys, linseys, negro cloth (cassinet), osnaburgs, plains, and flannels" with some being specifically marketed toward one gender or the other. For example, "linsey, also of cotton and wool, was designated for Negro women" (Ullrich 1985, 38). This kind of cloth was produced in both the North and the South, though the material produced in the North is perhaps the most well-known. It came to be called "lowell-cloth" after the most well-known place of manufacture, Lowell, Massachusetts. A participant in the *Narratives* project of the 1930s remembered "Us wore lowell-cloth shirts. It was a coarse tow-sackin'" (Foster 1997, 75). The *Slave Narratives: A Folk History of Slavery in the United States From Interviews with Former Slaves* (Botkin 1940) forms the basis of Helen Bradley Foster's work *"New Raiments of Self": African American Clothing in the Antebellum South.* Conducted between 1936 and 1938, the *Narratives* project was an endeavor to collect the oral histories of almost 2,000 formerly enslaved African Americans and was supported by the FWP (Federal Writers' Project). These interviews were frequently recorded, for better or worse, with dialectical spelling. In her work, as in this, Foster chooses to retain this spelling in an effort to avoid misinterpretation of the original source material.

When cloth was made onsite in the South, it was very often made by enslaved African American women. The cloth produced was generally used to make clothes for other enslaved individuals on the plantation or, in some cases, clothing for the master's family. Most frequently, however, homemade cloth (when it was used) was used in combination with factory-produced cloth in the production of clothing. Louis Hughes, born in 1843 and enslaved in Mississippi and Virginia, noted in the *Narratives* project that "each piece of [homemade] cloth contained forty yards, and this cloth was used in making clothes for the servants. About half of the whole amount required was this made at home; the remainder was bought, and as it was heavier it was used for winter clothing" (Foster 1997, 76). Making clothing was traditionally women's work, either by slave or free persons. Foster notes that the evidence from the *Narratives* project reveals that white women were often solely responsible for the production of slave clothing, as well as clothing that was worn by the family. "Miss Fannie and Miss Frances—that was her daughter—they wove such pretty cloth for the colored. You know, they went and made themselves dresses and the white and colored had the same kind of dresses" (Foster 1997, 108). Foster notes in her research that "Narrators mention that clothing was produced either by specially trained black women or their white 'mistresses' or by professional seamstresses who were hired for that purpose" (Foster 1997, 117). The labor in clothing production at home was typically divided, however, into several different tasks that were carried out by different individuals. One might be skilled in carding and spinning, another in weaving, one in cutting, and yet another in sewing. This process was a reflection of the division of labor found in the commercial production of clothing. Cloth would be purchased from a merchant, taken to a cutter to be cut into the proper shapes, and then a seamstress for finishing. Purchased, cut fabric might also be finished in the home after being basted by a skilled professional.

Two revolutionary advances in clothing production occurred during the Antebellum Era. The first was a growing movement towards a more uniform pattern drafting system for women's wear, which was the first step in a very long procession towards the mass-production of women's clothing. The other, also a key element in the ultimate mass-production of clothing, was the invention of the sewing machine. Introduced in the 1840s, the sewing machine was initially too expensive for most home use. Very few, if any, garments of the antebellum period are finished entirely by machine, in fact. However, the use of the sewing machine is seen in the long straight seams of skirts and side seams of bodices, as well as in men's and children's wear.

In 1820, scholars contend, the uniform tape measure was introduced (Zakin 2003, 91; Waugh 1964, 130; and Kidwell 1979, 2). In the past, tapes were used to mark only a specific person's measurements.

The information was not recorded in uniform inches. As Anne Hollander points out, "The tape measure, marked out in impersonal and universal inches that might apply its measurements to all and then compare the results...was used for the express purpose of making well-fitting suits for many unmeasured men at once, using a principle of common rules for masculine physical proportions." While men were the subjects of the initial usage of the tape measure, it would become an essential tool in women's pattern manipulation by the end of the period. Hollander continues, "Many new measuring schemes were invented by skilled and experienced tailors for the creation of variable patterns that would make ready-to-wear suits desirably well-fitting. Since Classical bodily proportions were part of the fiction behind Neo-classic suits in the first place, the plan served both an imaginative ideal and a very practical commercial purpose. Neo-classic suits were originally designed to augment chests and shoulders just a little, to suggest natural heroism with very subtle artifice, and 'perfect fit' was already a slightly fictional matter, even for bespoke examples. This fact helped make ready-made production easier to manage and gave it predictably excellent results" (Hollander 1994, 106). By the 1840s, a proliferation of drafting systems aided a new breed of clothier—the merchant tailors—in speeding up production, lowering costs and further standardizing American men's wear. The merchant tailor was a phenomenon unto himself. He represented the successful marriage of two distinct

Worth, the Father of Haute Couture

Although the label that would eventually become the House of Worth was founded at the tail end of the Antebellum Era, the importance of Charles Frederick Worth (1825–1895) and his revolutionary approach to fashion is not to be overlooked. Once a salesman in London and Paris textile and dry goods stores, Worth hit upon a clever idea for promoting the yardage that was for sale. By designing sample gowns and modeling them on his future wife in a Paris store, Worth was able to help clients more completely visualize their completed gown. This simple approach increased sales and the modern fashion designer was born. With Worth, you received the attention of no mere seamstress but a designer, an artist. His clients in Paris were offered a selection of skirt and bodice types from which to choose each season, each executed in luxurious and impeccably executed French silk. Wealthy women of America took notice. One extant example of a ball gown worn at the Prince of Wales ball, held in New York City in 1860, is attributed to Worth et Bobergh. Made from fabric woven in Lyon, it is exemplary of the mission set by Emperor Louis-Phillipe, and embraced by Worth, to reinvigorate the silk industry of France. "Well-traveled, well-heeled New Yorkers were, typically, among the first [American] clients of French couture" observes Caroline Rennolds Milbank. Worth's contributions to fashion were significant in other ways. In Anne Hollander's words, Worth was the "first man-milliner." The couture business he established in 1858 set the precedent for more than just the phenomenon of haute couture. He introduced a "dramatic new element" into women's fashion: clothes helped women become the "creations of men" (Hollander 1994, 116). With the advent of Worth, the making of a dress was no longer the domain of women. He combined the business of the dry-goods merchant with that of the seamstress, while adding a new layer of service or enterprise, that of the "designer." The creation of women's fashion was no longer a joint operation between client and dressmaker—now the dressmaker dictated what the client wore.

steps in the production of men's wear. The place where suits were made was now also the place where the fabric of which they were made was acquired—in essence, one-stop shopping was created.

For women's wear, the effect of the introduction of the tape measure was felt at a much slower pace. The introduction of widely available patterns was slow, beginning after the first American fashion periodicals began distribution in the 1830s. Initially, pattern diagrams were printed and even one-size-only patterns were available for purchase. The latter were expensive and both methods were difficult to use. As fashions became more fitted to the body, a need was felt for a more efficient means to attain a properly fitted pattern/garment. Claudia Brush Kidwell's study of dressmaker's drafting systems for the Smithsonian Institute goes into some detail about the variety of patented instruments and systems created in the Antebellum Era and after.

Care of Clothing

The care of clothing is equally important to its manner of production. One finds information about the care of clothing in the antebellum period in both anecdotal accounts and period publications. These often offer insight into not only how things were done but who was doing them. For example, *The House Servant's Directory,* the first book by an African American to be published by a commercial publisher, appeared in 1827 and offered advice to "free blacks" who might find employment as domestic help. Primarily addressing male servants, author Robert Roberts provides guidelines for "brushing and cleaning gentlemen's clothes," advice for removing stains and preserving fabrics such as wool and fur (Roberts 1827; Foster 1997, 129).

Of supreme importance in the care of clothing was the process of cleaning. Doing the laundry in the 19th century was no mean feat. It required several days and many hands to complete the task. Laundry day could be a family affair, enlisting the support of sons and daughters, as well as husbands in many cases, or it could be something that was hired out, either to women seeking employment, "free blacks," or in many cases, enslaved African Americans who were allowed to hire out their time for their own gain (or the gain of their master). Professional help in the form of laundresses might also be employed for this arduous task. This was true in both city and rural settings. The individual tasks, including making the soap and preparing the clothing, could be divided in a manner reflecting that seen in clothing production. "Hauling water was considered women's work, although young boys were often required to help" (Ritter and Feather 1990, 156).

Even as tasks were designated to certain members of the family, the day of the week on which laundry was done became a cultural norm. More often than not, a family's laundry was done on Monday. Women, as keepers of the home, took pride in presenting a fresh laundry at the beginning of the week for view to their neighbors. Preparation for laundry day began the week before with water-softening. Instructions for softening water for laundry day could be found in numerous periodicals of the 1850s—it was typically achieved through the use of wood ash or quicklime that was allowed to settle in the water and then filtered out (Ritter and Feather 1990, 160). The clothing would also be prepared in advance of wash day. It would be sorted "according to use, color, and the amount of soil" (Ritter and Feather 1990, 160). The process of stain removal was begun, including bleaching of yellowed garments. Pre-soaking clothes was also part of this process; "White clothes were soaked in cold water that had washing soda or lime added to help remove soil during the washing process" (Ritter and Feather 1990, 160). Common household ingredients were excellent multi-taskers and provided the means for stain removal as very few products were sold for this specific purpose. The ingredients could be stomach-turning, such as sour milk, or merely unpleasant-smelling, such as vinegar, while others could prove noxious or dangerous if incorrectly mixed. Oxalic acid, ammonia, or white alcohols in the form of gin, vodka, or unaged whiskey were all used in stain removal. Other issues arose with the treatment of colored clothing. Additional treatments were required to make sure that dyes did not become transient in the wash. Fixatives or mordants were used to set the dye. The clothing was soaked in a mordant solution and then frequently washed separately from all other clothes to reduce the risk of bleeding (Ritter and Feather 1990, 160–61).

In preparation of washing day, laundry materials were made at home. This included all the soap, dye and utensils to be used in doing the laundry. Two tubs on a board or table would be set outside in preparation for washing day. The water that was gathered was boiled with soap in order to create suds (Ritter and Feather 1990, 161). The process of actually doing the laundry began with the heating of the pre-softened water. This was done outdoors over a large fire, so that several gallons could be heated at once. All of the pre-soaked clothes would be rinsed and washed first. These were then wrung out and washed again. The second washing was typically more intense—a scrubbing board or manual scrubbing would be used to loosen any remaining soil from the garment. As the washing water cooled, the colored garments pre-treated with a mordant would be washed. The warm water would provide further protection from potential dye bleeding. All of the washed clothes would be rinsed in a separate water bath to remove any remaining soap. An additional rinse, referred to as a blueing treatment, might be applied to white garments before a final rinse. This, in addition to bleach, helped maintain the pristine whiteness of linen. All of the clothes were then dipped into starch, wrung out, and hung to dry. A sunny area would be preferred for drying clothes that required further bleaching while dyed clothes would be dried in a shady spot to prevent fading.

However, not every fabric used in the 19th century might stand up to such harsh punishment. Alternative cleaning methods were used for these delicate, often expensive, fabrics. Since these could not be washed with the regular laundry they required special, often labor-intensive, treatment. This kind of special treatment of clothing was more typically found in the homes of the wealthy, who could afford both the more expensive fabrics and garments and the skilled labor required to clean them. Clothing made of silk and those trimmed in the latest fashion were prepared for a kind of dry-cleaning, or in some cases, a gentle wet-cleaning. The arrangement of folds, trim and tucks might reduce the efficiency of the cleaning process, so garments were often disassembled before cleaning to prevent this. The pieces would be flattened, cleaned and then re-assembled before wearing again. This process may have encouraged women to alter the silhouette of their garments more frequently in order to keep up with the latest fashions. After all, if the dress is already dismantled, why not refine the skirt or change the line of the bodice before wearing it again? If dry-cleaning was required, absorbents of different kinds were used. These typically included French chalk, fuller's earth (which is still used today by some in treating stained clothing, though the material can be hazardous if inhaled), flour, magnesia, or cornmeal. These were rubbed into the fabric to absorb any oily or waxy soil and then brushed off to remove both the absorbent and the soil. If wet-cleaning was called for a variety of solvents could be used. These included alcohol such as gin or vodka, as well as turpentine. These would be applied to the fabrics to dissolve any matter soiling the surface. Then the fabric would be allowed to dry in the air to remove the odors associated with the solvent.

Once the family's laundry was clean, the work of laundry day was hardly over. The clothing must then be ironed. Without the convenience of electricity, this was a difficult and uncomfortable process. Sadirons were used in most households throughout the United States. Most would have multiples that might be used in rotation. These heavy irons, weighing between four and eight pounds, would be heated over the stove or in fire (Ritter and Feather 1990, 163). While one was in use, the others would remain in the fire to be picked up when it became too cool to be useful. There were also specialized irons for flounces, pleats and other trim. These were called crimping or fluting irons and were typically made to fit the narrow structures they pressed. Since starch was applied to clothing following washing, it would often adhere to the iron. This could be prevented by treating the bottom of the iron with wax after cleaning it with salt and paper.

After wash day, clothing was stored until it was worn. Built-in closets were rare in the mid-19th century and those that did exist were typically small. According to one contemporary source, a young girl in boarding school in Missouri in 1858 stated, "closets will hold only three to four dresses and then they get creased" (Ritter and Feather 1990, 160). More commonly, furniture and wooden pegs were used for clothing storage. Armoires, cupboards, chests of drawers, and trunks were all used to store clothing in both middle and upper class households. Wooden pegs hammered into the walls of the home were more commonly found in middle and lower class households. Out-of-season storage might occur in the attic, where clothing could be laid out horizontally over poles suspended from the ceiling (Ritter and Feather 1990, 160).

Consuming Fashion

A relationship between "consumerism and propriety" grew throughout the Antebellum Era. As Caroline Rennolds Milbank observed, "in a few decades [of the founding of the country] the dictates of etiquette had multiplied, reinforcing a newly strong relationship between consumerism and propriety. Rules of civilized conduct prescribed what ladies and gentlemen should wear at all hours of the day and for all types of occasions. Magazine coverage of etiquette was closely intertwined with that of fashion, and the advice given was so specific that an insecure customer paying close attention could purchase secure fashion footing" (Milbank 2000, 252).

So, for women, shopping became an acceptable pastime, particularly in those urban settings that afforded the broadest choice of stores and goods. Places such as Boston, Philadelphia, Washington, D.C., and New York City became veritable shopping meccas, gaining national and international reputations. Ladies might venture out to the shops without the aid of a chaperone and while there, were treated to "art exhibitions, lectures, and architectural novelties" (Milbank 2000, 248). Streets like Broadway gained an international reputation for being places where the most fashionable ladies might be met. James Fennimore Cooper wrote that New York and its promenade, Broadway could "safely challenge competition with most if not all of the promenades of the old world" (Cooper 1836, 194). New York was home to what was to be the first department store in the United States, owned by A. T. Stewart, as well as a number of "small but luxurious" (not to mention expensive) boutiques run by "modistes or couturiers, milliners, fancy-goods dealers, and jewelers" with windows of goods so alluring that they might "make the money leap from one's pocket" (Milbank 2000, 244). The establishment of Stewart was started in the late 1820s when he first began selling Irish laces. He expanded his store and his purview to include dress goods and accessories as well as items for furnishing the home. In 1846, he built his "Marble Palace" along Broadway and became synonymous with the last word in fashion.

In Washington, Mrs. Roger A. Pryor was shocked by both the amount and quality of shops. "There was Galt's, where the silver, gems and marbles were less attractive than the cultivated gentlemen who sold them; Gautier's, the palace of sweets, with Mrs. Gautier in an armchair before her counter to tell you the precise social status of every one of her customers and, what is more, to put you in your own; Harper's, where the dainty leisurely salesman treated his laces with respect, drawing up his cuffs lest they touch the ethereal beauties; and the little corner shop of stern Madame Delarue, who imported as many (and no more) hats and gloves as she was willing to sell as a favour to the ladies of the diplomatic and official circles, and whose dark-eyed daughter, Léonide (named for her godmother, a Greek lady of rank), was susceptible of unreasoning friendships and could be coaxed to preserve certain treasures for humbler folk.... At Madame Delarue's, if one was very *gentil,* very *convenable,* one might have the services of François, the one and only hair-dresser of note, who had adjusted coronets on noble heads, and who could (if so minded) talk of them agreeably in Parisian French" (Pryor 1904, 6). Mrs. Pryor goes on to describe an incident where Mme. Delarue's daughter awoke her in the middle of the night to give her a sneak preview of bonnets that had just arrived before other, more prominent customers, had the chance to see them. She was able to secure for herself "a 'divine creation' of point lace, crape and shaded asters before Madame had seen it. Otherwise it would have been reserved for Miss Harriet Lane [Pres. Buchanan's niece] or Mrs. Douglas" (McClellan 1969, 471).

And yet with all the opportunities to consume fashion, American women were still likely to be found wanting by foreign visitors. Frances Trollope observed that the dress budgets of American women did little to improve their taste. "Though the expense of the ladies' dress greatly exceeds, in proportion to their general style of living, that of the ladies of Europe, it is very far (excepting in Philadelphia) from being in good taste. They do not consult the seasons in the colours or in the style of their costume" (1832 2:134–35). Trollope was not alone in her criticism, if not of the expenditure of money than of that of time. The maid of honor to Queen Victoria noted "American ladies bestow those hours of leisure, which English women of the same class give to drawing, to the study of nature, and to mental cultivation, almost wholly on personal adornment" (Milbank 2000, 248). The cost of maintaining a fashionable appearance also consumed the national media. In *Watson's Annals* of 1856, one article rages against the rising price of high fashion in America, citing those of Philadelphia in the same year: "EXTRAVAGANCE IN DRESS: At this time a fashionable dry goods store advertises a lace scarf for 1,500 dollars! Another has a bridal dress for 1,200 dollars. Bonnets at 200 dollars are also sold. Cashmeres from 300 dollars and upwards are seen by dozens along Broadway. And 100 dollars is quite a common price for a silk gown. Think of such a scale of prices for 'un-idead' American women! Can the pampering of such vanities elevate the character of our women?" (McClellan 1969, 468). But the fashion consumer had been born and her desires could not be extinguished by pleas to return to more republican ideals.

The rapid dissemination of fashion information was in many ways to blame for this growing consumer culture. While in the previous century information about the latest fashions had often been the privilege of the elite few, women of the 19th century had unparalleled access to it. Even on the frontier, where women were far removed from civilization, news of the latest fashion spread like wildfire. Sally Helvenston (1991) notes that women of the frontier "eagerly discussed fashion among themselves," finding evidence in the memoirs of some of these women such as Elizabeth Brandley. "The latest styles in sleeves, overskirts or basques was a matter of much solicitude" in the growing frontier. Many times, the latest arrival to any frontier community was considered an "expert" on the latest fashions; regardless of their previous pattern of consumption, and was applied to for advice and information. One Oregon pioneer wrote: "Although I had now been absent from civilization—otherwise Ohio—for a year, I still was considered an authority on the matter of dress and fashion. I was consulted and acted as an advisor whenever a new cloak or gown was made" (Helvenston 1991, 146). Letters were full of the news of fashion. Newspaper clippings of the latest styles were sent through the mail to family and friends on the frontier. One need not wait for the latest letter from home, however, to review the fashion news. On the frontier, sources for fashion information also included general periodicals that carried fashion columns. These were produced within the new settlements but most often borrowed heavily from Eastern newspapers for fashion reporting. Subscription clubs provided access to magazines such as *Godey's Lady's Book, Peterson's Magazine,* and *Harper's Bazar* (Helvenston 1991, 146). These periodicals could also be viewed in public reading rooms throughout the frontier in hotels or "local milliner's or dressmaker's shops" (Helvenston 1991, 146). The purpose behind fashion commentary in frontier newspapers may have been quite different from that of their city counterparts, however. Mary Hudson, the editor of fashion columns for the *Kansas Farmer* stated that her purpose was "not...to report the very latest system adopted by fashion followers, regardless of good sense and economy, but to glean from all the sources at our command, and present in the *Farmer*...a plain description of serviceable, graceful, and economic costumes and garments" (Helvenston 1991, 148). Perhaps the most powerful way in which fashion information was transmitted in the 19th century was through the visual medium of fashion plates. For women, these were found in popular periodicals and were meant to aid the home sewer as well as the woman who employed the help of a dress-maker in determining the shape and trim of her latest gown. In men's wear, the fashion plate was meant only for the maker of men's clothes, not for the consumer. "Fashion plates depicting men's styles were not in fact designed for general consumption. They circulated instead in trade journals such as *le Mirror de Beau Monde,* the *Quarterly Reports of London and Paris Fashions, Taylor's Magazine and Quarterly Reports of Fashion,* the *American Report of the Fashions,* and the *Mirror of Fashion,* which published their illustrations in tandem with the technical details needed to make up the garments. Certainly, men had no intention of cutting and sewing the suits themselves: the illustrations, like the instructions, were intended for tailors" (Zakin 2003, 197). Outside of the brilliant Broadway and other avenues of America's most fashionable cities, local fashion trends were observed in some seemingly unlikely places. In Cincinnati, Ohio, for example, the churches were the catwalks, based on the keen observation of Mrs. Frances Trollope. "It is in the churches and chapels of the town that the ladies are to be seen in full costume...No evening of the week but brings throngs of the young and beautiful to the chapels and meetinghouses, all dressed with care, and sometimes with great pretension; it is there that all display is made, and all fashionable distinction sought.... Were it not for the churches, indeed, I think there might be a general bonfire of best bonnets, for I never could discover any other use for them" (1832, 1:100).

For 19th century women, fashion was consumed in ways very similar to those observed in modern times. Window shopping, perusing magazines, and discussing the latest trends were all part of daily life for most women. Only those who could not afford the luxury of leisure; those below the growing middle class, could not participate in this new phenomenon of consumer culture.

THE IMPROVERS: REFORM MOVEMENTS IN ANTEBELLUM AMERICA

Women in Politics

Women had been active in national politics since the birth of the nation. In popular history, their contributions are often minimized to reflect gender roles of the time. Young Americans are told of Betsy Ross making the first American flag or the steadfastness of Martha Washington. Women's contributions to antebellum politics have often been similarly maligned. By discussing the role of fashion in women's political lives, however, this volume does not mean to add to this tradition. However, the use of fashion as social commentary was one of only a handful of outlets for expression available to many women. Despite their inability to vote, women would often express party or candidate affiliation through their dress. For example, in 1829 when Andrew Jackson was elected president, "His lady partisans were to be distinguished by dresses and aprons of calico imprinted in great medallions with the very unhandsome head of their hero," notes costume historian Elizabeth McClellan. She continues to cite in her study on American fashion that extant examples of this "Jackson" calico can be found in the Historical Society at Newport, Rhode Island (McClellan 1969, 404). Their involvement in the temperance movement, the women's rights movement or the abolitionist movement could be similarly expressed through dress, the wearing of badges, or by adopting reformed silhouettes.

Among the loudest cries for freedom for enslaved African Americans were the voices of women who, at the same time, sought freedom and rights of their own. In a society where a wife was essentially the property of her husband, with her individual identity completely absorbed into his upon marriage, the road towards a more equitable society would be longer than the 40 years that comprise the antebellum period, however. (Volo and Volo 2004, 13)

Women's involvement in the abolitionist movement was viewed as an assault on the traditional values espoused by northerners and southerners alike. For many, such as President John Tyler, women abolitionists were not just attacking slavery but "the entire traditional social order" (Howe 2007, 433). When Congress instated a gag order regarding the slavery issue, abolitionists upped the ante by sending in more petitions. When southern representatives expressed contempt over the presence of women's signatures on these petitions, they were defended by people such as John Quincy Adams. "Women are not only justified [in circulating and signing petitions], but exhibit the most exalted virtue when they do depart from the domestic circle, and enter on the concerns of their country, of humanity, and of their God" (Howe 2007, 514–15). He took their cause to heart and encouraged the petition drives, coming up with new and different tactics to get them heard before Congress.

Dress Reform

It is in dress reform that the strongest link between fashion and politics can be seen. Dress reform was spurred on by a number of motives. Dress was seen by many reformers as the stumbling block between women and their greatest potential as individuals. The popular fashions of the period were cumbersome and were seen to support the submissiveness of women in society. The greatest proponents of this movement saw dress at the center of the growing dependency of American women. "Women such as Amelia Bloomer, Elizabeth Cady Stanton, Elizabeth Phelps Ward, and Abba Goold-Woolson...advocated the most radical changes in women's attire—namely the abandonment of the skirt in favor of the ease and comfort of a bifurcated garment" (Helvenston 1980, 32). But dress reform was an issue that was embraced for a number of other reasons. Health reformers, for example, were typically more concerned about the physical damage that fashionable women's dress might cause than its political or emotional burden. "They generally went beyond mere moralizing and attempted to point out to women the unhealthy aspects of the clothes they wore which needed change...[they] worried about what fashion might do to women's bodies" (Helvenston 1980, 40).

Among those concerns high on the list of health reformers was the custom of lacing corsets tightly to achieve a more narrow waist. Those against the custom included physicians such as Dr. William Alcott, as well as women who were also active in other forms of activism such as the Beecher sisters, Harriet Beecher Stowe (the author of *Uncle Tom's Cabin*) and Catharine Beecher. Dr. Alcott explained that "corsets impeded full expansion of the lungs in breathing, thus causing weakening of the lungs, shortness of breath, and poor circulation." He also "likened tight lacing to the Chinese practice of foot binding well known for its crippling effects" (Helvenston 1980, 41). The Beecher sisters included a list of ailments caused by tight-lacing in their arguments against it, including "curvature of the spine, displacement of the internal organs, weakening of the diaphragm, 'palpatations of the heart,' and consumption" (Helvenston 1980, 41). Women's footwear also found a place on the list of health reformers. Small, thin-soled shoes were cited for the pain they caused. The fashion for wearing a too-small shoe gained popularity as an expression of society's notion of the petite female stereotype. Of particular note was the blame they placed on the practice of constructing shoes that were straight, as opposed to those designed to fit only the right or left foot, a practice that was applied to men's and children's shoes as well as women's (Helvenston 1980, 41).

Mrs. Trollope, in her wry observations of the "manners" of the Americans, notably commented on their habit of dressing out of the needs of fashion instead of suitably for the season (1832). This complaint was shared by the health reformers. "Women's failure to modify their clothing according to the weather or climate was also stressed by the reformers. Death almost always was the final outcome of exposure from thin clothing." One reformer, Florence Hartley, claimed "many a fair head has been laid in a coffin, a victim to consumption, from rashly venturing out of a heated ball room, flushed and excited, with only a light protection against the keen night air" (Helvenston 1980, 41).

Fashionable skirts were also blamed for adding to women's ill-health and the spread of disease. Long trains, when worn outside, were faulted with catching and carrying unsanitary street debris. This was a mild complaint made by the health reformers in comparison to those more politically motivated. As Sally Helvenston observed (1980, 43), "More radical dress reformers found many more faults with the skirt [than health reformers]. It was considered too voluminous and difficult to handle, especially when spread over crinolines or hoops. Skirts also added unnecessary weight and were dangerously susceptible to catching on fire."

The Bloomer Costume

When discussing reform dress, the costume that comes to mind most readily and is, perhaps, of most significance to the Antebellum Era (and those that followed) is what came to be referred to as the "Bloomer costume." This ensemble was composed of a knee-length sacque or loose tunic dress worn over loose trousers, which were bound at the ankles. Despite its reform nature, the costume did nod toward fashionable attire. While it could be worn without stays, the Bloomer costume was worn with a number of petticoats to recreate the fashionably full skirt of the period.

This ensemble was not introduced to America by Amelia Bloomer, as one might think. Instead, women's rights activist Elizabeth Cady Stanton is far more responsible for introducing this reform dress to American women. She, in turn, was first exposed to it by her cousin Libby Smith Miller in 1851. The costume was first published as a sketch in June 1852 by Amelia Bloomer (a friend of Stanton's and fellow reformer) in her paper, *The Lily* after she had worn the costume for some time. Although she would eventually print a pattern for the "Turkish costume" (as Stanton coined it) or "the shorts" (as some women referred to the costume) in response to requests, it soon became known as the "Bloomer" for Amelia's role in publicizing it (Severa 1997, 87).

A cartoon about Bloomer wear leading to male behavior. Courtesy The New York Public Library.

The Bloomer costume was reviled by many men and women of the time, as well as many who would come after. Take Elizabeth McClellan's commentary on the costume for example: "Early in the decade [1850s] a novel and hideous costume was devised by Mrs. Bloomer, editor of a temperance journal in the United States, who went about the country giving lectures in 1851–1852, on Woman's Suffrage, and advertised the new dress henceforth known as the "Bloomer costume." By way of manifesting the independence of her sex she advised the women to adopt a part at least of the customary costume of the men" (McClellan 1969, 462). The fashion press of the period was one of the Bloomer costume's greatest detractors, however. In *Godey's Lady's Book* in January 1852, the magazine gives itself a proverbial pat on the back for turning its nose up at the Bloomer costume, "The 'Rome Courier' says, 'We have been much gratified that Mr. Godey has given no encouragement to the bloomer folly.' We were right. Even those who paraded our streets at night have given it up. The thing is dead.'" Joan Severa points out that "'Those who paraded our streets at night' refers to the torchlight demonstrations by dress reformers in support of the bloomer costume" (Severa 1997, 87). The Bloomer costume eventually found more success overseas, although in time the Bloomer's most ardent supporters gave up the style in the later 1850s as they felt the negative press it received was "injurious to their cause" (Tandberg 1987, 22; Severa 1997, 88). By the end of the 1860s, the fashion had disappeared.

When it was worn, the bloomer costume was often most successfully adopted by those in isolated circumstances, such as pioneer women. Many times it was worn for purposes far removed from the reform motivations that inspired it. Per Helvenston (1991, 147): "isolation not only affected fashion availability but also diminished social controls over traditional feminine apparel. For example, Adela Orpen and her aunt took the radical step of wearing bloomers on their isolated homestead because they experienced no social pressure to wear their traditional skirts." This absence of pressure quickly changed when they received a visit from a non-frontier friend. However, Adela reported that their friend quickly adopted the reform dress as well, and commented that she [their friend] "never wanted to go back to Boston, or anywhere else, but only to stay on the prairie and be a savage, it was so utterly delightful" (Helvenston 1991, 148). Other more subtle alterations to dress on the prairie might also be seen as echoing those of the reform movement. However, it is more likely that they occurred out of necessity rather than political motivation. "The mobility required for this type of work [physical labor on the homestead] meant that trailing or voluminous skirts had to be shortened or pared down, that corsets had to be loosened or eliminated, that patterned fabrics which concealed soiling had to be used, and that fewer trimmings which made garments easier to launder and iron were called for" (Helvenston 1991, 148–50).

ART AND CULTURE IN ANTEBELLUM AMERICA

Entertainment

For all levels of society, even those enslaved in the Southern states, social gatherings centering around dancing were the primary form of entertainment in the Antebellum Era. Parties and balls were favored among the wealthier members of society. Many times these would be in honor of dignitaries visiting the country. In effect, these visits placed the whole nation on display as they toured from city to city. One particularly important visit and tour occurred from 1823–1824 with the arrival of General Lafayette to the United States. He had been invited by President Monroe to visit the country he had helped succeed during the Revolutionary War. He was welcomed with "balls, fêtes, dinners, parades, etc." in every city he visited (McClellan 1969, 395). The clothing worn to these occasions was influenced directly by his presence. One example, a gown worn by Miss Amanda Nace to one of the balls in Baltimore, featured a badge with the head of "the distinguished guest on a white silk ribbon edged with gold fringe." A relative of Miss Nace noted that the gloves she wore were also inspired by Lafayette—"The head of La Fayette was stamped on the back of each glove" (McClellan 1969, 401). That Lafayette may have felt uncomfortable with these overt displays by his fans might be read in his reaction to being presented to the lady wearing the gloves. "As the old courtier bent over the hand of the wearer to imprint thereon a kiss in the old style, he recognized his own likeness, and with a few graceful words to the effect that he did not care to kiss himself, he made a very low bow, and the lady passed on" (McClellan 1969, 401).

Naturally, at the center of these entertainments was music. This was for the most part drawn from the works of European composers, especially in the early years of the 19th century. As the Antebellum Era dawned, American music began to take on a life of its own. The middle class emerged as one of the heaviest consumers of popular culture of the time and the demand for American music increased. Music served to display their possession of good graces and culture. In all "good" homes, an area reserved for polite entertainment—the parlor—often featured a piano or small organ, on which the family's young ladies might demonstrate their skills. Several themes emerged in American popular music. Parlor music, meant to be played amongst a close circle of visitors or friends, was sentimental and tended towards love themes. Songs and music of a patriotic and political theme were also popular. The evangelical awakening among the religious brought about compositions for church music and songs to be sung at Sunday school.

From 1825 on, "musical societies" emerged, with the aim to instill the appreciation of classical music in its members or to improve upon the quality of songs of a spiritual nature (Volo and Volo 2004, 254). A national appreciation of music, both sacred and popular, spurred on the creation of educational institutions centered around its instruction. The Boston Academy of Music was founded in 1832 and the school board for the Boston area soon incorporated musical instruction into its students' curriculum (Volo and Volo 2004, 255).

Music was also an integral part of slave culture. Requiring singing while working was a kind of watchdog system many overseers used to keep track of their charges. The voices of those enslaved raised in song while they worked were kept from spreading dissidence and unrest among their brothers and sisters at the plow. The style was typically a kind of rhythmic chant that might aid in keeping the pace of the work being performed consistent. Saturday nights on the plantation often brought a dance or social for those enslaved there. Despite being ripped from their motherland without any possessions, the enslaved African American population brought with it a rich heritage of African music. By the 19th century new instruments had been developed to mimic traditional ones and the traditional songs adapted to suit a largely English-speaking population. Other slave songs were a hodge-podge of traditionally "white" folk music. The melodies were often copied wholesale while the lyrics were changed to suit the fancy of those singing (Volo and Volo 2004, 278).

Art

A sense of nationalism helped inform the fine arts, particularly painting, of the Antebellum Era. As in music, patriotic themes were popular. Documenting important moments in America's young history became the occupation of many artists and the enjoyment of antebellum viewers. Other artists focused their energies on documenting the land and its people, particularly that of the new frontier. Many artists traveled and lived with American Indians and captured, often in an overly romanticized vision, their dying culture. In these portraits, traditional dress is almost always portrayed, sometimes in complete ceremonial regalia, in spite of the fact that many tribes had adopted more "Western" modes of dressing. Artists of the Hudson River School focused their energies on capturing the landscapes of the original colonies. Here, a heavily interpretative hand prevailed. Their sweeping panoramic vistas showed the beauty of nature in America, much as English pastoral painters of the previous century had done. Another theme, genre painting, emerged late in America. Beginning in the 1840s, as tensions over the abolition of slavery were mounting towards all-out war, paintings began depicting scenes of typical daily life in America. For many, this meant recording people exactly as they "found them," creating a canvas that carefully reflected the reality of life in America, both positive and negative (Volo and Volo 2004, 346). For others, genre paintings were full of stereotypical representations of "types" to be found in America, such as the enslaved African American cook or "mammy." Portraits, of course, were also a main staple of American artists. In the tradition of 18th century American portraitists such as Benjamin West and John Singleton Copley, antebellum artists captured the visages of some of America's most important people. Those of less historical significance were also recorded and were a favorite decoration of the middle class home, typically found hanging in the parlor. In the same vein, though perhaps not typically considered fine art, were the many silhouettes taken by both professionals and family members. These were executed in cut paper or drawn using a kind of shadow system and grid paper. These silhouettes were a less expensive way to indulge in the growing American custom of portraiture.

Other forms of folk art prevailed in the Antebellum Era, as well. The collections of American museums reflect the variety of hand-made objects produced in the era, from women's small fancy work to large, expertly stitched quilts and coverings. For women, the domestic sphere had become the center of life, not economic production. With leisure time becoming a symbol of class status, middle class women were left with time on their hands, as their household chores might be carried out by servants. Beginning in 1847, the *Godey's Lady's Book* introduced a new department called the "Ladies' Work Department." This featured patterns and instructions for making small fashion accessories such as purses, caps, scarves, decorated cuffs, and stockings, among other items. In a society where bourgeois women were being asked more and more to redefine their roles as women in the household, fancy work represented a return to a virtue defined by industriousness. The passing of one's leisure hours in sewing was touted as part of the definition of a true lady and the passing on of sewing skills to one's daughters would lead to the continuance of this virtue. As early as 1830, needlework, drawings, paintings, and "other useful articles" were to be found at agricultural fairs throughout the country, replacing the perhaps more utilitarian entries of homespun cloth, carpeting, and practical clothing of the country's early years (Zakin 2003, 184). The sewing that expressed virtue in the product of fancy work was highly contrasted with the underpaid sewing of the working class seamstress. Here, virtue was sorely tested by the poor conditions of wage-earning women, who might, through the low wages they earned, be forced into lives of dissolution and prostitution. In antebellum America, the ultimate irony existed in that the needlework of the homebound "lady" of society was more valued than the industrious production of the working woman, as it more clearly maintained the middle class morality of the 19th century.

Quilts and quilted textiles are among some of the most well-preserved items of handcraft from the antebellum period. Quilts served both a

Slave Quilts

The involvement of enslaved African American women in the production of textiles and textile goods was substantial during the antebellum period. Extant evidence of their production exists in museums across the United States. A particularly telling contribution to textile arts in America can be found when slave quilts are examined. Beyond utilitarian or artistic objects, these quilts often tell the story of woman's life in slavery. Without possessing the skill of written language, many of these women picked up the needle to tell their own story. Family histories as well as political, religious or cultural viewpoints are set down in many of these quilts. Many of these quilts might have been made to commemorate a marriage or death. The patches used reflect the kind of cloth that was available to those who were enslaved, whether it be of the highest or lowest quality. Fine examples of quilted objects were executed for use in the "big house" or home of their master, but these were equally made for use by the maker. They are all examples of the high level of skill possessed by many enslaved African American women, skills that are not to underestimated. Their quilts marry Western needlework traditions with aesthetic and spiritual expressions that are uniquely African American.

practical and an artistic purpose. They kept members of the family warm and served as decorative objects in the home. They, like other forms of sewing, provided a venue for demonstrating the skills of a young, marriageable woman. Several types of quilts became particularly popular during the antebellum period. Appliqué quilts enjoyed popularity early in the period, featuring whole motifs cut from fabric and stitched onto a white cotton background. These often reflected the taste for "Orientalist" inspired textiles or chinoiserie. Pieced quilts, in a variety of block patterns, were also popular in antebellum America. Color schemes such as red and green quilts were popular in the middle of the century. Album or signature quilts were made during this time as well, many times as gifts to members of the community departing for land in the new territories. Utilitarian quilts reflected ingenious use of leftover materials, as fabric was pieced in organized patch designs or, in some cases, in an almost crazy quilt fashion (though this style of quilt would not truly not rise to popularity until much later in the century).

Literature

The first decades of the 19th century witnessed the births of some of America's greatest writers. As the dust settled around the American Revolution, schools and colleges had sprung up, creating an atmosphere ideal for the production of a truly American expression in literature. Book production itself had changed as technology changed. The expansion of the industry allowed a few American writers to actually make a living at their craft as the Antebellum Era wore on. Literacy was on the rise. With more women receiving secondary education following the end of the Revolutionary War, a wider audience for printed matter was created. This was especially true in the North, where the bulk of book producers were located. The United States was slowly become a literate nation, desirous of its own literary heritage.

The men who stepped in to fulfill this need told stories of the young nation, either in the form of a new folk mythology or in tales of adventure and daring on the new frontier. We also see some professional women authors and editors emerging during this time, though the concept of women (particularly married women) working outside the home was still deemed inappropriate.

Among the great authors are Washington Irving, whose *Sketch Book* was published in 1819, at the beginning of the antebellum period (Irving 2001). This work featured short stories such as "The Legend of Sleepy Hollow" and the tale of Rip Van Winkle, all drawing on the history of the Hudson Bay Area and its Dutch forebears. These stories were quite popular—they embraced traditional values while poking fun at those who took themselves too seriously. James Fenimore Cooper was a contemporary of Irving but his work differed greatly from the other's. His style grew out of the epic romance tradition of such English authors as Sir Walter Scott (the author of *Ivanhoe*). His *Leatherstocking Tales* (Cooper 1985) created a different kind of American mythology. This time, the plot focused on man's struggle to survive on the new frontier. Among the female contributors to the new American literature that arose in the decades of the Antebellum Era were Catharine Maria Sedgwick and Harriet Beecher Stowe. Catharine Maria Sedgwick was among the earliest American women writers. Her work appealed to women in particular as she primarily produced historical romance novels such as *Hope Leslie* (Sedgwick 1842). Ultimately, however, her work was aimed at instructing the rising middle class through didactic tales that reinforced the new morality growing in 19th century America. Harriet Beecher Stowe may be the best-known American woman writer of the 19th century. Her *Uncle Tom's Cabin* continues today to be a book that inspires controversy (Stowe 1853). At the time of its publication, many in the South viewed it as a form of propaganda for the abolitionist movement and saw it as slander against themselves and their way of life. Those opposed to slavery held it up as written proof of the inhumanity of slave owners, helping to stoke the fires of contention between the North and the South towards the end of the Antebellum Era.

Transcendentalism is among the most well-known American literary movements. Its participants, the likes of Ralph Waldo Emerson, Henry David Thoreau, Walt Whitman and others, continue to be held up as examples of the pinnacle of achievement in the literary arts in America. Though the movement truly began in the 1830s, many who wrote as part of this movement were followers of Charles Fourier, or "Fourierists," as they called themselves (Volo and Volo 2004, 222). Fourier's followers led a crusade for social harmony. Like many who pursued a utopian view of life in America, they lived communally. However, they were segregated within the compound, divided into working groups representing forty different craft areas, including writing. The content of their work focused not on all that was heroic about human existence but what was philosophical and metaphysical. These writers actively sought the "inner light" in themselves and in all men through an almost religious pursuit of the written word (Volo and Volo 2004, 222).

References

Botkin, B. A., ed. 1940. *Slave Narratives: A Folk History of Slavery in the United States From Interviews with Former Slaves.* Washington, D. C.: Work Projects Administration.

Brooks Brothers. "The Founding and Future of an American Classic" http://www.brooksbrothers.com/info/founding.tem.

Cooper, James Fenimore. 1836. *America and the Americans: Notions Picked Up by a Travelling Bachelor.* London: Published for Henry Colburn by R. Bentley.

Cooper, James Fenimore. 1985. *The Leatherstocking Tales.* New York: Literary Classics of the United States.

Daniels, Roger. 2003. "The Irish Potato Famine and Migration of the Irish to America." In *Antebellum America: 1784–1850,* ed. William Dudley, 263–271. San Diego, CA: Greenhaven Press.

Foster, Helen Bradley. 1997. *New Raiments of Self: African American Clothing in the Antebellum South.* New York: Berg.

Fry, Gladys-Marie. 1990. *Stitched from the Soul: Slave Quilts from the Antebellum South.* Chapel Hill, NC: The University of North Carolina Press.

Helvenston, Sally. 1980. Popular Advice for the Well-Dressed Woman in the 19th Century. *Dress* 5: 31–47.

Helvenston, Sally. 1991. Fashion on the Frontier. *Dress* 17: 141–55.

Hemphill, C. Dallett. 1999. *Bowing to Necessities: A History of Manners in america, 1620–1860.* New York: Oxford University Press.

Hollander, Anne. 1994. *Sex and Suits.* New York: Alfred A. Knopf.

Howe, Daniel Walker. 2007. *What Hath God Wrought: The Transformation of America, 1815–1848.* New York: Oxford University Press.

Irving, Washington. 2001. *The Legend of Sleepy Hollow and Other Tales, or, The Sketchbook of Geoffrey Crayon, gent.* New York: Modern Library.

Kidwell, Claudia B. 1979. *Cutting a Fashionable Fit.* Washington, D.C.: Smithsonian Institution Press.

McClellan, Elizabeth. 1969. *History of American Costume.* New York: Tudor Publishing Company.

Milbank, Caroline Rennolds. 2000. "'Ahead of the World': New York City Fashion." In *Art and the Empire City,* eds. Catharine Hoover Voorsanger and John K. Howat, 243–57. New Haven, CT: Yale University Press.

Pryor, Mrs. Roger A. (Sara Agnes Rice). 1904. *Reminiscences of Peace and War.* New York: The MacMillan Company.

Ritter, Joann Gregory and Betty L. Feather. Practices, Procedures, and Attitudes Toward Clothing Maintenance: 1850–1850 and 1900–1910. 1990. *Dress* 17: 156–68.

Roberts, Robert. 1827. *The House Servant Directory, etc.* Repr., Wilmington, DE: Rhistoric Publications, 1969.

Safford, Carleton L. and Robert Bishop. 1972. *America's Quilts and Coverlets.* New York: E. P. Dutton & Co.

Sedgwick, Catharine Maria. 1842. *Hope Leslie, or Early Times in the Massachusetts.* New York: Harper & Bros.

Severa, Joan. 1997. *Dressed for the Photographer: Ordinary Americans and Fashion, 1840–1900.* Kent, OH: Kent State University Press.

Stowe, Harriet Beecher. 1853. *Uncle Tom's Cabin, or Life Among the Lowly.* Boston: J. P. Jewett and Company.

Tandberg, Gerilyn G. 1987. Towards Freedom in Dress for Nineteenth Century Women. *Dress* 11: 11–30.

Trollope, Frances Milton. 1832. *Domestic Manners of the Americans.* 2 vols. London: Whittaker, Treacher & Co.

Ullrich, Pamela V. 1985. Promoting the South: Rhetoric and Textiles in Columbus, Georgia, 1850–1880. *Dress* 11: 31–46.

Volo, James M. and Dorothy Deneen Volo. 2004. *American Popular Culture Through History: The Antebellum Period.* Westport, CT: Greenwood Press.

Waugh, Norah. 1964. *The Cut of Men's Clothes: 1600–1900.* New York: Theatre Arts Books.

Zakin, Michael. 2003. *Ready-Made Democracy: A History of Men's Dress in the American Republic, 1760–1860.* Chicago, IL: The University of Chicago Press.

CHAPTER 8

Women's Fashions

EVERYDAY AND SPECIAL OCCASION CLOTHES

The morality of women was of great concern to antebellum Americans, particularly to those writing the plethora of advice books and dressing manuals that were published during this period. As women were the moral center of the home, their spiritual integrity was essential to the continued well-being of the American family. As Sally Helvenston has noted in her work regarding dressing manuals of the period, "if women were mainly responsible for the upholding of high moral and religious values, then the degeneration of these values might mean that the nation was destined for destruction" (Helvenston 1980, 43). In this light, the hope of authors of these life manuals that their instruction would strengthen the moral center of the American home is clear. Concerns regarding the consumption of fashion ranked high among the most conservative of these authors. If women's attention to dress were to remain unchecked, their moral and religious values might be strained or tainted. Of particular concern to some was the origination of "dangerous" fashions. While men's fashions in early 19th century America were decidedly English in origin, the French style held sway over American women's taste. As the Antebellum Era dawned, however, the influence of the English style would ultimately become equally important in women's fashions as in men's. In the years before America's first fashion periodicals were published, English publications helped to fill the void. Though the magazines might be delayed in transit to the states, the styles represented in their fashion plates guided the trends in American fashion. It is important to recognize, however, that while English publications may have served as one of the primary influences on fashionable tastes in America, France was still an influence on women's clothing, if only through its distillation by the English. Several advice book authors saw these "transatlantic infections," whether they were English or French in origin, as "seducing women into a type of slavery" (Helvenston 1980, 43). In *Watson's Annals* of 1856, the crinoline is the subject of such guile, "We had hoped that our ladies would never again be brought to use such ill-looking, useless and deforming appendages to their dresses…[they are] as spellbound subservients to some foreign spell; one feels scandalized for 'the Land of the Free!'" (McClellan 1969, 467). It was not necessarily the fashions themselves that were objectionable but the money that was spent on them that made them objects of concern. As Helvenston notes, "the spending of American dollars on French and British fashions was condemned because it took away from American manufactures and the development of a distinctly American sense of taste in dress" (1980, 43).

Whether it was the English or French taste whose influence dominated American fashion is open to debate. Contemporary observers, such as Lady Stuart Wortley and Frances Trollope, seemed to notice that the French style was prominent, especially in the northern metropolitan center of New York. Upon her visit to New York in 1849, Lady Stuart Wortley noted that "Crowds of carriages, private and public, are to be seen in Broadway, passing and repassing every moment, filled with ladies beautifully dressed in the most elaborate Parisian toilets" (Wortley 1851, 147). Frances Trollope also observed the influence of the French on women's clothing in New York in the late 1820s. "The dress is entirely French;" she chronicled, "not an article (except perhaps the cotton stockings) must be English, on pain of being stigmatized as out of the fashion. Every thing English is decidedly *mauvais ton;* English materials, English fashions, English accent, English manner, are all terms of reproach; and to say that an unfortunate looks like an English woman, is the cruelest satire which can be uttered" (Trollope 1832, 211–12). Indications that American milliners and dressmakers were importing styles from the Continent also appear in America's first fashion periodicals. There is a mention of the practice of importing French styles in an 1849 issue of *Godey's Lady's Book:* "Embroidered crape bonnets are the newest [fashion]. They are both simple and elegant, and were introduced by Miss Wilson, one of the most fashionable Chestnut Street (Philadelphia) milliners, direct from Paris" (McClellan 1969, 458).

That American women were equally influenced by English tastes in fashion can be witnessed in some of the earliest issues of America's first fashion periodical, *Godey's Lady's Book.* These issues contain fashion reports drawn exclusively from English magazines such as *La Belle Assemblée* and *The Lady's Magazine.* Featured near the cover of the magazine, "The Latest English Fashions" described suitable dress by type, i.e. walking dress or carriage dress. The magazine was also full of reprints of English news and serial fiction. This continued until the October 1830 issue when a plate of "Philadelphia Fashions" was included at the beginning of the magazine. A one-paragraph description of the fashions followed, with a longer section on London fashions for both men and women after. By the next month, *Godey's* was including more reprints of news from American sources, mixed in with reprints of English articles. By April 1831, there were no descriptions of London fashions, only a plate of Philadelphia fashions followed by a description. Later in the issue, a plate of the latest London hats and bonnets is included without description. The source of the fashions seems to have alternated monthly between Philadelphia and London, but by 1839, not only did fashion plates appear more frequently in the publication but they were no longer specified as "Philadelphia" fashions, perhaps indicating that America had its own style that required no qualification.

Fashion plate from the October 1830 issue of *Godey's Lady's Book,* depicting the latest fashions from Philadelphia. Photography Courtesy of Los Angeles County Museum of Art, Anonymous Gift.

The location of America's fashion center is equally divided, in this case, between New York and Philadelphia. When considering American women's taste in fashionable clothing, Mrs. Trollope notes in her work that "though the expense of the lady's dress greatly exceeds, in proportion to their general style of living, that of the ladies of Europe, it is very far (excepting in Philadelphia) from being in good taste" (Trollope 1832, 134). Here, the city that *Godey's Lady's Book* would call home in the 1830s is awarded the preeminent position of fashion capitol in the United States. In 1843, however, the *Boston Transcript* reports on bonnets appearing in New York, having just arrived from Paris. This observation is followed by a synopsis of the latest fashions seen at a social event at the Astor House, placing New York at the center of America's fashion consciousness (McClellan 1969, 449). Perhaps the strongest argument for placing America's fashion capitol resides in its first fashion periodical. *Godey's,* being published in Philadelphia, would have naturally selected that city as its source on American fashion, but that does not disqualify it as the center of American fashion—in fact, it solidifies the point that in publication Philadelphia was more regularly featured for its fashions. Ultimately, however, New York was and would continue to be the preeminent shopping destination for the most fashionable women of America, and indeed the world. By the 1850s, it was firmly ensconced, alongside Paris and London, as one of the most fashion-forward cities in the world.

Main Garments

The basic ensemble for women throughout the Antebellum Era consisted of a gown or dress, wherein the bodice was attached to the skirt, or a two-piece dress, with the bodice separate from the skirt. Within this basic ensemble, however, a variety of construction techniques, silhouettes, materials and trim reveal the often subtle changes from decade to decade. The silhouette of women's dress changed dramatically from the beginning of the period, where the entire ensemble was less voluminous, to the end of the 1850s when the crinoline helped to create the large bell-shaped skirts so many associate with this period. Methods for attaching the bodice to the skirt, where a one-piece dress or gown is concerned, changed little from the 1820s to the late 1840s. Typically, these two pieces were attached to each other via gauging, a technique where a series of running stitches were applied to the top of the skirt and then drawn up to fit to the bottom edge of the bodice. The outside of each fold created by the gauging was whip-stitched to the bodice so that, when examining examples of this technique from the period, the result often resembles a series of intricately pressed and stitched pleats. As Norah Waugh notes in her seminal work *The Cut of Women's Clothes,*

Fashion as Souvenir

There was little innovation in the kinds of materials used in the construction of women's clothing throughout the antebellum period. Cotton and cotton blends figure prominently when examining extant examples of women's dress from this period, followed by wool, linen and silk examples. The research of scholars such as Linda Welters (1997), however, has turned up evidence of some unusual materials for women's clothing. Piña cloth, or cloth woven from processed fibers of the pineapple plant, was brought to New England communities as a souvenir of trips to Manila and other ports that were frequented by these shipping communities' residents. It can be found in collections along the Eastern seaboard in "women's dresses and accessories, men's shirts, children's clothing, dress lengths of fabric, fabric swatches, and fabric scrapbooks" according to Welters (1997, 16). Though women's clothing made from piña cloth was not commonly found throughout the country, it does serve as an interesting example of the multiple roles clothing played during this period. Piña cloth served as an "ideal memento" of these sailors' and ship's captains' voyages due to the "the fabric's association with the pineapple, a well-known symbol of friendship and hospitality in New England" (Welters 1997, 16). Welters goes on to add that "the hand manufacture of piña cloth contributed to its reputation as textile art, and enhanced its value as a meaningful gift or souvenir of the nineteenth century" (Welters 1997, 19). Native costumes that resembled women's fashionable dress, such as the embroidered neck cloths or *pañuelos* worn by Fillipina women, were particularly popular items. These resembled in shape and character the fashionable fichus of the 1820s.

"gauging is an excellent way of giving even fullness, but needs to be done by hand" demonstrating the often labor intensive methods of construction of this period (1968, 149). Radiating pleats were often set at the front of the wider skirt silhouette of the late 1820s. Slight differences in the arrangement of these pleats and gathering stitches can be observed in the 1830s and 1840s (and occasionally the 1850s), when the narrow gauging of the front of the skirt was offset by a series of deep pleats at the back. This construction aided in creating the very full skirt silhouette of these decades, culminating in the widest silhouette of the period with the addition of gathered flounces in the 1850s.

1820–1828

From the beginning of the 1820s, the silhouette of women's dress gradually moved away from the columnar line that marked the early part of the century. By 1825, women's skirts had widened towards the hem, no longer skimming the body as they had in the previous decade. The line of the bodice lengthened with the passage of time. At the beginning of the decade the waistline was placed high, under the bust, but by 1825 it had lengthened, almost reaching the natural waistline. The waist was also more clearly defined by the addition of a waistband connecting the bodice to the skirt or through the use of a wide belt. As skirts widened towards the hem, creating an almost A-line silhouette in the late 1820s, sleeves became more prominent to offset this wider silhouette. Beginning in 1820, the small, puffed sleeves of the previous decade gained in volume, with additional material gathered into the armscye at the top of the shoulder.

Bodices

The cut and construction of women's bodices in the 1820s consisted of two distinct styles. Norah Waugh (1968, 135) identifies the first, a style in which the front of the bodice is more fitted to the body, as being "cut on the cross and fitted by two darts running from the point of each breast in towards the centre front." The second type of bodice, wherein the front has a fuller appearance accomplished through gathering, was "cut from the straight of the material and the fullness was evenly distributed round the neck, but at the waist the gathers were drawn in towards the centre front." Regardless of the front appearance of bodices in this period, the back was always cut and constructed in the same manner. It consisted of two pieces on each side of the center back seam or closure, each cut on the straight of the grain. The side seams of the bodice back curved slightly towards the center back from the armscye. At the shoulder, the seam was placed towards the back of the bodice. As the line of the bodice lengthened towards the natural waistline, the waist front featured a slightly pointed center (Waugh 1968, 136).

Sleeves

As the overall silhouette of women's dress began to expand, sleeves became a prominent, and often disagreeable, feature. The focus of this voluminous fashion was consistently at the top of the sleeve. In order to achieve the leg-o-mutton sleeve (in fashion from 1825), a large quantity of fabric was required. Contemporaries observed that nearly as much material as made up the skirt of a dress went into the construction of these oversized sleeves at their height of fashion. Though it is no doubt an exaggeration, critics of this fashion often noted that "walking behind a pair of these sleeves one could always hear a curious creaking sound made as they rubbed together at the back" (McClellan 1969, 402). Gathered sleeves were often topped with flounces made of various materials, called *mancherons.* For evening, a long transparent sleeve of pale silk was inserted over the short puffed sleeve (Waugh 1968, 135). These would often feature cuffs constructed in the same fabric as the dress, giving the illusion of a bare arm trimmed with lace and silk.

Skirts

At the beginning of the decade, skirts remained relatively narrow, though a wider appearance began to be the fashion. Initially, the skirts were trimmed with flounces, without any alteration to the actual cut of the skirt, to create width. One passage from a contemporary fashion periodical excerpted in Elizabeth McClellan's work describes an "Evening dress of black crape, over a black satin slip made with a demi-train, and ornamented round the border with three fluted flounces of crape, each flounce headed by an embroidered band of small jet beads and bugles" (McClellan 1969, 375–76). The mention of a train most certainly implies that this dress was intended for evening wear. Before the decade began, a padded hem had been introduced to the skirt. This feature might also be alternated with wadded self-fabric trimming (most often in silk) placed slightly above the hem and applied around the circumference of the widening skirt, a style introduced before the middle of the decade. The padded roll would ultimately be replaced by a cotton facing applied to the hem, measuring about four to five inches. Hems remained short, as they had been at the end of the 1810s. Typically they would reach to just below the ankle or above the instep.

By 1825, skirts had become more triangular in silhouette. This line was created through the addition of two or more gores in the construction of the skirt. Norah Waugh notes that as the decade wore on additional gores might be added at the sides to create an even more triangular skirt silhouette. Her research also suggests that the addition of these gores did not change the fact that the back of the skirt was always cut on the straight of the grain and that the fullness was pushed from the center front towards the back with "the fullness which was gathered across the back being more concentrated at the centre back, and sometimes at the centre back only" (1968, 135–36).

Undress or At-Home Attire

In addition to the one-piece or two-piece dresses worn in this period, a woman's daytime wardrobe might be supplemented by pieces meant to be worn inside the home only. Among these, the pelisse dress was extremely popular. Similar in shape and construction to the redingote of the late 18th century, the pelisse dress of the 1820s was typically constructed with long sleeves, often topped with shorter puffed sleeves. The center front closure would extend from the top of the neckline all the way to the hem, which reached to the instep. This closure came in a variety of forms, from frogs of decorative braid to a simple system of hooks and eyes paired with decorative buttons. In her work on American costume, Elizabeth McClellan cites as an example a pelisse dress constructed in cambric worn by a young bride in Virginia the day after her wedding in 1823. She also notes that these favorites of housewear were worn over a false petticoat, which was trimmed in a manner similar to the pelisse dress (1969, 392). Another example (M.2005.89) can be found in the collection of the Los Angeles County Museum of Art (see sidebar).

Materials

White cotton muslin gowns remained popular in the early part of the decade. These were typically trimmed with embroidery, some more elaborate than others. Though the United States would become a central figure in the production of cotton, most cotton muslin gowns in this country from this period would have been made from materials imported from England. The finest cotton muslins came from India, as they had in the previous century. Silk is mentioned frequently in fashion periodicals of the period, in a variety of weaves and colors. Though silk was produced in the United States in the 1820s, it would not be fully industrialized until close to the end of the century. Like the finest cottons, the majority of silk products in this period would have been imported. Wool was domestically produced, and along with coarsely spun cotton, would have been a staple used in at-home weaving as well as in mass manufacture. Most women would have purchased their woven wool and wool-blend goods from local merchants who, in turn, would have procured them from a number of sources, both domestic and as imports from England. Fashionable colors would have been introduced each season or on an annual basis. In her review of American fashion, McClellan indicates that several new colors with evocative names are mentioned in correspondence from this era, including "nile green" and "Marguerite pink" in 1821 and "café au lait" in 1822.

Trimming of dresses was typically done using the same fabric used in the construction of the garment. This might consist of wadded trimming, such as that used on the hems of gowns in the early part of the decade or piping. Norah Waugh notes that in the early part of the decade, piping would have been inserted around the armscye and at the neck. By the late 1820s, this use would increase to trim all of the seams of the bodice, except for under the arm (Waugh 1968, 149). This continued until the late 1830s. Lace was also used in the ornamentation of dresses. Evidence of domestic lace manufacture at an industrial level can be found in newspapers and other periodicals of the period. The *Niles Weekly Register,* for example, includes a report about "Medway Lace" in its 1823–1824 issues. According to reports by the New York Statesman, two boxes of lace made in Massachusetts by Dean Walker & Co. were examined and found to be of the same, if not better, quality than that imported from England. The story goes on to relate the manner in which the manufacturer gained access to the technology that enabled them to compete with the internationally produced goods and bears a resemblance to the story of the introduction of power looms in the early part of the century. The lace was made "in a singularly constructed loom, made in this country, from the recollection of a similar machine examined by one of our artists in England, and who, by his genius and memory has thus obtained what he wished, without violating the law of England against the exportation of machinery" (McClellan 1969, 394–95).

Linings in the 1820s were typically cotton. The fashionable cotton muslin gowns of the early part of the decade were unlined, while gowns and pelisse-dresses of silk were usually lined with fine muslin. Stiffer cotton might be used in the lining of the fashionable *mancherons,* which adorned sleeves in the 1820s, to help maintain their shape. Evening dress constructed in sheer materials were worn over a separate slip constructed of silk, made with a fitted bodice and a skirt gored to match that of the outer gown (Waugh 1968, 148).

1828–1840

Silhouette

By the 1830s, the triangular line of the skirt had reached its peak, as had the width and fullness of the sleeves. The waist, by this time, had come to rest around the natural waistline, if only slightly above. This led to a silhouette in which the smallness of the waist was emphasized by very wide shoulders and a very wide hem, as if two triangles were placed apex to apex. It would not be until the very late 1830s, when the fullness of the sleeve was deflated, that the silhouette would gain a more rounded and less angular line.

Bodices

As the line of the bodice lengthened towards the natural waist, boning was used to maintain a straight line from waistline to shoulder. Norah Waugh notes that this technique was introduced around 1835 and was initially used at the center front of the bodice only. However, she observes that "by the late 1830s darts and side seams were boned" as well (1968, 149). The pieced bodices of the 1820s, trimmed with self-fabric piping at the seams, gave way to draped bodices, mounted on a lining. The construction of these bodices required the use of material cut across the grain line, which would then be draped in folds or pleats from the shoulders onto the fitted and boned underlining. These folds might fall straight from the shoulders to the waist, in diminishing pleats or crossing-over at the center front of the bodice, as if wrapped around the frame. As the neckline of the bodice widened to match the silhouette, the shoulder seam was pushed out onto the shoulder of the bodice. The back of the bodice continued to be fitted with curved side seams from the armscye to the center back.

Sleeves

The extreme width of the sleeve of the late 1820s and 1830s required additional support to retain its horizontal line. This was provided initially through stiffened underlinings. Ultimately, the addition of a "sleeve plumper" was required. These might come in the form of down-filled pads or boned supports that would tie on at the shoulder under the dress. This fashion, the large leg-o-mutton or gigot sleeves, continued to be a subject of much criticism. As Sally Helvenston notes, the large Gigot sleeves of the 1830s "were often criticized as one of the ridiculous extremes of fashion to which women unwisely subjected themselves" (1980, 34). Early in the 1830s, evening dresses also featured this exaggerated sleeve silhouette and were worn with a short, puffed sleeve. The fashion for a transparent oversleeve continued. When the width and fullness of the sleeve began to collapse around 1837, the excess material at the shoulder was gathered or arranged in pleats at the top of the arm. As the decade progressed, this excess material was eliminated and the sleeve became more fitted at the top. The fullness instead moved down the arm in the form of gathered flounces or bell-shaped bishop sleeves.

Skirts

By the end of the 1820s, skirt hems had lifted to their shortest length yet of the 19th century. Reaching to about the ankle, the skirt was cut without gores, creating a tubular shape. The fullness of the skirt was initially arranged in pleats that began at the center front and moved outwards toward the back. Around 1834, the hemline lowered and skirts became fuller. By the end of the 1830s, skirts were gathered or gauged all the way around the waistband and might extend to within an inch of the ground.

Materials

As the silhouette changed, so did the material of fashion. With the introduction of the draped bodice, large sleeves, and gathered skirt, the necessity for applied trim seemed to diminish. Instead, patterned fabrics in cotton, chintz, silk and wool blends were used, replacing the decorative elements with all-over pattern. For evening wear, silk was still the fabric of choice and sheer colored gauzes were much used. From the early 1830s, bodices were lined with a piece of cotton or other material, cut to the same shape as the bodice pattern. The pieces were basted and then stitched together at the seams. Norah Waugh notes that preference in lining material was given to "soft white cotton" throughout the 1830s (1968, 148). The American silk industry had made a little headway since the 1820s; apart from some home manufacture, the majority of silk produced in America was for use as "sewings" or sewing thread. Domestic mills might import silk thread for weaving but the majority of silk fabric used in the production of women's clothing was imported from the silk centers of Europe, namely Italy, Spain, England, and France.

1840–1860

Silhouette

As with most fashion trends, the seemingly limitless increase in the volume of sleeves in the 1830s was countered by a diminishing trend in the 1840s. This reduction in sleeves affected change in other aspects of the silhouette. As the volume of sleeves decreased, the volume of the skirt increased. The bell-shaped silhouette became the order of the day, whether it was achieved through multiple layers of stiffened petticoats, as it was in the early part of this period, or through the inventive cage crinoline of later 1850s. The deflated sleeves led the way towards a sloping shoulder line in bodices of the 1850s. The waist was kept small through the use of corsets, creating a silhouette where the fullness was always pushed downwards, towards the hems of sleeves and skirts.

Bodices

In the 1840s, bodices became more fitted, losing some of the draped quality of the 1830s, with the carefully arranged pleats stitched down from bust to waist. The line lengthened to below the waist, with a long, pointed bodice being the height of fashion for the 1840s. By the middle of the decade, the center front of the bodice was cut on the straight of the grain, which brought the bias of the material out to the side seams, allowing for a closer fit (Waugh 1968, 139). This change was accompanied by the use of side darts, resulting in a daytime bodice cut from fewer pieces, yet more figure-fitting. For evening, bodices were constructed most often of several pieces. Darts were eschewed in favor of a more carefully cut pattern that helped to obtain the low, shoulder hugging neckline that was most popular in this period for eveningwear. The draped *bertha,* or deep, falling collars of the 1830s continued to be in favor for eveningwear through the 1840s. The *bertha* collar was typically a separate piece, constructed on the bias and mounted on a lining before it was attached to the neckline of the bodice.

During the 1850s, bodices were raised back up to the natural waistline. This most likely occurred in response to the growing volume of the skirt, aided ultimately by the invention of the cage crinoline. A popular style for period was a *basque*—a bodice that featured a short skirt or coat tails attached at the waist. This style was present in the late 1840s but did not truly gain in popularity until the following decade (McClellan 1969, 461). This "jacket bodice" buttoned up the center front, as most of the day bodices of the period did, and was separate from the skirt. For evening, the neckline was wide and off the shoulders with a dip at center front. The draped *bertha* style maintained popularity into the 1850s with the adaptation that the neckline was also sometimes trimmed with bias-cut flounces of self-fabric. The evening waistline was pointed at the front and back. In the late 1850s, lace berthas gained in popularity through the influence of Harriet Lane, the niece of President Buchanan and First Lady during his presidency (McClellan 1969, 469). Indeed, many of the nation's tastemakers in women's fashions of the antebellum period came from the political circle.

As the circumference of the skirt increased, the waist diminished, requiring the use of clever cutting techniques to achieve this more fitted look. From the 1850s onwards, the center front pieces of the bodice were frequently cut with a curve, and with the additional assistance of bias along the center front seam or closure, this created a fitted silhouette.

Sleeves

In order to achieve the more close-fitting look of the 1840s, sleeves were cut on the bias or across the grain. By the middle of the decade, the sleeve began to widen below the elbow. Frequently, sleeves were worn with a short oversleeve. For evening, sleeves were very short and very fitted.

In the 1850s, the sleeve widened from the armscye to become the pagoda sleeve, an early and widespread expression of the regrowth of interest in *Orientalism.* As fullness increased in the sleeve, the material was pleated into the armscye, with the pleats stitched down. By extending the stitched pleats a couple of inches below the shoulder line, a sloped shoulder silhouette was created. By the mid-1850s, the bishop sleeve was introduced. This two-piece sleeve was gathered or pleated at the shoulder and the wrist (Waugh 1968, 140). For evening, the sleeve became a short puff, losing some of the tailored character it had in the 1840s.

Skirts

Constructed of several unshaped widths of fabric, skirts in the 1840s and 1850s were dome-shaped. The fullness of the skirt was gauged or gathered into the waistband, with the size of the gauge increasing towards the center back. As skirts gained in volume, they also gained in length—extending to the floor or instep. In the 1840s, gathered flounces were added in rows, increasing the visual presence of the skirt. By the 1850s, underpinnings such as the horsehair crinoline and the cage crinoline were used to add volume, eliminating the need for layers of petticoats (Ritter and Feather 1990, 158).

Materials

Cotton, wool—alone or as blended fabrics—continued to be fashionable through the 1840s and 1850s for daywear. Silk was also widely worn, for both day and evening wear. In their study on clothing maintenance techniques of the period, Ritter and Feather noted that in "*Godey's Lady's Book* and other primary sources, fashionable fabrics in the 1850s [for the upper classes] included silk in assorted weaves and prints, poplins, or wool grenadines, taffetas, and velvets," all of which were difficult to clean (1990, 158). Bodices continued to be lined with cotton, though by the 1840s a fine, glazed version of the cotton lining was preferred, perhaps to provide more stability for the fitted line of the period (Waugh 1968, 148).

During the 1840s, self-fabric piping was typically seen at the neck, armscye, waist, and sometimes along the bottom hem of the sleeves, but by the end of the 1840s, this trend had come to an end.

UNDERGARMENTS

At the beginning of the 19th century, the quest for the idealized Grecian figure produced a kind of revolution in women's undergarments. The sheer muslin gowns of the first decade of the century were best worn without corsets and, because of this, corsets were somewhat out of fashion until right before the beginning of the antebellum period. The shape and quantity of underpinnings changed greatly throughout the world and American women were not exempt from these changes. The small padded back bustles worn with the empire-waisted muslin gown of the 1800s continued to be fashionable through the 1820s until they were gradually replaced by layers of petticoats in the 1830s and 1840s and ultimately, the cage crinoline in the 1850s. Besides undergarments that shaped the female form, women's wardrobes were also home to a number of "unmentionables"—from drawers to chemises and camisoles; these garments changed little in construction and style throughout the period. Women of fashion in the United States would have worn several layers of undergarments between their skin and their gowns or dresses. These layers helped to protect their outer garments from wear and soil. As Ritter and Feather point out in their study of clothing maintenance in the 19th century, "The areas of the outer garment which could not be easily cleaned were protected from body soil by wearing white collars and undersleeves [in addition to other undergarments] that could be easily removed and laundered when soiled" (1990, 158).

1821–1840

> The mere items of tight stays, tight garters, tight shoes, tight waistbands, tight armholes, and tight bodices—of which we are accustomed to think little or nothing, and under the bad effects of which, most young women's figures are suffered to attain their growth, both here and in Europe—must have a tendency to injure irreparably the compressed parts, to impede circulation and respiration, and in many ways which we are not aware of, as well as by the more obvious evils which they have been proved to produce, destroy the health of the system, affect disastrously all its functions, and must aggravate the pains and perils of childbearing.
>
> —From a letter dated October 31, 1835 (Kemble 1882, 37)

The Chemise

Worn next to the skin, the chemise was typically made of a lesser fabric—either of homespun cloth or linen. In the first decades of the antebellum period, it was short-sleeved and unshaped, constructed without gores or darts. The chemise was worn under the corset and might extend to the knees or longer.

Drawers

Drawers had long been popular in France but had only recently gained footing in countries such as England and the United States by the 1820s. Made of cotton or linen, drawers were made as two legs held at the waist with a tie inserted through a small casing, without a seam through the crotch. These garments were not highly decorated in this period, as they were never meant to be seen.

Petticoats

The petticoat was a garment that could serve two functions at once—providing warmth while also providing support for the growing skirts of the 1820s and 1830s. It was sometimes worn with a bustle or small pad or padded roll tied at the waist, which was used to hold the full skirt of the period out at the back. Extra flounces might also be added to the petticoat at the back to perform the same function.

The petticoat could be constructed in one of two ways. The Cunningtons, in their 1951 work on underclothes, refer to a "long petticoat" that had an attached bodice. This garment could fasten at the front or the back while the "short petticoat," made without a bodice, hung from the waist and fastened with ties (130). Both of these styles were initially made of cotton but as the silhouette of skirts expanded, a heavier weight of fabric was required and the bustle was discarded. Starched cottons, quilted fabrics and wool petticoats would become the preferred style and the number of petticoats worn would increase steadily as the skirt silhouette increased. Petticoats stiffened with whalebone appeared in England as early as 1827; however, these do not appear to have made headway in the United States until the late 1840s.

The Corset

The beginning of the 19th century marked a change in the way corsets were worn and how they were made. From its rejection at the beginning of the century to its re-adoption at the beginning of the antebellum period, the corset changed in cut and construction. The length of the corset reflected the silhouette of the gown. As the waist lowered, so too did the line of the corset. Corsets were made of a strong cotton material. Early on they were composed of four pattern pieces, two for the front and two for the back, with gussets at the bust for shape. As the waist lengthened, the pattern became more complex, with a basque, or shaped piece over the hips, added in the mid-1830s. As the fullness of the skirt increased towards the 1840s, the length of the corset decreased. A broad busk held the figure in place at the front while the back was boned. Additional bones might be added as needed for the more stout of figure. Corsets of the 1820s and 1830s typically had shoulder straps and laced up the center back. Industrial innovation changed the way corsets were made, or at least what they were made of, in this period. The first metal eyelets were introduced in 1828 and the first steel-front busk fastening appeared in 1829.

The editor of the *Lady's Magazine,* Mrs. Hale, comments in 1830 on the proper materials for corset construction:

> Corsets should be made of smooth soft elastic materials. They should be accurately fitted and modified to suit the peculiarities of figure of each wearer. NO other stiffening should be used but that of quilting, or padding; the bones, steel, etc. should be left to the deformed and diseased for whom they were originally intended. (McClellan 1969, 414)

It would seem from extant objects and other accounts from the period that this advice was steadily ignored, though 1832 saw the invention of woven corsets by a Frenchman, Jean Werly. Whether these lightly boned corsets were widely worn in America is unclear. They did become popular in England and France and remained so throughout most of the rest of the century. This may indicate that they enjoyed the same level of popularity in the United States as well (Waugh 1970, 79).

1841–1860

> At the commencement of the Empire the fashion was very peculiar. Modern ladies of fashion who dress their slim bodies with skirts narrowly draped would tremble with horror if they had to appear in such finery as was then in vogue, and which was supported by a kind of frame with pliable steel springs, the size of which would scarcely admit of three women to be seated or to stand in a boudoir of a small house at a time.
>
> —Mme. Carrette in "My Mistress, the Empress Eugènie" (Waugh 1970, 135)

Mme. Carrette might easily have reflected the horror felt by American women of a generation before the antebellum period began at the appearance of the cage crinoline in the mid-1850s. But the growing width of the silhouette, which marked its beginnings with the start of the third decade of the 19th century, now required this almost architectural support. In addition to the multiple layers worn by fashionable women in America, a steel cage would be required to maintain the most fashionable silhouette of the period. As the Cunningtons note, "It was as though she [woman-kind] had become petrified into a monument which, however impossible it might seem, continued to expand" (1992, 136).

The Chemise

The chemise continued as one of the innermost layers of a woman's wardrobe. It changed only slightly from one decade to the next. During the 1840s and 1850s, it became slightly more shaped than in preceding decades and might extend as far as the knee. It continued to be of plain construction with only a little lace attached at the neck or sleeves for decoration. In addition to the chemise, a new garment was introduced. The camisole, first introduced in England in the 1840s, was sometimes called a waistcoat. This garment was worn next to the skin, under the chemise, and was intended to provide warmth to the wearer. To such ends, the recommended material for its fabrication was wool. It seems very likely, however, that many of the youngest fashionable women would have resisted wearing this warm and uncomfortable garment despite its perceived benefits to their health.

Petticoats

As the skirt silhouette expanded, the number of petticoats worn to support it increased. For the most fashionable line, these could number between four and six layers, the majority of which were of plain construction with very little or no trim. The outermost layer of petticoat might have more decoration as it was the only layer that might be seen by chance. This would typically take the form of quilting, embroidery or applied trim. By the 1840s, most petticoats were worn at the waist and the slip style petticoat fell out of fashion (though extant examples from the period do exist in limited quantities (Cunnington and Cunnington 1992, 145).

Drawers

Women of the 1840s and 1850s were advised to wear drawers that extended "down the leg as far as it is possible to make them without their being seen," though broadsides of the era suggest that women's drawers were making more appearances in public than etiquette might advise (Cunnington and Cunnington 1992, 148). As the circumference of skirts increased and the horizontal distance from limb to skirt hem extended with the addition of the crinoline, the likelihood of catching a glimpse of the drawers peeking out from underneath increased, making their decoration a necessity. Drawers could be made of wool flannel and wool blends or cotton and linen and became more highly decorated with lace, ribbon and other trim through the 1850s.

Corsets

By the 1840s, the line of women's corsets extended to well below the waist. The corset of the 1840s and 1850s was boned throughout with whalebone and, as it had been in decades prior, outfitted with a metal, wood or whalebone busk at the center front. Commenting on the gradual lengthening of the corset in 1841, the *Handbook of the Toilet* noted that "[t]he modern stay extends not only over the bosom but also all over the abdomen and back down to the hips…they have been growing in length by degrees" (Waugh 1970, 104). By this time, corsets had lost their shoulder straps and were most commonly fastened up the front with busk outfitted with clips and laced up the back to achieve a more precise fit. In fact, *Townsend's Parisian Fashions* noted in 1834 that "[t]he most elegant Ladies have adopted Corsets without shoulder straps and without whalebone; for full toilette these Corsets are made of white poux de soie" (Waugh 1970, 103). As the 1860s approached, however, the corset shortened as tight-lacing became less necessary due to the increasing width of the skirt.

When corsets fell out of popularity in the early part of the 19th century, the whaling industry began phasing out their transport of this commodity. But with the reemergence of the corset in 1820s and 1830s, the American whaling industry again made use of whalebone, or baleen, as one of its major products. And with the discovery of petroleum in 1859, whalebone became the exclusive product of the industry, as whale-oil became redundant. Thus the peak years in the 19th century for the American whaling industry were in the middle of the century; from the end of the antebellum period, the output of baleen declined. Unfortunately, the boon years for the corset whalebone industry levied a heavy toll on the whale population in the Arctic and the growing rarity of these animals caused the price of whalebone to increase steadily throughout the rest of the century and into the next.

In addition to corsets, women might augment or enhance their natural figures with devices such as bust improvers. These were introduced in the 1840s and were pads constructed of cotton or wool. Contemporary advertisements boast of their products' ability to transform any figure into the fashionable ideal: "To ladies: The zone of beauty for 18/6, that much improved article of ladies' toilet which imparts a sylph-like roundness to the waist without restraint or pressure" (Cunnington and Cunnington 1992, 147).

Crinoline

Strictly speaking, crinoline does not refer to the wired hoop skirt with which most associate this period. Instead, crinoline refers to the material of which the predecessor to the cage was made—*crin,* or a loosely woven stiff material with a horsehair warp and a wool weft. These undergarments first appeared in the 1830s but were not widely worn until the 1840s. As the silhouette expanded, the need for innovation in this arena was apparent. The 1850s saw American petticoats stiffened with whalebone (which had first appeared in England the 1820s) and cane, and ultimately, steel. Around 1856, the cage crinoline was introduced—a product of the improvements made in the processing of steel. This structural undergarment was a revolution—it was light and flexible, constructed of several concentric rows of steel held in place with vertical tapes (usually of cotton or linen twill).

The cage crinoline was perhaps the most controversial undergarment of the Antebellum Era. In the United States, as well as abroad, women were lambasted in print and elsewhere for participating in this fashion. Despite its detractors, however, the fashion dominated the remaining years of the antebellum period. Those who could not afford these new devices might imitate the style by stiffening their gowns through a lining of horsehair or by wearing several layers of stiffened or starched cotton flounces. Despite its ubiquity, there was one place in America where this fashion was sometimes abandoned. On the frontier, where the winds were quite strong, the cage crinoline might be dispensed with entirely, though many continued to wear it despite the havoc wreaked upon it by the winds. One settler, Anna Green White, who moved to a settlement outside Junction City, Kansas in 1851 noted that while magazines and newspapers indicated that hoops were "all the rage," "the Kansas winds made sad havoc with them and they were soon discarded [by those in Junction City]" (Helvenston 1991, 146).

OUTERWEAR

1820–1840

The spencer or short jacket fashioned after a masculine style remained popular in the 1820s in America. This style originated in the 18th century and followed the line of men's riding coats in their construction, with the elimination of the tails as its distinguishing feature. Long mantles and cloaks, or shaped outer garments, were worn, sometimes extending to the heel. McClellan speaks of examples with attached hoods stiffened with whalebone, to avoid damaging the ladies' elaborate hairstyles (1969, 376). Fringed scarves and woolen shawls were worn by almost every woman of every economic level. The light varieties, ornamented with embroidery, were reserved for evening wear while woven wool shawls, the best from Kashmir, were worn during the day.

Shoulder capes, which covered the areas exposed by the lowered neckline of the 1830s, were worn as morning attire by many women. Fur-trimmed mantles were in fashion for much of the decade, as were velvet pelisses. The pelisse as outerwear in the 1830s was often equipped with a double cape collar, similar to a man's greatcoat.

1840–1860

The wide cape of the 1830s was modified in the 1840s to become the *pelerine.* This elbow-length cape was often made from the same material as the dress with which it was worn, lined with the same glazed cottons used in the construction of the dress. For evening wear or more formal occasions, the pelerine might also be constructed of lace, net, or a sheer fabric, such as cotton lawn. A variety of surface decoration might be seen in these modified capes, from white-on-white embroidery to appliqué and applied tapes, and they were trimmed at the edge with piping, flounces, or lace. Other garments, such as the lace basque and the full-length cloak, are also featured in fashion plates of the decade, along with lace or silk mantillas and wrappers.

The quality of a woman's shawl often revealed her social and economic class. The patterned, woven shawls imported from Scotland and elsewhere were the provenance of the middle classes, while only the wealthy woman could afford the woven and embroidered shawl of Kashmir. To purchase one shawl of middling quality, a factory worker or "mill girl" might have to save several months worth of wages. Whether authentic or one of the many imitations, the patterned woven shawl of the 1840s was typically square in shape and would have been worn around the shoulders, folded into a triangle. Silk crepe shawls were equally invaluable in an American woman's wardrobe. These embroidered shawls were based on Chinese designs and were stitched in monochromatic colors. The most popular colors were white and black and were folded into a triangle as well, with the deep silk fringe cascading off of the arms and at the back. By the 1850s, the shawl was by far the most popular form of outer garment for women in America.

In those instances when a shawl did not provide enough cover for intemperate weather, fitted sacques, mantilla wraps or coats and mantles might be worn. In the 1850s, these were distinguished by a shorter skirt that was more flared, as well as fuller sleeves. Both of these concessions were required to accommodate the width of skirt and sleeve in this decade.

ACCESSORIES

A woman's accessories were often what visually defined her status in America. Where all but the wealthiest women in America would have worn pared down versions of the latest Parisian styles, stripped of most of their trim and featuring a less exaggerated silhouette, the addition of accessories would offer visual clues to the subtle differences in class, between the lady of society, the woman of the middle class and the independent mill girl. Throughout the antebellum period, the types and styles of accessories changed frequently, sometimes seasonally. To better understand those that were most important, they are here organized into four main categories: Headwear, Footwear, Carried Accessories (such as parasols), and Other Accessories worn as part of the ensemble (such as aprons, watches and jewelry).

Fashionable footwear was an area in which American women in the Antebellum Era strayed from the examples set by their European counterparts. As a group, women in America were more frequently shod in thin-soled slippers, even when their wear was wholly impractical. Foreign observer Frances Trollope, was astounded by their choices in foot and headwear. "They never wear muffs or boots, and appear extremely shocked at the sight of comfortable walking shoes and cotton stockings...They walk in the middle of winter with their poor little toes pinched into a miniature slipper, incapable of excluding as much moisture as might bedew a primrose" (Trollope 1832, 135). Nancy Rexford explains the American woman's dismissal of comfortable shoes as a reaction to the country's "fluid" social structure. American women were more bound to outward symbols of being a lady due to the lack of a clearly defined social stratum. In England, she conjectures, a woman might don a pair of comfortable walking shoes and have no fear of being thought unladylike or a member of a lower class, because after all, a duchess who "chose to cultivate her own garden" might wear what she pleased, i.e. sturdy footwear such as work boots, because there would be no doubt as to her rank in society. "She might be an eccentric duchess" in her rough work footwear, but as Rexford points out, "a duchess she was still" (Rexford 2000, 51). Regardless of the reasons for the proliferation of the slipper in America, these delicate foot-coverings seem even more uncomfortable to modern eyes due to the continued use of the straight sole in their construction. As Frances Trollope observed, American women of fashion favored silk stockings over cotton, even when venturing out of doors (Trollope 1832). Many times, these stockings would have been knit by the wearer or a member of her family and in some cases, the silk used might have been cultivated by the woman herself. The early antebellum period saw a great craze for the cultivation of silk worms and the home processing of their fibers was a common enough practice for there to have been publications centered around American sericulture techniques (see Marjorie Senechal's work in *American Silk: 1830–1930* [Field, Senechal, and Shaw 2007]). Trollope's statement does not apply to all women in America, however, as wool and cotton stockings from this period with firm American attributions are found in collections of historic clothing. They range in length from 17 to 23 inches and some incorporate knit-in patterns and ornaments such as beads.

1820–1840

Headwear

At the beginning of the 1820s, American women still clung to the neoclassical styles of headwear that had opened the century. Turbans remained the most popular form of headwear at the start of the decade. These were most frequently made of crepe or gauze. However, according to contemporary sources such as *La Belle Assemblée,* bonnets quickly became popular as the silhouette gradually moved away from the slim, flowing lines of the neoclassical (McClellan 1969, 374). The most fashionable bonnets were made of woven straw or chip and trimmed with ribbons at the brim and around the crown. Ribbon ties extended from the edges of the brim to fasten beneath the chin of the wearer. The brim extended forward on either side of the face, essentially obscuring a woman's face from view from the side. The capote bonnet combined the preference for the soft, unstructured headdress of the neoclassical era with the new trend towards more formalized styles. A soft fabric crown was merged with a stiffened brim to create one of the most popular styles of the early decades of the Antebellum Era.

The width and height of bonnets was at its summit in the late 1820s, as was the extent to which they were decorated with ribbons and flowers. The exuberant style of the late 1820s began to deflate in the early 1830s. The "bibi" bonnet, with a small crown placed at the back of the head and an open brim, replaced the soft-crowned bonnet styles of the 1820s. A skirt or bavolet was placed at the back of the bonnet to cover the small amount of neck that might now be exposed through the careful arrangement of hair in curls and braids.

Caps of white cotton might be worn as part of the morning costume but would not have been a visible part of street wear for American women early in the Antebellum Era. However, this accessory would eventually evolve into a badge of honor for the married woman and ultimately become the province of the elderly.

Footwear

Women's footwear changed very little from the dawn of the 19th century through the first decades of the Antebellum Era. The flat slipper that had replaced the high-heeled buckled shoe of the 18th century remained the most common type of shoe worn by American women. Because the hemline was higher in the 1820s, slippers tended to be more colorful and decorated than in following decades. A low, stacked heel became popular during the 1820s but its popularity did not survive the decade, with the heel once again lowering to flat in the 1830s. Rounded or oval-shaped toes were the norm until the late 1820s. At this time, slippers, seen under the shorter hemlines of the 1820s, maintained some of the color and decoration they had gained through the previous decades. These thin-soled shoes frequently featured pairs of loops along both sides of the upper through which ribbons were laced and then tied around the ankles. For walking dress, however, the tie shoe was a much more practical alternative. Whether they were fastened over a slit vamp or in the "open tab" style (where a tongue is inserted under the slit vamp), these shoes offered a somewhat more sturdy alternative to the delicate slipper. Boots were not very common in the early decades of the Antebellum Era. A significant change in footwear occurred at the approach of 1834, when the hemlines lowered and skirts were fuller, and the foot was rarely seen peeking out from underneath. Less attention was paid to the color and trim of shoes. The heel began to rise slightly through the 1830s, culminating in a low, stacked heel that would remain popular through the 1840s. Toes became more square and tie shoes were eventually overtaken by boots as the popular footwear for walking. Gaiters, or low boots with fabric uppers and leather toes and heels, were among the most popular designs (it was not until the 1850s that all-leather boots became popular) (Rexford 2000, 75). Side-lacing boots had replaced front-lacing ones in the late 1820s and continued to be popular through the 1840s. These were typically low-heeled, and extended high enough to cover the ankle.

American women, as part of their role as the "angels" of the home, held more stringently to the concept of the small and dainty foot than the English, thus so many more thin-soled slippers are the only extant examples of shoes of the time in American collections. Sturdy thick-soled work shoes are far less frequently found. Though Frances Trollope found much to ridicule in American women's habit of wearing the wrong shoes for the weather, she did find favor with their anatomy, "I must say in their excuse, however, that they have, almost universally, extremely pretty feet" (Trollope 1832, 135).

Carried Accessories

Of the accessories that might be carried by the American woman of the 1820s, the fan was perhaps the most luxurious. In her study of American fashion, Elizabeth McClellan cites the letter of a French woman discussing the manufacture of American hand fans. "A lady has lately arrived here from Louisiana, and has presented some of her friends with very Pretty fans, made of feathers, which fans were fabricated in that part of America. They are composed of 25 different feathers, each 7 inches long, ranged in a half circle, 12 belonging to the left wing and 12 to the right: these feathers all turned inward; and it is observed that in fixing one to the other the barbs of the second feather half cover those of the first, and so on to the 12th. The middle feather inclines neither to one side nor the other, but its barbs half cover the two feathers on each side of it. The stalks of the feathers are all stripped to certain height; and it is these that form the sticks of the fan; above and beneath each stick is a narrow ribbon the two ends of which, before the rosette at the extremity is formed, leave a loop, whereby to hang the fan on the arm, when not in use. The natural colour of the feathers of the different birds from whence they are taken, gives to the fan the appearance of a shell: the bowed-out part of the mount is painted with flowers or devices and the hollow part is held next the face" (McClellan 1969, 393–94). These elaborate constructions were likely intended for use on special occasions. It is less likely that the average woman in America would have carried a fan of this type with her, or even have possessed such an object. On the other hand, purses, as carried accessories, were much more likely to be on every woman's person. Many women's ensembles of this period might lack attached pockets, making the *reticule* or small purse a necessity. Made of knit silk or other fiber, or intricately beaded in patterns that reflected the waning neoclassical taste of the period, these small bags also reflected the skills of the woman who carried it. The construction of these bags might represent the final lessons in handiwork for a young woman, and fashion periodicals of the period published patterns for their construction.

Other Accessories

Fashion aprons, a more elegant expression of this utilitarian object, continued in popularity from the early part of the century through the early 1820s. Made of cotton lawn or sheer cotton muslin, the finest examples feature whitework embroidery or *broderie anglaise.* Here, too, was an opportunity for a young woman to display her needle skills for public consumption.

1840–1860

Headwear

Joan Severa, in her 1995 study of daguerrotypes and everyday fashion for Americans, suggests that caps of white cotton or day caps were worn by both young and old women in the early 1840s, for both day and evening wear. An "American authority" states bluntly that "[n]o unmarried lady should wear a morning cap; it is the mark, the badge, if we may so call it, of the young matron. And if the wife cares as much for her husband's admiration after marriage as before it, she will never dispense with this tasteful, coquettish appendage to a morning toilette" (McClellan 1969, 457). But written accounts of the dress of the unmarried mill girls of Lowell, Massachusetts, suggest that these consummate consumers of fashion also prized these simple, starched caps. From these assertions it would seem that, like the diminutive slipper of the period, the day cap had become a symbol of what it was to be a "lady" in America in the mid-19th century, whether in aspiration or realization. Severa goes on to note, however, that by the end of the decade the white cap had been firmly relegated to older women of society (1995, 10). Bonnets are more commonly seen in visual depictions of American women of the period, whether in daguerrotype or fashion plate. The deep-brimmed, close-fitting bonnet of the early decade opened up as the 1850s approached to become a shallower, circular shape. Straw and fabric-covered buckram continued to be the primary materials in their construction but the trim and decoration of the 1840s bonnet grew to include frilled silk net under the brim, often with an asymetrical arrangement of silk flowers, ribbon and lace. This fashion for underbrim decoration continued into the 1850s, when the silhouette was pushed further back on the head and the overall appearance was even more open and rounded.

Footwear

The broad, severely square toe introduced in the 1830s continued into the early 1840s. However this was replaced by the end of the decade by a more rounded square toe that continued to be in fashion for the next three decades. Slippers were the most popular form of footwear and, as skirt hems descended, became quite plain. As *Godey's Lady's Books* observed in 1849, "[s]lippers, as we have before said, threaten to supersede gaiters for the street. The toes are rounded, and the instep ornamented with a small bow, quite as our grandmothers recollect them" (McClellan 1969, 458). Heels had disappeared in the 1830s and this continued to be the fashion in the 1840s. The low, stacked heel did not reappear until the late 1850s, and then mainly on walking boots. Rosettes became a popular trim for slippers of the 1850s, despite the length of hems, and ribbon ties for slippers were narrow. When walking footwear was necessitated, the gaiter or boot was more popular than the tie shoe. The height of boots descended in the 1850s from well above the ankle to just barely covering it. By the late 1850s, boots made entirely of leather were the most popular—a style that would continue into the 1860s.

Carried Accessories

Purses continued to be an important accessory for American women when they were outside their homes. The making and decoration of these objects also continued to offer an opportunity for the display of an individual woman's needle skills. Some offer insight into the types of unusual materials that were used by some women in America. A reticule in the Los Angeles County Museum of Art's collection features beading of both bronze beads and dried cantaloupe seeds (M.54.20.1). The effect is of a beaded net over a silk satin ground. This kind of net effect can also be seen in examples of ring purses, or small coin purses that were worn on the finger, from the Boston Museum of Fine Art's collection. One crocheted example is strung onto an ivory ring and was constructed as early as 1840 (1981.125). Another, made of silk net, is more delicate in appearance and may have been made by a more accomplished craftswoman (43.1063).

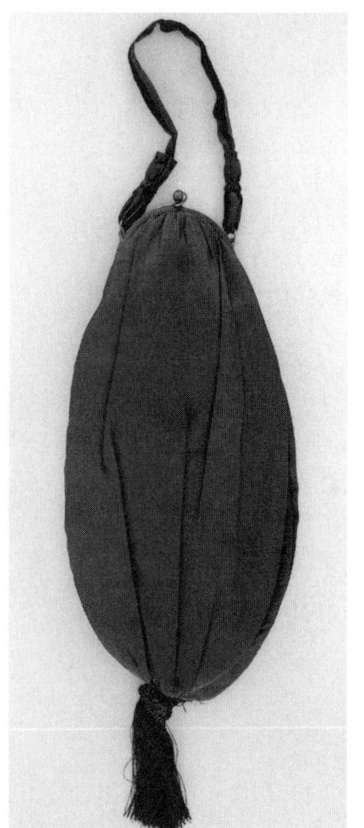

This combination of purse and parasol combines two accessories that the antebellum woman would have found indispensable. Courtesy of Los Angeles County Museum of Art, Anonymous Gift, M.85.240.82a-b.

The parasol was essential to any woman traveling out of doors. In the 1850s, these shrunk to a small size and featured a jointed handle, allowing them, as in the case of one example in the collection of the Los Angeles County Museum of Art (M.85.240.82a-b), to be easily carried inside one's handbag. One of the most "serviceable" colors was blue, with green also being favored (Severa 1995, 101).

Other Accessories

Most women of the 1840s took for granted that the wearing of mitts was reserved for special occasions, or so the lack of references to this custom in advice manuals and fashion periodicals would suggest. There is, however, plenty of visual evidence to suggest that this was a common accessory for evening and special occasion wear—Joan Severa (1995) cites a number of daguerrotypes where women are featured with these silk openwork fingerless gloves in either short or long lengths. A more sturdy covering was needed for outdoor wear. This need was met by gloves made of kid leather, which typically reached slightly above the wrist and were very tight-fitting. These, as well as the fine filet mitts in black, might be purchased commercially. Patterns for mitts were also featured in some fashion periodicals, indicating that they were sometimes made at home.

Collars and cuffs were a particularly important accessory in the 1840s and 1850s. Worn at the neck and wrists, where body soil was most likely to affect the appearance of their dress, collars and cuffs of washable lace and cotton were an essential part of maintaining a clean appearance. These were easily removed from the garment, washed, starched, and pressed and then reattached before the next wearing. By the 1850s, the collar was quite wide, to accommodate the fashionable neckline of the period. Additionally, the chemisette, a kind of dickey or decorative bib, was used to fill in the V-necklines of the 1840s. Known by a variety of names, including gimp, bertha and spencer (not to be confused with the short jacket of the 1820s), the chemisette was made of white sheer cotton, often featuring neat tucks or lace trim. This sleeveless garment fastened at the waist. By the 1850s, the chemisette had become indispensible, as V-shaped necklines plunged even lower. Another fashionable accessory required due to the changing styles of the 1850s was the undersleeve. As sleeves increased in width, shortening to the middle of the arm in some cases, a false sleeve was worn underneath. Typically, these featured a cuffed wrist and might be quite elaborate, with lace fill-ins or whitework embroidery.

Pen and watch sets were an accessory without which no young woman could be deemed a lady. Hung from a gold chain or black cord, the watch would be tucked into the waistline pockets of the skirt. A gold encased pencil would be suspended from the chain or cord, much like a man's watch fob. Bracelets are frequently seen in depictions of 1840s American women, however, though they were worn, earrings are not frequently seen in portraits or fashion plates until late in the 1840s and 1850s when the hairstyles changed, allowing them to be seen. A trend that was particularly popular in these two decades reveals something of the sentimentality of the Antebellum Era. The custom of making and wearing jewelry of plaited hair was widespread in the United States, so much so that companies advertised services that would manufacture custom pieces—simply supply your or your loved one's hair and choose the style and type of gold findings and your piece would be made to order. Instructions for the making of this type of jewelry were also published in women's magazines of the day.

HAIRSTYLES AND GROOMING

For the wealthy, grooming was not necessarily done by the individual lady. Instead, the skills of a professional hairdresser or lady's maid might be called on when arranging the hair. In a letter from Washington in 1834, a lady writes of one woman's evening attire and hairdress: "I was gratified by Julia's good looks. She was dressed in plain white satin, and pink and white flowers on her head. Her hair was arranged by a hair-dresser" (McClellan 1969, 424). For those American women for whom a hair-dresser was well above their means, even for special occasions, the proliferation of lady's magazines (from Europe in the early part of the period, and then America) provided ample visual reference for the self-arrangement of their locks.

1820–1840

The more natural look of hair of the neoclassical age of the early century gave way to ever more formalized styles. By the 1820s, hair was smoothly parted down the center and arranged into tight curls at the temples. These curls became increasingly elaborate as the decade progressed. The loose knot of hair worn at the back of the head during the first two decades of the 19th century also became more formalized, forming a looped knot of smooth hair placed very high on top of the head. The fashion for the antique in hairdressing did not completely subside with the dawn of these more formalized hairstyles, however. The ferronière, a form of hair jewelry made popular during the Italian Renaissance, came into fashion again toward the middle of the 1820s. This arrangement of a small jewel or other ornament suspended from a ribbon or chain at the middle of the forehead shared its popularity with jeweled combs (Waugh 1968, 138).

By the early 1830s, the arrangement of curls was accompanied by loops and knots of hair extending from both sides and the top of the head. These loops might take the form of smooth hair or, more frequently, as braided lengths. These were often looped over the ears and gathered into the top knot in an elaborate fashion. Because not every woman was blessed with a head of easily arranged locks, false hair rose in fashion. Frances Trollope offers another possible explanation for the immoderate (as she judged) use of false hair by American women: "I suspect this fashion to arise from an indolent mode of making their toilet, and from accomplished ladies' maids not being very abundant; it is less trouble to append a bunch of waving curls here, there, and every where, than to keep their native tresses in perfect order" (Trollope 1832, 134). The use of false hair, in turn, spurred on the use of another form of artificial hairdressing—hair dye. These early hair dyes were relatively inefficient, however, and as McClellan notes, the effects were often more comical than stylish. One correspondent of the time notes of a companion, "The restorative was applied and in two days' time the curls of the young lady, where the grey hairs had chiefly obtruded, were changed to an equivocal hue, bearing a near resemblance to the dark changeable green of the peacock's feathers...I cannot even now, though several years have passed, think of the ludicrous appearance of that patent coloured hair, and the mirth it created in our little coterie, without laughing heartily" (McClellan 1969, 410).

Pale skin continued to be prized among women, though this look must have been often achieved through artificial means and again, often with little success. During Frances Trollope's trip to America in the late 1820s, she documents the use of cosmetics among American women. "The ladies have strange ways of adding to their charms. They powder themselves immoderately, face, neck, and arms, with pulverised starch; the effect is indescribably disagreeable by day-light, and not very favourable at any time" (Trollope 1832, 134).

1840–1860

Hairstyles of the 1840s reflected the taste of earlier periods. Daguerrotypes of the period indicate that there were important differences in the styles of the 1840s from those of the early antebellum period. The center part continued to be the most popular style but the side curls of the 1830s were gradually replaced by smooth bands of hair looped and draped over the ears. These bands of hair might also be arranged into multiple braids and draped over the ears. Braiding or plaiting the hair was a popular form of hairdressing and those with especially long locks might arrange them in a coronet across the head. Large decorative combs and bejeweled hair pins were prized accessories for this style. In her remembrances of the 1850s, Mrs. Clay notes that even in the 1850s this style continued in popularity. "In 1858–59 the hair was arranged on the top of the head in heavy braids, wound like a coronet, over the head, and the coiffure was varied now and then with a tiara of velvet and pearls, or jet, or coral" (McClellan 1969, 469). The fashion for false hair had disappeared with these less curled styles of the 1840s and 1850s. Bangs were almost entirely absent, leaving the brow fully exposed.

RITES OF PASSAGE

Wedding Dress

The mid-19th century saw the introduction of many of the wedding traditions contemporary society continues to observe. With Queen Victoria's marriage to Prince Albert in 1840, a precedent for white wedding gowns and the wide use of orange blossoms in bridal trim was set. Before, and even after, this historic union, fashionable American brides might choose a dress of any color for their wedding day. In fact, there was often little to set a wedding dress apart from other special occasion or "best" wear. An example (44.247.1ab-.2ab) in the collection of the

Museum of the City of New York demonstrates this concept. Worn by Mrs. Peter Herrman for her wedding in 1855, the ensemble is in the style of a walking dress, constructed of green striped silk in a pattern of alternating stripes and green checks. Purchased from one of New York's shopping meccas, the Arnold Constable and Company store, this wedding gown is an example of how the "best dress" was sometimes worn for the wedding, not necessarily a special dress purchased for the occasion. In fact, many of the wedding dresses that exist in museum collections throughout the United States are only recognized as such through the oral history passed down through the families of the donors. This provenance allows for the following observations to be made about wedding dress of the Antebellum Era: the silhouette followed that which was fashionable at the time; the material used in its construction was typically the best that the bride or her family might be able to afford; and the dress, once worn for her marriage, might be worn by the American woman again for other special occasions, sometimes with trim or accessories removed to adapt it to the setting.

An 1838 example from Philadelphia does follow modern ideas of wedding costume. It is made of white satin and trimmed with blond lace. It was worn with short gloves, embroidered and fastened over the sleeves of the gown (McClellan 1969, 433). The use of lace in the sleeves indicates that this was a dress of no small expense. Fine, handmade lace in the quantity required to construct sleeves of this period would have been quite costly. That wedding apparel followed the latest fashion trends in silhouette is illustrated by another gown found in Philadelphia (McClellan 1969, 431). Worn by a Quaker woman at a wedding in 1837, it features the close-fitting sleeves that widened toward the wrist that were only lately gaining in popularity. The religious observance of the bride and her family did not necessarily dictate the style of her gown. Again, it was the prevailing fashion that most strongly influenced her choice. This is illustrated in the description of a Quaker bride's dress from 1834 in Philadelphia: "It is of white satin with short puffed (melon) sleeves, over which are full long sleeves of white silk gauze, fastening at the wrist" (McClellan 1969, 424). The seemingly more modest style of sleeves was not unique to the Quakers—the fashion for wearing sheer oversleeves was common. For a Jewish wedding of 1836, the bride's costume is described in terms that might apply to any fashionable ensemble of the year. Miss Sarah Hayes was married to Major Mordecai in 1836 at the Synagogue in Philadelphia, where she wore a gown "of the sheerest, filmiest India muslin we have seen, and was imported for the occasion by the bride's father, one of the leading merchants of the day. The slippers have square toes, the new fashion for 1836, and the short gloves are embroidered and originally were trimmed with blond lace to match the veil…the sleeves [of the gown] were originally puffed, a very fashionable style in 1836" (McClellan 1969, 430–31).

The dress of guests at a wedding did not follow special fashion etiquette, though the location of the wedding might dictate a more or less stylish mode of dress. A letter of invitation to a wedding in Washington, dated 1827, from Mrs. Mason to Miss Chew of Philadelphia, suggests that there were regional differences in the formality of dress required for social occasions such as weddings. "Let your dress for the wedding be as simple as you please.... Nobody here will make dress a matter of moment, and your wardrobe will pass unnoticed and unobserved unless you bring anything very extravagant. The prettiest dress you can wear at the grand occasion will be a white book-muslin trimmed with a wreath of white flowers, or with three rows of plain bobinet quilled double through the middle" (McClellan 1969, 403).

Maternity Dress

During the Antebellum Era, as now, pregnancy necessitated alterations to the fashionable silhouette in order to accommodate the woman's growing girth. As Gerilyn Tandberg observed in her work on women's clothing reform, "[p]regnancy...occasioned the desire for clothing more suitable than the fashionable tightly corseted costumes" (1987, 11–12). This desire was often fulfilled by the loose gowns or *wrappers* worn by many women, whether pregnant or not, for work. But women in this "delicate state" were not limited to work clothes during their pregnancy. In her research, Tandberg notes an 1840s example of a gown that retains a somewhat fashionable silhouette for the period but was clearly meant for a pregnant woman due to the addition of a draped and "flowing" front, in which was mounted a supportive underbodice with ties (1987, 16). Other examples of similar dresses can be found in the collection of the Los Angeles County Museum of Art. A dress (M.67.56.2) in printed cotton from 1840 has the full sleeves with narrow shoulders popular during the period and the printed fabric, with a moiré effect under a foliate branch design, reflects the growing taste for designs inspired by the East. The skirt is gauged up to within three inches of the center front where self-fabric ties are top-stitched to provide an adjustable closure. Here again, there is a boned underbodice of cotton muslin that extends to above the natural waistline, resting at about the middle of the rib cage, to accommodate the woman's pregnant belly. Another example from the same collection from 1845 (M.83.231.10) features the fashionable jockeys or oversleeves of the period. Constructed in silk, this dress features an unboned cotton underbodice.

Mourning Dress

That black was the symbol of mourning is evident in an 1842 description of mourning dress in America. A "[d]ress of black barege" with an underdress of "grey gros de Naples" is described, along with a "drawn bonnet of grey gros de Naples, trimmed round the face with a ruche of black tulle" (McClellan 1969, 444–45). The dress was described as being made in a style popular at the time, complete with the fashionably tight sleeves and *pelerine* that were the latest fashion. The trim of the bonnet is similarly fashionable, with the exception that black flowers are used in place of the more colorful silk flower trim found on less somber bonnets, with the addition of a grey feather at the crown. The accessories, black lace gloves and black panné de soie slippers, complete the look.

Women, in their roles as widows, bore the brunt of the required ceremony of mourning in the United States. When mourning a husband, a woman was expected to observe different stages of grief with her wardrobe. Beginning with deep mourning, which lasted up to two years, mourning attire was gradually lightened from all black to incorporate shades of purple, mauve or gray in the last stage, that of half-mourning. In between, a widow might enter full mourning for a period of six months to a year (or, in the case of Queen Victoria upon the death of her consort in 1861, the rest of her life) in which she would maintain a black wardrobe but discard the crape veil that had adorned her bonnet or headdress during deep mourning.

WORKING CLOTHES

With few of the modern conveniences that make housework a more amenable task, women in the antebellum period required a very different style of dress for completing the work required to keep the house running efficiently. Even on the elite plantations of the South, the lady of the house would have worn a work costume in great contrast to the fashionable attire that defined the rest of her wardrobe. Indeed, clothes for working in the South were "a great equalizer," as Gerilyn Tandberg (1987, 11) observed in her study of women's clothing in 19th century Louisiana. "The appearance of [women's work clothes] was closer to that of their house slaves than it was to their cherished fashion plates."

A number of alterations were made to the fashion of the day in order to create an ensemble appropriate for the many arduous tasks involved in maintaining a household in the 19th century. For example, the use of less expensive materials for work clothes was consistent throughout the period. These sturdy fabrics included wool blends such as linsey or inexpensive, American-printed cotton calicoes. Joan Severa observed that the surplus of printed or "factory" cottons in the United States made it the ideal fabric for work clothing, as well as for everyday clothing for the less well-off. "The enormous output of printed cotton in the United States in the 1830s and 1840s, and its consequent low price, contributed to the ability of low-income families to have new clothing. The 'factory cottons' sold for as little as nine pence a yard during the forties, and almost everyone could have a new cotton dress once a year at that rate" (Severa 1995, 5). These patterned fabrics were ideal for disguising the soil that might accumulate throughout the day or in the week between washing days. In addition to an alteration in fabric choice, the amount of trim used in such clothing was also diminished from what might have been the fashionable norm of the day. The purpose of this was two-fold: its absence decreased the overall cost of this work-a-day garment and also allowed it to be cleaned more quickly, without the need to remove costly trim such as lace before washing.

The silhouette was also altered, starting with the raising of hemlines. Even when skirts were at their shortest, during the 1820s, many women might have found them cumbersome for housework. Particularly in later years, when many Americans traveled west to homestead and skirt hems reached the ground, the need to raise them above a fashionable height was particularly high. Corsets might be worn less tightly laced or dispensed with altogether when engaged in housework and other vigorous activity. In the 1830s, the popularity of wrappers, or loose gowns of cotton or similar sturdy fabrics increased. This loose dress was tied or belted at the waist, giving the illusion of a two-piece dress while allowing for greater ease of movement. The cage crinoline of the 1850s was typically dispensed with when working and layers of petticoats were worn to fill out the full skirt instead. This was particularly true when outdoor work was required, especially on the frontier, and exposure to the elements such as wind might result in an embarrassing disarray of the silhouette for the wearer. Some women even took to wearing more controversial clothing for work, such as the "Bloomer" or Turkish trousers when traveling long distances or working on the frontier. Slippers might also be dispensed with in exchange for the moccasins worn by Native Americans (Severa 1995, 87).

MAKING AND ACQUIRING CLOTHES

The act of deciding what to wear in the antebellum period was not as simple as it might seem. With the proliferation of fashion periodicals in the early part of the 19th century, American women were supplied with more information about the latest fashions than ever before. Making these fashion decisions was often a function of where one lived. In towns and large urban areas, the dissemination of fashion information was not limited to fashion periodicals. In Cincinnati, according to Mrs. Trollope, the church was the primary setting for spreading fashion news through display. Other period sources indicate that a close communication with shop keepers, particularly in fashionable sectors of New York City, was another way to stay abreast of the latest styles in their community (many times these styles were imported by ship directly from Paris into New York's port). On the frontier and in less settled areas of the United States, communication with family back home was essential in keeping up with the latest fashions. Letters from settlers and homesteaders are full of questions about fashion. Sarah Everett, of Kansas, in 1855, "thought of asking for fashion news" amidst her other statements about family illness, finances, and the growing conflict between free state and slave state forces. One letter, written by her husband as she was ill, states: "Sarah says if Jane [her sister] has this Spring's basque pattern she would be glad if she would send it to her. She would like to know what kind of trimmings were worn and all about the latest fashions" (Helvenston 1991, 144). Newly arrived settlers were often seen as the arbiters of style in these frontier communities, whether they had been particularly skilled in the art of dress in their old hometowns or not. One Oregon pioneer was asked to supply her knowledge of millinery fashions from her recently departed Ohio community to members of her new frontier community: "I trimmed hats, literally for the entire neighborhood, and I knew less than nothing about millinery" (Helvenston 1991, 146). Frontier newspapers, which quickly sprung up where communities were formed, also carried news of the latest fashions, if only slightly delayed in their delivery. The process of making clothing decisions based on a presiding fashion persisted in even the most remote communities of the United States.

Assembling a wardrobe often required multiple steps and even many hands. There was little in the way of ready-made clothing for women of this period and typically the few types of garments available for purchase were for outerwear, such as loose sacque coats, or were accessories such as shawls, hats, and shoes. The dresses that made up the greatest part of any woman's wardrobe would have been custom-made for the wearer, either by the wearer herself, a member of her family or staff, or a professional dressmaker. In the South, where slavery provided a large workforce, many enslaved African American men and women found themselves making clothes for themselves, their master's family, and other enslaved individuals on the plantation. One former slave named William Branch recalled, "Marster's clothes? We makes dem for de whole fam'ly. De missis send de pattren [sic] and de slaves makes de clothes" (Foster 1997, 80). Most women in the North and parts of the South likely relied on the services of a skilled dressmaker when acquiring new clothes. Dress material would be brought to the dressmaker, where the style of sleeves, bodice and skirt would be agreed upon. Measurements would be taken and the pattern and fabric cut out. At this point, the cut fabric might be sewed into the finished dress or simply basted and given back to the client, who would then finish the job herself. Most American women had to look to their own dressmaking skills along the route to compiling their wardrobe. These skills would have varied from person to person and community to community throughout the United States.

While more information about the changing fashions of the period was available to women through magazines such as *Godey's Lady Book* and *Peterson's Magazine,* there was less published information on the actual construction of these garments. Information on cutting and sewing was more typically passed down and shared through oral history, or as Sally Helvenston puts it: "women set up networks to share knowledge of clothing construction and styling garments" (1991, 146). Few paper dress patterns were available for purchase, particularly at the start of the antebellum period. Many women drafted their own patterns off of an existing garment or borrowed those made by friends, relatives and neighbors. Catherine Beecher and Harriet Beecher Stowe instructed women of 1869 in how one might accomplish this task and their instructions echo the same methods employed by women throughout the period. In drafting a pattern for a bodice, a woman must "take out a sleeve, rip it to pieces, and cut out a paper pattern. Then take out half the waist [and make a pattern of that as well]...In cutting the patterns, iron the pieces smooth, let the paper be stiff, and with a pin prick holes in the paper to show the gore...and the depth of the seams. With a pen and ink, draw lines from each pin-hole to preserve this mark. Then baste the pieces together again, in doing which the unbasted pieces will serve as a pattern. When this is done, a lady of common ingenuity can cut and fit a dress by these patterns" (Warner 2001, 31).

Sales records and periodicals from the period indicate that pre-made paper patterns were sold starting around 1825. These first patterns were marketed more towards the professional dressmaker than the woman who would make clothes for herself and her family. The fashion plates published in *Godey's* and elsewhere offered little guidance in the construction of fashionable dress—certainly, the latest placement and quantity of trim could be deciphered, as well as the appropriate hem length, without the aid of a paper pattern, but little else. It was not until 1853 that *Godey's* would supplement their plates with "simple diagrams" showing the pattern shapes for bodices and sleeves. These were not easy to use, even by the most experienced seamstress, but they did provide some insight. *Peterson's Magazine* followed and improved upon the trend in 1855 by including inch measurements to "clarify the dimensions of the pieces." Magazines also began selling full-sized patterns of the gowns featured in their plates after the mid-1850s—these were available in one-size only, were made of paper, and were described as "facsimilies of the originals in color, trimming etc." and it was claimed that "at a distance, they would be taken for the garment itself. They could be worn in a tableau without being detected" (Kidwell 1979, 16). These first forays into paper dress patterns were expensive and ultimately of little use to the inexperienced home sewer. More and more the professional seamstress, or lady's tailor, was called upon, particularly for those clothes meant for special occasions. Women were increasingly stepping into this professional role and it is interesting to note that their increased presence played a large role in the evolution of drafting systems in the United States in this period. Kidwell notes that they helped to spur the development of systems that were simple and easy to use. In the early 1840s, many tools were invented and patented in the United States to aid in the conversion of proportions when cutting women's dresses (Kidwell 1979, 21). The invention and widespread use of the sewing machine assisted this growing trend towards easier to use patterns and drafting systems.

The amount of fabric required to construct a dress in the antebellum period varied widely from silhouette to silhouette. The final yardage needed hinged first upon the width of the fabric to be used, and second upon the style of skirt and sleeves desired. Fabric widths varied widely in this period. Silks were typically 19 to 24 inches while wool, cotton and blended fabrics were more often double that width. Once the fabric was selected, the fullness of skirt and sleeves dictated the amount of yardage required. Norah Waugh (1968, 149) provides examples of yardage requirements in her work, taken from research on extant garments or printed references: "Plain unshaped skirts—late 1820s, 90 inches wide; 1830s, 94 inches wide; 1840s, 126 inches wide; 1850s, 170 inches wide; 1850s, with flounces, 107 inches wide for foundation skirt, 129 inches for top flounces, 150 for lower one."

Even after the invention of the sewing machine, hand-stitched seams are likely to be found throughout most garments of the period—particularly in the curved pieces of the bodice. Long running seams were more well-suited to machine sewing, and these are more frequently found in women's skirts and sleeves.

Though ready-made clothing for women was not as widely available as it was for their male counterparts, the antebellum lady might look to a dry goods purveyor for some of her clothing needs. In these establishments she would find fabric and trim alongside fashionable accessories and other household goods. Indeed, the less form-fitting silhouette of the early 19th century had allowed some women's muslin dresses to be mass-produced, but by the antebellum period, when the fashion called again for a more fitted silhouette, this trend faded. Women might buy pre-cut and pre-basted skirts, particularly in the 1850s, which were accompanied by enough uncut yardage to complete the bodice and sleeves in the appropriate style. This was a trend that endured longer, lasting until the early 20th century. Other clothing items that did not require a more customized fit were mass-produced in the United States. These included items for outerwear such as shawls, cloaks and mantles as well as straw bonnets and bonnet frames, collars and cuffs, undersleeves (in the 1850s), and shoes and slippers. With the advent of the cage crinoline in the 1850s, women's underpinnings were added to this selection of clothing ready for purchase.

In the most fashionable cities and among the most fashionable women, footwear might be purchased from a boutique specializing in women's slippers, shoes and boots. These might include models made in the store, for the store by an American shoemaker, or imported from shoemakers overseas in London or Paris. They were still produced on a relatively small scale, not in any manner that might be deemed "mass-production."

"Recycling" in 19th-Century Fashion

The stuff of dresses—fabric, trim and notions—was a valuable asset. Clothing was not viewed as disposable as today's "fast fashion" may be. A woman might recycle last year's "best dress" into the latest fashion by making alterations to sleeves, hem, or even the bodice. She might freshen up a dress by dismantling it and "turning" the wrong side of the fabric to the outside. The finest imported silks were a luxury only a few women in America could afford, especially in the early years of the antebellum period. It is not unusual to find garments from this period constructed from fabric that was originally used for another ensemble. An example of this practice is found in the collection of the Los Angeles County Museum of Art where an 18th-century English silk has been used in a woman's pelisse-dress (M.2005.89) dating to circa 1823. The dress was worn by Julia Clark Taylor (1799–1846), a Southern woman from a prominent Colonial-era family. The textile dates to around 1765–1775 and was originally used in a dress from that period. In re-fashioning this cloth, the seamstress used the panels of material from the pleated back of an 18th-century open robe to make up the skirt, where some of the original pleating and stitch marks can be seen.

COMPOSITION OF A WARDROBE

Location and prosperity were factors in determining the extent of an antebellum woman's wardrobe. Those of limited financial means, often living in more rural areas where access to materials and services for the construction of clothing was limited, felt themselves rich in possessing as few as two changes of clothes. This scant wardrobe would include two one-piece dresses and as few a number of underthings. Frequently drawers were dispensed with altogether, as might be professionally made shoes if the individual's poverty were sufficient enough to warrant their absence even in the more chilly months. The addition of a best dress might distinguish between subtle differences in economic level in these rural areas.

For women with the means and access to materials and fashion information, the antebellum wardrobe could extend as far as circumstance might allow. The wardrobe on the opposite end of the spectrum from the rural woman's meager clothing collection might contain changes for each phase of the day: a morning gown for breakfasting and wear before venturing out for the day's calls, an afternoon, carriage, or walking dress for promenading through town on calls to friends or visits to the shops (either by foot or by horse-drawn carriage), and evening wear for the last meal of the day. Antebellum American women rarely engaged in horse riding, therefore equestrienne costume is fairly absent from some of even the most well-to-do women's wardrobes. The quantity and quality of the urban woman's wardrobe was determined by the portion of the family budget that might be spent on clothing.

AMERICAN INDIAN CLOTHING

In many ways, the clothing of American Indian women has been documented more profusely than that of their male counterparts. Traditions in materials, cut, construction, and decoration persist even today, providing insight into how and why certain styles of clothing were worn by tribal women in the Antebellum Era. Because of the intercommunication between many tribes inhabiting the same region of the continent, it is easiest to discuss their clothing in terms of geographic areas rather than by tribe. Naturally, there are differences in use of trim and material between tribes. However, the general silhouette is nearly always consistent.

Southeastern Region

Dress components of native women in the Southeastern region vaguely resemble those of white women of the same period. Essentially a two-piece dress, a wrap-around skirt of tradecloth or strouding was worn with draped shawl or cape worn fastened over one shoulder. The skirt was fastened to the waist with a leather belt (Paterek 1994, 6). The cloth used in their construction, referred to as strouding, was imported from Stroud, in the Stroudwater Basin or Gloucester region of England, and was typically made of wool and dyed either scarlet red or blue (Jennys 2004, 21). Ankle-high moccasins were worn by men and women and one early observer noted that an extra layer of hide was sewn to the bottom of the shoe to create a more durable sole (Paterek 1994, 6). Robes of skin and fur were worn for warmth during the winter months.

Northeastern Region

Contact with European influences can be dated back as far as the dawn of the last millenium, when Norsemen traveled to the northeasternmost tip of the continent. The dress of native tribes in the Northeastern region, therefore, was influenced by European styles well before the 19th century. A dress made of two hides was worn by most women in this region. Straps were stitched at the shoulders of the dress and the sides seamed together. Separate sleeves were worn, fastened at the neck and wrists. Leggings were worn knee-length and fastened with garters and ties at the ankles. Moccasins were worn, constructed in an ankle-high style of one piece of hide or in three pieces, either cuffed or drawn with a cord. Rabbit skin robes were worn by women in the winter months.

The Plains

Four styles of dress are traditionally found among the tribes of the Plains. The first, the sidefold dress, may be the oldest and was named this by art historian Norman Feder (Paterek 1994, 84). It was constructed of one large tanned animal hide, with a neckline of folded-over skin or, if constructed of two hides, it had two seams (one horizontal and one vertical at the side), with a seam at the neck over the left shoulder (Jennys 2004, 2). The two-hide dress was constructed by stitching the hides along the shoulders and under the arms down the sides. Here, the hair or fur of the animal where it was left on the hide acted as a decorative fringe along the sleeves and hemline of the dress. The development of the two-hide dress may be attributable to the abundance of hides during this time (Paterek 1994, 84). The three-hide dress was constructed of a skirt with two hides and a hide folded in half for the bodice. The skirt was then attached to the waist of the bodice. Tradecloth, or strouding, was also used in the construction of dresses. The shape of the dress mimics that of the hide dress (Jennys 2004, 3). Knee-length leggings were worn under the dress and were gartered directly below or above the knee. They were held in place with strips of hide or otter fur. Trim used in the decoration of Plains dresses included elk teeth, quills, shells, or the hair or fur of the hide (Paterek 1994, 84). Wraps of buffalo hide and other skins were worn as both protection from inclement weather and as ceremonial objects by both men and women. These were often decorated with paint or rows of medallions and pendants to indicate the wearer's marital or other tribal status. Moccasins were constructed with curved soles, to fit either the left or right foot. There were both soft-soled and hard-soled varieties worn in the Plains region, the hard-soled variety most commonly made from buffalo skin and constructed with a tongue. Moccasins with an ankle flap were most commonly worn by women (Paterek 1994, 85).

The Southwest

European influence in the Southwestern region dates back to the 16th century and invasion by the Spanish, led by Coronado. Many of the tribes' cultural traditions were preserved in a kind of underground observance, such that their own beliefs and customs remained somewhat intact despite the lifestyle imposed by the Spanish missionaries. With the annexation of the Southwest by Mexico at the beginning of the antebellum period, the tribespeople were given full rights as Mexican citizens. With the Mexican War in the 1840s, however, these rights were revoked by the conquering United States. Woven bast fibers had constituted a large part of the material from which clothing was constructed among the tribes of the Southwestern region. This trend continued into the Antebellum Era, when the clothing of tribal women in the Southwest was generally constructed from cloth. These were either made of wool or, as it became commercially available, cotton. Wraparound skirts and mantles were often worn over underdresses of cotton.

An example of the two-hide dress worn by women in the Blackfoot tribe. Buffalo Bill Historical Center, Cody, Wyoming; Gift of Mrs. Henry H. R. Coe, NA.202.376.

Western-inspired dress was frequently seen among Native American women in the 19th century, including a kind of two-piece dress made of printed or plain cotton, referred to as a "camp dress" (Paterek, 154). Trade blankets were worn as outerwear by both sexes and rose in popularity during the 19th century. Sandals of woven plant fiber were worn by both men and women and these were made in two types—round-toed and square-toed (Paterek 1994, 149).

The Northwest Coast

Cedar bark formed the primary fiber used in the construction of cloth by indigenous peoples of the Northwest Coast. Fiber was beaten and separated from the bark and then woven into the aprons, capes and blankets worn by the women. Tunics were also made from this fabric and then edged with fur. This style was worn by both men and women. Skirts of hide might also be worn over the apron of woven cedar bark. Shoes or moccasins were rarely worn, usually only for travel into the mountains. Capes were worn waist-length to protect against the cold and snow and might be worn in two layers; one tightly woven and worn close to the body, the other more loosely woven and worn as the outer layer. These were trimmed with fur at the neck and hemline. Cedar-bark blankets were also worn, and due to their water-repellant nature offered warm refuge from the elements. Fur robes were worn, however, as the fur trade persisted in this area, native people found them more valuable for trading than for wear (Paterek, 295).

CLOTHING OF ENSLAVED AFRICAN AMERICAN WOMEN

The reality of clothing for enslaved African Americans was a combination of customs imposed by the dominant white culture merged with those that "evolved distinctly from within the African American communities both as a reflection of the people's Afro-centric craftsmanship and sensibilities and as a reaction to their particular place in American society" (Foster 1997, 8). Clothing was a significant contributor to the enslaved people's ability to "build and stabilize their own communities as distinctly separate from the ever-present, threatening white communities" (Foster 1997, 15). The adoption of a Western style of dress was viewed by the white population as a civilizing process. History recognizes many instances where clothing has been used as an instrument of conversion, either to Christianity or more generally, a western way of life. Booker T. Washington noted that "[n]o white American ever thinks that any other race is wholly civilized until he wears the white man's clothes" (Foster 1997, 21). This manner of thinking was apparent in contemporary observations of African American dress, among freed and enslaved populations, by whites such as Frances Trollope who remarked upon the "civilized" nature of freed African Americans in the North. It was their more rigid adherence to a white or western dress code that was remarked upon as displaying their more civilized nature, when compared to adjacent white examples (Trollope 1832).

The influence of the English style on women's dress in America is extended unto the enslaved population, through their mistresses. Helen Bradley Foster notes in her study of responses about dress in the *Narratives* project that the Victorian sense of decorum as absorbed from English culture by American women was passed onto African Americans due to the fact that white women often dictated or at least played a role in creating the clothing worn by them. "It is clear that white women had a strong influence on some black women's sense of decorum and of suitable female dress. It was, after all, the Victorian era, and white American women still took their own cues about proper attire and fashion from Europeans, most notably English women" (Foster 1997, 169).

Distinctions in dress were made between those who worked in the houses of their masters and those who were involved in work outside.

Frederick Douglass observed on one plantation that "[t]hese [house] servants constituted a sort of aristocracy on Col. Lloyd's plantation. They resembled the field hands in nothing, except in color...The delicate colored maid rustled in the scarcely worn silk of her young mistress...so that, in dress, as well as in form and feature, in manner and speech, in tastes and habits, the distance between these favored few, and the sorrow and hunger-smitten multitudes of the quarter and the field, was immense" (Foster 1997, 138). In addition to being the recipients of the hand-me-downs of their mistress, female domestic servants might be dressed in a uniform of sorts, regulated by the white culture's idea of what a black servant should look like. This typically took the form of a white apron worn over a neat dress, with a neckerchief and cap completing the ensemble (Foster 1997, 141). It is interesting to note however, that the clothing of house servants was more regulated by the whites, and therefore less individuated, than that of the enslaved workers in the field. These individuals, while described as "fantastically dressed" by some contemporary white accounts, may have dressed in a style that was more in tune with the tastes and aesthetic sensibilities of African American culture of the time. "Thus, although Blacks who worked at jobs away from the big house apparently received less clothing and of poorer quality than that worn by domestic servants, this inequality may have been offset by the fact that they had more freedom of choice in what they would wear than did the seemingly more privileged domestic servants and carriage drivers" (Foster 1997, 145). There was also a distinction seen between those enslaved in rural areas and those in the more urban parts of the slave states of antebellum America. Peter Randolph, an enslaved African American in Virginia, born in 1820, noted that "the slaves in the cities...do very well...All can dress well" (Foster 1997, 77). These individuals would have had more ready access to money (acquired through hiring themselves out) and the machine-made cloth and ready-made clothing that it might be used to buy.

The main garment of an enslaved African American woman in the Antebellum Era would have been a one-piece dress. The most common silhouette was a longer version of the simple shirt worn by young enslaved African Americans of both sexes. The fullness of this long shirt would be gathered in with a belt or apron, the bodice would be relatively unshaped and the long sleeves cut in one piece with the body of the shirt. Susan Castle, an enslaved African American woman, remembered another common silhouette worn by her peers. "In summer time us wore checkedy dresses made wid low waistes and gathered skirts, but in winter de dresses was made out of linsey-woolsey cloth" (Foster 1997, 146). Another *Narratives* participant recalls not only the uniformity of dresses for enslaved women but the way in which material, and not style, differentiated the class of dress. "All the dresses was made a lot alike and most all of them buttoned up behind. If a person, white or black, had a calico dress in them days, they was dressed up. The home-spun cloth was, some of it, checked, and some striped" (Foster 1997, 111). Foster also notes that slave dress for women might be identifiable by the inclusion of a "large pocket attached to the waist of a dress or skirt" (Foster 1997, 171). Some formerly enslaved African Americans remembered using sack material to construct this pocket. There was a practical rather than a decorative reason for the inclusion of this large pocket (or pockets), as noted by one white observer's description of black domestic attire, "In these pockets, no doubt, Tyrah carries the keys to her workrooms since she would be responsible for the materials kept there" (Foster 1997, 172). Other *Narratives* participants provided folk beliefs for the presence of these pockets—"My mammy always wore and [sic] ole petticoat full gather at de waist band wid long pockets in dem and den to keep peace in de house she would turn de pocket wrong side out jes as she would go to somebody elses house," remembers Cora Torian. (Foster 1997, 172). Women working in the fields might supplement their wardrobe with pantaloons or pantalettes to protect their legs from exposure to the elements or harsh vegetation. Adeline Hedge, enslaved during the Antebellum Era, observed one manner in which these might be worn, "De women had pantelettes made an' tied to dere knees, to wear in de fields to keep dew off dere legs" (Foster 1997, 171).

Underwear was infrequently worn by enslaved African American women. In the winter months, hand-me-down male overalls from their master might serve as protection from the cold (Foster 1997, 147).

Slave woman traveling in the North explaining her loyalty to her mistress to two abolitionists, 1853. Courtesy The New York Public Library.

Fashionable underpinnings, such as hoops, might be purchased if money was available, though more frequently, enslaved African Americans who consumed this fashion made do with home-made versions. "My missus, she made me a pair of hoops, or I guess she bought it, but some of the slaves took thin limbs from trees and made their hoops. Others made them out of stiff paper and others would starch their skirts stiff with rice starch to make their skirt stand way out. We thought those hoops were just the thing for style" remembers Rivana Boynton, a participant in the *Narratives* project (Foster 1997, 170). Like underwear, outerwear for enslaved women would be reserved for the winter months, if it were provided at all.

Accessories often served both a practical and a decorative purpose. Jewelry might be worn for aesthetic or protective reasons. Helen Bradley Foster observes, "All cultures view 'beads and notions' as a way of beautifying the wearer, and an aesthetic sense about decorating the body is one obvious purpose for wearing such items. The contributors [to the *Narratives*], however, spoke far more often about another reason for wearing these kinds of objects on their bodies: the belief in the objects' protective powers" (Foster 1997, 174). In this way, jewelry often expressed a continuation of African dress styles and folk beliefs on American soil (Foster 1997, 175).

Shoes, or footwear of any kind, were not worn consistently by enslaved African American women in the Antebellum Era. As with the majority of their apparel, it was often up to their masters to dole out these highly sought after items. Based on testimony from the *Narratives* project, it is clear that some enslaved women fared better than others. If shoes were worn, they were often of coarse construction—sometimes made onsite by a specially trained enslaved man—and may have been more uncomfortable to wear than going barefoot. These brogans, as they are frequently referred to, were worn by both women and men, enslaved and free. Many participants in the *Narratives* project remembered winters without shoes while others noted that preference for better quality shoes was given to field hands over the domestic servants (in an apparent reversal of the typical pattern of finer clothing being given to the house servants) (Foster 1997, 224–26). Many times, footwear might be fashioned from rags or sacking, particularly in the winter months, to help shield the feet from frostbite and other injury. These might be made by the enslaved woman herself, or by someone else on the plantation, and were often not sanctioned by the master of the house. One *Narratives* participant noted that her master's wife made her "moccasins" when he refused to buy her shoes to wear during the snowy winter months. These were fashioned from "old rags and pieces of his [her master, Cargo's] pants" (Foster 1997, 239).

As with jewelry, headwear and the arrangement of the hair often represented a tie to African dress traditions. Women would wrap their hair with string in the style most frequently worn, then this would be covered with a kerchief (Foster 1997, 252). The strings would typically be removed for special occasions—Sundays, dances, other social occasions. Wrapped hair was for the work week only. The *Narratives* reveals four types of headwear most commonly worn by enslaved African American women—hats, caps, bonnets, and headwraps. Caps for women typically refers to "mob caps" or a "circular cloth drawn together with string to cover the hair" (Foster 1997, 255). Bonnets might appear in two forms—work hats made of plant fibers or cloth, held on with ribbons tied under the chin, sometimes called sunbonnets, or fashionable bonnets that reflected the popular taste of the time—typically the "poke" bonnet. These last were most certainly treasured items, possibly purchased with funds raised by hiring out or as hand-me-downs from the mistress (Foster 1997, 257). Headwraps were worn exclusively by African Americans in the antebellum period (Foster 1997, 272). They were worn by both men and women, however "over time…the form gradually became a type of hair covering worn only by Black women" (Foster 1997, 272). The style is most likely Caribbean, not African, in origin. In Louisiana, this style was referred to as a *tignon* and was part of the legislated wardrobe for women of color in the 18th century. Regulations passed in 1786 "forbade 'females of color…to wear plumes or jewelry'" specifically requiring them to wear "their hair bound in a kerchief" (Foster 1997, 273).

The amount and quality of clothing owned by enslaved African American women varied from person to person. While Lila Nichols recalls that, "We had just a few pieces of clothes an' dey wuz of de wurst kind," Jane Lassiter remembers, "Our clothes wuz home made but we had plenty shiftin' clothes" (Foster 1997, 14). The quality of clothing for enslaved African Americans can be best understood through comparison with that worn by contemporary members of the white population. It is important to note, however, that these comparisons vary from state to state and situation. Many times, the clothes are similar or of exactly the same manufacture and quality—particularly those worn for working days by both the plantation owner's family and those enslaved by them. Mollie Dawson, an African American born into slavery in 1852 noted "Marser Newman and his folks wore a little bettah clothes den de slaves did, but de clothes dat dey wore fer every day on de farm was jest like ours, but de clothes dat dey had fer special occasions was made outten de best cotton and was bettah made den ours, and sometimes dey would buy cloth at de sto' and makes dey clothes to wear away from home" (Foster 1997, 76). The differentiation between work clothes and best dress was often little more than the application of additional care such as pressing or starching. One enslaved woman remembers, "Us wore de same on Sunday as evvy day, 'cept dat our clothes was clean, and stiff wid meal starch when us got into 'em Sunday mornin's" (Foster 1997,

126). Some enslaved women could boast of nicer clothes for Sundays, however, they were still of a quality inferior to many of their white contemporaries. "De white ladies had nice silk dresses to wear to church. Slave 'omans had new calico dresses what dey wore wid hoop skirts made out of grapevines" (Foster 1997, 137).

As has been noted, the acquisition of clothing by African Americans was often entirely out of their control. Some enslaved individuals might be given an allotment of clothing on a regular or seasonal basis as "the more ordinary procedure on many plantations was a seasonal distribution of specific types of clothing...many told of receiving clothing twice a year: a lighter set suitable for warmer months, a heavier set for colder months" (Foster 1997, 146). Others were able to purchase additional clothing items with money earned by hiring themselves out—many times these clothes would be reserved for Sunday or special occasion wear. Among the most valued of any enslaved woman's wardrobe were those clothes made from store-bought cloth or purchased ready-made from the store (Foster 1997, 77). Clothes might also have been given as a reward for good performance. Masters might reward the woman who picked the most cotton, or additional clothes might be given for giving birth to a child (here, the reward was for increasing the number of slaves owned by the master). One *Narratives* participant remembered, "Every time a Negro baby was born on one of his plantations, Major Walton gave the mother a calico dress and a 'bright, shiny silver dollar'" (Foster 1997, 176).

References

Cunnington, C. Willett and Phillis Cunnington. 1992. *The History of Underclothes.* New York: Dover Publications.

Field, Jacqueline, Marjorie Senechal, and Madelyn Shaw. 2007. *American Silk 1830–1930: Entrepreneurs and Artifacts.* Lubbock, TX: Texas Tech University Press.

Foster, Helen Bradley. 1997. *New Raiments of Self: African American Clothing in the Antebellum South.* New York: Berg.

Godey's Lady's Book. July-November 1830, April-May 1831.

Helvenston, Sally. 1980. Popular Advice for the Well-Dressed Woman in the 19th Century. *Dress* 5: 31–47.

Helvenston, Sally. 1991. Fashion on the Frontier. *Dress* 17: 141–55.

Her Many Horses, Emil, ed. 2007. *Identity by Design: Tradition, Change, and Celebration in Native Women's Dresses.* New York: Collins.

Jennys, Susan. 2004. *19th Century Plains Indian Dresses.* Pottsboro, TX: Crazy Crow Trading Post.

Kemble, Frances Anne. 1882. *Records of Later Life, Vol. 1.* London: Richard Bentley and Son.

Kidwell, Claudia B. 1979. *Cutting a Fashionable Fit.* Washington, D.C.: Smithsonian Institution Press.

McClellan, Elizabeth. 1969. *History of American Costume.* New York: Tudor Publishing Company.

Paterek, Josephine. 1994. *Encyclopedia of American Indian Costume.* New York: W. W. Norton & Company.

Rexford, Nancy. 2000. *Women's Shoes in America: 1795–1930.* Kent, OH: Kent State University Press.

Ritter, Joann Gregory and Betty L. Feather. Practices, Procedures, and Attitudes Toward Clothing Maintenance: 1850–1850 and 1900–1910. 1990. *Dress* 17: 156–68.

Severa, Joan. 1995. *Dressed for the Photographer: Ordinary Americans and Fashion, 1840–1900.* Kent, Ohio: Kent State University Press.

Tandberg, Gerilyn G. 1987. Towards Freedom in Dress for Nineteenth Century Women. *Dress* 11: 11–30.

Trollope, Frances Milton. 1832. *Domestic Manners of the Americans.* Vol 2. London: Whittaker, Treacher & Co.

Ullrich, Pamela V. 1985. Promoting the South: Rhetoric and Textiles in Columbus, Georgia, 1850–1880. *Dress* 11: 31–46.

Warner, Patricia Campbell. 2001. 'It Looks Very Nice Indeed': Clothing in Women's Colleges, 1837–1897. *Dress* 28: 23–39.

Waugh, Norah. 1968. *The Cut of Women's Clothes 1600–1900.* New York: Theatre Arts Books.

Waugh, Norah. 1970. *Corsets and Crinolines.* 2nd ed. New York: Theatre Arts Books.

Welters, Linda. 1997. Dress as Souvenir: Piña Cloth in the Nineteenth Century. *Dress* 24: 16–26.

Wortley, Lady Emmeline Stuart. 1851. *Travels in the United States, Etc. During 1849 and 1850.* New York: Harper & Brothers.

CHAPTER 9

Men's Fashions

> The age is, perhaps, forever gone by, when a privileged class could monopolize finery of garb; and, of all the civilized nations, it were least possible in ours.
>
> —Nathaniel Willis, *New Mirror,* Oct. 21, 1843 (Zakin 2003, 105)

In the early 19th century, the English style came to dominate men's town fashions throughout the western world. This style relied heavily upon the use of what formerly had been country wear; namely, tailored coats of wool broadcloth and other more functional articles of dress. As the Antebellum Era dawned, a wholly American style in men's dress was yet to be determined, but the citizens of the growing Republic were anxious to define it none the less. Opinions, sometimes contradictory, were expressed in the press and popular fiction, and diarists and letter-writers of the period also contributed to the discussion of what made the American man. One thing was clear, however—the search for fashion, or novelty, was as an integral part of what shaped American men's wear. The *New-York Mirror* proclaimed in 1823, that Americans were "perpetually in search of something *new;*" "everything that tells of hoary antiquity" was not in line with this emerging American ethos (Zakin 2003, 108). The few instances where antebellum men appeared in forms of dress that harkened back to the Revolutionary period were most frequently ceremonial, and therefore worn for the purpose of making a statement rather than participating in fashion. When James Monroe appeared in "small clothes" or breeches at his inauguration in 1821, it reflected his role in the Revolution and, in the way that coronation garb of the monarchy in England reflects the royal lineage of its sovereigns, was meant to bestow a sense of history on the still-young country. With powdered wig and buckled shoes, Monroe presented the perfect image of the Revolutionary War hero that helped to tie his presidency to those who had preceded him (Howe 2007, 91). And though it may have been comparable to the spirit of coronation apparel, it also offered a striking contrast to the dress chosen by George IV for his coronation the same year. Where Monroe chose the simple costume of the recent past, George IV borrowed from his Tudor and Stuart forebears in requiring his attendants to adopt the fashion from over 300 years prior to his coronation. Wearing paned trunk hose and ornate doublets, these "costumey" ensembles conveyed the pomp and circumstance that was warranted at such an event. Monroe's subtle historicizing was more in line with the democratic spirit of the United States. Monroe was not alone in adopting Revolutionary styles for effect. Daniel Webster, the senator from Massachusetts, "had a feeling for the theatrical" it has been said. For public occasions, he would don the trappings of an 18th century gentleman; knee breeches, waistcoat, and stockings, helping to secure his reputation with some as all that was civilized and learned about the law (Howe 2007, 369).

The emerging American style also rested on the rejection of all sartorial signifiers of servitude, such as livery. Ideally, these and other "badges of 'servility,' 'barbarity,' and personal dependence" were to be absent from any pervasive style that might be defined as American (Zakin 2003, 213). As is illustrated by the appearance of the poorest and those actively enslaved during the antebellum period, this was more frequently only an idea and not necessarily the actuality of all men's dress in America.

In fact, the most pervasive concept defining an American style was one of homogeneity. Style equality in men's wear became a uniquely American phenomenon or, as Lady Emmeline Stuart Wortley observed, "A mob in the United States is a mob in broad-cloth. If we may talk of a rabble in a republic, it is a rabble in black silk waistcoats" (Zakin 2003, 207). The participants in this blending of class through similarity might have complained of living in a "nation of black coats," as merchant tailor Nathaniel Willis had, but they were still complicit in its formation and dispersal through their participation in the growing ready-made men's wear industry.

If the ladies of America were meant to be the mannequins of display for their husbands' or fathers' wealth, American men were meant to display their gentility through their conformity to the fashionable norm. To be well-dressed as a man was to disappear among the crowd.

As the *New-York Mirror* advised its readers, "Dress so that it may never be said of you, 'What a well-dressed man!'" Upon his visit to the United States in 1842, Charles Dickens was feted as the exemplary gentleman of the 19th century for achieving this. The same newspaper remarked, "Mr. Dickens was dressed very neatly—so well, indeed, that we cannot remember how" (Zakin 2003, 192). Neatness and a good fit were the hallmarks of the properly dressed gentleman; this was the legacy of Englishman George "Beau" Brummell. Brummel was at the forefront of a trend towards a simplification in dress. What made him a "dandy" at the turn of the century, namely precisely fitted garments and a thorough attention to cleanliness and neatness in appearance, informed the expectations for the appearance of gentlemen of the mid-19th century. As Anne Hollander has observed, "elegance had shifted entirely away from wrought surfaces" by the early decades of the 19th century, to a focus on "fundamental form" and "natural simplicity" (1994, 90). The dandy of the Antebellum Era, instead, became a man who was overtly "super" fashionable. The fit of his coat was too close, his gloves too small and his pantaloons too tight—his clothing was not designed to allow him to perform the most basic and required function of this new industrial age, "produce." Zakin also identifies the "b'hoy" of the Bowery as the working class equivalent of the upper class exquisite or dandy. Here, it was the preference for overtly showy or attention-grabbing fashions that defined him as outside the accepted norm for gentlemen of the period. His brightly colored garments drew the gaze of those around him, as the dandy's tight-fitting silhouette did, and this was the greatest sin of dress a man might commit in antebellum America (Zakin 2003, 194).

"The Physiology of Dandyism" as depicted in the February 1852 issue of *Graham's Magazine*. Courtesy of the New York Historical Society.

DEMOCRATIC FASHION AND THE READY-MADE MAN

Of a piece with the simple and uniform American aesthetic was the movement towards the mass production of clothing. Men's clothing was the first to be successfully made and marketed, aided by the fact that silhouettes and sizes could be easily standardized. "Excellent ready-made suits were originally an American phenomenon" Hollander says, further separating the American man from the English man by the latter's adherence to a bespoke mentality (1994, 107). English observers were quick to point out that "in the New World,...American gentlemen..., were already becoming very hard to distinguish from American farmers, shop-keepers and artisans who were appearing in the park or at church in well-cut, well-fitting ready-made town clothes [by the 1820s]"—thus serving the democratic ideal of America's forebears, whether the true man of fashion appreciated this or not (Hollander 1994, 107).

The widespread availability of mass-produced suits, along with the accompanying reduction of prices, helped to create a seemingly more democratic mode of dress for men in America. The differences between upper and lower class men's suits were subtle but still detectable. The ready-made suit changed the role men played in assembling their wardrobes. The client of a bespoke tailor would trust to his tailor the fit and overall look of his suit. The purchaser of a ready-made suit must use his own judgment, and therefore train his own eye, to determine if the mass-produced suit he was purchasing was constructed well and had an over-all good appearance. As Hollander points out, "the American farmers who looked just like gentlemen in 1820 were obviously the ones who knew how" (1994, 108).

Through foreign eyes, it seemed that the Americans had achieved a mode of dress in their country that adhered to their republican virtues, as Stratford Canning, the minister from Great Britain commented in 1820. He observed,

> Breeches and silk stockings are not infrequently worn of an evening, but these innovations are perhaps confined to the regions of Washington. Even here the true republican virtues have found refuge. At the Foreign Office, trousers, worsted stockings and gaiters for winter. In summer a white roundabout, i.e., cotton jacket, sans neck-cloth, sans stockings and sometimes sans waistcoat. The Speaker of the House in the United States sits in his chair of office wigless and ungowned. (McClellan 1969, 577)

Mrs. Seaton, an observer during Mr. Canning's visit to the United States noted the difference between his dress and those of her fellow Americans. "The contrast between the plain attire of President Monroe and Mr. Adams and the splendid uniforms of the diplomatic corps, was very striking" (McClellan 1969, 578). But the simplification of men's dress would become a matter of state when, in 1853, the *Marcy Circular,* written by Secretary of State William L. Marcy, called on American diplomats abroad to adopt the "simple dress of an American citizen" (Moore 1912, 88). This meant a black coat worn without a cape, with a gold star on either side of the collar, worn with black or white breeches. The ceremonial *chapeau bras* and sword remained as part of this official dress. The sharp contrast between the black-suited American diplomats and the heavily embroidered and historicized dress that was more common in the courts of Europe proved detrimental to their diplomatic mission. American's clothing abroad was meant to exhibit restraint in decoration and expenditure but ultimately, the prescriptions for simplicity of the *Marcy Circular* hindered the acceptance of American diplomats in Europe's courts—they were perceived as disrespectful and inappropriately dressed. Their simple black suits made them appear as if they were wearing the current style of livery in Europe and, as Dick Tinto observed in the *New York Times* in 1854, "Why should [American diplomats] dress as to appear like Lord Cowley's servant?" (Tinto 1854). Marcy's policy, as the *New York Times* Paris correspondent had hoped, was later dropped.

What ultimately defined men's fashion in antebellum America was uniformity of shape and color. From *Things as They Are in America,* a travel book from 1854, the dress of members of the House of Representatives is described: "There was little diversity of costume. A black dress coat, black satin waistcoat, and black stock." This costume was meant to satisfy the needs of day to evening wear, from work to entertainments. The adoption of the frock coat as business wear would further this ubiquity of form (with the lounge suit fully supplanting all in the later 19th century as the formula business suit that continues to dominate men's fashion) (Milbank 2000, 251).

EVERYDAY AND SPECIAL OCCASION CLOTHES

Main Garments

The *Mirror of Fashion,* a men's wear trade journal in the 19th century, put forth that the well-fitted suit "discloses the shape of the figure, and yields to the conveniences of locomotion without restraint to limb, muscle, or joint, and yet without the inconvenience of carrying a surplus of cloth" (Zakin 2003, 83). These would be the watch-words for silhouettes for men throughout the antebellum period. In the 1820s, the ideal male form featured a long torso with a tight, nipped-in waist contrasting with broad shoulders. Coat sleeves were gathered into the armscye, accentuating this breadth, and the small waist was made to seem smaller still by legwear that was gathered or pleated into the waistband to create a curvy hipline. The 1830s silhouette did not alter much except for the elimination of gathering in the sleeves of coats, which were worn tight to the arm. The shoulders continued to appear broad compared to the still-small waistline, which was slightly raised. The hips were no longer full, as the line of pantaloons and trousers became taut and smooth.

An example of the typical silhouette of the well-dressed American man, woman, and girl of the 1840s. Picture Collection, The New York Public Library, Astor, Lenox and Tilden Foundations.

Contemporary critics and fashion historians alike have concluded that the silhouettes for men of the 1820s and 1830s are perhaps the most feminine for men of this century. Indeed, when describing a fashion plate from 1833, Elizabeth McClellan (an early 20th century fashion historian) refers to the ensemble as an example of the "extreme of lady-like dressing" for men (1969, 583). The 1840s saw the pronouncement of the chest and the further lowering of the waistline for men. Men are shown as slim in fashion plates; still with a somewhat pinched-in waist but with their chests puffed out to an almost absurd degree. The figure would become more substantial as the decade continued, as the ideal masculinity was redefined into a more mature figure. When the waist-line dropped for men in the 1840s, it settled there for the 1850s. The chest appears less exaggerated in fashion plates of this decade, though coat skirts remain full.

Coat, waistcoat and legwear all tended to be of different materials and colors at the start of the 19th century. Appropriate colors for coats included dark colors such as blue, green, brown, and black, and sometimes even a deep red. This began to change when black and dark blue were determined to be the most appropriate colors for formal evening coats, until at last black became the most accepted color for evening.

Broadcloth reigned as the material for most coats during the 19th century, with other tightly woven woolen fabrics such as kerseymere also used. Facings of velvet or satin were frequently used, though the collar and revers might also be faced with the same material as the rest of the coat. Legwear generally called for a lighter weight fabric as well as one in a lighter color. For these, merino and jersey-like woven fabrics were used for the winter and sturdy cotton or linen was preferred for summer. Patterned fabrics were popular for trousers and jackets of the late 1840s onwards. After 1840, evening dress pantaloons or trousers were always black. Until that time, they might be white or black, constructed of wool kerseymere or cashmere. Ditto suits or suits where pants, coat and vest were all made of the same material did appear with some regularity in the later decades of the antebellum period. The sack suit of the 1840s, when constructed as a ditto, was almost uniformly black wool, as would become the norm for business dress of the late 19th century.

Coats, 1820–1840

The dress-coat had been adopted for day and evening dress occasions by the start of the 19th century. This tail coat was cut in horizontally just above the waist and could be either single or double-breasted. Quoting from contemporary sources, Waugh (1964, 113) notes that the construction of the dress-coat should reflect a close fit. "It should, if anything, be even too small to meet across the waist and chest, so that it may sit open and display the waistcoat, shirt and cravat to the most advantage." The smoothness of this longer body silhouette was achieved through the placement of a seam at the waist, attaching the front tails to the front body. The rest of the coat was constructed in three seams, placed at center back and at the two sides. Darts were added in the 1830s when the waistline descended—these were placed at the sides below the armhole. The collar was large and stiff, padded at the front. The sleeves were gathered at the top during the 1820s but this, as has been noted, was eliminated in the 1830s. Riding coats were worn as fashionable day wear and, as their name suggests, for the activity of riding. In 1816, a new coat style for men appeared, the frock coat. Historians believe that this coat was military in origin, since its early incarnations buttoned all the way up the front to the neck. It had a fitted body and skirts that reached to about the knee and would become the most important garment in a man's wardrobe by the end of the period.

In the 1830s, the pilot coat or paletot was introduced into menswear. The pilot coat was a loosely cut garment that had no seams across the waist. The skirts were cut in one piece with the body of the coat and it could be worn as both a main garment or as a piece of outerwear. As a main garment, it typically fit more closely to the body.

Coats, 1840–1860

By the mid-19th century, the frock coat or surtout was more popular in America for day wear than the dress-coat. Declared "the most comfortable garments that ever were invented" by Nathaniel Hawthorne in his *American Note-books* of 1841, frock coats were exemplary of the importance and evolution of fit in men's dress of the 19th century (Hawthorne 1896, 249). Frock coats were generally looser in fit than the dress coat and were frequently constructed without a waist seam. Everything about this garment seemed to connote ease in movement, with looser sleeves at elbow and wrist and boxy shoulders. That is not to say that it was not without shape, indeed the frock coat also fit closely to the body, but its less restrictive construction and lighter material gave it a more casual air. These were typically made from light-weight, soft materials such as linen or cotton-wool blends; "stuffs," as Hawthorne noted when referring to his frock coat that was worn to fair in Brighton in 1841, and were almost always unlined (Hawthorne 1896, 248). But even this more casual style was accompanied by the standard accoutrements of hat, tie and vest, as it became the standard business dress for American men of the late antebellum period.

The dress-coat has changed little in principle since the 1840s—only minor alterations to sleeves, collars, tail length, etc. have been made through time. The darts added in the 1830s became seams in the 1840s—"the body of the coat now had five seams and was made from six separate pieces" as Waugh noted in her work on men's tailoring (1964). This would become the norm for men's coats "with fitted bodies and separate skirts or tails" of the 19th century (Waugh 1964, 113). Sleeves were long and narrow, fit high under the arm, and were closely fitted through the body.

The 1850s saw the body lengthen further and the whole become more sleek. The dress-coat was slowly being supplanted by the frock coat even for formal occasions in the 1850s. Also rising in popularity for more formal occasions was the riding coat, though it wouldn't fully replace the frock coat for day time formal wear until the 1880s. Here, instead of a straight, horizontally cut-in waistline, the front edges of the coat were sloped towards the side seams. By about the middle of the decade a fuller silhouette came into fashion—the width was a complement to the women's cage crinoline silhouette of the late 1850s. From 1854 a wider silhouette could be seen in the frock coat, as well as other coat styles, which were cut looser and had broad sleeves attached at a high armscye. Lapels became wider to complement these changes and the collar sat lower on the neck.

Vests

Waistcoats, or vests, as they were referred to in antebellum America, typically reflect the fashionable line of men's coat bodies for any period. Where they might differ from this garment was in their length and the type of material from which they were constructed. From the mid-1820s through the 1850s, the vest waistline was slightly pointed, instead of straight across as had been the fashion until then. Reflecting the taste for standing collars in shirts and coats, vests featured these as well until about 1830. McClellan mentions a particularly fashionable style of vest for the early 1830s being made of white silk with "large black spots, bound with galloon and made with a deep rolling collar" (McClellan 1969, 584). As the ideal male figure changed, the construction of the vest changed with it. Waugh notes, "In the 1830s and 40s the fronts were padded and a small dart into the armhole and another under the lapel helped to give the fashionable rounded-chest look." She also notes the fashion for layering that appeared in the early decades of the period in both England and America, "From 1820 to 1840 two or more waistcoats were often worn at the same time" (Waugh 1964, 115).

In the 1840s, vests were often made with shawl collars and in a double-breasted fashion. They might also have been made with notched collars and constructed in either single or double-breasted style, or sometimes collarless and single-breasted. The fashion for ditto suits or vests constructed of the same material as the pants and coat continued into the 1840s although many men wore vests of a contrasting fabric.

By the 1850s, "vests tended to be double breasted…often with notched collars, though shawl collars are [seen] as well" (Severa 1995, 105). A taste for patterned woven fabrics in vibrant colors had grown by the end of the era. This style was particularly present in vests intended for best dress. Most daytime vests were constructed of black wool; the same fabric used in the construction of the pants and coat. In warmer months, contrasting lighter vests became popular. If the weather was particularly warm, a single-breasted style might be favored. Severa, in her survey of early photographs of everyday Americans, notes a taste for checked fabrics in the late 1850s. These vests might be worn with trousers of a larger checked pattern (1995, 105). In contrast to this display of pattern and color, white and cream-colored vests were also fashionable in the 1850s.

Legwear

Breeches, which extended to just below the knee, were worn with the tail coat for daywear until around 1830. This somewhat antique style would continue to be worn by those in less fashionable circles well into the middle of the century. They were constructed with a fall front or flap below the waist, which fastened with buttons.

Pantaloons were worn until around the 1850s and replaced the early fashion of breeches for formal wear. They were tight-fitting and extended to the ankle, where they buttoned to achieve a fit like a legging. Straps would extend under the instep, over the stocking, to keep the pantaloon leg taut and smooth—though this was not done for formal wear, where the stocking was worn over the pantaloon.

Trousers had been introduced into men's fashion in the early part of the 19th century. These were almost indistinguishable from pantaloons in their tight fit, except that the leg tended to be cut straight from the calf down. Their length extended to the shoe, and instep straps were used to keep the legs taut until about 1855. By about 1825 they were generally worn for day wear. In the 1840s, trousers began to be constructed with a fly front instead of the fall front. They were worn low, sitting around the natural waist and accentuating the long line of the coat of the period. They were usually made of wool or wool blends. Black was the most popular choice for dress wear. More casual trousers might be made of sturdy cotton twill. The line of the trouser tended to be narrow throughout the period, though there were wider leg variations. The fabric of these wider-cut trousers was pleated into the waistband and fitted at the ankles. This style became known as "peg-top" trousers in the 1850s. Trousers with a wide leg, worn without a crease, extended to the toes in the early part of the last decade of the Antebellum Era. By the 1850s, all men's leg wear was made with a fly front. In her survey, Severa notes that "[p]laids, checks, and lighter-colored trousers were popular with the 'natty' dressers by mid-decade" (1995, 105).

Undergarments

While women of the 19th century had come to rely upon their undergarments to help them conform to the most desirable shape of the period, men were increasingly dependent on the structure of their outergarments for correcting figure flaws. It was the interfacings, padding, and canvas employed by the tailor that helped mold the male form into the fashionable shape throughout most of the Antebellum Era. The "desired male shape" was built into men's garments (Zakin 2003, 197). However, there were those men who did rely on underwear to help their bodies conform. In the early 1840s, it was not uncommon for the well-dressed man to prize underpinnings such as corsets as much as his female counterpart. Corsets were essential for all but the most youthful figure to attain the fashionable nipped-in waist of the period. These were most certainly more commonly found in the wardrobes of the well-to-do man of fashion than in the average American. Padded vests would also aid in creating the puffed chest of the early 1840s silhouette.

Shirts

Shirts were still considered "underwear" in the antebellum period—a man would not appear in his "shirt sleeves" in public, and even in the most casual environment, the shirt was at least covered by a vest. Some in the 1820s were constructed without collars, though this trend became more widespread as the period wore on. The separate collar was starched and worn turned up and deep enough to appear over the neckwear. In the 1820s, it might be tied on instead of buttoned to the shirt. These detachable shirt collars represented another kind of democratization in men's fashions. The appearance of clean, starched linen had always signified the wealth of the wearer—to have the funds to pay someone to clean and starch a large wardrobe of shirts so that one was always cleanly presented was a sign of prosperity. The detachable collar replaced the need for a whole wardrobe of shirts and cut down on the laundry bill as well. To maintain a neat appearance, one must only replace the collar and not the whole shirt. And collars were much more moderately priced than shirts—one might buy half a dozen for half the price of a medium quality shirt. By the 1850s, disposable paper collars that imitated the look and feel of linen ones offered an even cheaper option. These could be worn and discarded for half the price of a linen collar that would then require the cost of washing and starching.

Dress shirts throughout the period were typically more ornate, even if plainly so. In other words, they were more likely to feature tucks or embroidery on the center panel or, in the case of the 1820s and early 1830s, a ruffle. Joan Severa notes that the proliferation of detachable shirt accessories extended beyond the shirt collar to include other parts of the shirt as well. In 1840, she describes the "tailored, white cotton shirt" as having "narrow set-in sleeves and sometimes a pleated linen bosom." This "bosom" or center front panel might be purchased as a separate, pre-starched accessory, according to merchant advertisements of the time (1995, 20). It would typically feature a series of vertical tucks on either side of the center front, though there are styles where this section is plain. The separate collar would attach at the back of the shirt, buttoning underneath the tie.

In the 1850s, pattern and color entered the male wardrobe in greater profusion. This trend was reflected in the variety of shirts that were available. The standard white shirt was advertised alongside those made in stripes, checks, small prints, and solid colors. These shirts might be made with collars or with buttonholed bands to attach a separate collar. Cuffs were also made as separate, detachable pieces. These were starched and buttoned on. The collar of the 1850s shirt was moderately sized with a slight downturn over the necktie. Severa (1995, 105) notes the continued trend toward more ornate dress shirts in her survey. "Dress shirts were made with pleated, stiffly starched bib fronts, and separate fancy shirtfronts of this type could be purchased."

Drawers

In the first two decades of the period, drawers for men can be found in long and short variations, reaching either to the knee or to the ankle. These were made of calico, cotton, worsted wool, or, for the warmest variety, in a thick silk. The legs were attached separately to a waistband, and the crotch was split. In the last decades of the period, drawers for men tended to be ankle length, with many being made of a stretchy stockinette or knit cotton material. These drawers could be fastened with buttons or ties at the waist. Many did have an overlap at the front but the crotch seam was still split. Braces or suspenders were used to keep both trousers and drawers from falling down. These intimate accessories were often the subject of ladies' fancy work and were frequently made as gifts by women to the men in their lives. The intimate nature of these accessories suggests that such gifts might signify a romantic attachment.

Under Vests

A kind of sleeveless undershirt appears in the 1840s and 1850s as an under vest. As mentioned above, these were frequently padded to help achieve the puffed-out appearance in the chest that was so prized by their fashionable wearers. The under vest was made of wool and initially meant as a layer for warmth. These were worn under the shirt, next to the skin.

Dressing Gowns

A new invention of the Antebellum Era, and the product of a growing industrial economy, was the category of business dress. This class of dress would become the uniform of men well into the 20th century. This new category made the difference between street wear and at-home wear for men even more pronounced, and for most, even more cherished. In domestic circles, dressing gowns had risen to popularity among the well-to-do in the 18th century as banyans imported from India and the East. They continued to be popular at-home wear, entering the wardrobes of the middle class as well from the 1820s on. Their Eastern origins continued to be reflected in the stylized Orientalist designs of the fabric used in their construction.

Nightshirts. For sleeping, most men possessed nightshirts. These were simply a longer version of the day shirt. They were meant for sleeping; made with a plain collar and undecorated. This sleeping ensemble might sometimes be worn with a knit night cap for warmth.

Outerwear

Coats were worn by most men out-of-doors, irrespective of weather. Norah Waugh divides the styles worn into two distinct types. The first was the surtout or greatcoat, which was typically double-breasted "with the fronts cut straight but the side seams and shoulder seams towards the back like the dress-coat" (1964, 114). The skirt of the coat featured a pleat at the front with the back left open for ease of movement when walking and riding. This style was worn very long, reaching down to the ankles. The collar style changed with the fashion of the day and a shoulder cape was sometimes added. From 1823–1830, a full skirted greatcoat with a deep cape was the style and in her study of American dress, McClellan notes that velvet was frequently used to face the collar (McClellan 1969, 581). The second style Waugh identifies was a less formal one, a kind of loose boxy coat. The coat was wider at the hem than under the arms, creating an A-line fullness that was then either belted or held in place at the back with a strap. The front closure featured buttons or, more commonly, a tab closure. Waugh notes that this style was worn with layers of shoulder capes (1964, 114). She also cites other variations on these two styles: the frock greatcoat, featuring a waist seam, which was introduced at the middle of the century, and the paletot, a shorter version of the greatcoat (Waugh 1964, 114). Long cloaks were also frequently worn, lined with contrasting material. These were particularly popular in the 1820s.

Accessories

Headwear

Hats were an essential part of men's wardrobes in the Antebellum Era. It was almost taken for granted that a man would be seen with one, even if he carried his hat in hand while indoors or as a show of respect. For daywear, the shape of headwear changed from decade to decade. "High" hats or top hats were made wide at the top, narrowing towards the hat band in the 1820s. These were typically made of beaver fur. In the 1830s, these hats were still made of fur though they were not always found in black. McClellan notes that examples of gray and white beaver hats were particularly fashionable for daywear in the first half of the decade. The shape of these hats changed as well in the 1830s, becoming more straight up and down. (McClellan 1969, 585). In warmer climates, palm leaf hats were favored. These were particularly fashionable for men in the summers from 1826 through the 1830s. This fashion, and their production, extended beyond the southern states and into New England, so much so that *New England Magazine* commented in 1831 that "Palm Leaf Hats are manufactured to a surprising extent in New England, but principally in Massachusetts" (McClellan 1969, 585).

The rise in popularity of the palm leaf hat was due largely to the high tax levied on imported leghorn straw hats, another warm weather staple, during the 1820s and 1830s. The palm leaf hat was a product of cottage industry, with young girls making them domestically from leaves imported from Cuba. They were naturally of varying quality, were sold to "country merchants" and then gathered together to be sold in America's big cities (McClellan, 585).

Joan Severa (1995) notes a variety of caps and hats featured in daguerrotypes of the period, including knit caps, peaked wool caps, and bowlers. The beaver top hats of the 1820s and 1830s were out of fashion in the 1840s, and had been replaced by black silk top hats. In the early 1850s, a tall, straight-sided soft felt hat in off-white was worn for day. The "Wide-awake" was a popular style throughout the 1850s. This was a "black hat with a broad, stiff, horizontal brim and a tall, malleable crown" (Severa 1995, 106). Caps continued to be worn for casual wear. These could be knitted or made of wool felt with leather bills, or even cloth caps in a style similar to those worn by railroad engineers. By this time, business dress called for the bowler hat or the top hat. For dress wear, the top hat was still the most appropriate form of headwear.

While an antebellum gentleman might find himself clad in the black suit of the ready-made revolution, at home he would find an outlet for more expressive dressing. The night cap had long been worn as an article of undress, worn out of practicality when the fashionable wig was removed and the hair underneath, worn cropped, did not provide enough warmth for the head. It, like the banyan or dressing gown, was part of the growing exotic or Orientalist look of the 18th century, and was often replaced with a structure that was more turban than cap in keeping with that look. The night cap provided a ready surface for ladies, who became expert at the art of needlework in polite society, to ply their needles and create nightcaps with floral, vegetal and organic motifs embroidered all-over. In the 1850s, the nightcap was replaced with the smoking cap. Diane Maglio, in her work on men's smoking caps of the period, notes the continued use of orientalist motifs in these at-home accessories. American women were advised to their proper decoration by the editors of *Godey's* and *Peterson's* magazines. These small caps, ornamented with their own needlework, were "an article of ornament that is really useful" in their estimation, making them the ideal gift for men (Maglio 2000, 11). The smoking cap of the 1850s was typically constructed of dark-colored velvet and embroidered with motifs in gold thread. The flat crown might be surmounted by a tassel, in the style of a fez, to complete the exotic look.

Neckwear

Stocks, which were originally part of military costume, entered fashionable use in the 19th century. A shaped band that fastened at the back of the neck, the stock was constructed of stiff material such as woven horsehair or buckram. The center front seam was shaped to contour the neck. The most extreme versions of the stock reached high onto the cheeks and would even extend to the chin in the front. McClellan mentions that these high stocks were in fashion at the end of the 1820s and well into the 1830s. After around 1840, the fashion fell out of favor with younger men and stocks were generally only worn by older gentlemen.

Cravats, or large square or triangular pieces of fabric, were usually made of lawn, muslin or silk. These were then folded into a band and starched and arranged around the neck in a variety of styles. According to Waugh, "[b]lack or coloured cravats were considered very undress, patterned white might be worn for half-dress but they always had to be plain white for balls and soirées" (1964, 119). She also notes that an additional stiffener in the form of buckram or whalebone might be worn under the cravat to help maintain its high-reaching shape. There were a variety of ways to tie the cravat, an art perfected by the English dandy but not as widely observed in the United States. Waugh mentions a simply tied cravat referred to as the 'à l'Américaine' in her work on the cut of men's clothes (1964, 120). McClellan also mentions the 'americaine' as one of the more popular methods for tying a cravat, along with the Napoleon, Mail-coach, Osbaldestan, the Irish, and the Mathematical methods (1969, 573–74). According to Waugh, the 1850s saw the conformity of the cravat develop into something that more closely resembled the necktie—a "made-up band...might be moderately broad and tied in a flat bow or folded and fastened with a pin, or there was a very much narrower version, the 'shoe-tie,' which also tied in a bow or was knotted with long ends" (1964, 120).

Beginning around 1840, neckties entered the fashion vocabulary for American men. These were wide, soft and tied in a "small horizontal bow knot" or appear as a "stock form of a thick silk scarf [that] is sometimes seen folded and tucked into the vest fronts" (Severa 1995, 21). These could be light or dark, and were generally made of silk. String ties were also worn.

In the early part of the 1850s, a stiff silk tie, two-inches wide, was tied horizontally in a half-bow form, with the ends extending on either side. Severa conjectures that "[t]his kind of tie was possibly achieved by folding a silk square in from two corners diagonally to form a thick scarf" (1995, 106).

Late in the last decade of the Antebellum Era, the tie became narrower and more horizontal. Softer silk ties are also seen in this period, as well as narrow black ties.

Footwear

Wellingtons, a specific style of boots, were worn from around 1815 to 1850 "[T]hese boots were made of calfskin and fitted close to the leg as far as the knee and were worn under long trousers fastened with strap beneath the sole of the boot" (McClellan 1969, 574). The Hessian boot, which got its name from the style of boot famously worn by Hessian troops, was fashionable through the 1840s. This boot was cut higher in the front and ornamented with a tassel just below the curved upper edge of the boot. In the 1840s short pull-on boots with a square toe and a low broad heel were worn, always in black. Low shoes were worn as well as boots. These were tied for day wear, slip-on for evening. They were almost universally made of black leather and worn with a square toe and a low heel or none at all.

Hairstyles and Grooming

The short and unruly hairstyles of the first decades of the 19th century slowly gave way to a more structured style. In the 1820s, men's hair was worn full on the top, loosely parted to one side and cropped fairly closely at the back and neck. Side burns could be expected in most men but otherwise faces were clean-shaven. The 1830s saw a continuation of the wavy curls of the 1820s; the hair was "worn in loose waved locks over the forehead, and side whiskers" (McClellan 1969, 583). Early fashion plates from the 1840s show clean-shaven faces, perhaps a nod towards the cult of youth prized early in the century. A short beard might be seen as the mature man became more fashionable at the end of the decade, mustaches and sideburns are more commonly depicted. Mustaches were substantial, "mostly horizontal with downward-twirled ends" (Severa 1995, 23). The volume and curl that had dominated men's hairstyles of the early antebellum period slowly gave way to a more plain, closely groomed style. By the end of the 1830s, hair was cut ear-length and parted to one side. This in turn was replaced by a sleekly oiled front wave style in the late 1840s—a wave of oiled hair that rose high on the forehead. This style continued until the end of the Era. Macassar oil was most popularly used to achieve this look (Severa 1995, 23). In the early 1850s, most men were again clean shaven, but full beards became popular towards the end of the decade. Young men of the mid-1850s adopted a slightly more refined look with a goatee-style fringe starting under the cheeks and extending along the jawline. The highly oiled front wave hairstyle of the 1840s and early 1850s was gradually replaced with a side-parted style, and then combed away from the face. Hair was cut longer at the end of the decade, reaching to the collar and covering the ears by 1857.

Wedding and Mourning Dress

The *Gentleman's Guide to Politeness,* one of the many etiquette manuals that appeared for the rising middle class in the mid-19th century, advised men that the proper dress for weddings was a "dark claret dress coat together with a white ribbed-silk vest" (Zakin 2003, 196). There were fewer requisites for proper dress for men than women during times of mourning. The dark suit that had become their uniform was almost all that was required. Armbands might be worn for a period of a few months to a year by a man who had lost his wife. After this period of outward mourning, the widower was free to remarry and resume his normal manner of dressing. In fact, remarriage was highly desirable, particularly if he had young children to care for. Hatbands for men were generally worn as a sign of participation in a funeral if not during a period of mourning. These might be worn in black or white silk, if the deceased were a young girl. Crape hat bands would replace the silk bands for close relatives of the deceased as time progressed. The level of intimacy with the deceased might be reflected in the width of the band worn—the closer the relative, the wider the band.

WORKING CLOTHES

In the early days of the Antebellum Era and in the remote areas of the expanding United States, work clothes resembled the hunting clothes of the previous century. On the frontier, leather hunting shirts and breeches were the norm in the 1820s.

As time wore on, the working man's dress became less rustic and benefitted from the growing textile industry of the United States. Both jean and denim were manufactured in the North and both are mentioned as suitable fabrics for working clothes. These terms were not interchangeable then as they are today. In fact, they describe two different kinds of fabric. A textile mill in Columbus, GA advertised a variety of materials to meet the needs of planters; they offered "Planters' Cassimere- (Jeans) colored, black, brown, green, &c. [and] Planters' Plains—colored, black, brown, green, &c." Jean or truck was also advertised as suitable fabric for planters (Ullrich 1985, 38). This jean fabric would have been woven of cotton, with warp and weft of the same color. Pants and overalls made from denim were worn by workers, both free and enslaved. Denim was also made of cotton, however the warp and weft threads were typically two different colors—one being white. This sturdy material would become the fabric of choice during the gold rush of the later 19th century, spawning the most famous American fashion innovation—jeans or "waist overalls" as they were originally called in the patent received by Levi Strauss and Jacob Davis in 1873 (Levi Strauss & Co., 2)

Work shirts of the Antebellum Era resembled the dress shirts of the previous century—that is, they were smock-like and made without a shoulder seam. The neckhole and placket front were bound and a plain shirt collar was added, with the fullness of the front of the shirt gathered into the collar. These full shirts would be tucked into the trousers. Full sleeves were gathered at the shoulder and into cuffs at the wrist, with gussets added under the arm to provide ease of movement. These were made of patterned woven material or solid colored fabric and might be bought ready-made or, more frequently, made at home. An oversized smock was also worn as work wear—made popular by the immigrant communities arriving from places such as Great Britain, Scandinavia and other parts of Europe. This was usually worn over a full set of clothing to protect the wearer during work. It would reach below the waist and have a loose, soft collar or band. Fallfront trousers with high waists were mass-produced in the 1840s and were also part of the working man's wardrobe. They were advertised as being made of cotton, linen or wool and wool blends in neutral colors. Brogans were the shoes most often worn for work, again by both free men and those enslaved. These rough shoes were made with thick, unyielding straight soles. Their hard leather uppers might feature a copper toe for added protection during work.

Gold miners of the late 1840s and 1850s, though from disparate classes and cultures, seem to have adopted a working dress that was almost uniform. One man, in a letter to his wife in 1849, says that his appearance is so altered that she might not recognize him and other workers in their "woolen or striped shirts and broad brimmed hats" (Adams-Graf 1995, 60). The uniform is described as this broad-brimmed hat worn with a flannel shirt, rough trousers and tall boots (in contrast to the low boots worn in more "polite" society).

By the mid-1850s, past fashions were being relegated to the status of work wear—that is, the sleeker dress silhouette of the 1840s was the work silhouette of the late 1850s. The work shirt was still loose in fit, like the smock, and might be made of wool or cotton. This would be worn with a vest, tucked into the trousers. The work smock was still worn as well, as a cover for clothes underneath. It was made long, sometimes to the knees, and of heavier material (white cotton or linen in the Northern states, others were made of wool or tweed and most were of home manufacture) and was never meant to be tucked in.

MAKING AND ACQUIRING CLOTHES

Ready-made clothing for men was available in a wide variety of materials and colors. A man could purchase almost the entirety of his wardrobe from merchant tailors, whether he was urban-dwelling or provincial. As has been noted, the largest center of production in America was New York, but these products were dispersed with some effort to all corners of the growing nation. Many advertised in the penny press that orders could be sent as far as the new territories and as drafting systems enabled ever more standardized sizing, a gentleman might take his own measurements and submit them for a near-custom suit. Custom tailors did not disappear altogether, however the line between skilled tailor and merchant tailor began to blur as more and more ready-made products were made available at cheaper and cheaper prices.

But even with the proliferation of ready-made garments for men at all levels, there were still some items of clothes that were made at home. These included men's linens or undergarments—shirts in particular. The fact that shirts were more consistently made inside the home made them one of the cheapest commodities in the men's wear market. This created an unfortunate circumstance among tailoresses or women seamstresses—shirts were priced at consistently lower price points, creating the need for cheaper and cheaper labor if the merchant was to make a profit from them. Women provided the cheapest skilled labor available in the North and even though the shirt sewers organized in the later decades of the antebellum period, their cause for higher wages and more humane working conditions was not met with any great success.

The use of homespun cloth, or cloth woven at home, was more prevalent in the southern states. Robert Shepherd, who was enslaved in Georgia, noted that his master wore a white linen "duster" (which probably resembled a riding coat, as he describes it as being in the cutaway style with long tails) made from plantation-made cloth (Foster 1997, 137).

COMPOSITION OF A WARDROBE

The composition of a man's wardrobe was shaped by his particular role in society. Zakin describes the wardrobe of the urban gentleman in this passage from his work on the ready-made industry in American: "civic-minded men wore dress coats in the evening and surtouts in the morning [that is, during the work day]. They owned riding coats, greatcoats, and something called a duster, which was 'the most desirable possible for wearing in railroad cars.' There was a proper time and occasion for gloves, collars, cravats, hats, demi-toilette, morning pantaloons and vests, single-breasted frocks, a business coat, breakfast dress, and shooting and fishing costume" (2003, 195–96). Though the urban gentleman's wardrobe might contain more than the average working man's, it could be expected that his would also contain at least one "better suit," usually in black. Severa identifies many of these in her survey of daguerrotypes from the period; they were "usually a sack suit with fly-front trousers and matching vest, if only for weddings, funerals and the occasional formal photograph" (1995, 21).

The hard-wearing wardrobe required by a miner in the 1850s was as follows:

> "2 blue or red flannel overshirts, open in front, with buttons. 2 woolen undershirts. 2 pairs thick cotton drawers. 4 pairs of woolen socks. 2 pairs

> of cotton socks. 4 colored handkerchiefs. 2 pairs stout shoes, for footmen. 1 pair boots, for horsemen. 1 pair shoes, for horsemen. 3 towels. 1 gutta percha poncho. 1 broad-brimmed hat of soft felt." Plus everything to clean and maintain this wardrobe and the man himself, such as soap, mending gear, combs and brushes. (Adams-Graf 1995, 60)

A laundry inventory of a wealthy English gentleman of the late 1820s reflects the difference in the amount of clothing owned by the well-off compared to the middle classes. When detailing his undergarments, the laundry list of August 1829 includes: "Day-shirts, 29. Night-shirts, 5. Night-caps, 9. Flannel drawers, 2 pairs. Calico drawers, 4 pairs" (Cunnington and Cunnington 1992, 123). Compare this to the wardrobe of one of the many young men who were flocking to the cities to participate in the growing white collar work sector of the new American industrial economy. Upon arriving in New York, one would-be clerk possessed "two pairs of stockings, one vest, one pair of pantaloons, one dress coat, one surtout, three cravats, one pair of boots, and 'apologies for a shirt'" (Zakin 2003, 111). His wardrobe would need supplementation, however, if he were to find employment in the city. This might require purchases similar to those made by another clerk, A. L. Sayre, over the course of 1849, when he purchased three vests, a dress coat, a linen coat, and an overcoat, along with multiple collars and cravats, all purchased in the "city departments" of New York's clothing retailers. In addition to these, he bought linen cloth yardage from one merchant before taking it to a cutter and then a seamster to construct two pairs of pantaloons (Zakin 2003, 112).

AMERICAN INDIAN CLOTHING

Masculine dress among American Indian tribes often served both a ceremonial and a practical purpose. The destructive attitudes toward indigenous people adopted in the Antebellum Era proved the undoing of centuries old traditions among many tribes. Evidence regarding the dress of many of these tribes is, where it exists, sparse at best. Though there were many, often subtle, differences between the dress of different tribes, it is possible to discuss commonalities in the general silhouette of men's dress within geographic regions.

Southeastern Region

The tribes of the Southeastern region of the United States were treated particularly harshly during the Antebellum Era. By the end of the period, many of the tribes had been either completely destroyed or removed from their homelands and dispersed to new territory. A fusing of styles occurred among tribes forced to occupy land in the new Indian territory of Oklahoma. The basic dress of men of the Southeastern region consisted of a breechcloth made of strouding, a woolen cloth imported from England, and thigh-length leggings. Ankle-high moccasins were worn when traversing areas of high water but, for the most part, tribe members went barefoot. Skin matchcoats were worn during the cooler months of the year, made from a variety of different animals. A sash might be worn around the waist or over one shoulder, trimmed with tassels at the ends. Skins were often dyed colors such as red, green, blue, yellow or black. Because of their early introduction to European travelers (as early as the 17th century), tribes in the Southeast adopted European dress earlier than others. A series of paintings done in the early 1830s show indigenous men visiting the nation's capital, dressed in the latest tailored looks for men with accessories to identify their native roots (Paterek 1994, 8). Turbans adorned with feathers were a popular addition to the male wardrobe of the early Antebellum Era.

North American Indians as depicted by George Catlin, 1830s. Courtesy The New York Public Library.

Northeastern Region

The tribes of the Northeastern region suffered early from the corruption and devastating force of the European influence. Few tribes survived into the Antebellum Era. For men, the breechclout was the primary form of apparel. These were fitted, with flaps hanging down in the front and the back. They were often decorated, either with quillwork or embroidery. Leggings were tied on, longer in the winter months and knee-length in the summer. These leggings might be incorporated into the moccasin during winter, to form a single garment.

The Plains

As largely nomadic tribes, portability was a priority in the traditional dress of the Plains Indians. Skins were the main material for apparel and were worn in the form of apron-like breechclouts, leggings and moccasins. Tanned skin leggings were folded and tied around the legs, often with a fringe at the end of the thigh. As the Plains Indians came in contact with traders, European garments such as shirts were incorporated into their dress. Tribes in other regions of the United States, such as the Great Basin and Plateau regions, adopted the dress of these nomadic tribes.

The Southwest

As it was part of Mexico at the beginning of the Antebellum Era, what is now the Southwestern United States did not come into this country's possession until the late 1840s. Though the Mexican government had afforded the indigenous tribes equal rights as citizens, the United States was less kind once it had taken ownership of the land. The use of loom-woven textiles in the production of clothing distinguishes this region from others. Breechcloths were made of woven cotton, though European dress in the form of cotton shirts and trousers quickly entered the costume of the tribes of the Southwest. Wool blankets, worn as an outergarment, are still the most well-known aspect of this region's attire. Exhibitions of Navaho blankets continue today.

The Northwest Coast

The mild coastal climate called for little in the way of protective apparel for the tribesmen of the Northwest coast. However, the fur trade brought trappers and trade companies to this region early on and the influence of European dress was seen in the Antebellum Era. Traditional dress for men had included woven bark tunics, though the trade blankets of the Hudson Bay Company quickly became a staple of the tribal wardrobe.

CLOTHING OF ENSLAVED AFRICAN AMERICAN MEN

Typical clothing for enslaved men, particularly those working in the fields, was a long loose shirt worn with knee-length pantaloons. Many times the shirt was referred to as a "banyan" or a "binyan," the same term (Indian in origin) applied to white men's dressing gowns (Foster 1997, 165). This shirt was constructed in two pieces, with the sleeves cut in, and gathered at the neck. The shoes called brogans, which were also a part of the regular working man's wardrobe, were worn by both male and female enslaved African Americans. Typically these were not store-bought but made onsite by enslaved individuals who were trained in the skill of shoemaking. Many ads seeking freedom seekers or runaways in the Antebellum Era mention shoemaking as a particular skill, and frequently the quality of the shoes made is noted as being "rough" or "coarse" as in an 1820 ad placed for John Allen who was described as a "rough shoemaker" who "may perhaps work at that trade" following his escape (Meaders 1997, 334; Parker 1994, 696) These were sturdy and most likely uncomfortable hard-soled tie shoes with uppers made of leather and the soles made of unyielding wood or thick leather. The *Narratives* project participants frequently mention these shoes as uncomfortable and even damaging to the feet. They recount episodes of having to use extraordinary measures just to wear the shoes, such as heating the leather by the fire and applying handfuls of tallow or fat to soften them up in order to get them on their feet (Foster 1997, 233). Adding to their discomfort, these shoes were most likely made with straight soles, designed to be worn on either foot and, very often, were made in a limited number of uniform sizes instead of being custom made. Red leather is mentioned most frequently as the material of their construction. Frequently, particularly in warm weather, men (as well as women) went barefoot. Shoes were among the articles of clothing doled out on a seasonal basis by many slave owners, given once a year for wear during the cold winter months. These might be made onsite by a skilled slave—many of the ads for runaways or freedom seekers mention skilled cobblers or shoemakers. Boots were often worn by men, though these were frequently the hand-me-downs of their master or his children. Sun hats were worn during the warmer months. These, like the palm leaf hats popular within the general populace, were woven from plant material. Stocking caps or brimmed caps were worn by men in the winter.

The fabrics used for the production of clothing for enslaved men ranged from factory produced fabrics to homespun materials. Among the factory produced materials were kersey, which was made of either all cotton or a blend of cotton and wool, and produced in three different grades. Ullrich notes that the grades were advertised to satisfy the needs for clothing for enslaved men in both "the house and in the field" (Ullrich 1985, 38). As with enslaved African American women, there were differences in the clothing and material alotted men who worked in and out of the plantation house. This is illustrated by the narrative given by Ellen Claibourn, who was enslaved in Georgia during the Antebellum Era. According to her testimonial, the house servants were dressed in factory produced cloth while the field hands wore clothing made from homespun (Foster 1997, 139). Frederick Douglass noted a significant disparity between the clothing of both men and women working in close proximity to whites and those who were more removed, observing that the men on Colonel Lloyd's plantation "were equally well attired from the overflowing wardrobe of their young masters" as there female counterparts (Foster 1997, 138). Jim Johnson, who was enslaved in South Carolina and Texas, notes that the only store-bought clothing he ever wore was hand-me-downs from his master's boys. Still, these second-hand items were a step up from the standard wardrobe of the field hand; as he notes, "I had store-bought clothes give to me, too. 'Course dey is what young Marse Eddie or George have wore, but dey is better'n what most slave folk wear" (Foster 1997, 139).

The quantity of clothing possessed by any enslaved African American man might depend on a number of factors, including the beneficence of his master, and his access to funds (typically through the hiring out of his services for pay). The importance of clothing can be felt in the numerous advertisements placed for freedom seekers or runaway slaves. Used primarily as an identification tool, the clothing described in these ads also reveals how freedom seekers may have used dress to disguise themselves on their road to freedom. Not only is the clothing worn by the freedom seeker described but frequently these ads include a laundry list of ensembles that might also be worn on the road to freedom. These items were sometimes described as being "stolen" from the master, and in these instances, they are typically noted as being of higher quality than what one might expect to find on an enslaved African American of the period. Most frequently, these freedom seekers are described as wearing homespun clothing or, as often, hand-me-down clothing in a style no longer in fashion, such as leather breeches or a souvenir hat from Lafayette's historic visit in 1824 (Parker 1994, 719).

The use of livery, in America at least, was seen as a sign of servitude, and therefore inappropriate for any citizen (read as free white male) to wear. It was a "costume of service, a most demeaning badge of servility" (Zakin 2003, 206). In the rare cases in which it was worn in America, it was by enslaved (and sometimes free) African Americans. Most often, this signified either aspiration by the people who forced the uniform upon the enslaved or as a form of theater. In the free states, the use of livery as a theatrical spectacle was especially the case when "two Ethiopians" were dressed in "scarlet coats, cocked hats, plush breeches, and white stockings" and put on guard at the opening festivities of a new store on Broadway in 1844 (Zakin 2003, 206). In Maryland, the Charles Carroll house was distinguished by the appearance of "no less than three servants in livery," which to the contemporary observer seemed quite grand as she had "not seen a servant in livery in the country, and you cannot think how grand it appears to me" (Hall 1931, 158).

Outside the use of livery, many enslaved African American men described the dress imposed upon them as a uniform, particularly those engaged in jobs in close proximity to whites. Because the quality of the uniform dress of coachmen, in particular, was higher than most slave clothing, these individuals were often afforded more freedoms. William Grimes remembers wearing his coachmen's uniform through the streets of Savannah in the evenings, despite the curfew imposed upon most blacks in that city. "I have frequently walked the streets of Savannah in an evening, and being pretty well dressed, and having a light complexion...I would walk as bold as I knew how, and as much like a gentleman" (Foster 1997, 143).

References

Adams-Graf, John. 1995. In Rags for Riches: A Daguerrian Survey of Forty-Niners' Clothing. *Dress* 22: 59–68.

Cunnington, C. Willett and Phillis Cunnington. 1992. *The History of Underclothes.* New York: Dover Publications, Inc.

Foster, Helen Bradley. 1997. *New Raiments of Self: African American Clothing in the Antebellum South.* New York: Berg.

Hall, Margaret Hunter. 1931. The Aristocratic Journey. ed. Una Pope-Hennessey. New York: G.P. Putnam's Sons.

Hawthorne, Nathaniel. 1896. The Complete Works of Nathaniel Hawthorne, Vol. 9: Passages from the American Note-Books. ed. George Parsons Lathrop. Cambridge, Mass: Riverside Press.

Hollander, Anne. 1994. *Sex and Suits.* New York: Alfred A. Knopf.

Howe, Daniel Walker. 2007. *What Hath God Wrought: The Transformation of America, 1815–1848.* New York: Oxford University Press.

Levi Strauss & Co.—History. "Levi Strauss & Co. General Timeline" http://www.levistrauss.com/Downloads/levis_timeline.pdf

Maglio, Diane. 2000. Luxuriant Crowns: Victorian Men's Smoking Caps, 1850–1890. *Dress* 27: 9–17.

McClellan, Elizabeth. 1969. *History of American Costume.* New York: Tudor Publishing Company.

Meaders, Daniel, ed. 1997. *Advertisements for Runaway Slaves in Virginia, 1801–1820.* New York: Garland Publishing.

Milbank, Caroline Rennolds. 2000. "'Ahead of the World': New York City Fashion." In *Art and the Empire City,* eds. Catharine Hoover Voorsanger and John K. Howat, 243–57. New Haven, CT: Yale University Press.

Moore, John Basset. 1912. *Four Phases of American Development.* Baltimore, MD: Johns Hopkins Press.

Parker, Freddie L., ed. 1994. *Stealing a Little Freedom: Advertisements for Slave Runaways in North Carolina, 1791–1840.* New York: Garland Publishing.

Paterek, Josephine. 1994. *Encyclopedia of American Indian Costume.* New York: W. W. Norton & Company.

Severa, Joan. 1995. *Dressed for the Photographer: Ordinary Americans and Fashion, 1840–1900.* Kent, Ohio: Kent State University Press.

Tinto, Dick. Diplomatic Dress. How the Marcy Circular Strikes an American in Paris. *New York Times,* April 19, 1854, NYTimes, http://query.nytimes.com/gst/abstract.html?res=9D02E3D9153DE034BC4152DFB266838F649FDE

Ullrich, Pamela V. 1985. Promoting the South: Rhetoric and Textiles in Columbus, Georgia, 1850–1880. *Dress* 11: 31–46.

Waugh, Norah. 1964. *The Cut of Men's Clothes: 1600–1900.* New York: Theatre Arts Books.

Zakin, Michael. 2003. *Ready-Made Democracy: A History of Men's Dress in the American Republic, 1760–1860.* Chicago, IL: The University of Chicago Press.

CHAPTER 10

Children's Fashions

The end of the 18th century had brought great changes into the lives of children. The works of philosophers such as Rousseau inspired enlightened parents to consider their children not as miniature adults, but as developing minds and bodies in need of a childhood to help shape them. As the 19th century dawned, this concept of "childhood" was still relatively new, but as the Antebellum Era began, American children, particularly those of the rising middle class and upper classes, were enjoying more physical freedom than previous generations ever had. Gone were the swaddling clothes that had bound infants. Quilted and corded corsets were still a part of most children's upbringing but small children were no longer expected to wear miniature versions of their parents' clothes. Instead their clothes were now designed to allow for easier movement as they explored their world. American children naturally transitioned into more mature clothing as they grew older, with each step marked as a rite of passage. As the era progressed, the clothing of early childhood became even looser and less restrictive, diverging substantially from the fashionable silhouettes of grown men and women of the time. The clothing of older children did reflect adult fashions but were much more likely to be adapted to the needs of the children wearing them through the shortening of hems, the use of hard-wearing fabrics, and other alterations that helped to define a clearer line between children's and adult fashions of the 19th century.

The Swaddled Child in Antebellum America

Swaddling, as it had been practiced since the Middle Ages, was all but given up by the majority of the population in the United States by the 1820s. William Dewees notes in the preface to his *Treatise on the Physical and Medical Treatment of Children* in 1825 that "we cannot but regard the now almost universal banishment of swathes, and stays, as one of the greatest improvements in modern physical education" (Dewees 1858, vii). He was echoed by Dr. John Eberle in 1833 when he observed, "the custom is now universally abandoned by every civilized people" (Helvenston 1981, 32). The use of swaddling bands did continue among many of the immigrant populations recently arrived in the United States. These bands were often elaborately decorated with whitework or colored thread embroidery and were often treasured family heirlooms that were passed from one generation to the next. In addition to the physiological rationale behind the use of swaddling bands, some immigrant populations continued this custom as a protection against less corporeal threats. Among the recently arrived, Italian immigrants often brought with them embroidered swaddling bands such as those found in the collection of the Heinz History Center in Pittsburgh, Pennsylvania. Swaddling was practiced among the Italian immigrant community as a protection for the newborn child from the evil eye or *malocchio*. Another example of elaborately patterned swaddling bands resides in the collection of Kansas State University. It also was used by an Italian family who took part in the western migration of homesteaders.

EVERYDAY AND SPECIAL OCCASION CLOTHES

Infants

The clothing of infants was often designed to protect them from the potential for present illness or the prospect of future ill-health. Mothers were given conflicting opinions on what type and amount of clothing was best for the health of their newborn. Some advocated using as little clothing as possible in an attempt to "harden" the child. This type of hardening often involved allowing the child to stay in a wet diaper for extended periods of time or, in the case of older children, encouraging them to keep their wet shoes and socks on after venturing out in inclement weather. This was all advised in an attempt to make the child healthier in later life. The authors of these advice books felt that the new generation of Americans were too often coddled and not exposed to the harsher elements of life, and that their constitutions would be weakened because of this. They portended that the American population at large would suffer due to their ill health, if mothers did not act to prevent it. Other authors of advice books for American mothers promoted just the opposite—the use of warm clothing was advocated to protect the child from the elements and drafts and insure a healthy constitution in later life. The use of wool was largely recommended in these manuals and the layering of petticoats and blankets was called for by this method's proponents. The layette described below was made to err on the side of generous coverage for infants of the antebellum period, rather than acquiesce to the few layers suggested by those who encouraged the hardening of children.

The Layette

Preparing for the arrival of an infant in antebellum America might mean months of work assembling the clothes that would make up his first wardrobe. Though there was some superstition about gathering the things needed for an infant before the birth, the amount of labor required in stitching together gowns and petticoats would have certainly called for some advance acquisitions. An infant's first wardrobe required most of the same types of clothing required by adults and children, such as undergarments, main garments, and outerwear, as well as accessories.

Underwear

Naturally, diapers were an essential part of every infant's wardrobe. A diaper, or "napkin" or "square," would be made out of cotton or linen toweling—a fabric with a thick woven structure ideal for absorption. This might be worn under a triangular piece of waterproof fabric, such as wool, referred to in England as the "pilch." This would offer some protection for the outer garments to prevent them from becoming soiled. It is important to note that the safety pin was not introduced until the late 19th century. Until that time, straight pins were often used to fasten diapers. Naturally, the practice of using straight pins as fastenings for even the most docile of infants raises questions of safety. Contemporary manuals for mothers often advised utilizing fabric ties or cord wherever possible when fastening the diaper. They also advised caution when inserting straight pins and instructed mothers on the proper angles to use when doing so. Other authors went further, suggesting that an infant's diaper be sewn on and re-sewn each time the child was changed (Helvenston 1981, 35–36).

Though many American mothers had given up swaddling by the 1820s, a "binder" was still applied by many. This garment was meant initially to provide protection for the umbilical stump as it healed. Constructed of a four to six inch wide strip of bias-cut cotton or wool flannel, the binder would be long enough to wrap around the infant's abdomen at least once. These were typically worn for up to four to six months after birth, suggesting that their use went beyond meeting the needs of the healing belly button. It was also said to provide "support to the bowels, prevent rupture, and provide warmth" (Helvenston 1981, 33). Should the term "binder" suggest otherwise, mothers were advised against wrapping the binder too tight as this might result in hernia or pain and discomfort.

In her research into the advice dispensed to American mothers on dressing their children, Sally Helvenston notes that there is little written in manuals about the use of corsets for infants in the antebellum period. There are, however, numerous advertisements for infant corsets in women's magazines of the period, which suggests that the practice of using corsets on even the youngest children did persist in some way. These ads claimed that the corset was "valuable for infants and children, affording ease and comfort, supporting the frame, and directing growth"

(Hale 1854, 265). The corset would have been worn by both sexes during infancy. These corsets were typically made of quilted or corded cotton and included shoulder straps and a tie closure at the back.

Whether a corset was worn or not, a linen undershirt would have been one of the layers closest to the infant's skin. This garment was open at the back and the petticoat was often pinned to it. The petticoat might be made of wool for extra warmth. At least one petticoat was always worn, though some mothers might have used more layers during winter months or when the outer gown was made of particularly lightweight or sheer material.

Day and Night Gowns

The neckline and sleeves of an infant's main garment, the long gown, seem particularly skimpy in light of the advice mothers were given about layering. The neckline was typically cut low, in a square shape, and the sleeves were very short, taking the shape of overlapping petals or else made up of short puffs, sometimes falling off of the shoulders. A long skirt, up to forty inches in length, was gathered into a short bodice and trimmed with self-fabric robings as well as embroidery. Long sleeves could be tied onto the gown for outdoor wear and were the norm for nightgowns for infants. The length of skirts and style of trim changed from decade to decade during the antebellum period. In the 1820s, the robings were arranged in perpendicular tucks and were widely spaced on the gown. By the 1830s, the robing trim resembled the arrangement of the stomacher and petticoat found in women's dress of the previous century. Taking the form of two triangles meeting at their apexes, the robings might frame whitework embroidery. By the 1850s, the gown had grown in length. For those who could afford the luxury, these gowns were elaborately embroidered, with nearly half of the fabric covered in this style of ornamentation. Christening gowns, a garment that marked one of the first milestones of a young infant's life, were nearly twice as long as the standard gown for infants. In addition to the cotton and linen that had been used in infant's clothing throughout the early part of the century, the 1820s saw the introduction of embroidered machine net as a popular material for infant's gowns. Children of less wealthy parents were outfitted with much simpler gowns, made up of less yardage and less expensive fabrics such as printed cotton or flannel. These were typically constructed in one piece, wherein the bodice and skirt were one, instead of two separate pieces joined at the waist. The skirts would be tied at the back with strings or might be arranged more evenly through the use of drawstrings and a casing at the waist.

Older infants were dressed in aprons to help protect the fabric of their gowns as they began to crawl. These sleeveless garments were made in a similar fashion to children's pinafores but were outfitted with a drawstring at the hem in order to fully cover the skirt as the infant crawled. As a protective garment, these were typically less ornamented and made of simpler materials than the day gown they covered.

Outerwear

Cloaks and fitted blankets were the standard outerwear for infants throughout the antebellum period. Merino wool was a favorite material for these long cloaks, which were lined with a layer of wadded cotton and silk. Embroidery was employed as decoration, along with swansdown or fur. A hood might be separate or attached to this garment to provide additional protection from the elements. The traditional baby's bonnet was the other main form of headwear for infants of the antebellum period. These caps were close-fitting and trimmed with ruched lace and ribbons.

Older Babies

A smock without waist seams replaced the long-skirted gown of early infancy between four and eight months of age, though Sarah Hale of *Godey's Lady's Book* advised mothers to take the time of year into consideration when transferring their infants into "short clothes." "It is not advisable to expose the little creature to the chance of taking cold in the severity of winter, or the inclemency of fall and spring. But somewhere between the ages of four and eight months the newcomer seems to crave a freer use of limb than the [long gown] will permit" (Helvenston 1981, 35). This would have allowed the growing child to gain his legs a little easier. These smocks were often made with a raglan-style sleeve and neckline that were drawn and tied with a cord, to enable easier changing. Additionally, the long gown of infancy might be altered to accommodate the baby's changing body and needs. Sarah Hale advised her readers to let the gown out at the waist and shorten the hem by tucking the skirt up into the waistband to allow for its continued wear into this next stage of life (1854, 256).

Girls

Main Garments

After leaving infancy, young girls would be dressed in short dresses. These generally featured short sleeves and would be worn with drawers and pantalettes. The pantalettes, which were in fashion from 1818 until the late 1840s, were made of different fabric and trim for everyday wear and dress wear. The dressier variety are more commonly seen in portraits and fashion plates—these are made of white cotton and trimmed with lace and embroidery or deep ruffles of self-fabric that had been starched and pressed. The everyday pantalette was generally made of humbler materials such as calico or nankin and had less trim. Whether for dress or everyday wear, the pantalette was worn long through most of the period, reaching to the top of the gaiter shoes until about the mid-1840s. In the 1850s, a sacque or loose smock-like dress was worn by both young boys and girls. This garment buttoned at the neck and was made without a waist so that it might be worn with or without a belt gathering its fullness.

It was the length of a girl's hem that signified her age more than the style of her dress. In fact, girls' dresses of the antebellum period resemble those of their adult counterparts in the style of the sleeve, bodice and skirt. An example of a girl's dress from the Henry Ford Museum (88.0.1190.1) illustrates the similarities between girl's and women's clothing. Constructed of yellow silk taffeta around 1840, the dress was intended for best wear and features the same wide, open neckline and short sleeves of women's evening dresses of the 1840s. The bodice is pleated into a pointed, high waistline that rests around the natural waist. The design does not take the needs of a young girl of six or eight into mind—the wide neckline necessitated excellent posture to keep it in place and the thin, delicate fabric did not offer much in the way of protection from drafts or stains.

The full skirt silhouette of the 1830s and 1840s was achieved for girls by the addition of flounces as well as through the wearing of multiple layers of petticoats or crinoline. Over her skirts, a girl might wear an apron or a pinafore. Her apron would have been in the style of her mother's fashion apron and could be made of silk or fine muslin, trimmed with lace or embroidery. The only difference was the addition of shoulder ruffles or frills. The less-well-off might have made do with aprons of less expensive materials, such as printed calico or patterned cambric, trimmed with narrow frills at the shoulders. Similar to aprons, pinafores were constructed with both a front and a back. The side seams were left open from at least the waist down and fastened at the neck. *Godey's* advised mothers of the 1850s that the pinafore offered an excellent alternative to fancier clothes in the summer months and might be worn with just a "waist" or undershirt and drawers (Severa 1995, 107). Another alternative to the dress was the zouave ensemble. These became popular in the 1850s with the introduction of the zouave jacket. The jacket was worn with a full skirt and a white blouse or shirt underneath.

Teenage girls in the antebellum period would have dressed in the style of their mothers, with the exception that their hemlines were shorter. By the time a girl reached puberty, she would have gotten rid of her pantalettes, a moment marked by some as a rite of passage. Harriet Farley included this moment in her poem, "The Patchwork Quilt" when identifying the various scraps of clothing included in the title object, "down in this corner a piece of that in which I first felt myself a woman—that is, when I first discarded pantalettes" (Severa 1995, 1). From puberty on a girl would have worn a fully boned corset like her adult contemporaries. It was their skirts and headdress style that set teenage girls apart as being not quite grown-up. In a daguerrotype from Historic Northampton, Mary Frances Stebbins is shown at the age of 14 or 16. In this image, she wears a woven check dress, which was most likely made of silk. In her commentary about this image, Joan Severa notes that Miss Stebbins "is still a bit too young for a full-length skirt" and asserts that "this dress comes only to mid-calf" even though the hemline is not revealed in the image (Severa 1995, 39). Mary Frances is accessorized as her older contemporaries might be—a lightweight plaid shawl is worn and a gold chain can be seen around her neck while she carries a watch or locket in her hand. Her hair, however, is done in a more youthful style. It is parted down the middle and looped up in braids at the back. It is this detail that reveals the sitter's age, despite her otherwise "adult" clothing.

Undergarments

Little girls and teenagers alike wore a number of layers under their clothing throughout the antebellum period. Drawers were worn by all ages, once beyond infancy. Unlike adult versions, girl's drawers were sometimes attached to a buttoned or tied bodice with shoulder straps. The drawers were still built in the split leg style, without a crotch seam. The chemise would have also been worn, as well a corset of some kind. Corsets for younger girls tended not to be boned, but constructed with heavy padding and quilted or corded to help retain their shape. As girls progressed in age, boning was introduced. Corsets for children tended to have shoulder straps, even when the fashion for adult women lacked them. Petticoats were worn by girls as they were by their grown-up counterparts. As the silhouette widened, more petticoats were added until, in the 1840s, the horsehair crinoline petticoat was more widely used. After its introduction in the mid-1850s, girls over the age of seven would adopt the cage crinoline to help retain the shape of their full skirts.

Outerwear

In the 1820s, short-waisted spencers continued in popularity for girls of all ages. Worn with the raised waistline of the early decade, these were eventually discarded for the pelisse in the 1830s. The pelisse resembled a dress in its lines of construction but opened down the front in the style of a coat. It was most often constructed of light weight cotton for summer months and of warmer materials such as wool for winter wear. Shawls continued to be popular for most of the period, for both girls and women. Triangular shawls of plain woolen fabric tended to be the norm for outerwear for girls of lower economic standing, while the Kashmir shawls imported from India and parts of Europe were worn by those whose parents could afford them.

Accessories—Headwear

As girls advanced in age, their bonnets began to resemble those of grown women more and more. As young children, sunbonnets, made of calico and stiffened with rows of cording or quilting, were frequently worn to protect them, as the name suggests, from the summer's sun. Hoods, lined and quilted, were worn in winter. More expensive examples were often made of silk.

Boys

Main Garments

Clothing for young boys of the antebellum period differed quite significantly from their older male counterparts. In fact, it is accurate to say that little boys' clothing had more in common with their mothers' than their fathers' wardrobes. Toddler boys were dressed in dresses similar to those worn by their toddler sisters. Short-skirted, most often with short sleeves and low square necklines, these were worn with drawers. Boys' dresses did tend to differ from girls' dresses in the color of fabric and amount and type of trim used, however. Examples in collections throughout the United States where a firm attribution can be made to a young boy rather than a girl, indicate that boys' dresses were more plainly trimmed, often with rows of buttons or braid in a military style. Typically these dresses were made in solid color or plaid fabrics. The most popular combination of colors for fabric and trim was red and black, though there are examples where more colorful trim was used. At the Henry Ford Museum, a boy's dress of circa 1850 is made of red wool and trimmed with purple silk appliqué and piping. Though they do not survive, it was probably worn with drawers as well as undersleeves, as these were in fashion at the time for women's dress.

A more masculine alternative to the short dress for slightly older toddlers was the tunic suit. These first appeared in the 1820s and were worn throughout the rest of the period. The tunic differed from the dress in that it opened from the waist down and was worn with long trousers or pantaloons instead of drawers. Tunic suits were made of a variety of materials, though the most popular appears to have been merino wool, with trousers made of white linen or matching fabric. In the 1820s, these tunics were constructed with short sleeves, reflecting the style in women's fashions of the time. The leg-o-mutton sleeves that were fashionable in women's wear of the 1830s were also used in little boys' tunics of the same decade. These tunics tended to resemble men's greatcoats, as the skirts were pleated into the waist, instead of being gathered, and the neck was open to reveal an open-collar shirt below. The tunic skirt silhouette of the 1840s became fuller, resembling women's silhouettes of the time. Eventually, the tunic evolved into the sacque of the late 1840s and1850s, which was worn by both boys and girls. Short sleeved sacques were reserved for the youngest boys, with longer sleeves added as the child progressed in age. The sacque-style of dress or tunic was particularly long-wearing, and therefore more economical than other styles, since the looseness allowed for the boy to grow into it. Sarah Hale advised her readers in 1859, "For little boys hovering between dresses and the first pair of 'pantalooons' we recommend short trowsers or drawers of white linen, cambric sacques of plain colors, pale green, blue, pink, or buff, with a narrow edge of white braid in parallel rows. They should be made low in the neck, very loose, and with short sleeves. A broad belt of patent leather will confine them sufficiently at the waist" (1859, 191).

Skeleton suits had been introduced in the late 18th century, and while tunic suits seem to have largely supplanted them, they were worn during the first half of the antebellum period. The skeleton suit was made up of a short-waisted, tight-fitting jacket that buttoned at the waist to a pair of high-waisted trousers. Typically, the jacket was constructed of a contrasting material—a popular combination was dark blue for the jacket and white for the trousers. The skeleton suit was worn with an open-collar shirt. In the 1840s, a one-piece coverall in

Fashion plate depicting fashionable children's clothing alongside their adult female contemporaries. Picture Collection, The New York Public Library, Astor, Lenox and Tilden Foundations.

the spirit of the skeleton suit was worn by boys. Here there was a "trapdoor," or arrangement of buttons and buttonholes, at the seat of the coverall instead of a waist-level opening. These were worn by boys around the age of four or five and were constructed with sleeves and collars to suit the season—short and loose for the summer, long and high for the winter.

The Eton suit offered a variation on the skeleton suit style meant for older boys. Here the trousers or pantaloons buttoned to a shirt or suspenders, under a short jacket. An example from the Henry Ford Museum, made of silk, is trimmed in a military style with buttons. In the late 1850s, Knickerbockers became a popular fashion for unbreeched boys. These short and loose trousers were worn gathered into a band below the knee and might have been worn with a shirt and jacket by the boy too old for dresses or "frocks" but too young for a proper suit.

Anywhere from the age of 4 to 10, American boys marked their first rite of passage into adulthood with the discarding of petticoats and the adoption of breeches. The importance of this moment in a boy's life was captured most picturesquely by early 19th century poets, Mary and Charles Lamb, who wrote "Going Into Breeches" in 1809.

Joy to Philip, he this day
Has his long coats cast away,
And (the childish season gone)
Puts the manly breeches on.
Officer on gay parade,
Red-coat in his first cockade,
Bridegroom in his wedding trim,
Birthday beau surpassing him,
Never did with conscious gait
Strut about in half the state,
Or the pride (yet free from sin)
Of my little MANIKIN. (Lamb and Lamb 1903, 365)

When deemed old enough, boys would be "breeched," or allowed to wear their first suit of clothes resembling those of his adult father, with jacket and pantaloons or trousers cut to the fashionable style. The reason behind dressing younger boys so differently from their older counterparts is, to a certain extent, unknown. Helvenston notes in her work (1981) that explanations vary from stylistic concerns to superstitions. It might be that the wearing of dresses by little boys reflected "the influence of women who were chiefly responsible for child care." Ancient beliefs in evil spirits might have been behind the tradition of dressing little boys in dresses—"in order to deceive the evil spirits who preferred to inflict their mischief on the much-prized male child." Helvenston's own conclusion may be the most correct, when she considers, "perhaps the use of nondifferentiating dresses was due to much more practical considerations such as their reusability or the ease of changing the diapers of young toddlers in dresses" (Helvenston, 1981, 41). Whatever the reason behind childhood skirts for boys, the moment they were left behind marked a boy's passage into the ranks of men, he was a "happy lad" now that he could "run, or he can ride, And do twenty things beside, Which his petticoats forbad" as the Lambs observe in their verse on breeching. The girlish games of infancy and toddlerhood were to be left behind and the stalwart character of the American man taken on.

Even once childish skirts were discarded, the open-necked shirts of early childhood continued to be worn through early adolescence. In the 1820s and 1830s, boys as young as four might be breeched. They would then wear short-waisted jackets with trousers over the open-necked shirt, often with a ruffled collar. One popular jacket shape lacked tails and had a pointed waistline. An example of this can be found in the collection of the Henry Ford, made of heavy cotton twill and trimmed with soutache and buttons. For older boys, open-necked shirts were worn with jackets that resembled the fashionable line for men of each decade. A boy's first pantaloons were constructed with a fall front instead of a fly closure. It was not until he was in his teen years that he donned this style of trouser. In the 1830s, most boys over the age of 10 were breeched and wore a suit consisting of loose-fitting pantaloons, a waistcoat over a white shirt, and a short jacket that reached to the waist line. McClellan describes an ensemble for a breeched boy of the 1840s as a "small jacket, open and rounded in front, of dark velvet, cloth, or cashmere, with buttons of the same. Small square linen collar turned over, a ribbon necktie. Loose trousers of blue and white striped linen" (McClellan 1969, 517). Older boys of the 1840s wore a sack coat or sack suit, the precursor to men's business suits of the later 19th century. The jacket and pants might have been constructed of the same material, as a "ditto" suit or the jacket might have been made in a contrasting fabric.

Undergarments

Boys' undergarments do not differ largely from those worn by grown men. Drawers were worn by all but the youngest boys. These were typically made as two legs attached to a waistband. There was no crotch seam and buttons and tapes were generally used to secure them at the waist and below the knees. In later decades, an additional undergarment was added to most young boys' wardrobes, particularly in the cold months of winter. The vest, a type of under-waistcoat, was sometimes made of wool or thick cotton and its primary purpose was to keep the body warm.

The Mourning Child

The act of mourning was one shared by even the smallest children in antebellum society. Even the clothes of infants might be altered to reflect the sadness at the passing of a close relative. As with adults' mourning dress, the closeness of the relative to the child would dictate the level of mourning expected from him. The long white gowns of infants were trimmed with black fabric to indicate their participation while children suffering from the loss of a parent were expected to dress in deep mourning for the requisite amount of time before allowing a little color to enter the wardrobe once again. In half mourning, a child's black clothing might be trimmed with shades of purple, mauve, or gray, but rarely with a combination of more than two of these colors.

Outerwear

Overcoats were worn by antebellum boys in cooler weather. These were tailored more loosely, to allow for movement over the round coat or jacket that was worn as a main garment.

Accessories

Headwear

Hats were an essential part of dress for both men and boys in the Antebellum Era. Boys' hats, however, differed greatly from those worn by men. In the first two decades of the period, boys wore broad-brimmed hats with the brim turned up at one side, trimmed with a feather plume. Lancer's caps were also popular. Hats for small boys were often in the same style as those for young girls, such as the broad-brimmed straw hat that rose to popularity in the 1840s. As boys progressed in age, so did the maturity of their headwear, until it resembled more closely that which was worn by grown men of the time. Adolescent boys could be seen wearing the top hats that were popular among fashionable men in the 1840s.

Footwear

For all children of shoe-wearing age, buttoned gaiters appear to have been the most popular form of footwear. These low boots were constructed of fabric with a leather heel and toe. Girls might also wear slippers with ribbon ties for more formal wear. Stockings of silk, cotton, and wool were worn by all children. The lower economic classes were often forced to forego shoes if they could not afford them. White stockings were worn through most of the period, though colored, horizontally striped stockings are seen in daguerrotypes of the 1850s. These were more common for everyday wear.

Hairstyles and Grooming for Boys and Girls

Though the silhouette of girls' clothing might have reflected that of their elder counterparts, their hairstyles were significantly different. In the early decades of the Antebellum Era, girls generally wore their hair neatly parted down the middle of the head, though there are rare instances where a side part is worn. Short curls were dressed on either side of the head, but while older women may have employed false hair and other forms of grooming trickery, young girls' hair was typically only styled with curling papers and fire-heated curling irons. After the mid-1830s, pigtails and braids were in fashion, worn on either side of the head and tied with colored ribbons. By the 1840s, the fashion for middle parts had faded and the hair was typically pulled straight back off of the forehead. Fabric-covered steel headbands might be worn.

In contrast, boys' hair was dressed more closely to the prevailing style for grown men at any time during the Antebellum Era. The primary difference between young boys and their older contemporaries was length. Boys' hair was worn longer and slightly less groomed than older men's. This changed as the child matured. Just as breeching served to mark a boy's passage from infancy towards manhood, the cropping of hair would mark his entrance into the world of men.

MAKING AND ACQUIRING CLOTHES

Most children's wardrobes would have contained both homemade and store-bought or seamstress-made clothing. In most families, the fabric for children's clothes would have been purchased at a local store, though the use of homespun fabric for children's clothing did continue into the Antebellum Era. Fine cottons and silks were reserved for dressy, special occasion clothing. Examples of specialty fabrics can be found in extant children's clothing, such as those surveyed by Linda Welters in her study on the use of piña cloth in American fashion of the 19th century. She identifies three examples of fashionable children's clothing made of "pineapple silk" or *piña* cloth from the 1830s and 1840s, all of which are associated with coastal towns or prominent shipping families of the East Cottons (1997, 16). Less expensive fabrics, such as the "factory cottons" produced in the North, were used for everyday wear. In fact, these factory cottons were cheap enough to enable families of low economic means to afford new cloth for clothing their children at least once a year. Children's clothes might also be made from fabric purchased for another purpose or from recycled fabric from adult clothing. An example of a childs's dress with pantaloons from the Henry Ford Museum, dated circa 1850 (00.4.3585) is made from pieced scraps of printed cotton and has been altered, perhaps for wear by multiple children within the family.

Like their mothers, girls' clothing was generally made at home or with the aid of a skilled seamstress. Patterns for dresses were shared among neighbors or kin and a favorite dress might be ripped apart in order to draft a pattern for a newer one. Girls' dresses were frequently featured in women's fashion magazines, offering the same communication of fashion information directly to the consumer that was afforded to women of the era. These images might be used to distill certain trends into a practical reality, eliminating expensive trim or superfluous volume from the Paris- or London-inspired plates to achieve the more toned-down look that was quickly becoming identified with American style. Very few items for girls would have been purchased as ready-to-wear items, and these would also have been in line with what was available to grown women. Items that did not require as precise a fit would have been available, such as cage crinolines and underpinnings, shawls, and outerwear. Unlike girls, however, many of the items worn by older boys were likely to have been products of mass production. Along with men's clothing, boys' clothing was among the first to be mass-produced on any real scale. These ready-to-wear garments were mostly manufactured in the East, in cities such as New York, Boston, and Philadelphia. Shoes for both boys and girls were mass-produced by the 1840s, though girls from wealthier families may have gotten their slippers from the same boutique shops where their mothers shopped.

COMPOSITION OF A WARDROBE

Infants

Superstition might have prevented some mothers from laying aside too many items of clothing in advance of a child's birth. It is hard to imagine, however, how a new mother would be able to acquire the amount of clothing required for a small infant if some preparation was not done in advance. Much like today, quantity was the watchword when it came to an infant's wardrobe. Since infants soil their clothing quite frequently, multiples of all necessary items of clothing were required. Those items worn closest to the body, such as diapers, petticoats, and undershirts, were required in larger numbers. If the mother was financially and physically able, she might build a wardrobe in multiples of a dozen of each piece of the layette, with a surplus of cloth diapers kept on hand. This was particularly important since in most households, the family washing was done on a weekly, not a daily, basis.

Girls and Boys

The taste for fashion in young children did little to determine the extent of their wardrobe. Instead, a family's financial standing played a much greater role in shaping the wardrobes of its children. The typical girlhood wardrobe for an average or lower income family contained at least one print gown with one or two pinafores or aprons to be worn over it. One pinafore or apron was reserved for best wear and the other used for everyday wear, protecting the dress underneath from soil. Printed cottons were favored for little girls to minimize the appearance of dirt or soiling between washings. For families that could afford it, silks that would wear well and turn easily were also a requisite part of a young girl's wardrobe. Drawers and underthings were to be found in slightly greater quantity, though among the poorest these might be few or lacking entirely. Wealthier young ladies, naturally, would have been afforded more clothing as well as a greater selection of fashionable accessories and outerwear.

The finances of a family also dictated the extent of the wardrobe for young boys. A family with relatively small means would be able to afford two changes of clothing, one for everyday and one for best wear. These ensembles consisted of main garments in the silhouette most befitting the child's age, whether it was a dress for the unbreeched boy or a suit of clothes for an older child. Again, drawers and shirts would be expected to figure in slightly larger quantities, though drawers might be entirely lacking in the wardrobes of the most poor. Shoes might be absent entirely during the warmer season, especially if the finances of the family were particularly meager. The proliferation of ready-made clothing for boys at all levels of quality and price made boys' clothing slightly more accessible, though, and, as has been previously noted, the cheap factory cottons produced in the North enabled even the poorest families to afford at least one new dress for their daughters on a yearly basis.

AMERICAN INDIAN CLOTHING

The Indian Removal Act of 1830 brought about a heightened interest in the way of life of the native population. Antebellum white Americans were particularly fascinated with the swaddling practices of many American Indian tribes. The tradition of "papoosing" was represented in both the literature and art of the time. This refers to the practice of binding infants to stiff boards or cradles, which were then worn on their mother's backs. This practice had both practical and aesthetic purposes. Papoosing was done in an effort to ensure perfect posture as the child matured. Also, when worn by the mother, the papoosed infant was kept near while the mother engaged in the active labor required in sustaining her family. Early costume historians focusing on American dress, such as Elizabeth McClellan, include descriptions by contemporaries of the dress of American Indian children. One such description comes from an English traveler to Washington, D.C. in 1832 who encountered a group of Indians (the specific tribal affiliation is not identified, nor is the region from which they hailed mentioned in the account). He describes a meeting between himself and a young boy and girl traveling with the group. "The girl's costume consisted of a sort of printed bed-gown without sleeves, fastened close up to the throat; trousers, moccasins or leggins [*sic*] of deerskin, worn generally by the Indians, and the whole covered by a blanket...In each ear she wore two large earrings. Fastened to the crown of her head was a piece of blue ribband. The boy...also wore a blanket...but instead of a bed-gown rejoiced in a long coat, the tails of which reached almost to his heels" (McClellan 1969, 589). The influence of European dress can be seen in this description, with the use of printed material in the girl's dress and the tail coat worn by the young boy. The use of animal skin in the production of clothing for both adults and children continued among many tribes in the United States, particularly in the production of moccasins for children. These were generally made by women and this practice was frequently adopted by both white Americans and African Americans who came into contact with American Indians when making foot coverings for their children.

AFRICAN AMERICAN CHILDREN'S CLOTHING

Young enslaved children were often furnished with very little clothing, many times going without clothing until a more mature age was reached. "[F]or the children, nothing was furnished them but a shirt; for the older ones, a pair of pantaloons or a gown, in addition, according to the sex. Besides these, in the winter season an overcoat, or a round jacket; a wool hat once in two or three years for the men, and a pair of coarse brogan shoes once a year" according to James L. Smith, who was enslaved in Virginia during the antebellum period (Foster 1997, 150). Frederick Douglass observed that "the children unable to work in the fields has neither shoes, stockings, jackets, nor trousers, given to them; their clothing consisted of two coarse linen shirts a year. When these failed them, they went naked until the next allowance-day. Children from 7 to 10 years old, of both sexes, almost naked, could be seen all seasons of the year" (Foster 1997, 151). The appearance of naked children was more common in rural areas, as the urban slave owner was less likely to risk offending his white neighbors' modesty by allowing (or forcing) his child slaves to go naked. As with adult enslaved African Americans, nudity was imposed on children very often as a form of punishment or as a tool of enslavement.

The most common form of clothing for enslaved boys was the shirt. The shirt was constructed in two pieces, with a hole cut at the top for the neck and partially slit up the sides to allow for freer movement. The shirt reached to the knees. It was worn in all seasons, by most accounts. Only in rare instances are the wearing of breeches or pants mentioned in reference to young boys—these were generally referring to times when young slave boys might be sent into more public spaces, such as town, on errands. Then the shirt would be tucked into the waist, to resemble a more formal shirt. The shirt might be made of homespun or factory cloth (the "lowell-cloth" that many in the *Narratives* project mention would have been made in the North out of Southern cotton, especially for use in the production of slave clothing). The predominance of this single-item wardrobe for small children, and boys especially, gave

The clothing of enslaved African American children was often handed down from the slave owner's children, frequently ill-fitting and ragged. Courtesy The New York Public Library.

ARRIVAL FROM MARYLAND, 1859.

ANN MARIA JACKSON AND HER SEVEN CHILDREN—MARY ANN, WILLIAM HENRY, FRANCES SABRINA, WILHELMINA, JOHN EDWIN, EBENEZER THOMAS, AND WILLIAM ALBERT.

The coming of the above named was duly announced by Thomas Garrett:

Arrival from Maryland, 1859. Courtesy The New York Public Library.

***Children of Commodore John Daniel Danels,* by Robert Street, c. 1826. This painting shows the range of clothes for male children from the dress of infancy through to the coat and trousers of early pre-pubescence—it is interesting to note that the clothing worn by the African American boys depicted here is the same as their white counterparts, though perhaps hand-me-downs.** Courtesy of The Maryland Historical Society, Baltimore.

birth to a nickname applied to young, enslaved African American boys. They were frequently referred to as "shirt-tail boys" or "shirt-tail fellows" (Foster 1997, 153). Enslaved boys were also afforded a similar rite of passage shared with their white counterparts. Though lacking in the pomp that might accompany a white boy's breeching, enslaved boys between the ages of 10 and 15 (sometimes, unbelievably, as late as 21) would be given pants for everyday wear. The same feeling of pride would accompany the simple breeches worn by slave boys as expressed by white boys upon the arrival of this more mature fashion. Examples of clothing for adolescent boys are described in many of the advertisements placed by those seeking runaway slaves during the Antebellum Era. One such ad describes the dress of a 14-year-old boy named Green in Virginia in 1820: "He had on a blue round about jacket and pantaloons" (Meaders 1997, 330). The "round about jacket" described was probably quite similar to those worn by white boys of the same age and era.

Young enslaved girls wore the same singleton shirt worn by young enslaved boys, though when worn by girls it was more frequently referred to as a "dress," even though it was in fact the same garment. Recorded narratives seem to reflect a disparity between the passage of female adolescence and the acquisition of more gendered clothing for enslaved girls. Many describe the clothing of older enslaved females as similar to the singleton shirt, only longer. Printed calicoes were more expensive than plain cloth and the wearing of dresses made from them indicated that the girl or her family (whether white or black) had access to money and stores. Most clothing for enslaved children was made from homespun cloth. This was especially true in the territories, where access to factory-made cloth was limited. Della Mun Bibles, who was enslaved in Texas in the 1850s, noted that this homespun material could be striped or checked and was usually dyed blue or brown. In her account she observes that differences in status among the children were indicated by the material used. "All the girls, young girls, bout fourteen and over, wore blue; the children on the yard, white and colored, wore brown most of the time" (Foster 1997, 111). Advertisements for runaway enslaved children placed in newspapers of the era frequently mention clothing worn as made from homespun cloth. Elijah, an 18-year-old wore "thin homespun apparel" when he escaped in 1833 (Parker 1994, 317–18). Tom, 14, wore "dark yarn homespun clothes" when he made his escape in 1820 (Parker 1994, 460). Differences in status among enslaved children were often reflected in a manner similar to that of their adult counterparts; young house servants were typically dressed better by their masters than children old enough to work in the fields.

Like their adult counterparts, there was often little difference between the clothing of children who served as house servants and that of white children. The composition of their wardrobes frequently reflected a similar amount and quality of clothing. For example, in an ad placed for a runaway slave in 1826, a 16 year-old girl named Peggy is described as having "one calico and one cambric dress" (Parker 1994, 303), the notable fact here being that she had two dresses. Here the calico dress might represent her best clothes while the cambric would have been for everyday wear. The similarity in wardrobes between white and enslaved African American children who served in the house might be put down to the frequent passing-down of used clothing to slaves. Charles, a 16 or 17-year-old runaway in 1829, wore "a fur or hair cap, a neat frock coat, originally olive but had faded, and been patched under the right arm: his pantaloons were fine black cassimere, but considerably worn" when he made his escape (Parker 1994, 315).

There were some items, however, that can be specifically identified as unique to the enslaved African American culture of the Antebellum Era. These items, such as beaded necklaces, tend to be linked to folkloric traditions and believed to possess protective powers. China berry beads were commonly worn by enslaved African American children to protect them from illness. They were also worn by older women, though more often for a decorative, rather than protective, purpose. Other unusual items might be worn for the same purpose. One participant in the *Narratives* project is paraphrased as noting that "children wore moles feet and pearl buttons around their necks to insure easy teething" (Foster 1997, 175).

References

Dewees, William P., M.D. 1858. *A Treatise on the Physical and Medical Treatment of Children.* Philadelphia, PA: Blanchard and Lea.

Foster, Helen Bradley. 1997. *New Raiments of Self: African American Clothing in the Antebellum South.* New York: Berg.

Hale, Sarah, ed. March 1854. *Godey's Lady's Book:* 265.

Hale, Sarah, ed. August 1859. *Godey's Lady's Book:* 191.

Helvenston, Sally. 1981. Advice to American Mothers on the Subject of Children's Dress, 1800–1920. *Dress* 7:30–46.

Lamb, Charles and Mary Lamb. 1903. *The Works of Charles and Mary Lamb, Vol. III Books for Children,* ed. E. V. Lucas. London: Methuen & Co.

McClellan, Elizabeth. 1969. *History of American Costume.* New York: Tudor Publishing Company.

Meaders, Daniel, ed. 1997. *Advertisements for Runaway Slaves in Virginia, 1801–1820.* New York: Garland Publishing.

Parker, Freddie L., ed. 1994. *Stealing a Little Freedom: Advertisements for Slave Runaways in North Carolina, 1791–1840.* New York: Garland Publishing.

Perry, Claire. 2006. *Young America: Childhood in 19th-Century Art and Culture.* New Haven, CT: Yale University Press.

Rose, Clare. 1989. *Children's Clothes.* London, B. T. Batsford.

Severa, Joan. 1995. *Dressed for the Photographer: Ordinary Americans and Fashion, 1840–1900.* Kent, Ohio: Kent State University Press.

Welters, Linda. 1997. Dress as Souvenir: Piña Cloth in the Nineteenth Century. *Dress* 24: 16–26.

Glossary: The Antebellum Era

armscye: The place at which the sleeve and the body of a garment are seamed, also the measurement of the circumference around shoulder joint.

banyan: A man's dressing gown; the name derives from the Hindu merchants who originally sold this garment of Eastern origins to the Western market.

basque: An extension of the waist of the bodice, reaching below the waist and flaring outwards.

bertha: A wide, deep collar (generally detachable or separate) that follows the neckline of a bodice.

bifurcate: To divide into two parts. In women's wear, the term bifurcated generally refers to skirts that have been seamed into two legs.

bishop sleeve: A sleeve in which the upper portion is fitted to the arm with pleats or gauging releasing into a full, soft sleeve below the elbow, typically gathered into a wristband.

breechclout: An apron-like garment worn by Native American men.

breeches, also called knee breeches: Men's pants that are fitted through the thighs and reach to just below the knee. These would be made with a fall front and the material from which they were made varied within the period, including leather, plush, and cotton.

busk: A stiff insert used to stabilize the center front of a corset. It could be made from steel, whalebone or wood.

bustle: During the antebellum period, a small pad worn at the back waistline to bring more fullness to the back of a gathered or gauged skirt.

cage crinoline: See crinoline.

chapeau bras: a hat form similar to a bicorne, of a purely decorative nature, rarely worn, usually carried under the arm as the name suggests.

chemise: woman's undergarment, may be sleeveless or worn with short sleeves.

chemisette: a kind of dickey or partial underbodice, worn particularly when the fashionable neckline plunged at the center front.

chintz: printed and glazed cotton or cotton blend fabric.

crape: Fabric of silk or wool, generally crimped in appearance, reserved for wear during mourning.

cravat: A square-shaped cloth, usually of linen, folded and tied in one of several distinctive styles.

crinoline: A stiff material, generally made out of horsehair, which was used in supportive underskirts in women's wear. When the steel hoop underskirt appeared, it was called the cage crinoline as its function was the same as the crinolines worn prior to its invention.

dandy: A gentleman consumed with the practice and art of dressing well. By the antebellum period, the term dandy had given way to others, such as *beau,* to describe men obsessed with dressing fashionably.

ditto suit: A suit in which all three components—pants, vest, and coat or jacket—are all made of the same fabric.

Eton suit: A suit with a short, single-breasted jacket that ended at or slightly above the waist, worn by small boys. The style is English in origin, having derived its name from the uniforms worn by boys at the Eton School.

fancy work: Handwork done for purely decorative or ornamental purposes. May have a wearable function, in which case the term is only applied to those articles that are elaborately embroidered or otherwise hand-decorated.

ferronière: A chain with an attached pendant or other ornament worn at the center of the forehead. The style first appeared during the Italian Renaissance but was briefly fashionable during the antebellum period.

fichu: A shawl-like accessory, typically made in white linen or cotton with embroidered or lace trim, worn across neck or shoulders and sometimes criss-crossed around the waist.

Gigot sleeves: See leg-o-mutton sleeve.

layette: A collection of clothing and accessories assembled together in preparation of the birth of a baby.

leg-o-mutton sleeve: Also called Gigot sleeves, a sleeve that is full at the shoulder and tapers towards the wrist.

linsey: A wool-cotton blend, sometimes called linsey-woolsey.

Lowell-cloth: A term applied to rough, sturdy cloth manufactured in the North for use in the production of clothing for slaves.

mancherons: Decorative shoulder extensions or epaulettes.

mitts: Fingerless gloves worn as a fashionable accessory. During the Antebellum Era, they were often made of lace, net, or knitted.

mob cap: A round cap, gathered at the crown, creating a short ruffle around the circumference of the cap.

pantalettes: This term may refer to both the drawers or extensions of the drawers, trimmed with lace at the hem.

pantaloons: A term applied to men's pants in the early 19th century. Generally refers to long, tightly fitting leg coverings that may or may not be made with a loop under the instep.

parasol: A carried form of sunshade, usually made of silk and trimmed with beads or lace.

pelerine: A short cape-like garment, generally made of the same material as the dress, constructed with long lappets.

pelisse: A full-length coat, worn as outerwear by women and girls.

pelisse dress: A dress in the form of a coat or pelisse. This garment typically fastened down the center-front with a series of buttons, ties or hook-and-eye closures.

reticule: A small hand-bag or purse.

skeleton suit: A suit for boys with contrasting pants and jacket that fastened at the waist with button closures.

soutache: Braid trim.

spencer: A short coat worn by women and girls. The style derives from fashionable men's wear of the late 18th century.

stays: A another term for corset.

stock: A stiffened neckband that fastened at the back of neck with ties or a buckle.

strouding: Dyed woven cloth of wool. The name is derived from the place in Gloucestershire, England where much of the cloth was made. It was then imported and most popularly used among Native American tribespeople.

swaddling cloth: A long strip of fabric or narrow woven cloth, sometimes decorated with symbols or ornamental embroidery, used to snuggly wrap infants.

whitework: A form of embroidery executed in white thread on a white background fabric.

wrapper: A loose gown, typically fastening up the center front, commonly constructed in cotton or cotton blend fabric.

Resource Guide: The Antebellum Era

PRINT RESOURCES

Adams-Graf, John. 1985. "In Rags for Riches: A Daguerreian Survey of Forty-Niner's Clothing." *Dress* 11: 59–68.

Aldrich, Winifred. 2000. "Tailor's Cutting Manuals and the Growing Provision of Popular Clothing, 1770–1870." *Textile History* 31 (2): 163–201.

Arnold, Janet. 1964. *Patterns of Fashion: English Women's Dresses and Their Construction, c.1660–1860.* London: Wace.

Arnold, Janet. 1974. *A Handbook of Costume.* New York: Macmillan.

Ayres, William, ed. 1993. *Picturing History: American Painting, 1770–1930.* New York: Rizzoli.

Bassett, Lynne Zacek. 2001. *Textiles for Clothing of the Early Republic, 1800–1850: A Workbook of Swatches and Information.* Arlington, VA: Q Graphics Production Co.

Baumgarten, Linda. 1991. "Plains, Plaid and Cotton: Woolens for Slave Clothing." *Ars Textrina* 15: 203–21.

Brackman, Barbara. 1989. *Clues in the Calico: A Guide to Identifying and Dating Antique Quilts.* McLean, VA: EPM Publications.

Campbell, Edward D.C., Jr., ed. 1991. *Before Freedom Came: African-American Life in the Antebellum South.* Richmond: Museum of the Confederacy.

Coon, Anne C. 1995. "The Bloomer Costume: Fashion Reform, Folly, and 'Intellectual Slavery.'" *Rochester History* 57 (3): 18–24, 28.

Cunningham, Patricia, ed. 1993. *Dress in American Culture.* Bowling Green: Bowling Green State University.

Cunnington, Cecil Willett. 1990. *English Women's Clothing in the Nineteenth Century.* New York: Dover.

Cunnington, Cecil Willett, and Phyllis Cunnington. 1970. *Handbook of English Costume in the Nineteenth Century.* London: Faber and Faber.

Cunnington, Cecil Willett, and Phyllis Cunnington. 1992. *The History of Underclothes.* New York: Dover Publications.

Cyr, Paul Albert. 1996. "The Progress of Bloomerism." *Spinner: People and Culture in Southeastern Massachusetts* 5: 134–41.

DeMarly, Diana. 1990. *Dress in North America.* New York: Holmes & Meier.

Edwards, Lee M. 1986. *Domestic Bliss: Family Life in American Painting, 1840–1910.* Yonkers, NY: Hudson River Museum.

Field, Jacqueline, Marjorie Senechal, and Madelyn Shaw. 2007. *American Silk 1830–1930: Entrepreneurs and Artifacts.* Lubbock, TX: Texas Tech University Press.

Foote, Shelly. 1980. "Bloomers." *Dress* 5: 1–12.

Fontanel, Beatrice. 1997. *Support and Seduction: The History of Corsets and Bras.* New York: Abrams.

Foster, Helen Bradley. 1997. *New Raiments of Self: African American Clothing in the Antebellum South.* New York: Berg.

Fry, Gladys-Marie. 1990. *Stitched from the Soul: Slave Quilts from the Ante-Bellum South.* New York: Dutton Studio Books.

Godey's Lady's Book. 1830–1860.

Harris, Kristina. 1999. *The Child in Fashion, 1750 to 1920.* Atglen, PA: Schiffer Pub.

Harris, Kristina. 2001. *American Victorian Fashions in Vintage Photographs, 1855–1910.* Mineola, NY: Dover Publications.

Helvenston, Sally I. 1980. "Popular Advice for the Well-Dressed Woman in the 19th Century." *Dress* 5: 31–47.

Helvenston, Sally I. 1990. "Fashion on the Frontier." *Dress* 17: 141–55.

Helvenston, Sally I. 1991. "Fashion and Function in Women's Dress in Rural New England: 1840–1900." *Dress* 18: 26–38.

Hemphill, C. Dallett. 1999. *Bowing to Necessities: A History of Manners in america, 1620–1860.* New York: Oxford University Press.

Henkin, David M. 2006. *The Postal Age: The Emergence of Modern Communications in Nineteenth-Century America.* Chicago: The University of Chicago Press.

Her Many Horses, Emil, ed. 2007. *Identity by Design: Tradition, Change, and Celebration in Native Women's Dresses.* New York: Collins.

Holt, Marilyn Irvin. 2003. *Children of the Western Plains: The Nineteenth-Century Experience.* Chicago: Ivan R. Dee.

Howe, Daniel Walker. 2007. *What Hath God Wrought: The Transformation of America, 1815–1848.* New York: Oxford University Press.

Jennys, Susan. 2004. *19th Century Plains Indian Dresses.* Pottsboro, TX: Crazy Crow Trading Post.

Kesselman, Amy. 1991. "The 'Freedom Suit': Feminism and Dress Reform in the United States, 1848–1875." *Gender & Society* 5 (4): 495–510.

Kidwell, Claudia B. 1979. *Cutting a Fashionable Fit.* Washington, D.C.: Smithsonian Institution Press.

Lakwete, Angela. 2003. *Inventing the Cotton Gin: Machine and Myth in Antebellum America.* Baltimore: The Johns Hopkins University Press.

Maglio, Diane. 2000. "Luxuriant Crowns: Victorian Men's Smoking Caps, 1850–1890." *Dress* 2: 9–17.

McClellan, Elizabeth. 1969. *History of American Costume, 1607–1870.* New York: Tudor Publishing Company.

McDowell, Colin. 1997. *The Man of Fashion: Peacock Males and Perfect Gentlemen.* New York: Thames and Hudson.

Milbank, Caroline Rennolds. 2000. "'Ahead of the World': New York City Fashion." In *Art and the Empire City,* ed. Catharine Hoover Voorsanger and John K. Howat, 243–57. New Haven, CT: Yale University Press.

Montgomery, Florence M. 2007. *Textiles in America 1650–1870.* New York: W. W. Norton & Company.

Nelson, Jennifer Ladd. 2000. "Dress Reform and the Bloomer." *Journal of American & Comparative Cultures* 23 (1): 21–25.

Paterek, Josephine. 1994. *Encyclopedia of American Indian Costume.* New York: W. W. Norton & Company.

Perry, Claire. 2006. *Young America: Childhood in 19th-Century Art and Culture.* New Haven, CT: Yale University Press.

Rexford, Nancy. 2000. *Women's Shoes in America: 1795–1930.* Kent, OH: Kent State University Press.

Rinhart, Floyd, and Marion Rinhart. *The American Daguerreotype.* 1981. Athens: University of Georgia.

Ritter, Joann Gregory, and Betty L. Feather.1990. Practices, Procedures, and Attitudes Toward Clothing Maintenance: 1850–1850 and 1900–1910. *Dress* 17: 156–68.

Rose, Clare. 1989. *Children's Clothes.* London, B. T. Batsford Limited.

Safford, Carleton L., and Robert Bishop. 1972. America's Quilts and Coverlets. New York: E. P. Dutton & Co.

Severa, Joan. 1995. *Dressed for the Photographer: Ordinary Americans & Fashion, 1840–1900.* Kent, Ohio: Kent State University Press.

Steele, Valerie. 2001. *The Corset: A Cultural History.* New Haven: Yale University Press.

Tandberg, Gerilyn G. 1985. "Towards Freedom in Dress for the 19th Century Woman." *Dress* 11: 11–30.

Trollope, Frances Milton. 1832. Domestic Manners of the Americans. Vol. 2. London: Whittaker, Treacher & Co.

Ulrich, Pamela V. 1985. "Promoting the South: Rhetoric and Textiles in Columbus, Georgia, 1850–1880." *Dress* 11: 31–46.

Volo, James M., and Dorothy Deneen Volo. 2004. *American Popular Culture Through History: The Antebellum Period.* Westport, CT: Greenwood Press.

Warner, Patricia Campbell. 2001. "'It Looks Very Nice Indeed': Clothing in Women's Colleges, 1837–1897." *Dress* 28: 23–39.

Waugh, Norah. 1954. *Corsets and Crinolines.* New York: Theatre Arts Books.

Waugh, Norah. 1964. *The Cut of Men's Clothes, 1600–1900.* New York: Theatre Arts Books.

Waugh, Norah. 1985. *The Cut of Women's Clothes, 1600–1300.* New York: Theatre Arts Books.

Welters, Linda. 1997. "Dress as Souvenir: Pina Cloth in the Nineteenth Century." *Dress* 24: 16–26.

Worrell, Estelle A. 1979. *American Costume, 1840–1920.* Harrisburg: Stackpole Books.

Zakin, Michael. 1998. "Customizing the Industrial Revolution: The Reinvention of Tailoring in the Nineteenth Century." *Winterthur Portfolio* 33 (1): 41–58.

Zakin, Michael. 1999. "A Ready-Made Business: The Birth of the Clothing Industry in America." *Business History Review* 73 (1): 61–90.

Zakin, Michael. 2001 "Sartorial Ideologies: From Homespun to Ready-Made." *American Historical Review* 106 (5): 1553–86.

Zakin, Michael. 2003. *Ready-Made Democracy: A History of Men's Dress in the American Republic, 1760–1860.* Chicago, IL: The University of Chicago Press.

MUSEUMS, ORGANIZATIONS AND USEFUL WEB SITES

The Boston Museum of Fine Arts
Avenue of the Arts
465 Huntington Avenue
Boston, Massachusetts 02115-5597
617-267-9300
www.mfa.org

The department of Textile and Fashion Arts contains examples of American and European fashion from the 19th century, some of which are viewable online through the museum's collection database.

Costume Institute of the Metropolitan Museum of Art
1000 Fifth Ave. at 82nd St.
New York City, NY 10028-7710
212-535-7710
www.metmuseum.org

The Costume Institute holds exceptional examples of 19th century fashion from America and Europe and with the addition of the Brooklyn Museum of Art's Costume Institute collection it has become the pre-eminent collection of American fashion. Examples of dress from the Antebellum Era may be found on the museum's Web site.

Eli Whitney Museum
915 Whitney Avenue
Hamden, CT 06517
Phone: (203) 777-1833
http://www.eliwhitney.org/

An experiential museum built on the site of Eli Whitney's factory, the Web site includes pictures and information about Whitney's cotton gin.

The Henry Ford Museum and Greenfield Village
20900 Oakwood Blvd.
Dearborn, Michigan 48124-5029
1-800-835-5237
www.hfmgv.org

With an online and fully searchable illustrated database of the Museum's collection of costume, The Henry Ford offers researchers the ability to view examples of American dress from the Antebellum period. This collection is particularly rich in examples of children's dress.

Kent State University Museum
PO Box 5190
Rockwell Hall
Kent, OH 44242-0001
330-672-3450
www.kent.edu/museum

The Kent State Museum collection of fashion and decorative arts are exhibited regularly through thematic exhibitions. The "Visual Dictionary of Fashion," which is available online, includes examples of dress organized by date, from 1800–1829, 1830–1839 and 1840–1859. Each record includes multiple views of these objects, many of which are from America. The collection is available for research by appointment.

The Los Angeles County Museum of Art
5905 Wilshire Boulevard
Los Angeles, California
1-323-857-6000
www.lacma.org

The department of Costume and Textiles at LACMA is an encyclopedic collection of fashion and textiles, with a particularly strong collection of European and American fashion of the 19th century. The Doris Stein Resource Center, housed in the department and available to researchers by appointment, includes print materials such as early American fashion periodicals and loose fashion plates, many of which are also available for view through the museum's Web site's Collections Online.

Old Sturbridge Village
1 Old Sturbridge Village Road
Sturbridge, MA 01566
1-800-733-1830
www.osv.org

With a collection that includes items from the 1830s, the Old Sturbridge Village living history museum features a gallery with rotating exhibitions which may include items of dress. There is also an online collection database which features over 400 objects relating to dress.

The Smithsonian Institute
National Museum of American History
Kenneth E. Behring Center
14th Street and Constitution Ave., NW
Washington D.C.
202-633-1000
www.americanhistory.si.edu

The museum's Web site features collection highlights and online exhibitions. The collection includes examples of dress of both ordinary and extraordinary Americans from the 19th century including pieces worn by the First Ladies and Presidents of the United States of America.

OTHER USEFUL WEB SITES

The Costumer's Manifesto: Regency and Empire Fashion and Victorian Fashion Costume Links. Ed. Tara Maginnis.
http://www.costumes.org/history/100pages/regencylinks.htm;
http://www.costumes.org/history/100pages/victlinks.htm
This site provides a fairly comprehensive overview of fashion history information available online with links to related Web sites.

Digital Gallery. New York Public Library.
http://digitalgallery.nypl.org/nypldigital/index.cfm
The New York Public Library provides a database of English and French fashion plates from the early 19th century from their collection, which is searchable by date as well as content.

Fashion Plate Collection. University of Washington Libraries, Digital Collections.
http://content.lib.washington.edu/costumehistweb/

A database of fashion plates sorted by time period including the Georgian (1806–1836), Romantic (1825–1850) and Victorian (1837–1859) periods.

Women in America, 1820–1842.
http://xroads.virginia.edu/~HYPER/DETOC/FEM/home.htm
Includes descriptions of women's roles and lives in the Antebellum period, searchable by topic and author, including a section on Appearance and Fashion.

FILMS

Jane Eyre

There are multiple film and television adaptations of Charlotte Brontë's work, each with its own strengths in representing period costume. Though the novel is set in England, the costume portrayed in the following films represents a somewhat accurate portrayal of that worn by middle-class Americans in the Antebellum period.

Jane Eyre (TV mini-series), DVD. 1983. Directed by Julian Amyes. Distributed by BBC Warner. Unrated.

Jane Eyre, DVD. 1996. Directed by Franco Zeffirelli. Distributed by Miramax. Rated PG.

Jane Eyre (Masterpiece Theatre) (TV mini-series), DVD. 2006. Directed by Susanna White. Distributed by WGBH Boston. Unrated.

OTHER PERIOD FILMS

Gone with the Wind, DVD and Blue-ray. 1939. Directed by Victor Fleming. Distributed by Warner Home Video. Unrated. Adaptation of Margaret Mitchell's iconic 20th century novel about life in the Antebellum and Civil War-time south.

Queen (mini-series), DVD. 1993. Directed by John Erman. Distributed by Warner Home Video. Unrated. Adaptation of Alex Haley's novel about his grandmother, Queen, the daughter of a white slave owner and an enslaved African American

Nightjohn, DVD. 1996. Directed by Charles Burnett. Distributed by Echo Bridge Home Entertainment. Rated PG-13. Story of enslaved African Americans and the quest for literacy during the Antebellum Era.

About the Author

MICHELLE WEBB FANDRICH is a fashion and textile historian and appraiser. She holds a MA in Visual Culture: Costume Studies from New York University and a BA in Art History from the University of North Texas. She has served on the curatorial staff of the Metropolitan Museum of Art and the Los Angeles County Museum of Art. Her published works include *La Dernière Mode: Blogging Fashion* (2007) and *Costume Worldwide: A Historical Sourcebook* (2008).

Index